HEARTS SET FREE

Our freedom for which Christ Jesus died

shared by the Apostles Paul, James and John

Norman Grubb

WRITINGS BY NORMAN GRUBB

Biographies...

C.T. Studd, Cricketer and Pioneer

Alfred Buxton

Edith Moules, Mighty Through God

J.D. Drysdale, Prophet of Holiness

Rees Howells, Intercessor

Abraham Vereide, Modern Viking

Jack Harrison, Successor to C.T. Studd

Books & Booklets on WEC...

After C.T. Studd

Christ in the Congo Forests

With C.T. Studd in Congo Forests (U.S.A. printing)

First the Blade

Modern Crusaders

The Four Pillars of W.E.C.

Mountain Movers

Spanish Guinea

Ivory Coast

Penetrating Faith

Ploughing Through

The Price They Paid

A Mighty Work of the Spirit

This 'n That

Books...

Touching the Invisible

The Law of Faith

The Liberating Secret

The Deep Things of God

The Spontaneous You

God Unlimited

Who Am I?

The Leap of Faith

Continuous Revival

The Willowbank Story

Modern Crusaders

Nothing Is Impossible

Yes I Am

Booklets...

The Key to Everything

Romans 6-8

Are We Still On Target?

Throne Life

It's as Simple as This

The Secret of Suffering

No Independent Self

Intercession in Action

Books published after his Homegoing...

Knight of Faith Volume I

Knight of Faith Volume II

My Dear C.U.M.B

The Japan Talks

The Meaning of Life

Think on These Things

Journeys of Faith...Old Testament Lives...their lives AND our lives

Hearts Set Free...NT Epistles

Please visit our website for Norman Grubb's writings as well as others who share Christ as their life...

www.normangrubb.com

www.christasus.com

thesingleeye.wordpress.com

Hearts Set Free is dedicated to three saints who have been instrumental in ways too numerous to mention these last twenty-five years in my effort to publish additional works of our friend and mentor, Norman Grubb.

Judy Dunn...who has walked with me in faith, encouragement and *incredible* hands on work. Without her the previous seven books would scarcely have made it past my heart's desire to publish them.

John Bunting...who stood by me always cheering me on in spite of walking out his own *deep* intercession. When **God** was ready to take him into a redirection for the final twenty years of his life John willingly gave his medical practice away and left his family to go to Africa in hope and fulfillment that just *one* African would come to know Christ as *their* life. In the end John was like Abraham – *only* seeing the promise by faith, which God had spoken to him.

Linda Bunting...for always supporting me in faith, and with ever-wise counsel as issues came up with each publication. John's 'call' became Linda's just as Linda's in meeting Norman Grubb in 1968 eventually became John's also.

John and Linda are a couple after God's heart, who gave up *all* in countless ways to follow His call. I can truly say they have had hearing ears, seeing eyes and hearts completely given to God's **cross** and glorious plan for their lives!

"And surely their works do follow them."

ACKNOWLEDGEMENTS

A very special thanks of deep gratitude to those who have made this final book a reality...by recording, transcribing, entering electronically, proofing, giving me their opinion on an issue, and just simple encouragement – Judy Dunn, Linda Bunting, John Bunting, Sara Tinetti, Harriet Wearren, Carol Foster, Ole Henrik Skjelstad, Dan Powers, Marian Sandbek, Rhonda Oldland, Glenda Lauter, Patty Hattaway, Nick Cabiness, Darlene Breed, Tony Maden, John Collings, Laurie Hills, Millie Baldwin, Bette Ketcham, JoAnn Parker, Roel Velema and Margie Godfrey...and especially to Norman Grubb who could not but follow the still small voice of the Holy Spirit in creating these recordings for future generations. And I cannot leave out my husband, Gary, for always being there in whatever I need.

"There is an element in the gospel of Christ
so disturbing
that the world will forever reject it,
but never forget it;
and the Church will forever waiver between
patronage and persecution.
Yours is the present,
for the world will ridicule or crucify us;
but I think the future is ours."

"The Gold Cord" ......
Brother A. Vida Schudder

TABLE OF CONTENTS

Foreword...xiv

Introduction..xx

Romans..1

II Corinthians...111

Galatians..167

Philippians...203

Hebrews...217

James..265

I John...295

Afterword...353

Back Cover...355

About the Author..357

FOREWORD

John and I were asked to write the Foreword to this final book of talks of our friend and mentor, Norman Grubb, who we consider to be the premier mind of the 20th Century! Norman was a modern day Paul and Martin Luther, believing that a second Reformation was at hand. Before John could contribute to this Foreword God took him Home. I write for John, posthumously, having been married for 63 years, knowing that he would trust me to speak for him. We met Norman at the same time, but since our lives were taking on new vistas our needs were widely divided. He was just beginning the practice of his surgery career, and I had taken on the responsibility of building our home and raising our four children. Needless to say the weight of both drove us in different directions, but looking back, we each came to see the wealth of love and guidance that pressed us to faith and brought us home to the Living Spirit of **Christ** *in us*.

Writing my thoughts of Norman, who became my deep confidant and friend in working closely with him for 40 years, seemed daunting! His writings have been the key for us which unlocked the door into the true treasure chamber of what Paul called "the mystery of godliness." What did that really mean? Paul wrote to the 'top line' saints of Ephesus, who already knew Christ in a saved and Spirt-filled relationship, but they still needed "the eyes of their understanding to be enlightened." Norman was the beginning of that enlightenment to us; eventually taking John and me into what I would daringly call the ultimate of understanding. Here at last was what our lives were really all about!

It was after reading Norman's books and 'catching' what he was saying about 'Only One Person in the Universe' and how we humans fit into that Person, that I read the letters in the New Testament with the eyes of my heart – my faith switching from 'performing' a Systemic Theology to catching the Person of Christ, living in and as me! The way in which Paul wrote his epistles could be read as law. What Norman did for us was transform our faith from self effort to the Living Spirit of Christ as us. His writings have been the key which gloriously gave life to these New Testament Epistles.

Norman brought us the Living Christ and His Holy Spirit revealing that we are now – "Crucified with Christ" and Christ is living as us – Galatians 2:20; "Living letters written in our hearts, known and read of all men" – 2Corinthians 3:2; "He that is joined to the Lord is ONE spirit" – 1 Corinthians 6:17; "For me to live is Christ" – Philippians 1:21; "Rejoicing in filling up that which is behind of the sufferings of Christ" – Colossians 2:24; "What can separate us from the love of God, in Christ Jesus" Romans 8:38; "Counting it all joy with many trials and temptations...knowing that we may be whole, complete, needing nothing" James 1:4; and "He that is born of God cannot sin" 1 John 5:18.

At 20 years of age I began to read the Bible and voraciously searched and studied to get into a deeper living relationship with the Lord. It was my driving force in life and became my God. Being an urgent seeker of the 'deeper life' teachings plus reading and trying to make it all fit into living by the 'letter of the law' rendered me hopeless. All the knowledge I acquired left me with a past forgiven and a future secure, but present tense living found me in Romans 7 crying with Paul, "Oh, wretched man that I am, Who will deliver me from this death?". Reading and learning 'about' Jesus without knowing the present tense Person of Christ living in me had become a dead letter. I actually had to put the Bible to rest for a season. Prior to meeting Norman, I had not read the Bible in two years. I can remember asking the Spirit if I could begin reading again. His reply was, "Not yet. There is a deeper condition in your self-effort to achieve within your own strength that needs to be addressed." Being utterly helpless to perform one more thing, I gave up and said to God, "I'm through with You. If You don't come and cause me to walk in Your ways, I will die and go to hell, but it really won't matter because I'm living in it!"

All this time John was watching my newfound 'love', Norman Grubb, who had taken me and a few of my fellow seekers aside to explain "the way of God more perfectly". And just what was the more perfect way? None other than our positional truth of Galatians 2:20...and then the remedy of the human condition, which is solved in Romans 6, 7 and 8. In doing so the "eyes of our understanding" in Ephesians 1:18 are opened to the unlimited vision of the Spirit – to know that it is the Holy Spirit Himself, Who came into the body of Christ Jesus in the resurrection, bringing to the forefront God's final benediction on *us,* as His sons.

I will say it took John a bit longer to give up his mindset of being a 'sinner saved by grace'. When I asked Norman why, this was his reply. "John is a big negative; leave him alone. When God gets him, he will be a big positive." What far reaching insight he had, because that is exactly what happened to John, who in the beginning fought Norman's message, but at the end of the day, gave up *everything* for it.

****

John…

Norman came into my life in 1968 when my wife heard him for the first time. His message of Christ in You was so contrary and radical to the teachings I grew up with, that I became very circumspect and afraid he was speaking heresy. But my wife, for her own reasons, was 'full steam ahead' and in due time Norman became my friend, and the driving force that turned my life upside down to take his very message to other countries in the world.

It was Norman who showed me the wonderful mystery 'Christ in you the hope of glory.' I had to come to the point where I was ready to admit that I could not do anything. Once I saw it I began to live by faith, truly and utterly cast upon the Lord. My guilt had been condemning me for years but when finally I gave up and said, 'It's not I but Christ' that was the point where I started to come free. The major problem disappeared as I started to move with the Lord. It was miraculous. Norman was so influential at that time, not that he sat down and talked a lot to me, but he pointed the way, and the Holy Spirit was able to lead me into these precious truths such as Colossians 3:3, "Your life is hidden with Christ in God."

At a crossroads in my life, I was beginning to have thoughts of having missed a 'call' to go to Africa as a missionary. My friend, Tony Ketcham, flew me to see Norman and when I said to him, "Norman, have I missed something?" His reply was this: "John, DON'T TOUCH IT. When it is of the Spirit you won't be able to NOT do it!" A great relief came inside my spirit and I was freed for the time to let it be. Then a day came in 1995 when I heard the 'CALL' from the Holy Spirit to go to Africa, and just as Norman had so wisely counseled me, my only answer could be, "Here am I; send me."

John's one and only letter to me…

"My Dearest Darling,

Well I started this letter just like Norman, I knew he had inspired me to come here, but I didn't think his ol Irish baloney would come out of this typewriter. Ha Ha. No, there is not a day that goes by I don't think of him, and C.T. and how it was when they were here. The changes are great, but the culture remains the same. I have found that it is the major difference, and the major hindrance of them seeing total truth. As you said they are too tied to their old ways of religion, but I know that the Spirit is bigger than their old ways, and by faith they will know and I see it NOW. As Norman would say, "It's just a little mist on the mountain."

  With all my love and His love -
  John

Norman and John are now together living in the light and life accomplished through the years they lived here in a negative dark world – each gloriously fulfilling the part God had created for them before their birth. As he does in each of his writings, once again, Norman brings untold wealth to these Epistle letters for us!

Revelation 14:13…

"And I heard a voice from heaven saying unto me, "Write, Blessed are the dead which die in the Lord from henceforth: Yea, saith the Spirit, that they may rest from their labors; and their works do follow them."

The Apostle John's words from the book of Revelation speak of Norman Grubb and John Bunting as well as countless others and the writers of these phenomenal New Testament letters – Apostles Paul, James and John. Today each of us is a "living letter" writing our own epistle to be read of men. Norman Grubb's "works do follow" him in ways too numerous to mention around the world…in the writings he penned and the lives he impacted with the TRUTH of the gospel given to him in 1920 in Africa…"I live; yet not I, but Christ liveth in me…"

Linda Bunting
January 2021

INTRODUCTION

Hearts Set Free is the final book I shall publish of Norman Grubb's writings and talks. My main objective has been to share his boundless wisdom and to provide an alternative and necessary voice to the body of Christ, now and for many future generations, in order that they may gain deeper insight into the *complete* gospel of Jesus Christ. Norman was a true visionary in things of the Spirit. What he gave us went *far beyond* our being "sinners saved by grace." He told of a life of freedom and fullness in Christ as being one of righteousness, holy and blameless, saints *kept* by grace because Another died for us, and *now* lives our life! He brought the truth that the Cross of Christ ushered in a **new covenant** of the *living* Spirit – not one of mere words, nor of the letter of the law, and also not simply a 'Jesus of history', but *this* is the gospel of the resurrected, ascended, *living* Christ found in the letters of Paul, James and John...AND in us!

The writers of *these* Epistles wrote to *establish* the followers of The Way...the churches at Corinth, Ephesus, Philippi, Rome and Jerusalem...as well as to establish *us* in the knowledge of the *finished* work that Christ *accomplished* for mankind. I pray that as you read you'll "be given a *spirit of wisdom and revelation* and that the *eyes* of *your* understanding be enlightened". Norman Grubb has brought these 'eyes' to these Epistle letters for countless seekers over the years.

Never would I have dreamt in 1995, after Norman's death a little more than a year earlier, that beginning to actively pursue my desire to publish a book of his letters would consume the next twenty-five years of my life, and turn into not one, but three books of letters, and five more of his writings and talks comprising eight books in all! As God ever so slowly and precisely causes us to walk in His ways, His plans begin to take form before our eyes and reveal to us His magnificence in ways too marvelous to imagine! He says, "This is the way; walk ye in it" and *miraculously* we do! These years have been an adventure of faith, frustration and joy, as well as a real treasure hunt, as the Lord turned up one surprise after another, bringing the reality of God's fulfillment and faithfulness in ways I never imagined.

The following is from one of Norman's letters in *Knight of Faith Vol I*…

"You will be seeing the new "title" we are using for U. L. [Union Life]

The Twentieth Century Reformation…

Luther gave us Paul's Romans 5.1   Justification

Union Life gives us Paul's Col. 1.28 COMPLETION (or "Perfection")"

Norman believed a **Twentieth Century Reformation** was at hand…one even *more powerful* than Martin Luther's in declaring, "The just shall live by faith." He believed *this* reformation would happen *in* each believer as they *saw by revelation* that *they* were Christ in 'their unique form' and that His Holy Spirit was living *in* and *as* them in every single aspect of their being, which sadly, is seldom *fully* discovered. He saw that the church, which in its beginning walked in this newfound freedom after the coming of the Holy Spirit at Pentecost, had since become 'grace for the lost, but law to the saved' – that having a 'sinner mentality' presses us to try harder to *become* holy through more prayer, quiet time, bible study etc, etc, etc. until it all crashes in a dead end! Norman revealed, however, that Christ boldly told us *we* would live in a new covenant…a new way of life other than by an outward law. We would *be* the branch expressing the LIFE of the Vine – Christ; a temple containing His LIFE! Hebrews tells us this life IS one of rest. "There remains a rest to the people of God. For he that is entered into his rest, he has also ceased from his *own* works, as God did from His." There is a rest…it is the rest of a *total* Gospel!

It was in the jungles of Africa in 1920 that God began to reveal Himself in a revelatory way to Norman and his life was forever changed. After answering the Spirit's call to bring the saving love of Christ Jesus to the Africans, he feared he was bringing them just another set of rules and doctrines, and also found he was *completely unable* to love them as he knew God wanted. He cried out to the Father to give him more love. God clearly spoke back to Norman giving him two scriptures – I John 4:8 that God *is* love and saying, "*I* am love; I won't give love to you, but *I* will *be* love in you", and Galatians 2:20, "I am crucified with Christ: nevertheless I live; *yet not I but Christ liveth in me*; and the life I now live in the flesh I live by the faith *of* the Son of God who loved me, and gave Himself for me." Norman suddenly knew it was not *his* love, not *his* life and not *his* faith!

He knew there was a *vast* difference between what he had seen of these scriptures before *this* moment of the Holy Spirit's *revelation*. What he had seen previously was his *position* in Christ, but now he saw oneness with Christ as *his condition*! For him it was the difference of the light of the sun at first dawn against the light of the sun at noonday!

Norman always sought a total truth, which he saw revealed in Jesus Christ. To Norman *total* meant a *perfect* God – Father, Son and Spirit – living in His *perfect* creation – human beings! As the Holy Spirit began to mature him and lead him into truth upon truth, building on his Galatians 2:20 revelation, he began to realize the tragic condition of the body of Christ. Spiritual activities...all good in themselves...had become a 'way' of self-effort to become a better Christian. He saw the body of Christ living as though Romans 7 is the truth about them. It is an *existence* of sin and condemnation...always trying harder and failing. He brought us the 'key' that *when* we have a separated consciousness, we also believe we have a false independent self who can sin *or* do/be better. It was *this mindset* that caused the Apostle Paul to cry out in Romans 7, "Who will deliver me from this body of sin and death!"

Paul *found* his answer in that Jesus Christ *had* rescued him and he *now* lived a Romans 8 life – one of *no condemnation* – one of *unity* and *oneness* and *freedom* and *victory*! It is *this life* that Norman explained thoroughly and encouragingly in his writings, sharing and ever-wise counsel, which he gave to anyone who hungered for more than what they had known in the past. How to begin to walk in this union is each believer's dilemma. Norman taught us that it was only and always by faith as we agree with God in what *He* says about us – we need a Savior; when we believe, Christ becomes *our* life; He sent His Holy Spirit to lead us into all truth and live through us in *His* absolute perfection – *our* oneness with Christ and our lives hidden *in* and *revealing* HIM!

Jesus promised this same oneness to us, which He spoke about in John 17, as He prayed a final prayer to His Father before going to the Cross. His prayer that we might live in the *same* oneness as He did with His Father – doing as He saw the Father do and saying as He heard the Father say. It was *this* life of union that Norman proclaimed far and wide!

****

For many of us Norman was our first encounter with "unconditional love" in another human being...bringing us into the presence of the sacred. He stretched and expanded our perceptions of God, of life, and of our own humanity in every way imaginable. He was a *living reality* of *our freedom* for which Christ Jesus died. By example and encouragement, he taught us to become people of faith...finding God and *His* ways by 'seeing through' *all* that life brought to us...through our temptations, fears and actions of others, past our weight of self-condemnation and heartaches, and *into* God being in each and every circumstance. What Norman saw about himself, he saw about each of us, and what he believed, *we* became emboldened to believe...first for ourselves and then for *our* world! He was truly our "epistle written in our hearts, known and read of all men".

The beautiful litany we find in Philippians 4:8 - honorable, right, pure, lovely, good repute and excellence, also aptly describe the man we knew as Norman and his 'way' with those around him, those who came to him for counsel, and also with any situation which arose. He was the truest friend, mentor and encourager. His encouragement, correction or praise was our path to *trusting ourselves*. Norman never drew attention to himself and sought no 'followers'...but always emboldened each person with the truth that *they* had the Answer within – "Christ in you, the hope of glory!"

In one of his letters he lifted a woman to *see* the truth about her wholeness...

A dear friend came to me last night and said, "Will you bless me?" "Well", I said, "I'll tell you, you've got the Blesser inside you. So you don't need my blessing." He's forever *your* blessing! You see we enter into a new relationship. We don't *need* the outside. We know we need it for fellowship and joy and friendship, but not for an increase...maybe for confirmation...not for greater reality. You can't have a greater reality. You can't have a greater – *you* are Christ in human flesh. Can you have a greater than that? *You are* the living Christ in human flesh! You're the living God expressed by your humanity. That's what this vine-branch union means! A branch is the vine expressed in its branch form...and we are the vine expressed in our branch form. So what's the Lord seeking to settle us into – a permanent, conscious relationship in which there never is a lack again.

In *Hearts Set Free* you will find Norman's commentaries on Romans, II Corinthians, Galatians, Philippians, Hebrews, James and I John. In each one we see Norman's desire for *our* wholeness, just as he gave to his friend in writing to her. I have begun each chapter with comments pertinent to each Epistle using Norman's words from his letters, books and other writings and talks which I have published.

Norman's usual encouragement in signing his books was often a shock to those who still had a divided consciousness –

Not God and...
but God only!

****

The title, *Hearts Set Free*, comes from an email exchange with my dear friend and Tennessee poet extraordinaire, Dan Powers, when he wrote to me, "Truly they are high apostles of the heart set free". Immediately my spirit leapt giving witness to *Hearts Set Free* as the *title and truth* of Norman's gift to us all! The exquisite cover photo is the work of gifted photographer and dear friend, Ole Henrik Skjelstad of Norway, who also provided the photograph for *Think on These Things*. He had appropriately titled it *Silent Night*. It perfectly depicts that all of heaven and earth were settled and silent after Christ's death and resurrection ushering in the New Covenant. Ole Henrik's photo was 'captured' for the book cover by graphic designer, Sara Tinetti, who also created the incredible cover for *The Meaning of Life*. Sara also graciously and efficiently stepped in to do the margins when I discovered the publisher no longer did them!

Hearts Set Free was made possible in the same way as the *Old Testament Journeys of Faith...their lives...AND our lives*. In the early 1970's some of Norman's friends asked him to do a series of talks on the great lives from the Old Testament and on the New Testament Epistles. They gathered in homes and Laurie Hills recorded them. These audio cassettes were copied by the hundreds and I am sure many still exist. They have been shared, recopied, transferred to CD's, and posted on our website dedicated to the life and works of Norman Grubb www.normangrubb.com. I have delightedly shared them with other sites such as Lighthouse Library, Sermon Audio and Sermon Index and they are now widely shared throughout the Internet. After they were transcribed, I once again, did my 'creative editing' with *italics* and **bolding** words, as well as using three dots (...) or a dash (–) to separate Norman's impossibly long sentences and stream of *knowing* into something more easily read and understood.

In looking through my files for these Epistle letters I found an early unpublished writing of Norman's exploring *Christ as All in all*. You can find it on our Norman Grubb website along with Martin Luther's commentary on Gal 2:20.

May you have blessings of revelation, peace and joy and may a new 'settledness' come over you as you read of Christ, *your* life!

Love in Christ, *our* life...

DeeDee Winter

ROMANS

I am deeply convinced, although it sounds awful to say so, that even our deeper life teachers are not really giving the clear foundations, and as a consequence they put many hearers into bondage, because their emphasis to exhort the believer to get on with his consecration, prayer life, witnessing, etc. (really an exhortation to a **Romans 7** life!) rather than unveiling to him a Christ who is all, and will surely mold those who recognize Him in their allness in them, into the pattern of life He intends to live in them.

Knight of Faith Vol I

We are told to "have the faith of God" (Mark 11:22, margin). What is God's faith? We **looked** at **Romans 4:17**, and there it was in print: God calling the things that be not as though they are! And the Spirit causing us to believe, with His believing as ours.

Intercession in Action...
Think on These Things

They had to have a broken self...they had to be broken as sinners and broken as selves. So **Romans 6** deals with our *sins* out. Romans 7...our self out...it's a comeback, but broken from the center of independence.

Now **Romans 8** is the chapter the other way around...Oh, it isn't *you* living. It's the living **Christ** living in you. You're a new person...not just a new person yourself...that *self* of yours which *was* captured by a spirit of error – you *were* a vessel containing the God of wrath. You're *now* the same vessel containing the God of mercy, Christ...but your **self** is under new management. It's in a new relationship. It's in a *conscious* relationship with the living Jesus Christ, living God – living *you*...as you, in you. That's Romans 8! Christ dwells in you. The Holy Spirit dwells in you. You're not in the flesh...you're in the Spirit!

The Meaning of Life

Norman Grubb

ROMANS

We all know that Paul's letter to the Romans was his most complete and comprehensive presentation of what he spoke of right from the beginning of Romans as the good news of God for the human race. It centered around His Son – Who was demonstrated to be His Son by the Spirit of Holiness, and by His resurrection from the dead, and by His relationship to the human family which came out of that.

Romans is a letter, so it had to be tightly presented...it couldn't be expanded too much. It is a letter which had all the great *facts* of the good news of God. It is in somewhat shortened form. He doesn't expand on the great basic facts... probably couldn't in one letter. He expanded upon it in other letters in the Bible, and as the other writers of the letters have done.

So, I'm going along with Romans and where I feel it would be good to expand, which is quite often on some of the great main issues, I will do so maybe by one word – sin, law, grace, redemption, and the "walk" in the Spirit, but when they are mentioned, my plan shall be to stop...and sometimes quite at length...and go back and look further at what is meant by those great words...in what sense they are real to us. So I shall deviate to some extent from the letter, and then come back to it...and so will cover chapter by chapter...but not in *any* means in total detail. It will be somewhat in a survey fashion linking these great facts presented to us in the letter. So, it is from that angle that we are approaching it.

After Paul had made his preliminary words of welcome and introduction to the Roman Church to whom he was writing, he moved straight into his presentation in the sixteenth verse of the first chapter – that he was ready to preach the Gospel to Rome also, and that he is not ashamed of the Gospel of Christ..."For it is the power of God unto salvation to everyone who believes, to the Jew and also the Greek."

Then, he starts off by presenting the fundamental fact that there is a Living God Who we are told in other scriptures, "He is Spirit." He presents Him to us here as in relationship to us in which we can know *of* Him, because it says that the truth of God in 19 is manifested *in* us, not *to* us. So, straight away he presents the fact that He is Spirit. In other scriptures we find that our true selves – our inner person is spirit. Spirit co-related to spirit.

3

Therefore, there is in all humans this basic means by which we can be in a relationship with Him. This is given us as our foundation here. The way in which He manifests Himself is *Spirit manifested through form*. So, it says in this twentieth verse that He, the invisible Person, *is* manifested by these *visible forms*, which we call creation. All the visible forms around us are the evidence to our inner self...this invisible Person is manifested by these forms. We are able to see something of the grandeur of Him – such as perfection, power, beauty. His very power and deity are shown to us...the visible manifests the invisible...so that we are without excuse. We are able to know what we can touch, see, and feel. These are all outer forms of The One Person in the Universe - Whose *Spirit* is manifested in created forms!

He then goes on to say that instead of being in *harmony* with Him, we are in disharmony. He being harmony, everything is basically in perfect harmony. We are in a discordant relationship with Him – disturbed relationship, which he speaks of as being in the wrath element of God, not the grace element. Wrath is when things go wrong, which is when things go wrong in us, so that we are in disharmony. We have a *distorted* relationship, not a harmonious relationship.

He goes on to state the fact about the human race which needs further explanation – that is that something has happened to us. That instead of having thankfully, worshipfully relating all things with ourselves and that situation to Him and worshiping and glorifying Him, we relate them to ourselves. Something so *happened* that our attitude to creation is (we bring this into reality by our own opinions) what he calls here, our "vain imaginations" where we profess ourselves to be wise.

So, there is an element that's taken over in the human race of *self*-appreciation, *self*-explanation of our universe. That which we worship are self-forms, human forms which relate to the kind of things that we are in our selfish condition. So, we have gods which this human race is made of, which have expressed its fallen desires. So there are gods or images which have expressed themselves in fleshly action or in perverted spirit action of hates, jealousies, revenges and so on. Theirs are the gods which are really self-images, because it permits us to do those kinds of things ourselves...because we have made gods of flesh, gods of lust, gods of hate, gods of murder, gods of fear. We fulfill those same things in our nature.

So, he goes on then to describe in the first chapter the most drastic form. We run into perverted sex. Because *all* is love...God being love...everything, therefore, is a form of love. If our love has come apart from God, Who is self-giving love, then it has become in us a form of self-loving love which expresses itself in forms of self-gratification. The strongest physical form of love being sex, we express it in perverted sex. So, it gives the strongest description in the Bible of men and women in their perverted sex forms in those early verses of Chapter 1, when God gave them over to their uncleanness through the lusts of their hearts. And, then having described something of the excesses of perverted sex running rampant, what is so common today, homosexual forms, he then moves on to *spirit discords.*

In Verse 28 it says, "God gave them over to their reprobate minds" as well as a perverted body. In the reprobate mind He gives a whole list of them, such as hates, murders, rebellions, un-thankfulness, malice, cruelty, a whole list of them. The kind of condition we have gone into is that we *delight* in doing these things. For it says at the end of the chapter, "not only do them, but have pleasure in doing them." We find ourselves destroying life, because we have the death sentence passed on us for doing them.

We find our distortion in life as self-pleasing self, instead of being in relationship with God, Who is self-giving love. Yet, Paul also states we still remain *His*. He has just given us over to those things. We're still **His**; He's just given us over to be torn to pieces by these expressions of God's wrath...by these misuses of the human self. And, the best description we get of the consequence which is the operation of the wrath of God in us is in that statement at the end of the twenty-seventh verse which says those who do these things "receive in themselves that recompense of their error which was meet." It comes out into us, the wrath operates in ourselves. Our discordant spirits or our corrupted bodies produce their corrupted effects on our spirit or flesh, in our selves.

Our discordant spirits or corrupted bodies produce their corrupted effects on our spirits or flesh, and the recompense is the wrath of God. It operates in us because we are beings of God; we are made in His image. Therefore, being in His image we can misuse the image. The *wrath* is *in us,* because it is in this 'image' form of God that discord has taken place, not in His own harmonious Self.

He follows on in Chapter 2 by turning his attention to those who by the operations of God's mercy and grace, through the centuries have come into some light because we know from other parts of the Bible the light of God has dawned and has been shining in the human race right from the very beginning, right from the time of the Fall itself, and right through Abel to Abraham and on through the nations which come out of Abraham to whom God began to reveal Himself in both grace and truth – grace and law. So, there are whole areas of people who knowing through these revelations something of God's ways and God's truth, still would have conformed themselves to a better way of being a self. Not knowing Him still forms His better way of *being* – "Oh all right, I'll be a moral self".

So, there is the hedonistic self, pleasure-loving self of Romans 1, and there is the ethical self of Rom. 2 and they are both self. They are both self-affirming, self-pleasing, self-gratifying self. The *proof* of that is when you are like that, you will think yourself superior to those who do rotten things and you judge them. What you are really doing is you judge yourself – for this reason – that we *all* do these kinds of things in different ways. We may pretend that we are not. The only people who can be capable of judging are also mentioned in Chapter 2. They are those who *have found* a way of repentance. In verse 4 they have found that God's goodness, forbearance, long suffering leads you to *repentance* and then to a new purpose in life. He says there *are* those who being a fallen-self have known it was wrong to be a fallen-self...whether in ethical pride or in physical corruption...repented of being such and sought a way of mercy. Where there are such, they *never judge* because they say, "I'm just like that myself." So, judging proves you have not been that. Because if you have been, yourself, a repentant person, you *don't judge* a person who is seeking to find a way out of that, whether they have found the way of mercy or are just seeking it.

So, Paul speaks of those who *have sought* the *right way* of life in Verse 7 of those who may not have *found* yet, but who *seek* glory, honor, peace and immortality and are in pursuit of Eternal Life. If you're a judge you can't be one of those, because you only judge because you *do* those things yourself, but you try and pretend you don't. So you *hide* it. You point your finger at the other person doing them and pretend that you don't. The person doing that is really judging themselves. If you are a person who has moved out from this false way of self, you don't judge it...simply because you've been that yourself and you know there isn't any *hope* for you. It's only in mercy and repentance. You look upon those who do those things just as yourself for perhaps they haven't yet found the way to repentance and mercy as you have.

He goes on in the middle of this chapter to say there *are* those who have never known the ways of the law of God, who we call Gentiles, who have that law somehow in their hearts. They too, sought a better way of life knowing they shouldn't be this wrong kind of person. He does stick in a word of mercy for them, because he says, "It is only God Who knows the secrets of men." He also says, "The day will come when God will judge the secrets of men by Jesus Christ according to the Gospel." So, we leave their destiny with Him.

So, the second chapter is a turn around on the ethical people. You hide your fallen nature...your self-gratifying, self-seeking nature under the pretense of being a *high* kind of person, when you are *still* a self-person – you run things for your ends your way – being part of what you are. You do the same things yourself.

He actually turns on the Jewish people and says, "The very name of God is blasphemed by you" because people can see you are not going to persist in what you claim to be, because you can't be – because self can only follow its own way. He ends by a little touch in that second chapter by saying only an *inward change* is truth – that which changes *you* is Truth, not that which changes your conduct. If you are a fallen person it is still self-conduct. If it is moral or immoral conduct it is still self-conduct. Therefore outer religion, outer law is no more helpful to you than false forms of living. He ends by saying the only true circumcision is circumcision of the heart. It isn't your outer law that changes you.

Verse 28 says..."He is not a Jew who is one outwardly, neither is that circumcision, which is outward in the flesh. He is a Jew who is one inwardly and circumcision is that which is one in the *heart*, in the spirit, and not in the letter; whose praise is not of men, but of God."

The way it *strikes* him...he says that truth is inner because truth is *Spirit* truth. The heart is for the express purpose of the Spirit and God is Spirit and we are spirit. And, it is only when there is an inner relationship there can be the truth.

Finally, he gathers it all up together in the presentation that *all* men are in the grip of what he begins to now call *sin*. He hadn't called it sin; he had called it ungodliness, at first. It now comes under the name of **sin**. He begins to use that word in Chapter 2 and heads it up in the first part of Chapter 3 by various quotations from the Old Testament. The *final declaration* of total depravity of this fallen human race because depravity is self-loving self, whatever form it takes. It comes out in *all* expressions. It says "cursing

7

bitterness, feet swift to shed blood, destruction, misery in our ways. The way of peace we don't know. No fear of God before our eyes; our throat is an open sepulcher." Those are quotations in Chapter 3, Verses 12-18, where it says, "All have gone out of the way, all have become unprofitable." He names that under the title of sin, when we come into contact with the law. Until there's been *known law*, we have been doing those things but didn't know that it was sin. Verse 19: When law comes in "every mouth is stopped and the *world* is guilty before God." We recognize in v. 23 "That all have sinned and come short of the Glory of God."

Now that takes us back as sometimes I'm moving off of the descriptions written in the Roman letter seeking to put these conditions of the relationship of God to the human race in a more complete form than Paul *could give* in a shorted letter. He had told us where sin began in a brief reference in the 5th chapter where he says "that by *one* man sin entered the world and death by sin—so death was passed upon all men—for all have sinned." That's verse 12. That takes us back for a moment into the original purposes of God and where we as the human race fit into those purposes, where we have gone wrong and later how we can come right. We find from other scriptures that it *always was* the purpose of God to have a *vast* family of sons. We find for instance in the first chapter of Ephesians where it says, "We are chosen by Him, through the adoption of sons chosen in Him before the foundation of the world."

So, when we go back to the origin of things as given in other scriptures...right back to their first historical presentation in the early chapters of *Genesis*...we find that this one Living Person in the universe, Who was in the beginning...Whom we are told of by Jesus, is Spirit. We are told by John His total character is love, which means He is a Person, Who is *just* for others. True Love is the nature *in us* in which we exist to perfect everybody and everything within our reach! It is the outgoing drive of our being into service for others rather than pleasing of ourselves. And, it always was from eternity, it always *had been* the means by which He can manifest Himself through eternity by His manifested form, which is His Son.

So, the Universal, Unknowable, Invisible, Unapproachable Father can be known by a knowable, visible, approachable form of Himself, which is His Son, the Only begotten Son of God, which we speak of as the manifested form of the Deity. It always was His purpose, through His Son to bring into being a vast family of sons. God in reproduction, in manifestation, is God the Spirit! From the Father, through the Son, God the Spirit comes into being so that in Creation the *Spirit* of Creation moved upon the face of the waters. All creation came into expression from the Spirit. The final form of creation was the bringing into being of the Son-family in His own image. We then follow through from other scriptures and we find that His ultimate purpose which has been a fixed fact from Eternity is that His Son should both bring into being this Universe then He hands over this Universe **to** His Son for His inheritance.

Therefore, the Son is the One Who will be the agent by which the Father will fulfill *whatever* His eternal purposes are through eternity in the *whole* universe. That is told to us in other scriptures...one particular one is Heb. 1:2 speaking of His Son Whom He appointed heir of all things, by Whom He has made the whole world.

Then later on we are told in other scriptures which link up to Him through grace, that we are co-sons, co-brothers, and co-heirs. What He inherits, we inherit. Therefore, His eternal purpose always had been that the Invisible One should manifest Himself through His visible form, expressing Himself as Love in visible form. That the One and the ones joined to Him should be the eternal Love expressions of the Father in fulfilling whatever His ultimate purposes are in the Universe. Being love, all His purposes are perfection and completion, that all should be what it is meant to be in harmony, the give and take of love, love relationships; this is to be fulfilled through eternity by His Son-family.

We then move on to the historical description of the creation of the Son-family, human family, and the first means by which as persons made in His image, we begin the process by which we become established as persons. By that I mean the Bible means that there *can be no manifestation* in the nature of things except by a relationship between *opposites*. Thus, the first statement made in the Bible in the very beginning is "dark and light," because a thing can only be known by its opposite. So, the first word in *Genesis*, we read, "Darkness was upon the face of the deep." Then the Spirit of God said, "Let there be light and there was light." The reason *being*, which we can recognize, by normal faculties, a thing can only be known by its opposite. Light can only be known because it isn't dark; truth can only be known because it isn't a lie; love can only be known because it isn't hate; sweet can only be known because it isn't bitter; *Yes* can only be known because it isn't *No,* and so on. And, the relationship between the two is that the *positive swallows up the negative* and finds that its most basic strength is swallowing up the negative. Love is love, because it is not hate. It swallows up the possibility of being hate, and all that possibility moves into the potential of love...and so through *all* the pairs of negatives.

Thus, the Bible says in 2 Cor. 5, "Life swallows up death." Life is only known because it swallows up death; its strength is that it replaces the possibility of death by life. Therefore, a person can only be a *conscious person* when he is confronted with all the opposites of life, and gets them into their right relationship – where the positive is swallowing up in the positive, and it's getting its strength by swallowing it up. The supremest, the profoundest revelation of that fact as a person is in our personhood...starting with God's Personhood. We're conscious *persons* made of love because God is love, and love is desire. Now I am a conscious person with desire. I must satisfy myself; otherwise I can't be a conscious person. Now I am confronted with the two alternatives: Should I, as desire/ love, satisfy myself by getting everything for myself, be a self-getter, a self-seeker, self-accumulator...*or* should I satisfy my self's desire by being a self-giver, by being the means by which other people can have *their* needs met? Will my *self* find its answer in being a person who always meets my own needs no matter what happens to others or will my self be satisfied by being one who can be the means by which others may have *their* needs met?

That's why that is such a profound revelation in the Bible that this eternal Person has stated He has something in His own eternal nature which He couldn't do. It is a very startling statement to make of Him, Who is the source of all things. If He is all things He can do all things, can't He? If He is Omnipotent, Omniscient, Omnipresent, can't He do so? Yet, here in the Bible it comes out twice over. In Titus Chapter 1 and in Hebrews 6. It says that it is one thing that He Himself can't do – He can't lie! In Hebrews says it's *impossible* for Him to lie! Heb. 6:18. Now *here* is a confrontation of the two opposites in God. A liar, being the form of a person who is going to gain his own ends at any price...no matter what happens to his neighbor. When it says that God can't lie, it is saying that there is in the very *being* of God, a settlement between the opposites. Being a self-affirming Being of the universe, the I AM of the universe, He *could* have been a Person who'd get everything for Himself, everything for His own ends (self-pleasing self) because that is what a liar is...or He *can* be the alternative – which is a self-giving self, and express all His self-pleasure in self-giving, rather than being in self-getting.

That's why one of the men who may have had the greatest insight into the Being of God, the great German mystic, Jacob Boehme, had this diagram...not of Jesus Christ, but of the Eternal God with a Cross in it, because there is *eternal* death in the Eternal Being – because He could have been a God Who was Self for Self. It said that He determined to be God who is a Self for others. He has *died* to being what we would say is the negative self, to be the positive. Because if we say that God is *perfect*, what He is, is positive. Therefore if He is perfect in love, only love is positive. Self-giving love is positive; self-loving love is negative. Self-giving love is life; self-loving love is death. Self-giving love is total fulfillment. Self-loving love is total corruption. So, we have here the basis of our revealed universe in the *revealed* Person of whom the universe is infinite forms of manifestation.

Therefore, we *now see* that in His purposes always had been by His only Begotten Son, and through His only Begotten Son bringing in a vast family who would be leveled up to His level as co-sons, and co-brothers by whom He'd fulfill His *eternal* manifestations; eternal expressions of Himself in whatever power, love operations that there are still to be. Those persons *themselves* must be settled in this same *reality of being* in which He is settled. They must be as fixed in their love, which is the self-giving love...and in them there should be this same Cross and the death to being possible people of self-loving love. If, therefore, that had to come into being, if we can use such terms for eternal facts (in the Eternal Deity), it *certainly* had to come into us, who are temporary forms – sons. That is, therefore, *why* we have in the first historical presentation of the birth of the creation of the human race (we call it the birth of the human race) the Father putting His first members of that family into a garden in which *everything* expressed His unending givingness! It all was theirs to benefit by, but He had also to put in that garden an *alternative,* because they must discover that life is only known by its alternatives, and the relationship of the two alternatives. Therefore, it *had* to have the symbol of the two trees. One tree symbolizes the conception of Eternal Life. The other one, "If you do this you will surely die" – eternal death.

That is why it is also given us, this remarkable revelation, that before there ever was a human race there were other beings that were made as sons...sometimes spoken of as seraphim, angels (we don't know much about spirit beings), spirits in heavenly places...at least some of whom who had the same quality of choice that we have. And there was *one* who was given us in the Bible. He is often spoken of in the Bible under different terms. He is called the "spirit of error" in 1 John 4; he is called the "prince of power of the air" in Eph. 2 He is called the "god of this world." That is in 2

Cor. 4:4. And, other terms like that all give him an actual title. He is called Satan or the devil or in Revelation, the "accuser of the brethren." His pre-existence is revealed to us in those two famous passages by prophecy in Isaiah 14 and Ezekiel 28.

Usually prophets had the future unveiled, and they would see forward in the future. *Occasionally* a prophet would have the past unveiled, and would see back into the past. These are two occasions that the prophets Isaiah and Ezekiel had the background veil opened, and they went back. They saw the origin of evil as a person created in relation to the Father and to be the agent by which the Father would manifest Himself. He was to be the bearer of light. Light is what manifests. He was to be the one who manifests the Father in His love. But, he as a *person*, although we do not know what kind of a person, could only confirm his personhood by standing between these two opposites. And so, he is revealed to us as one made in outstanding perfection, equipped with all the beauties and powers. That is in the Ezekiel 28 passage. But, in the Isaiah 14 one as using his love expression for his own ends, and setting himself to be the one who would live for himself and be his own self-fulfillment and therefore, his own god...and he would *replace* the God of the universe. This is the one then, who is revealed to us in *Genesis* in the form of the serpent, whose very character of a serpent gives the idea of his subtlety, who is *necessarily* used by God to lead the originators of the human family into the necessary discovery of *their* personhood, and the consequence of their establishment as a person.

So, he is the means by which our human first father and mother come to know what it is to be a person and to be confronted by the necessary two alternatives – a self for self or a self for others. They came to find themselves by being tempted to have something which the Father had said that they were not to have. This was the subtlety of Satan to tempt them, to say to them, "The Father is not being good to you as He should be, and there is value in the fruit of this tree which He says that you shouldn't take." That had the *consequence* of arousing conscious desire in them...and only by a *conscious* desire can we come to know who we are. By their *conscious* desire Adam and Eve came to know their appetites. The fruit looked good to eat. They had all that can come...the gift of sight. It was pleasant to look upon. We develop from use in life of sight. They had a mind which could be stored with new forms of knowledge. By no *other* means could they find that they had body and human potential and mind. They were also then confronted with these two alternatives – the way in which self can be for itself, or the way in which a self can be for others, in their case, for the will of God.

Because we see that the whole universe is *fixed* in this fact that He who is Author of the universe is fixed in self-giving Self. The opposite can only be evil, and only what He (God) is, is good. Therefore, that is why love is good. Self-giving love is good; self-loving love is evil. So, here they moved into Satan's way of self-for-self, partly by deceit on Eve's part; partly by deliberate choice by Adam, who freely chose to go the evil way, Satan's way of self-for-self. The true significance of the two alternatives being presented in the form of fruits of a tree is that what you *eat* takes you over, becomes you, and therefore, by the invitation to *eat* the fruit. What you eat goes within you and becomes you.

Therefore, if they had done...which we, by another process and not by the symbol of the fruit of the tree, but we by the atonement of Jesus Christ have received Jesus Christ...if they had taken of the True Fruit, the Genesis scripture says they would have received Eternal Life. That is how we *know* the fruit is only a symbol because we know Eternal Life **is** the Living Person...God in His Son form. He is The Life. We know that the fruit symbolized receiving Eternal Life—really receiving Him, Who is Eternal Life. Therefore, to receive the right fruit, is to receive Him, Who is the symbol of Eternal Life. To receive the wrong fruit is to receive him, who is the symbol of the opposite, the evil life which is really the death-life, because *all* that isn't God in love is death...only we call it life. The only true life is forms of self-giving love which is God. All other forms of self in self-loving form is *death* and we call it life with its present corruption and ultimate destiny.

So, we see this fundamental fact referring back to the *self* that Paul spoke of in *Romans* 1. It is compulsively a self-for-self, but *basically* it is not its *own* self. It is a human *self* expressing a divine self, because the false one has called himself a deity. He is called the "god of this world" because he was only a creature, but in the Garden it says that he was an originator. He brought into being a *quality* of person which was *unknown* in God, a person who is self-for-self...and therefore, he is called the god of this world. Therefore, humanity became a container of the deity of self-centeredness. That is an important fact! The deity that you contain, you express, because the whole Universe is an expression of deity. Only, inanimate things can only just automatically express deity. A tree is just a tree. We may say it is God in a beautiful tree form, but it can only be a tree. A person is like God Himself. We can have unlimited forms of expression because we are free selves, but we are *always expressing* the deity we contain. That is why all the words, as we move on, about the relationship of man to God, whichever god it is, are the relationships of the container to the one he contains. That is why we are called vessels in Rom. 9. A vessel is the container of the water within the container. So, in Romans 9, it is called a "vessel of wrath" or a "vessel of mercy." Wrath comes from the discordant life, the satanic life. That means the vessel contains the god through whom the discordant life comes, which ends in lost Eternity. The vessel of mercy is the *same vessel*, but it contains Him through whom harmonious life comes in mercy. That's Jesus Christ!

So, we see that the human is always a vessel. Later on Jesus speaks of the human as a branch; therefore He speaks of Himself in relation to the human as the True Vine...the branch expressing the Life of the True Vine – the Personhood of the True Vine. But, that implies that there is a false vine. If He says, "I am the true vine," the implication is that Satan is the false vine of which we humans were the expressions of the satanic nature.

As we're still remaining on that subject and its importance, it might be good to complete it; in the sense that the most dangerous effect of the human race indwelt by the satanic spirit (the spirit of self-centeredness, spirit of error) is that he moved the human race by deceit, into the false concept that we are just "independent selves." He himself claimed to be independent. Of course, he was only a creature of God. He *claimed* to be independent. However, he infected the human race with that same spirit of independence. So the human race doesn't know, in its fallen condition, that they contain the spirit of error. They just think they are people living their own lives, their own way. That leads on to an error dealt with in later chapters of Romans.

It's also important to note (understand) by the history (happenings) in the Garden of Eden that there's a **fundamental** difference between the deity person who by the symbol of fruit...entered into humanity...a self-lover, and God Who is an other-lover. Satan chose in his center and became fixed in his center as a "self-getter." He fixed himself to be his own god. So, he became fixed as a self-loving self, just as God is fixed as a self-giving self, who cannot lie. So, Satan fixed himself as a self-loving self who cannot be true. Jesus said, "Satan is a liar from the beginning." His nature is self-loving self.

The human race did not cast God out from our inner center. That is why it is important to see that Eve was deceived. She didn't *know* what we can know by hindsight. We *know* she knew the Father's love, but she didn't realize in any real certainty the implications of what would happen if she followed the invitation of the serpent...nor did Adam, because Adam really only followed Eve. (Which men have been doing ever since...laughter!) As Eve went that way, he chose...not willfully to defy God...but so as to remain with his mate. The *importance* of that being, the fall of *man* was in the flesh, where the fall of Satan was in the spirit. Now, that affected the spirit of man, because that is the whole man, so we'd become captive, although we hadn't given our spirits over to Satan. We followed the flesh, and of course the flesh belongs to the spirit...and in that sense since he is the spirit of error, he *took a hold* of our spirits, but he wasn't able to *unite* our spirits to himself. So, the Bible never talks about Satan in union with humanity. It talks about the spirit of evil working *in*, not totally *united* to.

That is why the human race *basically* remains what it always was, in the image of God. They are lost *sons*. The Bible speaks of Adam as a son of God...lost sheep. Jesus will speak of the unsaved Jews as "the lost sheep of the House of Israel" and phrases of that kind. That is why there remained in man's "inner center" what John 1 talked about, "As the light that lights every man that comes into the world," the *inner knowing* that we belong to God and have our being in Him, and being able to respond to Him. That is why, also, when the meeting first took place in that Garden (after Adam and Eve had fallen), God didn't hide Himself from man. He sought man out. The Bible says about Him, "As walking about in the cool of the day." It was Adam who hid from God. It was Adam who projected upon God the wrath that he was feeling. The wrath was really in *himself*. He knew he was wrong; he projected it upon God as if *God* was the angry one. That is what we have done ever since. And, in that is a sense in which God has permitted Himself to *be* regarded as the angry one...because we couldn't *see* the right...so therefore, it was *good* for us to understand in a sense that He *was* angry, because we were really *in the wrong*, but the anger is really in ourselves. The wrath took place in us...but only in God's mercy.

Therefore, God called Adam, "Where art thou? Come out from hiding." When He got them together His only *wrath* was on Satan, because as we see later on, God has to *hate* something which is fixedly evil. Love *does* hate; love must hate its opposite! The opposite, which was *fixed* in the opposite, was hated. Therefore, He had to say, "You are cursed, you are symbolized like a serpent, eating dust, crawling on the ground, you are cursed." He never said that to man! All that He said to Adam and Eve was "You'll have sorrow. You are My people; you have gone wrong. So, you will have sorrow to find you're wrong. There is a straightaway in *you*; there is the Ultimate Savior. You can find Him now."

He said to Satan, "I've put enmity between thy seed and her seed and her seed," or Satan's seed. What is Satan's seed? Satan infected us; he impregnated us with his false nature, so we become expressions of Satan's nature. But beneath that expression of 'Satan's nature' we are the 'seed of woman' and in the 'seed of woman' is Jesus Christ from eternity "the Lamb slain from the foundation of the world." So also, being in the seed of the woman...hidden there when we are prepared (conditioned) to receive Him...the One Who destroys Satan, destroyed the works of Satan. That's why of the very first two sons of Adam, one was redeemed. The first known redeemed person is Abel, who knowing his false condition, knowing his need of forgiveness, presented a sacrificial lamb, and this was taken up by God as a *symbol* of the fact that he was presenting himself for God's mercy through Jesus Christ. So Abel was pronounced righteous, God *testifying* in his gifts. So a first 'child of Adam' found the way to grace and deliverance in God.

So now we're seeing I've gone into length about that for this purpose...what Paul means when he talks about ungodliness, and then he calls it sin. So ungodliness is anti-Godness. He has described that with its appalling consequences, in the physical misuse of love, and the mental and spiritual misuses of love; turning into self-interest and self-gratification...and so we get the Romans 1 description of fallen humanity, which is given over by God that we may find that we are wrong. It doesn't say God turned His back on us. He just gave us over temporarily. God is there watching. He is there with us. He just given us to..."Alright you'll find out." There's a difference in "God *gave*" and not He said, "I'll throw you out." We are His lost sons; we're His prodigal sons, His lost sheep. So, this gives us a little more fundamental understanding – what it means – *why* are humans so ungodly; why we're self-loving selves, why we build our own gods like ourselves, so that we can live like the old Greek gods, so full of flesh adulteries, and hates, and murders – so we follow *our* adulteries, hates and murders. We have built our gods to suit ourselves, have affections for ourselves and do the same things they do...so the Baal worship and all the filthy worship of the heathen, *or* the worship of the golden calf – inquisitive self...or the worship of self-glory in the temple – *my* temple. The only fall is projecting *myself* – *my* temple, *my* god. The final stunt of the human self...making himself god as a projection of self-loving self, self-affirming self.

16

He gives us glimpses of the *totality* of the Fall – what it really is which we will see later on. It's the expression of the *false deity* expressed *through* humanity, and thus, that is the nature of humanity. The *only nature* humanity can have is the deity whom he expresses, because humanity is the vessel, the branch or the body compared to the head, or the temple in which the god worships...always a means of expression of the deity. And, the only **nature** humanity ever has is the expression of the deity of whom humanity is the manifestation...and we the manifestations of Satan. As we shall it later on, we will see it more clearly.

Now we get the coming in here back in *Romans* of the coming of the law...coming to a special race who could be prepared to *know* the difference between sin and righteousness (of God and devil) among whom the Savior could come and fulfill the atonement. The race which started from Abraham...and could be known in a *certain sense*, as we read, by those who *weren't* the children of Abraham by some responses of an inner law, because we all remain in the Being of God...although we're lost, we have our living and moving and being in God. Thus you have people like Socrates who distinctly felt that there was a right and wrong, and sought to align himself with the right as best as he knew how. All through the ages of man there has been this type as referred to in the Bible, as those "who by patient continuance in well-doing to *seek* for glory, honor and immortality." And we presume that was the *set of their being* even in their fallen condition. God meets the *set of their being* in that He meets them, when God shall judge the secrets of men. Whether they had *set of their being*, like Socrates, was for the right of the few who knew how to find it. He *didn't* know, but he *sought*. That day God will judge the secrets of men by Jesus Christ...calls it "my Gospel"...the means of grace for them.

Now we come in, having established in these early chapters of *Romans* (up to Verse 19 of Chapter 3) the sinfulness of sin, the *lost* condition of man, captives of the devil, expressions of the devil and therefore going to the devil's destiny, if they remain his captives. Slaves, incidentally, another of the illustrations used in the Bible of man's condition. When we move on to Romans 6, we find men are either slaves to sin or slaves to righteousness. Slaves to Satan, to the being through whom we express the life of sin *or* slaves to the Being Who expresses the righteousness of God. Therefore *again*, humans are the slaves under the dominion of our boss and fulfilling the purposes of the one who owns us.

17

In Chapter 3, we've had the introduction of the law. Rom. 3:19. We know what things the law says to those who are under the law. "Every mouth will be stopped and all the world will become guilty before God. Therefore, by the deeds of the law shall no flesh be justified in His sight: for by the law is the knowledge of sin." So here we have another great principle inserted in a few statements like this by Paul in this *Romans* letter.

That also takes a little backtracking and *understanding* by us in what *form* and for what *purpose* this law came in. We find that it is the first stage by which God can prepare a human race for the reception of grace. It is the first preparatory step that leads to grace. Paul doesn't go into this in detail in this letter at this level. We have to go back to fit that in by seeing how the God of all grace, of perfect self-giving-love Who only exists for the perfection and betterment of everybody, first approached the human race in its blindness by one man. There had been traces of light *before* one specific man, and that was Abraham. Abraham had been conditioned. Abraham had forefathers – Seth and so on, right on to Abel and to Adam and Eve – but with the rest of his family had fallen into idolatry. So, we read in the book of Joshua that Abraham was among his family in Ur of the Chaldeans who had given over to idolatry – this idolatry being some form of self-magnifying self.

There *was* an area of response in Abraham. I think there is an area of response in *all* men, because we haven't totally fallen. There remains an area in which God can appeal to us in which God *did* reveal Himself to Abraham, and said that through Abraham He would restore to the world His blessing in which He told him that if you identify yourself with Me now, I will appear to you as the God of glory. Abraham saw the glory of it. "I'll bless you and make you a blessing. And in you all families of the earth will be blessed." So we have here the moving out of the *universal* grace of God from the first man to whom He could get within hearing distance of His purposes. So, we see the *falsity* of any idea that God was anything like a punishing wrathful God. We will see later on how He had to *appear* like that for His purposes, but He appeared to Abraham, who was the one to whom He could reveal himself, the God of *all* grace. He says, "As you identify with Me, not only will I bless you, but indeed shall *all* families of the earth shall be blessed. Through *you* will come the complete restoration of the *harmony* for which the human race had been created." Harmony which is found in God's love-nature by us...that can come into being.

So, through Abraham He began a family to whom and by whom He began to express His grace, His faithfulness...whom in their response of faith He counted as righteousness. As it says, "Abraham *believed* God and it was counted as righteousness," which means that the Eternal Christ was imputed to Abraham before there was a historical Christ. Because the only way in which a fallen sinner can be righteous is in the righteousness of Christ through the atonement. Therefore, the "Lamb slain" was "slain from the foundation of the earth," in Spirit before He came into history. Here and there, there were men who *could* move in and find the efficacy of atonement in the Eternal Christ, which had not yet taken place in the historic reality of the Cross.

So Abraham, Isaac, and Jacob began to come into being. This family, this nation who received *partial* light...to a few, full light...in preparation for the *fullness* of light to come, when Jesus came. This was the Israelite Nation. That is why we hold them in *special* veneration. And, the day is going to come when *all* Israel again shall be saved, and why Paul always puts his *first* objective is to bring the Gospel to God's *privileged* people, if they could take it.

But, here came (if we may call it that) the *problem* that God had, or we had, which must be the preparation for grace. And that was our blindness would be removed, so that we may understand that we are in the need of grace – grace being the free gift by which God could *accept us back* in Jesus Christ. So, this privileged people of whom Jesus Christ was to be a member in the flesh, and *all* the early apostles to whom, therefore, we owe *everything* in what we now know of grace. He *had* to come to them by means of *radical* self-exposure which would indeed mean centuries of self-exposure, negative self-exposure...and that was when He got His people to Himself when He said He was going to meet with them on Mt. Sinai after the miraculous deliverance, probably a couple million of them from slavery in Egypt. There He began to speak to them through His anointed servant, Moses, who had been through an *individual experience* in which he had come into the grace of God, at the burning bush. He, himself, had to learn the difference between a self-affirming Moses, and a Moses who contained God...the Other Self, which he did at the burning bush.

And there we see around Mt. Sinai the next state of the *necessary exposure* of the blindness of self. We said, "Satan deceives," because we think we are right when we are wrong. Deceit is worse than blindness. Blindness is you just don't know. Deceit is when you think you *do* know when you don't. This made them think they were a credit to themselves, a self-affirming, self-reliant self...and therefore had to *meet* them on Mt. Sinai through Moses and He had to *say* to them a word of great grace. "I have brought you out here" he says in that Exodus chapter "on eagles' wings, like an eagle carries its young on its wings. I have brought you out to safety. You are my *favored* people in all the earth. You are not only my favored people; you are to *be* those by whom the world knows that they can be favored. You are to be a *kingdom of priests.*" Priests are the ones who were to reveal the grace of God to all the world. As He said to Abraham, "In you, shall all families of the earth be blessed."

First of all, there had to be the *exposure* to us humans of our *deception* concerning ourselves. Therefore in this interview of God with the people of Israel through Moses, which is in *Exodus* Chapter 19, He then went on quite quietly to say "You're blessed, thy gift to Me; you are to be a blessing so long as you obey My voice, and fulfill My covenant. I made a covenant with you; fulfill it**."** Now of course, that *immediately* brings up the response of self-relying self. That is exactly what He wanted! Blind self-reliant self says, "Oh, I can do it." Self, not knowing it's self-for-self...and so He says, "That is it then. We'll make this covenant now." It was here in this *Exodus* 19th chapter that they gave themselves away when they came back and they said (verse 8), "All that the Lord has spoken, we will do." So, here was the exposure of the blinded-self that *thinks* that it is self-sufficient, and can fulfill the laws of God and be worthy of the promises of God. God *had* to put it in the form of self-reliant worthiness because He had to expose self-reliance. Of course we know now that our worthiness is not relying on our self. That couldn't come then because He had to expose this false satanic self-reliant, self-affirming, self-sufficient self! So, they answered gaily and said, "*All* that You have said, we will do."

It was after that, that God gave the law to Moses. Up to that time, He had only met Moses and the children of Israel on the basis of this free grace. "You are special treasure to me; I have brought you out on eagles' wings. You are to be the light and blessing to the world. But, you must keep My covenant." He had to insert that to *expose* self-reliant self. Here came the answer – self-reliant self.

Here came the giving of the law on Mt. Sinai. We usually know it as the Decalogue, the Ten Commandments to Moses on those tables of stone, which the Bible late on says were given him not by God Himself, but by an angel. It says that in Galatians and in the speech of Stephen in Acts 7. The reason being that God is *pure love,* and He cannot give Himself *as God* simply in the form of "Thou shall not." It has to be a reflected *form* of God, which was all at the moment that the fallen world could take to *find out* their own fallen condition, which is only a stepping stone to grace. So it says in Gal. 3:19, "The law was ordained by angels in the hand of a mediator." Later on in Moses' meeting with God on Mt. Sinai it was face to face. But, that was when grace came. That was when He gave him the pattern of grace in the Tabernacle. It shows *always* grace, *always* acceptance and *always* His presence for those who are in faith relationship with Him. So, there He met him and spoke as a man speaks to his friend, but not when He gave him the law. That was given as a representation in angels.

So, here came to the children of Israel the necessary means of *exposing sin as sin*. So, in Romans 3:20 "By the law is the knowledge of sin" which *had* to be the first stepping stone into grace, because when we become we honest then we are confronted by the law of God...the commandments of God...we confess we're guilty. So, it says here, "*All* the world may become guilty before God."

That is why Jesus said that the first step into Himself must be by coming to the light, where He Himself had fulfilled the reconciliation necessary, which could bring us from our sin condition to our justified condition in the presence of God. That couldn't be, first of all, until we are confronted by the Light. Light exposes things as they are. Jesus said in John 3, "No one is condemned by their sins. They are condemned because *Light* has come into the world and men loved darkness rather than Light." They would not come to the Light, hated the Light less their sinful condition be exposed. That's why there has to be repentance before there can be faith, because repentance is a change of mind about myself, not about God.

Paul has presented us, in *Romans*, with the first necessary stage to us being what we were created to be, failed to be through the Fall, and re-created to be in Jesus Christ – liberated sons of God...the means by which He manifests His own personal self-loving, self-giving Self through eternity.

Now it is at *this* moment that Paul turns from the exposure of our sin condition to the remedy in the *blood* of Christ...not yet the body of Christ, but the blood of Christ. We'll read about the *body* of Christ in Rom. 6. We're now in the third chapter and this is where Paul brings in the *reality of the blood* and *the necessity of faith*. So he says in Rom. 3:25, "Being justified freely by His grace through the redemption in Christ Jesus: Whom God has set forth to be the propitiation through *faith* in His blood, to declare His righteousness for the remission of sins that are past, through the forbearance of God." (Not yet sin...*sins*...specific acts of the breaking of the law of God; sins, not yet sin. We discuss sin later on.) The removal of our guilt, and the consequent penalty of those who have sinned...it is said here to be through faith in His blood. He doesn't in this letter (which I said is in a sort of shortened form) give all the explanations of *why* we can have this propitiation through faith in His blood, and thus that God can declare His righteousness for the remission of our sins of the past...and be both just and the Justifier of him that believeth in Jesus.

That is why it is important to realize this is the first stepping-stone into our grace and saved relationship with God through Christ. Not the finalizing of it, just the first stepping-stone. The reason being, that as we've seen, we've been so *blinded* by the deceit of Satan into a self-affirming self with his *deepest* form of a self-righteous self, which is when we receive some *external* approaches to God by the requirements of the law and external forms of religion and in our self-righteous self if we think we're outwardly *supposed* to conform to these standards of the law...outward religion...therefore we're acceptable to God...which is a lie in it itself, for we have already seen in a previous chapter that we, who would *say* that we are in the right relationship with God are really unrighteous. When we come down to here we are the sinners. We are the liars. We are the adulterers. We are the haters. We are the murderers and so on.

So, our first move *in* is when we come to this exposure of our *sinful* condition in the form of the sins we've committed. Perhaps I shouldn't use the words "sinful condition" because we haven't come, so far, as to see sin in its *inner* essence yet (which is our self-loving-self) but we see its *products* which are the sins. The law pinpointed the products, and we come to the point when we recognize them, and therefore recognize our guilt. We've also known those to whom the law has come, that, that produces the consequences of the curse...and *death*. Galatians speaks of the *curse* of the law – those who have committed sins. James explains, even if you have committed *one sin*, you are guilty of a broken law. Just the same as a person in the law of a country, if he commits one sin, he is guilty of breaking the law of the country. And, therefore, we have this *destiny* of being under curse, explained to us in other scriptures, the "eternal hell" which is described by Peter as being the condition of being of "spirits in prison." This is very significant, because he is taking us *deeper* there than we know when we first commit sins. The *real* prison of a person is his self.

If freedom is God in His self-giving Self, bondage is a self in its self-loving self. So it is a self-getting, self-seeking, self-preserving, self-justifying self – *that* is his hell! That is his prison; we are always imprisoned by self-loving self. That is why we can *taste* some of the pains of hell in our life down here, when they take the form of our self-reactions and our resentments, hates, fears, and so on. We are touching the meaning of "spirits in prison" which is the condition of hell - a condition given us in John's revelation, the book of Revelation, as being a "lake of fire"...remembering the physical is only a *dim outline* of the true condition. In Revelation gold is *transparent*, while our gold is a dull thing. Yet pure gold, the streets of the City of God are *transparent* gold...pure gold. We have a dulled form of gold, so we only have a dulled form of fire. Pure fire is something much worse.

It has to come as a *symbol* to us of a body burning, but the *true fire* is these "spirits in prison." And we know a little of that, thank God, down here. That's why hell is spoken of as something which operates **in** us in one statement, and that is in James where it speaks about us as having a fallen tongue...a blasphemous, vile, cursing tongue. It says it is set on the fire of hell. Therefore, hell is the *inner principle* which is *causing* me to use my tongue in these expressions of hate and revenge or whatever they may be.

However, the first form the principle of sin, which is *self-centeredness*, is seen by is in sins. We're too blind to see our self-centered condition or the *being* which is causing us to be a self-centered person. That is beyond our sight, but we *do see* the products...and that's where the outer law came – because you *have* lied, you *have* committed adultery, you *do* what is equivalent to murder, you *do* worship anything except God, etc. Now we have the first presentation of the *coming among us* of the Redeemer. It is first mentioned to us here. Paul said his gospel's concerned as the revelation to us of His Son, evidenced to be the Son of God by the resurrection from the dead. And, *here* we have Christ Jesus coming in, "Being justified freely by His grace through the redemption that is in Christ Jesus."

We move on later to a presentation of Christ Jesus as the true Adam for us...we find that in Rom. 5. We don't go into detail of that *now*, because we will pick it up then. We are, therefore, in Paul's statement taking it for granted that we *understand* that Jesus Christ came in the flesh. Paul doesn't speak in Romans of the Virgin birth; he speaks of in Gal. 4:4, where he says, "He is made of woman, made unto the law." He just moves us into the statement, implying His incarnation. Here he speaks of Him only as a completed Person, as a Savior. He doesn't take us through the backgrounds of His being the *one* Person Who never became a vessel of Satan, who rejected the temptations of different kinds to yield to Satan's voice, both in the wilderness and the ways in which it says, "He was tempted in all points as we are." Temptation is enticement. He rejected those enticements. So, He *never became* either a child of Satan...or a vessel that contained Satan...or a branch of the satanic vine. He remained His Father's Son.

The *blood* of Christ, however, means that we know of His history, the propitiation through His blood, that He *voluntarily* offered Himself first to be a physical sacrifice...what John the Baptist had previously called "The Lamb of God," and that there would be a *physical* crucifixion and a *physical* shedding of His blood. The *necessity* of that being, "that the wages of our sins are death." He must fulfill that *same* way of death if He is to be the One Who took our place, and removed the necessity of us going that *same* way. The *full significance* of death that is important for us to grasp is that it's not a physical. It had been said to Adam and Eve, as we read, "In the day you eat of it, you shall surely *die*." Well they didn't die physically. We are told in Eph.2 "We are *dead* in trespasses and sins." We have not died physically. Paul said in 1 Tim. 5:6, "But she that liveth in pleasure is dead, while she liveth." So it is not physical. So we realize what we *really are* is spirit! Our soul clothing which is our reasons and emotions; the body activity is merely the *clothing* of our *real self*. So, the *real* death is the death of the inner spirit. But, the inner spirit never dies. It is immortal. So it goes into a death condition, and remains in a death condition. The *seriousness* of death is not our physical; it is the destiny of our spirit.

The Bible presents us as spirits *either* in our fallen condition joined to Satan, and therefore goes to the realm of Satan, which is called in the Bible "where the spirits are in prison." We recognize the *real* prison is our self-centeredness. Or, if there has been a way of redemption, we move among those who are called in Heb. 12:23 after physical death...we are among "The spirits of just men made perfect." "Spirits of just men" means that my *real* self, by having become a justified self, perfected in Christ, is among the company of the justified and perfected in Christ...in Mount Zion. Therefore, that *means* that if the Lord Jesus Christ, God's Son, Who later on we find is called "the Last Adam," to represent the human race (later on in 5) is to remove from me the effects of my sins (judgment, curse, judgment, guilt, death)He must go that way of death. And, that way of death is only *incidentally* the body. So He went the way of the body, which is the outward evidence that He really died. That's what we speak of as the shedding of the blood.

That's why it is important in the history given us of Calvary, when they *saw* that He was really dead, they didn't break His legs to kill Him, as they did the two thieves. Instead they pierced Him, because He was already dead, and "out came the blood and water" which was the evidence that it was really a dead body.

The importance to us in the totality of this blood redemption is that it's not *real death*. Death is the destiny of the spirit! That's why it is important to know that the Bible says, first of all by prophecy in the Psalms and then by quotation in the first speech after Pentecost, that He went to hell, the place of the "spirits in prison." In Acts 2 when Peter, speaking in his speech before the people of Jerusalem, quoting what David said about Jesus in Psalms 16:10, "Because Thou wilt not leave my soul in hell, neither wilt Thou suffer Thy Holy One to see corruption." It says in another place that it was *impossible* for death to hold Him...that death couldn't hold Him. But it *does say*, in this I Peter statement that I briefly referred to, that He went and preached to the spirits in prison. "Being put to death in the flesh, but being quickened by The Spirit by which He went and preached to the spirits which were in prison." So, we know that He was there!

The perfection to us means He went *all the way* we are destined to go by the *outer* fact...we are not yet concerned about our inner condition, but by our outer condition. Our inner condition *caused* us to commit these sins, and therefore break the law and be under a curse and go into the death which was part of that curse – death not being physical death, but spirit destiny. He went *all* the way and then the resurrection is the evidence that all had been completed – to be for all the sins of the world. "This is the Lamb of God who takes away the sin of the world," John the Baptist says. "For our sins," Peter says...only our sins, not sin..."takes away the **sin** of the world." "Bore our sins in His body on the tree" – that was Peter's remark.

The human race is a multitude of sins – its necessary destiny as a human race. It couldn't hold Him! Not just because He was God's Son, but because Satan never could 'get' Him. And because He *was* God's Son, Satan had no hold on Him – it was impossible to hold Him. "He was *raised* from the dead by the glory of the Father." That statement is made in Romans 6:4"...raised from the dead by the glory of the Father." He couldn't raise Himself as a man because He represented lost man, lost sinner. Lost man cannot raise himself so it says He was *quickened* by the Spirit..."raised from the dead by the glory of the Father." Now that means as representing us, *all* that could come to us as a consequence of sin is disappeared. It shut the gates to hell to us, to all humanity, to all mankind. Thus in 2 Cor. 5:19 "to wit, that God was in Christ reconciling the *world* unto Himself (the whole *world's* reconciled) not imputing their trespasses to them; and hath committed us unto the word of reconciliation." Therefore, God said, the whole *world* is reconciled. He doesn't impute the trespass of *anybody* to them. So it is a *total* redeeming act by the One, we could say who could act because He was the Creator and Originator of the human race. Therefore, He *could* represent the human race, where one man, human, couldn't represent another.

The consequence being, therefore, that resurrection gave us our justification. The blood meant He went the way we go to an eternal destiny, death of body leading into eternal destiny of "spirits in prison." The resurrection gave us our justification, as if we had never sinned. So in Romans 4:25 he goes on to say, "Who was delivered for our offenses and raised again for our justification." *Justification being a far greater work than forgiveness.* You can forgive and not forget. "Justification isn't there. Justification means the thing isn't there; it has disappeared. All that has been done is disappeared. I don't see it there. There's nothing in the record! My record's *clean*.

Therefore, in Jesus Christ He makes it as if we've *never* sinned! We are righteous...as He *is*. That's at this point, the inner righteousness, but what is called *imputed* righteousness. We are seen in God's sight as if we hadn't sinned. It doesn't yet refer to the fact of how we cease to *be* people expressing sin – sinfulness. That comes in a little later now. Expressing our outer position and condition...in other words God was not *imputing* our trespasses to us. That was said of David and said of Abraham in the Old Testament. Because the One Who went the way we went, went *all the way* into hell, was delivered (as it were) the doors of hell closed before Him, and the resurrection means you are accepted – the 'thing' as if it isn't there. So He was raised again for our justification.

So this is the presentation in this somewhat shortened form, very *definite* form, by Paul – that we have come under guilt, and the guilt is confirmed to us by the law. All the world is guilty, but they don't know that they are guilty until the law comes to them. *Then* they know that they're guilty. That's why Jesus came under the law as a law-person and then went as a law-person, as if He was us, into death and hell and rose again for our justification.

That completes in Romans 3 the presentation of the totality of the first form of our total salvation, the outer form in which our sins, guilt, wrath, judgment, hell, destiny are wiped out in this One, as the Lamb of God taking away the sins of the world!

Paul then moves on to the *centrality* of this word – faith. Of course, there again now, we come across a great thing to be said. He said at the end of this third chapter, he spoke about the One Whom God has set forth to be a propitiation through faith in His blood. Where is boasting? It's excluded. By what law, of works? Nay, by the *law of faith*. That's in Romans 3:27 – the *law* of faith. Therefore, that's a principle that takes some further examination which is not given us in detail by Paul, except that he exemplifies to us in Chapter 4 what faith *is* ...against our self-effort, against our doing things by our own initiative...from relying upon our own deeds – works. He illustrates that to us by the final great act of Abraham's faith, when it said towards the end of this 4th chapter of Romans that we can understand faith by Abraham. And also we come to understand that it doesn't depend on *law* because Moses came *long after* Abraham – 400 years after.

So, law wasn't God's grace! Law came to expose *us*, not to reveal Christ. *That is what we get wrong*! Law didn't come to expose God. That is why God didn't give it. It came by an angel. It was outer form...that's what my *character* is, because we've got to find what His character is before we can find Him! We were not prepared to find Him until we qualify His character. We've got to qualify His character as 'this': (His character is what *we* know, and of course, LOVE fulfills *all* law. But you couldn't use those terms *then*.) He had to specify righteousness by saying what we should *not* do such as...you don't thieve, you don't lie, you don't commit adultery, you don't murder, you worship only one God and so on. Because in our childish condition that's all we could see. We have to be called on it... but you *have* lied, you *have* committed adultery, you *have* hated, you *have* coveted, you *have* worshipped other gods, and so on...never have stopped. By the *law* is the knowledge of sin. The real God of course, God Father of our Lord Jesus Christ, is the God of grace. And, grace means free gift to the undeserving...free gift to the undeserving. So, incidentally he is saying there, Chapter 4 of Romans, the difference between works and faith. This is the final *danger* as well as the final *privilege* of religion and high standards...that self has to be satisfied so that we take *danger* upon ourselves to justify ourselves. We think we can justify ourselves because we are attached to certain *church laws*, certain commandments and so on. That can still be the danger right among us Christians, as it was among the Jews, to take on certain forms, as if the forms meant something!

He exemplified faith as coming in this instance to Abraham physically at a time that was beyond physical possibility. This is the occasion given us at the end of Rom. 4, the faith of Abraham where God had said, "I'll make you a father of many nations." God said that..."Quickened the dead and called those things which be not, as though they were." He said that to Abraham when it was impossible for them to have a child, where it says that his body was now dead when he was about 100 years old and Sarah and the deadness of her womb at 90 years of age where it was *impossible* for physical fulfillment of this word – "Now I have come to you, you are to have a son." So it says this is given to us as a *standard* example of faith. You may say it is an *extreme* form, and therefore it is extravagant to offer an extreme form; it would be better to offer an example in a simpler form. And that's where it says, when this word came to Abraham from God, "Against hope, he believed in hope that He might be the father of many nations." It gives there the *processes* of faith that he wasn't weakened in faith by considering his own condition. That's the first step when you don't consider your own condition, because that is hopeless. It says (Romans 4:19) "And being not weak in faith, he considered not his own body now dead when he was about a hundred years old, neither yet the deadness of Sarah's womb." So faith's first step is, "I'm not going to be influenced by my sight or my reason...my outer reaction." We say that's hopeless; it's impossible.

Paul then says that faith moves on. It will stretch *in,* and will take an *impossible promise* and not stagger at it. That is the next move in the spirit. In a sense you are moving back from soul to spirit. With soul – emotions and reason it is impossible...as well as with the body...impossible! Impossible! *Spirit*, which is in tune with God, is talking about Abraham. His faith was in tune with God. In his spirit he can take this promise of God which is *ridiculous* and not stagger at it because God *says* so...because he has the promise of God so he wouldn't stagger. So it says, "He staggered not at the promise of God." Then it says faith had its *consummation*. He was strong in faith when he *gave glory*...when he said, "Okay, it is going to be!" So faith had these phases. He had rejected being controlled by the outer appearances when it was ridiculous. It moved him into saying "God does the impossible and in this condition, in this situation where the impossible is available to me, I am going to take it; and therefore I'll take it! I speak a word of faith"...which it refers to later in Romans about the word of faith.

Being strong in faith giving glory to God; being fully persuaded that what He had promised He was able also to perform...because when there is that word of faith there comes the inner witness – "He that believes hath the witness in himself." And, we come to see – He'll do it; He'll do it! So that the *link* to word of faith and giving glory to God was the inner assurance that will come to pass. "Therefore it was imputed to him for righteousness."

In other words what that meant was now he *totally* conformed himself to the promise of God. He was totally delivered...any idea of any idea of *self-reliance* is destroyed. How can you rely on a body in that condition! So, he couldn't rely on himself. He relied totally on the promise of God, against his body condition, and against Sarah's body condition. That was what was imputed to him as righteousness, because he was confirming the righteousness of *God*...because when God says a thing...that's it! Righteousness just means right. God is right. Paul then says that it was written as a *standard example* to us of what this faith is...of which is what this chapter is concerned. It means that we know this *first stage of redemption* comes about when we consider not our sins – like Abraham considered not his body. Our sins? Our sins are sins. That means we have first of all admitted our sins, and have now moved into repentance. We have changed our minds and admitted our sins, and are guilty before God. We are *done for* then with all these guilt upon us of wrath and judgment. We do **not** consider that. We *stagger* over to the promises of God! We move over to the presented fact of the shed blood of Jesus Christ, and the resurrection which confirms that in that shed blood and resurrection – all that *should* come to us through our sinful condition...this is *out!* So, we stagger not at the promise of God...and then by the *folly of faith*, we praise God!

Faith always is the moving in *against* appearances, against our *condition*, and of course that is great to be found in that condition, because that means that we have come free from this false show of self-righteousness. The law has had to operate on us first to get us out of this – "Oh, I'm all right; I have fulfilled the laws." I've got to square up I'm *not*! I've come to the light with my sins. So, I have moved *out* from this false concept of self-righteousness. That's what the law is *meant* for...to move into the recognition of our sinful condition. Then in refusing to *recognize* my sinful condition, I transfer my believings about my sinful condition into what God says about His Son Jesus Christ. This is presented to us in the gospel and by the *meaning* of the blood and resurrection. I say to myself God *imputes that* for righteousness. Therefore, in God's sight, I am that one who is as if I was

Jesus Christ and I have never sinned. Now we know that this is the *first stage* of this redemption.

The fourth chapter shows us the difference between false works, which is the subtlest and highest form of self-loving self – "I am all right anyhow," and especially if I have religion! We know that millions of us have gone through that and that has to be destroyed in us by the operation of the law. I can't be honest without the law. That is why there had to be a law. Law is the knowledge of sin, and sin *acknowledged* moves into repentance, faith, righteousness and justification.

We then move in to the finalizing of this which we commonly speak of as the new birth, the new creation in Christ, although, that term is not used in *Romans* when Paul describes the effects of this faith-relationship. This is where we also learn what is not in Romans – that faith produces substance. It is not in *Romans*. Faith is substance. It becomes something substantial to us. That is why we always say by faith, "I'll come to this home this evening." Now faith becomes substance to us and we are in this home. Faith moves us into something which is available and desirable because faith is the free move that we take into the thing and it comes to pass. And, then we don't say, "I'll *be* in this room this evening." We are here. I *am* in this room. Faith has become substance. Now Paul is saying the *real* substance is – you are a spirit person, which is *inner* self. God is that inner Self of Spirit; God is Spirit; we are spirits that knew *Him*...that inner Self...that's where there's inner circumcision and so on.

Paul continues in the fifth chapter to say that the *consequences* of moving in to a faith relationship with Christ crucified and Christ risen *is* Pentecost! Pentecost means the *Sprit* comes into us and confirms to us the relationship we have moved into by faith – into Christ Jesus. So Romans 5 moves in and says certain things happen to us by the Holy Ghost, which is given to us. He has not been mentioned before...and what the Holy Ghost has given to us in Romans 5 is a certain Spirit that says, "We know."

The first is a *peace* with God, because we have rightly discovered our disharmony, which is the wrath that we have been in – our separateness from God in a sinful condition, and our lost destiny. We have been *rightly troubled* with our sin condition and its destiny...and being justified by faith...ahhhhhhh, *God accepts me.* "Oh, I'm all right." It is as if I had never sinned! Peace! I have moved into *harmony* with the Eternal Being, Whom I should from the beginning have known. There was that in me which *could* respond in the beginning, as we read. I've moved back into *harmony*. I've begun to move back into harmony with the universe...because God is The Universe. God is our originator.

We have moved back into a Person of Whom the universe is just a form. We have come into center! We have peace with God through our Lord Jesus Christ. We have a *sense* that things are right. We move out of disharmony and distortion into proportion and harmony...peace...it's as is all is right...peace. We *all* know that who are born again. With that a sense of acceptance, which is access by the same faith into "the grace wherein we stand." We are standing! It isn't just a whim; it is permanent – condition of relationship with God – our Father, our home. We are children of God, and so on in whatever form it has taken. And then Paul adds you have necessary things you must go through to become a *stabilized* person, because you are going to be the heir of God's universe. You're going to be a stable expression of Him to the universe! So *you* have to become established and stable as God Himself is established – you *cannot sin*; you *cannot lie*. We have become "cannot" people too. We are beginning to become that. We don't quite know much about it yet. We have come to a *relationship* but not a union, yet. We have come to Him, Who died *for* us...'outside' us. So now the blood is Christ 'outside' us. It's 'set forth'; that's why the expression is 'set forth'. That's used in both Rom.3:25 "God had set Him forth" and it is used in Gal. 3:1, "Why don't you avail the truth and realize that Christ Jesus has ever been set forth, crucified among you?"

We are still external people. We see our sins, we see a Savior on a Cross, and the resurrection, and we are presented with the consequence...the effects of that. It has taken *faith*, because it is only faith that can believe in resurrection. So we have moved into the *Spirit realm* out of the flesh realm, because crucifixion is flesh realm. Resurrection is Spirit realm! Anybody who believes history can believe the crucifixion. Only people who have gone *beyond* human history can believe resurrection. Therefore, the world thinks that it is absurd. We have moved into the *absurdity* of faith, the *foolishness* of faith. We have moved into a Spirit condition. That is why the Holy Spirit has touched us. We have now moved into our first relationship with Him, Who is the Source of the universe. Who are we but the 'outer forms'. So, we're moving now in the Spirit dimension, sometimes called heavenly dimension. It's first form *still* somewhat out from us. Because we have seen our *sins*, we have this peace with God and we know that we're accepted, so we don't go about worrying about our sins. We'll *stand* in His grace.

31

We have a hope. We haven't quite yet got the glory in our souls, maybe. We have the *hope* of glory. We are going to move to this perfection. That's the main *for* us...*perfection!* Where "Eye has not seen, nor ear heard or entered into the heart of man what God hath prepared for those who love Him." So we have glory on the way to glory! We haven't got the final glory yet – "Christ in you the *hope* of glory." We haven't even got that yet; we're just hoping for the glory here. We're in the first stages of babyhood. And, then we get this shock that we have to become established. We have to become *far* more settled in who *you* are than Who He is. So we are going to be banged about in all kinds of ways! There will be all kinds of things to frustrate you, disturb you, and bother you and upset you. These are called tribulations. You are to learn a *very big* thing; when you get settled you are to *glory* in tribulations! We won't do that until we've gone *far enough* to see the value. The value here is that tribulations – you are *stuck* in something – works patience. You wait.

I have just seen my friend, Hobart Smith, who is a building contractor in a very big way. I moved in to his life about ten years ago when he had taken a stand in Charlotte. He wouldn't advertise on Sunday. Apparently all big builders do their transactions on Sunday. He, was a good Baptist...he has other ideas of Sunday *now*. He was a good Baptist – he kept his Sundays. It was a great *thing* at that moment; his friends thought that he had failed...he shook them up. They said, "You've *failed*." But, he took his stand in faith, and then he had to be encouraged in his faith. He said to me, "Can it work?" So, I began to *show* him, that if you walk with God, faith means *God's* doing things and you move into situations where you can say, "*God's* doing it."

You don't have to be a business man and have your business operations, because your *real* basis is *God* doing things through your business things. So he moved into faith and I remember things happened. There came a crisis just before this recent recession and a then on the verge of taking a very big estate. (I think it cost about a million dollars, around Raleigh. He was a Charlotte man.) Should he take this big piece of land and build? I don't know anything about business of course. I do know a little about faith. So, I knew the faith side and he knew the business side. So I went with him and I said, "Yes, it *looks* to me as if God is giving you the opportunity. All right, your *faith*...move in...dare to say, and be strong in faith; God has given you that thing!" He couldn't prove a thing. So I was advising him maybe wildly, maybe truly. Well, he has come back now. "Brother Norman, I *proved* these principles work. They just work! I went to the *verge* of bankruptcy. My chief competitor has collapsed and gone. I just today am finally selling that whole business off at an enormous profit. The whole Raleigh situation has come *perfectly* through! I am not meaning I *settled* at one point. You see it through life; it has affected my whole family. We have seen how you trust God in situations and God comes up on top *every time*! You will win your poker games every time." So now of course he has become stabilized. That's an illustration of what I mean.

So tribulation worketh patience; it didn't happen in a moment. It's taken about ten years for this to come to its satisfactory ultimate end. But on this level it has come through. Patience means, "Alright, I don't know, God is in it somewhere. Let's stick at it. God's in it somewhere." Patience works experience. This *happened*; it happened! All right it happened once; it will happen again! *Hope*...see? Tribulation works patience; stick it out! And, so you have begun to say, "It's all right, go on with it." Against all these storms go on; don't see evil. See a good God through everything. Then it happens. "Oh, it's happened. I've got experience. I've got experience it happened! I can prove it again." Hope. Then it says, "Hope doesn't make ashamed," because it's graduate seepage of God loves. Now you're moving. Not just God had mercy and grace on your mercy, but God loves; God loves. God has a love relationship with you and you with Him. So, it's beautiful and works out together. God's beautiful verse is in Rom. 5:5. "This *love* of God is shed abroad in our hearts by the Holy Spirit which is given unto you." So, it is not referring now to *our* love for Him, but *His love for us*. We are now moving into the fact that there is a God of love operating in us, so we come to be God-lovers, which is the Spirit of God in us. As the light dawns on us we get more and more conscious of the *expansion* of love. Love is for a person that is against you in every way – a person who is helpless or rotten...an *opponent* to you. *That's* who God loves!

He moves on in this chapter...this is how we see what God's love is to us in Christ. We are helpless; we were rotten in our sins; we are antagonistic. "Scarcely for a righteous man will one die, peradventure for a good man someone might dare to die but God commandeth His love toward us when we were sinners." We were *rotten* in our condition. And a little later on we find we were *rebels*; we were *enemies*, but Christ died for us. Then he moves on...he says we have been justified by His blood...*now* you can see that. Now you're justified by His blood, *therefore*, you realize you have been saved from wrath. That *wrath* business is out. Being justified by His blood...you are safe there. But, then he goes on to say, "But *now* you are

33

saved by His *life.*" Therefore, the Person Who *died* for you – in His death you've come you have come clear. You're sure clear in His life! He's got you now. He's the One who has things in hand, so you are *saved by His life.* That moves you on to rejoice in God Himself. Your *joy* is in God now. He is no longer some fearsome Being. It is now a loving free family relationship in God! You're moving freely into God! Now that's what he presents to us as the first, the *elementary evidences,* very precious evidences of a new birth, but still somewhat in an outer relationship – peace, and knowing where we stand in God's presence, and having tribulation and knowing that God comes through and therefore God loves...even going to the Father and know we are saved by His life and that He'll keep us (little Father) and therefore we can begin to enjoy God (little Father).

Now Paul says that we have to go *far deeper.* We have to open a *whole new area.* That starts in Rom. 5:12. He says that you're a new being; you're the *product* of a new being. You're *something more* than just an individual who has got a relationship. He says we're all beings by the law of nature, the law of God. You see, the originator always produces its own kind. Cats produce cats; carrots produce carrots and so on. This is the law of nature. Fathers produce sons. You're linked in with that area of the family – Genesis 1 talks about "after their own kind." Fish after their own kind; birds after their own kind...because this is the law by which creation works.

He is now saying, therefore, we were caught up by our forefather..."By one man sin entered the world and death by sin: and so death passed upon all men, for all have *sinned.*" Then he goes on in another paragraph to say sin was *there,* and death was *there,* even though he didn't know the law. The law made sin, even though it was not really known as *sin.* It was known as right and wrong, but not as the word sin, which means a personal relationship with God – until the law came and made this relationship.

He is now saying we are now *part* of a new Adam! He is not called the last Adam here. Paul called Him the last Adam in 1 Cor. 15...the same right as Paul...the Last Adam! But the first Adam *is* called a *figure* in vs 14... "*Death reigned* from Adam unto Moses, who was the *figure* of Him who is to come." So, you see, God always had a *pattern.* So the human relation under Adam was a pattern, which was to move to the original of which this *is* a pattern. So the human race under Adam was a *pattern* to move on to the original. This was the first Adam; we're all part of that first Adam's race. It's called in 1 Cor 15 "a living soul"...because soul becomes spirit of a *sunken soul.* We are born **spirits.** Heb. 12 says that He fathered our spirits! Spirit, you know, is the I am, because God is the I AM. He's Spirit...the I am which says that I *know*, I *desire*, I *will* – *that's* I am! That is my inner self. I know, I love, I desire, I choose, I will. That's a person! Anything I ever *do* comes from my knowing something, my desiring something, and my moving into it which is choice, or faith. That's a person...God or man. All the rest are forms.

So we know what we are because it says He fathered our spirits, and because we are created in His likeness. Yet, in Adam we are called living souls...*because* the soul is the expression of the spirit. Soul is my reason which seeks to express my knowledge...and my emotions which express my love...and my body, outwardly. Now, becoming a living soul means that we have sunk into self-centeredness. Soul is what *I* think about it...what *I* feel about it and so on...and what *I* act about it. That is soul, body...the two together. And, so it says in 1 Cor. 15 Adam, the first Adam, was made a living *soul*, a self-soul. The spirit was sunk in there; spirit is there, but it was more or less sunk in it. You don't know much about spirit and you'll find the world doesn't know much about spirit, scientists don't talk about spirit; they talk about soul...many psychologists. Spirit is unknown until you '*touch*' spirit...practically unknown. Mind you, it is coming back. That is why personally I welcome much more this 'age' than mine. I mean that I go back to the era that was pure materialism. The atom was only just discovered. A *thing* was thought material...was reality. What's that stuff about some mysterious force? *This* is what's real. Because atomic science broke that up and we began to move into another *whole realm* of something beyond this! Even though atom may be called spirit-material in a certain sense, but we have gone beyond that now.

I've just had a very interesting book given me written by a couple of scientists called *All is Light*. It says all that we call under different terms is really light. Well, of course, that takes us straight back to the very simple fact that light's a Person. That's what science doesn't know! They know *divided* light which has got positive/negative, which becomes electricity and so on, but they do not know *pure light* is God...a Person! That's something they don't *know*. Now we are moving! So the ultimate universe is, as we have said all along, to be light — a Person. God is light. Of course scientists won't take this unless they've had a Person to person relationship! That's where we fall out of that.

So the Spirit is made more or less to go into the trash can. We don't know much about it. Men might laugh at it or accept it as coming back a little. That is why I say I prefer a person who fiddles with occultism and things like that because they are at least occupied with things of the spirit...maybe a false spirit will lead you to the True Spirit. You are getting nearer to reality when you touch the spirit realm than when you touch the matter realm. Matter is only outer *form*, which to me is interesting. So, we're saying the passage in 1 Cor. 15:45 says, "The first Adam was made a living soul, the last Adam a quickening spirit." So, we are seeing how in the first Adam, which is a figure, we are made *people* and the whole point was that we discovered that we are wonderful people. We have tremendous potential and we only look at this world without the relationship to God and see *tremendous* potential! Look at any room; see the inventions and realize the tremendous potential. We have hardly begun to *know* the potential in investigation, invention, application, reproduction and material. Tremendous potential...we know *that*! *That's* living soul.

The last Adam is the quickening Spirit. Now that's the other one here, the figure of Him Who is to come. He is called just, "Him that is to come." He isn't called here by His name, Adam...but He is in 1 Cor. 15 by Paul, "A quickening spirit" – that means life going *out*; living soul – life's come *in*. I am a living soul. I have got what I have taken. I *use* what I take – "A quickening spirit" means something flows *out* of me. I am another kind of person – outgoing to other people; not in-taking to me. *Another type of person*...no, that is this other *One*. Now this is presented to us as a heredity relationship to a *whole new* family of spirit, a *new kind of person* and you *are* what your ancestor is. Now it's getting beyond outer sins; you *are* what your ancestor is. If one died for all then all are dead, and if one has caused offense, then we are all under condemnation...then the judgment and bondage. Death reigned by one; death reigns over us. We are under bondage. We are slaves. So, we are *all* caught up in the by-products, shall we say, of our ancestor, Adam.

Therefore, if we are caught up by our "living soul" ancestor, we *are* caught up by our *new "quickening spirit"* ancestor. This is what Paul is now saying. Now we move on to a Person, not to the things you *did*, which produced certain effects, which have been removed in the blood of Christ. And so, externally speaking, as it were, you were justified, but it was *more than external*. It has happened! **The Spirit has come into you.** You've begun to have a relationship! You know about its outer effects; now move **in**! He says by the same One you have entered a new relationship. He says it is *staggeringly great* because you were just common; you were just a human...a creature. The *new One* is God's *own Son* – Deity! We've moved into a *Deity relationship* from a created relationship. It's *staggering*! And so he says this "abounds"!

Certain things happen to you through Satan. In this next chapter Paul says God's grace *abounds*, *abounds* because He has lifted the human race back to what He always intended it to be. It *can* be because we *are* spirits. Spirits can be tuned to Spirit. Can be! We can move back into sonship...in fact as we *know* in John 10...in fact into *godhood*! It was Jesus Himself Who confirmed in Jn. 10 when they *challenged* Him and said they were going to stone Him, because He called Himself God, because He said God was His Father. He quoted His own Psalm and the Psalmist said of you, "You are gods!" This grace of God in Christ Jesus *comes right down and picks up* the human race right into this.

Yet, we *had* to go the other way to know who we are. You have to know the opposite, be delivered from the opposite, and be disillusioned by the opposite or you may go back to it. That's why I always use the illustration of competency. Training always means you know how to discard the wrong use of a thing and be able to do it right – the wrong use of your tools, the wrong use of your teaching, the wrong use of whatever it is. You have to know the *wrong* use to discard it...and competency is the right way to do things. You cannot, therefore, have the right way to do things unless you have the opposite, and the right has swallowed up the wrong. You're *competent* now, competent. We are competent sons of God, now, but we had to go through this period, and that is where (we didn't say at the time)it is said that God had foreordained His Son in 1 Peter 1 to be the Lamb *slain before the foundation of the world*. He had to *die* for it, which *showed* God had the whole thing fitted up, *including the right use of the devil* - the devil being an agent by which He put us through certain *necessary negative* conditions and only by them could we be 'fitted' to experience and settle into the opposite...the positive conditions in Christ. So, there had to be the falling away, since He had already foreordained His Son before, and we had to enter into the fallen condition. But, it is important that He's called "the last Adam," because that means that He is the progenitor of the race and then the race becomes what the progenitor is. They go together.

So, the remaining of this fifth chapter is about that abounding grace – where judgment came for one sin, justification's come for many sins. If through the sin of one man death grabs us and we are slaves to deat**h,** and therefore life is aimless, because what is the use of life after all, if there is no aim to it? It says in the seventeenth verse by the gift of righteousness *we reign! We* *reign* in life because we are not managed by an aimless life...but imagine an in*filled* life! We reign in life and *we* are now expressions of God fulfilling His purpose of grace and love in our present day.

We have an adventure of grace and love and fulfillment because we begin to find that *other love is fulfillment,* and thus we are able to be the blessing to others...and we are conscious of the blessing. And *all* men...there it is *to all men* to the *whole* race (Verse 18 of Chapter 5) "condemnation is to all men; righteousness and justification of life is come unto all men." And not only is Paul's message is not only imputed righteous (only a touch)...*made* righteous! Verse 19 says not only were we imputed sinners, we were *made* sinners; we became that. We go back to what we heard in the spirit – the inner false deity expressing himself by us...this inner operation where we expressed the false deity, the spirit of error. We were made sinners. We were sin in essence. We were an expression of sin. We haven't touched sin yet. We only touched sins. And *here* we're made righteous! So we *became* who we are – righteous people, right people. We *are* right people! Made Righteous! It says when the *law* came...then God's grace...it seemed to make sin worse. It made sin real! That made grace real. The law came that *sin* might become sin! "Where sin abounds, so grace much more abounds." So grace *reigns* now! Where sin reigned over us and grabbed us, grace now reigns. Free...grace means we are in God's *freedom* – *we* are in God's life. We are *new* people in Christ, under *new* dominion, under *new* management, under *new* manifestations of the *new* Spirit of Life...instead of the old spirit.

Now He made that as a preparation; now He has set a condition. You see the possible condition of sin, more than sins. We have met the sin *condition* in Adam. Adam was a sinner. We are sinners...a *condition*. So He moves into Romans 6 and says, "Should we continue in that sin condition?" He isn't talking about sins. *That is a very important point.*

In other words, this is that point that he doesn't bring out, which I have spent some time in bringing out because I think it is so important. The sin condition is the *condition* of the **sin spirit** *in the human.* It isn't fundamentally human. The human never has anything fundamental. The human is always the agent. He is always the branch to the vine, the body to the head, the temple to the indwelling God, the slave to the master. He is *always* in that area. The vessel is what it contains. So the human is only the agency, and the human always expressing the agent *inside* the agency. Remember sin is the spirit of sin, the spirit of error...the god of this world who has come into us and joined himself to us *inwardly* and expresses himself through us. So we are branches of *that* vine – a body operating *that* head or vessels expressing *that* foul water flowing out of us. Paul doesn't touch on that. It's John who touches on that. It fits in here. But he's saying now looking at that – our sin condition, our sin condition, not sins. Then he says, "I know; now we get a new one!" He says we are **dead** to sin! *Now* this is something altogether *different*.

That brings us into a *whole new* concept – not He died for my sins, but **I'm** dead with Him! What's that mean? He goes into a new level of understanding which we are *supposed* to know. "Know ye not that we were baptized into His death?" Well it shows that they knew this all once – the two together. But, it says something *profoundly different*! It is one thing to say Christ died *for* me. It is another thing to say, "When He died, I died." What does that mean? That is something *far deeper* than taking my sins. It means the sin condition! Now that can't mean anything personally to me unless I 'get' it. Sin condition is **not** *me*; it is [like] a virus...a person who is expressing sin by me. In other words sin is the principle of self-centeredness expressed through me. Now this is where we begin to see it. This is where I bring help in (if I may) from John and Jesus Himself, because John had this *freeing* insight into inner truth...clear insight. It was *he* who said some of these things and it was *he* who spoke about sin more in terms of the person who expressed that nature, Satan. He was speaking of the devil. So, when you look in 1 Jn. 3, he says the devil sinned from the beginning. Oh, *that's* where sin is! He is talking about the sin of the devil – the *devil* sins!

So, he's taking it a bit further. He says sin is a *person* expressing a false way of life. Holiness is The Person expressing the right form of life – that's God. In other words other-love is the right form – is God. Sin, self-love, is the devil. In the same chapter, I John 3, which takes us a good way on that line, he *defines* sin by one very good statement. He says in I John 3:4, "Sin is the *transgression* of the law." Sin is the transgression of the law. Those few words put it into focus. What is law? Well, the law we use is what a person is, how he works. The law of God is supposed to be what the nature of God is. That's the laws. The real law is the *nature* of God – is love. We know, who know the *ultimate*, love fulfills *all* laws. So the detail laws of the Decalogue are only put there because we are children.

It works like this: you shouldn't do this, you shouldn't do that. When you have gone *beyond* the Decalogue, you go to love. Love fulfills *all* laws. That's why God is love. So, we know that the *real* law of the universe is a Person

Who of Whom *everything* is an expression of love. That is why we have a new insight on the whole universe. We begin to see...don't see the negative. We begin to see beauty in *everything*. Because we begin to see little bits in a different way...maybe a little disturbed en route...but we are seeing, not the disturbance, but the beauty is everywhere. We see a Person expressing every form of love. We get a whole *positive* outlook on life! That's the law. The law is how things work, how the universe works...a Person of *love*.

What's transgression? Sin is transgression of the law. Transgression can't be a dog transgress, a tree transgress. Only a *person* can consciously transgress. So, transgression means someone saying, "I'm not going to be that!" And, it says sin is *that*. What's sin? Sin is therefore not a thing. Sin is a *person* who says, "I won't *be God* in other love. I'll be myself for myself. I'm a self. I can be the other way. I'll be that." Sin is the opposite of God! If God is the Person of self-giving-love, whoever began this sin business was the person of self-loving-love. That's what Satan *is*. So, it's the *same* chapter that says, "The devil sins from the beginning." He commits sins of the devil; the *devil* sins form the beginning! In John 8, he said he's a liar from the beginning.

Now *why* do I make it something of this? Because, you see, if I *catch* it, if I just say *sin*, as Paul puts that – I mean while I *sin* it's something that's part of my makeup. How do I get rid of my makeup? That's where we get this *false* concept that fits right into the evangelical churches, which is two natures. It is taught by those who use that Bible commentary, *Scofield's*, and *all* the Bible schools. All the evangelical Bible schools teach two natures. If you think *you* are the sin and *you* are the righteousness, well...you are sort of vague...you're *both*, you see. You have got it *wrong* – I am sort of *both*! *No, we are not; we are not either. That's* the answer – we know we're either, because, sin is the person, the deity, who expresses himself *through* me...or right is the Right Person expressing Himself through repentance. I am the agency of the person expressed *through* me. So, sin or righteousness isn't me. It's the person to whom I am so linked. I am an expression of *Him*. That's the truth of life!

Look at the statement that Jesus made. He made it *perfectly clear* to my mind in John 8:43, where he had been confronted by the Pharisees who were of course refusing to accept what He was saying. He turned to them and said, "Why do you not understand my speech? Even because you cannot hear my word." Now listen...*why* you can't understand My word, "Ye are of your father, the devil." They had been saying they were children of Abraham. Well, that outer stuff is nothing; it is what you are *inwardly*. This is *startling*! There is another father then. We say we of our Father, God. There is another father. That is startling! He hit it. He said, "You have another father, his name is the devil." And, then He goes *further* and says, "The lusts of your *father* ye will do."

I find that illuminating.

If I just think I am sin or *I* did those things, then how can I get free from...I do that thing? Well, I say it never was me. It was the lust of *my father* I did and acted. My going to my lusts, my going to my hates and my wrongs was really the motivating spirit *causing* me to do those things. That is another focus on things. That is the vessel of wrath. It is the false vine through the branch. I got great light again from 1 Jn. 3 when he made that little remark which again put it in focus for me. He had been saying in 1 Jn. 3 about the children of God, and the children of the devil...and then he says about the children of God, "This is the message ye have heard from the beginning that we love one another." Then he says, "Don't be like Cain who was of that *wicked one* and slew his brother."

Now, when I read that, I stopped and said, "Why did he put in that phrase, "that wicked one?" Why didn't he only say, "Don't be like Cain?" Because, it wasn't Cain who slew his brother. Because *inside* Cain was the spirit of Satan who was the murderer, and Jesus was quoting the murderer. He says in 8th chapter of John, "He's a murderer from the beginning." This is the murdering spirit in Cain which *caused* Cain to murder Abel. Now I am bringing things back into focus. So, now I come back into Rom. 6 where it says, "Reckon ye also yourselves to be dead to sin." This is something different. Sin, mind you, is the principle of self-centeredness, transgression of the law as a person who says, "I will be for myself." The 'original person' is sin and we are in that sense an expression of sin, the person who says, "I will be for myself. I won't be like God is." Now he says, "How shall we that are dead to sin (Romans 6:2) live any longer therein? Know ye not that so many as were baptized into Christ Jesus were baptized into His death? We were buried with him by baptism into death—that like as Christ was raised up from the dead by the glory of the Father, so we also should walk in the newness of life." Rom. 6:3,4. In Verse 6, it says, "Knowing this, that our old man *is* crucified with Him that the body of sin might be destroyed that henceforth we should not serve sin." Now I'm getting a little closer.

So the body which sin motivated has been destroyed as an *agency* for that motivator. Now I begin to see something of the *body* of Christ. Now we have left the blood. The blood you never find mentioned again in Romans 6-8. Never mentioned; it's out. That settled our *sins*. He is dealing with the sin principle now, which is the spirit of self-centeredness manifested through me. Now he says we are talking about the *body*; we are baptized into His *death*. We were *buried* with Him. We were *crucified* with Him. All these words come here.

So now we've got in a **new** relationship where we participate in, *not the blood*, **but the body**. We didn't partake of the blood. That is out! That is what the shed blood indicated, going to hell, death and sin and sins. This is the *body!* So, now he said that we participate in the body. *Why?* Because the body is that which contains the spirit. He says the body of sin has now been annulled. It means the body through which sin motivates might be annulled.

Now I am getting closer. Through that false fruit there came into my body, my being, my person, this false spirit. Like the Holy Spirit's now in my body. Well, this is the false spirit in my body *motivating* me! Now I move into this *tremendous* further revelation of Jesus which is only perfectly put in II Cor.5. It seems as if Paul was involved in being intercessor for people. His life was being poured out for the Corinthians. An intercessor can see farther. He can see himself being involved for people. It was here apparently that Paul in II Cor. 5:14 saw this great truth. "Don't you *know*, that if one died for all then were all dead?" Oh, this isn't Him dying for our sin. This is – if He died I died. What does that mean? We already said He died for sins and descended into hell. Paul said, "Wait a minute, if He died *I died*. If he died for all, I died. He represented the whole race. Now, therefore, if I rise, I am risen with Him." He talks about what the new creature he is then – cut off from the old. And, being in that new creature *position*, it's wonderful – we know no man after the flesh...know not anything after the flesh...only new creature. That is what the next verse is, 16 and 17 of 2 Cor. 5. Then Paul says, "Now I have explained it to you." In Verse 21, "For God made Him to be sin for us, who knew no sin." Sin not sins. Now we are getting somewhere. Sin is the principle of self-centeredness, the *person* of self-centeredness occupying the body. We saw that. Now when Jesus Christ was made sin, what does it mean? It means *that Body* on the Cross was our body...our bodies, an agency for sin! We express through our bodies and our personalities, sin. Therefore that Body represented all of us, which has in it the deity of self-centeredness, the false spirit.

The whole **point** of the death is - out goes spirit. Now we're getting somewhere! It says in Rom. 6, "We are buried with Him." Now this is important, "We were *buried* with Him by baptism into death. Knowing our old man is crucified with Him that the body of sin might be destroyed." Buried means no spirit, of course. So a buried person has no spirit. (Now we're getting somewhere.) So a dead, buried person has no *spirit*. That's why it says, "Now therefore in that ye died, ye died unto sin once." *Not died* **for** *our sins, not* **for** *our sins at all.* Died **unto** sin meant that body dies to spirit. If that spirit happens to be Mr. Sin, Mr. Self-centeredness, if he is the spirit in you, that's out! Now he says, "Do you see what happened? That was *you* on the Cross. It wasn't just He died for your sins. It goes deeper. You move into union, now. That was you! When He died as *you*, He died as the whole race, which was motivated by the spirit of sin, which got into us from the Fall. Now when He died representing us He *died* **to** sin. Out went that sin! So, the body as a dwelling place for sin is annulled. It's no longer a dwelling place for sin.

In the resurrection, of course, that Body becomes a dwelling place of the Spirit of God, quickened by the Spirit and, therefore, if that Body represents us, we have now become a dwelling place for the Spirit of God. So, there has been a *replaced* god...so we move into the fact that what we call salvation is really only exchange of the motivating person within us. If the motivating deity within us is the spirit of self-centeredness, and in Christ's death representing us, he is *out*...into the dead body comes the new Spirit. The new Spirit is the motivating Spirit of self-giving-love – *God!* So the *living God* replaces the false God in **us**. So the Gospel is a change of gods. The God in us is the One Who motivates us! That's what he's saying...Paul says, "You see, you can't go on sinning because you are under new motivation, new management. You've got a new Person! You were Mr. Self-centeredness; you **had** to live by Mr. Self-centeredness! You can only be what the person inside you is. Therefore you can't be Mr. Self-centeredness." We are not talking about temptation now, although you may slip into an area like that you can't *live* in it. You can't be self for self again...after you have been born of God's Spirit. So you have moved in to find who you are. "The love of God is shed abroad in your heart." So the new *drive* of your life is that you are for God, Christ, and people...and how you can begin to be a blesser of *others* in life instead of a person who is always seeking his own blessing and so forth.

So he's saying, therefore, *count* on this as a *fact*. The word 'recon' is a banking term – like you have cash in the bank. Count on that as a fact...that you're *dead* in Christ to being under control of the sin spirit, who motivated you to be self-centered in all its forms. It might have been a righteous self-centeredness *or* a false righteousness. It is all the same thing. Count on it now that you are dead unto sin but alive unto God through our Lord Jesus Christ. It hasn't been quite cleared up as yet; wasn't meant to be at this spot. The emphasis more is to be on the death; we'll get that *out*. Romans 6 is the *death* chapter; you're **out** in the old. You *are alive*; it doesn't say too much about that. You are alive unto *God* and so you *yield* your members now *in your freedom* as agents of *righteousness* instead of being what they were – agents of sin! Your members have become your humanity, your **being** – because of *that* your emotions, your appetites and your will have become *expression* of the God of other love. Your basis becomes that you are the servant of others, as He is. Then Paul says, (This is where the agent arises; he slips in something there, because Paul saw through.) "You see sin won't have dominion over you now because you are not under the law, but under grace." That's a new thing he's put in there. We had the law *out* as exposing sins, and then Jesus Christ taking the curse of the law, and therefore the guilt is out and all that. We had *that* lesson in the blood of Christ.

Now accept the law of behavior. Paul now says, "Now in this present life (Now I talk about this present *new* life, which is Christ in you, not the old one in you.) sin will not have dominion over you because you are not under *law*." Why does he say that? *Very important!* Then Paul diverts for a moment and says, "Now all you who are saved then, if you are not under the law, you can do what you like." People argue with that, "You can do what you like." You *can* when you know what you are, of course. "Shall we sin because we are not under the law, but under grace? God forbid!" Because in the new life when you know it...you're a *slave*. You've changed bosses." That's the important line there. He says the actual fact is, of course, you're not under 'boss sin'; you're under 'boss Christ' now! You were under 'boss Satan'...now you're under 'boss Jesus.' Your life is run by your boss in the old idea of slavery. And so he shows how you've become *free*...from the old life to the new one. You obeyed by faith in that doctrine Verse 17: "You were slaves to sin (the spirit of sin in you) but you obeyed from the heart that form of doctrine that was delivered to you." You obeyed from the heart the fact that you *have* believed in Jesus Christ your sins are wiped out and you've gone to the Father now and recognize that Jesus Christ has taken you over. This is somewhat *new* and hasn't been properly settled yet, that you are under new management. So, you're freed from the old one and you are now under the obligation of the new one. That needs further discussing.

Then he reminds us when you were in the old life you were free to see what you get. In the old life you were free from grace...free from grace. What'd you get? Just a mess! Aren't you ashamed! Look back on those things. What fruit did you get out of that? Just the sins of which you are ashamed! We know that don't we? Those things are *death*! We look back and know these things are this fruitlessness, this emptiness to say the least. That's the old false freedom you had – freedom from being God's man to being the devil's man. Now it is been changed around...the freedom from being the devil's man to being God's man. That's why Paul indecently put it in...to show us how ridiculous to think that you could continue in the old... because you can't when the new boss has taken over.

Now that doesn't really solve our problem *yet* so that's why he then moves into the famous seventh chapter of Romans where he discusses freedom from the **law**. Now he said from *sin*...we've done that...also free from sins, in the blood. Freedom from **sin** if you recognize that you are identified in Christ. You are out of the spirit of **sin**, who caused you to sin. You are parted from self-centeredness.

You get that 'play', don't you? Sin is that you are impossibly self-centered; sins are occasional products. **Sin** is the principle that you live by. You *cannot* be born again and don't live by the principle of "I'm for self." That was broken at the Cross. Your sins, you may slip into occasionally. That's only sin**s** and we'll deal with that later on. But, you cannot *possibly* be for self or you are not born again! If you are born again the new spirit of self-giving-self, the spirit of Christ, has taken you over and you are under this *new compulsion* as seen in 2 Cor. 5. If you have come into this new life in Christ, "From now on we recognize no man according to the flesh," you see *all* men as the potential of what they are meant to be – either redeemed or they are meant to be redeemed. They can be. You have a new outlook on the *world* – how you can be an agent to *bless* people and please God! You don't even know *yourself*...you're a new *self*! Just think of that...under this new dominion!

Then Paul brings up this troublesome spot you've got to get right...that's the law. He says the law was God's *potent* way, *powerful* way in which He confronted us with whom we *really* **are** in our unsaved days. You see we never were devils. We were *children* of the devil, *servants* of the devil, *agents* of the devil. We weren't devils; we hadn't become **fixed** devils. A *fixed devil* means that we say in the spirit, "I'm that; I am for myself, period." According to the Bible, a *fixed* devil can't be changed...can't be reached; he has become **fixed** in the opposite. We're *deceived, tricked, captured*; we became captives. The devil didn't *make* us; he stole us. "Led captivity captive." We were the devil's captives; now we're God's captives! That's why God can speak to us. That's why the Holy Spirit can get at us, because underneath, our *real being* never was the devil's. Paul said in his great Act's 17 speech where he said the *whole* human race is in Him...they belong to Him. "In Him we live, move and have our being." Our basic being is a form of God's being! Because we are *free* persons, I *can* reject being God's. I do not accept that I am God's. I operate my being as for myself, but it really is His, because as God's being, I know that I am being what I ought to be. That is the beginning key of the lost person. We are not lost to the extent that we don't know what we ought to be. We have that conscience that lights us. That is very important! We aren't lost in the sense that the *devil's* lost. He is eternally lost. We can become so, and while we remain so, we *can go* that way, but we are not basically **fixed** as that.

Now it's on *that* level the law comes in. Now the law comes in and *demands* us. It's a little uncertainty in Romans 7 who the old marriage was to. I don't think he makes it clear. He's saying you *were* married and under certain laws, so that marriage puts you under the law. In death you're free. We are not free to marry somebody else unless there is a death of your mate. Now he says in that marriage there are demands made of you. It *looks* as if he means your marriage is to the law. You *could* say it was marriage to sin...I'm not sure. We were *bound* to sin; we were *captured* by sin. I don't think the Bible makes that plain. What I mean is in that sin condition *thank God* the law came to me. "You belong to Me, so you *shouldn't* do that; you *mustn't* do that." So there is always this *guilt* attitude – you shouldn't be doing that. So, we try to escape the law and pretend that it isn't there.

Thank God there is guilt in all humanity! We *know* what we ought to be. That is why we always try to make the best of everything, because we know that we ought to make the best of everything. We say we ought to have brotherhood; we don't want brotherhood. Thank God that is in us, deeper than our sins. That is the way of sense, because there is some cohesiveness in humanity, because underneath we know what we ought to be. We are God's underneath. We are lost sheep, prodigal sons, and that's where the law operates. In our old life it *got* at us...those of us who were within reach

46

of the law. It said, "You shouldn't be that, and you know you shouldn't be!" Then we try and run away and hide and pretend, but underneath, thank God, nobody is happy or at peace who is a fallen person because there is a *law* there...maybe in a sense in which our real marriage is to the law. We aren't really law. It is the law of God and legally you can't be. The reason you can't be is because the devil enslaved you, but you really belong to the law of God. Maybe that's what it means, because he then says "In the death of Christ you've come **dead** to that because that only came to you when you were caught by this false person. When you're caught up by Satan, and you began to be an expression of Satan – self-loving self – in that was its law. It says "You ought to be that." It never lets us alone.

While we were in that possession under Satan the law gets at us. Now, the subtlety was, Satan made us think we were independent. You know, yourself, not one in a *million* of us, in those unsaved days, thought that Satan was **in** us! We probably thought we did the works of Satan and admitted influence of Satan, but saying it was Satan living his life in me, Oh no!!! We say other people have demons. We don't say that we have them.

So you see it is a deeper truth than is known. That's where we have been deceived. The Bible says, "Sin deceived you." I told you that *deceived* is a very serious word. Blindness means that you just don't know. It also says that darkness was blindness. We don't know who we are. Sin makes you think you are who you are not. That's *far* worse. Satan says, "I'm for myself." Satan has light. Jesus said this very subtle thing in the Sermon on the Mount. He said, "If the light which is in you is darkness, how great is the darkness." You think that you are in the light and you are in darkness. That is much worse! "If the light which is in you is darkness, how great is the darkness." And you think it is right. That is where *we've* been. We thought we had light! We are decent people and so and so. We had *no idea* we were motivated by Satan! We don't take what Jesus said, "You are of your father the devil." We don't accept that at all! We don't accept that we are doing it for lust. We regard ourselves as *responsible*. We don't see that we have a motivating demon/devil inside us. We don't know that! *How deep it is.* We don't know that.

Now the subtlety of that has been, it has made me think I'm myself. I'm just myself. I'm just, if you like, a selfish self. I've sinned; I've sinned. Okay! Therefore, my problem is because I thought I was a self-reliant-self...and of course, the law was getting at me...and got me, and got me under conviction I became saved, but I *still* think that I'm a self-reliant-self. That's

47

where my mistake is. I still think, "Well, I'm saved now, I am God's." This is a very subtle thing because the *whole* of this life claims self. "The whole of this world lies in the wicked one." He says, "You do what you want." Everything in life is: "Follow your own way; make your reactions; do this." We can't help it. That is human life. We'll always have it! Everything is disturbing us in self-reactions. All life is – worry about this, fuss about that. Life can be nothing else!

Now, while I haven't got this separation from that *death* within my spirit right I think that *I'm* a responsible person and I shouldn't do this. Now I *still remain* where the law is. The law is there while I think I am independent. If I'm deceived into thinking I'm independent, the law is still there! A law says if you can run yourself, run it. That is what the law is – Okay, do it! This is what you couldn't be, of course. The law came in, Satan got us, but we think we're running ourselves. We didn't see we were being run about by Satan. The law says, "Don't steal, don't lie," then we go and do it, of course. So the law is *always there* while I am under this false apprehension I am an independent self, which is what Satan made me think. Satan became what he thought was independent. Of course, he is a servant of God, but he tries to by-pass that one. So, we may be like that. Now do you see that subtlety?

I've come into a redeemed life. I know Christ as my Savior. I have the "outer" right. I might even say to a point that I'm dead to sin. I might even go so far as to say that I am not controlled; I doubt it. I doubt that I have any understanding of Rom. 6 at all in that first stage. But, of course I'm not governed by Satan, I know I am governed by Christ. But, I have this idea, "I will be better. I am better. I must not react. I must govern all my reactions." Now the moment I do that, that's law! And, the law says, "Follow me." Then I'm caught! Because, you see, independent self serves itself. That's the 'me' of it. So, while I think that I'm independent, I am tempted to be angry. I'm angry! I can't get rid of it. I'm grabbed by the thing, because that's part of me. I think I can't escape it. I may say Christ is there to help me, but while I think I'm *there,* as a person responsible, then I struggle with all my fusses and all my temptations, because I think I shouldn't be like that! So it goes with that *whole period* of life. We are bothered by, "I shouldn't be like that. I don't *want* to be"...and this is the famous Romans 7. "I don't want to be...shouldn't do that and go and do it. **I'm in a mess**!"

Paul says he first found himself overcome by covetousness. Paul's a very high man. You see it when you read Philippians. He was righteous, blameless. He really was a legalist; he really was a moralist. He had total ethics, except for self-loving-self which is the 'highest ethic'. He hadn't got that one, but everyone else he'd got. He was only caught by covetousness. It suddenly occurred to him, "Oh, I'm fine; I shouldn't covet." Covetousness isn't an outer sin. It is an inner sin. Well, you can't manage an inner sin if you are for self. He said here it is in Rom. 7:7 the law said, "Thou shall not covet." Verse 8 says, "Sin, taking the occasion by the commandment, wrought in me all manner of concupiscence." The law of sin was death. In other words, when the law says I shouldn't covet, I want to covet everything. I was caught by that inner desire that beat me. I shouldn't lie; I shouldn't steal; I shouldn't commit adultery...but I shouldn't desire? That's too much! I can't handle that one! And, you're **caught**...by law...because law says, "You shouldn't do it." While you're 'there' you shouldn't do it. Then you're in trouble.

Then Paul says, "This is how sin gets you. Sin plays this trick on you. You *think* that you're an independent perso**n."** You may think you're a new person in Christ. All right, you're a person, but you haven't got it; it's Christ in you doing it. You haven't got it. You know He is there, but you have to get it clear, that the One running your life is He. You've got your relationship; you haven't got your union yet. It's a union relationship. You have Him in an inner relationship, but not in union. You may think that you're an outer *devil*, but you still have this *same* question bothering you. Then you see temptation comes saying, "You shouldn't" and now I'm guilty! Paul went through, "I shouldn't do this; I've done that and the other. I'm all caught up. I shouldn't do it. I shouldn't do it! Oh dear! I'm guilty, etc."

This is what Paul's saying he went through in this Romans 7 letter. He gives a whole description of what he shouldn't do. "It isn't I; it is sin that dwelleth in me." He says, "I delight in the law of God after the inward man." Rom. 7:22. **"I delight in my inner man, my inner spiri**t.**"** That is where Christ is and yet, this thing gets me because, you see, he doesn't *know* he's not he, but Christ. And while he thinks that he's 'himself' then sin gets him, because sin is an independent self. While I try to fight my own battles, sin gets me because the desire of my flesh gets me...couldn't conquer them. So, I couldn't get this thing right. Inside me I didn't want to do them. Yet, somehow as I followed on I couldn't conquer them; I couldn't conquer them. That chapter is full of "I"...until he said at last in verse 24, "I am a wretched man!" "Oh *wretched* man." Now of course that doesn't mean a rotten man. He was that, like we all were. He may not be rotten, but he may be wretched. We go through a period where we are not rotten, but we are wretched when we haven't handled this thing right, and we haven't seen somehow how to make it work. This was how it was in Paul's life in the 24th verse when he suddenly saw he couldn't do it. "Who shall deliver me from this body of death? I can't do it!" At last he found it! He was *conditioned* now...I can't do it! Who'll deliver me? And, then he found his answer was in the replacement inside him; he may have known (the old Satan was out by the Spirit of Christ) the Spirit of life. "The law of the Spirit of life in Christ Jesus has made me free from the law of sin and death." Then he says the Spirit of God dwells within us. So the main point that Paul gets to is that while I'm independent even though I do think I may not governed by Satan, I think that I'm independent. That's a lie. There's no such thing as an independent person; there never *was* an independent person. This chapter talks about a change of marriage. Romans 7 says you *were* married to sin and law...saying in all things you shouldn't have done that thing at all – now the guilt. I said, "That's out in Christ's death! That old man's gone! You have a new marriage! While you belonged to independent self the law gets at you. The law says, "I shouldn't" and then when you did, you were guilty.

Now when you have died in Christ, you have died to sin and law. This is a very important point in Rom. 7, "You have died to the *law*; you've become dead to the *law* by the Body of Christ." Why? Because, the law is there while I'm under Satan – while I think that I'm independent and can run my own life. The law comes in and says "You shouldn't do that." So, while I'm related to Satan and, therefore, to sin, the law gets me and tells me to be that which I can't be. What is that? The law is there to tell me...but I can't be better. Now, when I found that through the death of Christ I am not only dead to sin dwelling in me, but I am dead to the law. This latter is there saying, "Don't. You must not, etc." *Now* I'm not paying any attention because I have a new marriage in place of the old spirit of error telling me to do something, I have the new Spirit of Christ in me. That new Person being my life is Christ!

When you know that the real Person in you is Christ, it becomes a 'know-how' to you. You know that your real Person is Christ...we cease from the independent reaction we used to have. That's our trouble. When we have an independent reaction – I shouldn't do this; I shouldn't do that. The law says "Yes, you should and no, you shouldn't." You're all mixed up with independent self *and* law...and you're guilty! You struggle and can't do it. When you have moved into the new life...when it becomes conscious to you that the real you is Christ in you, the Spirit of God in you...you don't listen to independent self anymore. You're *dead to law*. You don't listen to independent self. Why? Because, you live a life under Christ's control – this new union. When things turn up that are contrary to that instead of saying, "I shouldn't do so and so," you say, "Well, that is just my outer reaction." Then I go back to Christ and Christ handles it. So, you aren't fighting that "You shouldn't do that." You accept it. You accept your temptations as a springboard for faith. They used to be a springboard for self-effort. That was our trouble. Our temptations used to be "I'm a saved person...I shouldn't be angry; I shouldn't have the wrong thoughts; I shouldn't be resentful; I shouldn't be so tense; I shouldn't handle life wrong; I shouldn't have wrong relationships and all the rest of it. I shouldn't! See I've got that idea and then the law says, "you **should**" and then we're caught! I'm living a lie of the *delusion* of independent self. There's no such thing! There's no such thing. It's an illusion. Romans 7 is an illusion. We have moved from an old marriage to a new one. In the old marriage, there was sin and law. In Jesus Christ you are dead, not only to sin, but to the law which says "you ought, you ought, you ought." That's out! That belonged to us when we were the wrong person.

You cease to be in that condition now. In the new life the Person in you is Christ. Now, there will come to you all kinds of temptations. Now you no longer say, "You ought," you say, "I have it clear now, this is Christ's management." So, you accept your temptations as your springboard. If you are worried, you don't say, "I ought not to be worried." That is not you. My humanity is pulling at me. What temptation does is it pulls me back to an illusory self. You see when I have got this thing right my 'new' union is "not I, but Christ." I have moved over now into Gal. 2:20 which is mentioned in other terms in Romans 6.

My new self is this law of the Spirit of life, the principle of the Spirit of life; the spirit of life is the 'me' in me. He is the Spirit of Life – my life's me. The Spirit of Life is me. It came through Christ delivering me from the old through His death and resurrection. It says that you are not in the flesh; you are in the spirit if the Spirit of God dwells in you, which is Christ dwells in you. He's replaced you. In the old relationship through Satan I'd got the false idea that I was independent, which was a lie anyhow, because we were expressers of Satan. I just thought I was independent and running my own show. And the Law kept saying we shouldn't do it. I get my sins went out with the blood of Christ. But I still have this deception. I may think I'm not under Satan in the extent of control. But as I've said – that's the lie. The lie is the idea that I'm independent; that's a lie. So I come over to the new life and while I think I'm independent, the law's still there saying, "You shouldn't." What do you say? I say that I'm not managing this; YOU are managing this. You *don't take guilt*. You don't take "I shouldn't." I *am* angry...OK God handles that. You accept the temptations and say, "I'm worried." Okay, God handles that. You are not there fighting your body. Your body actually turns right around and your body becomes precious to you. It becomes an asset. But, temporarily in the area you haven't got so far as to see the positive body. You tend with Paul to see the negative. You have been through the stage; you have been fighting against your failures and your weaknesses and your strains and stresses, and you are more conscious of the failing self than you are of Christ in you. You haven't got that settled yet. This is Romans 7:8.

So in Romans 7 we have this *false* consciousness. Somewhere it dawns on us. Somewhere Paul had a dawning..."Oh wretched man...I *can't* do it. It isn't me running this thing any longer." He saw through the illusion thinking he ought to *be something*...and then when you are if you think you're an 'independent' self, self's got you. He cut that off – that 'ought to be.' Why? Oh, because actually I never was that. There never was independence. He missed that! From the moment you're born again you've got a new marriage. That's what you don't know! You've moved from death to resurrection – that's the new marriage! It's death you walked in the old marriage, and resurrection in the new marriage. But you don't know that. You know you belong to Jesus, but you haven't got the other thing right. You haven't got that outlook right. So you think you run your own self – fighting. That's the lie. You may not have realized you were governed by Satan in that sense. Doesn't matter...*except* that when you've got a false union you can conceive a new one. *If you recognize I **was** indwelt by Satan, expressing him through me, it is easier to move into and say,* "Now I'm indwelt by Christ. He's handling it through me." **There's a change of union.**

We can see it better that way, but we didn't know that false union – so alright we haven't died. Because we've had this idea I was a sinner, now I'm cleansed by the blood of Christ; I'm justified. I'm still a person – that's my fault. I'm still a person – that's a lie. I have moved *from* a person indwelt by Satan to a person indwelt by Christ. The god in me has changed. The *motivator* in me has changed. That I haven't got clear.

In order to get that clear, we have to go through a miserable period in which we mistakenly think I'm 'there'. I'm no longer the bad person I was, but I think I *ought* to be different. This "I ought, I ought, I ought." So we have to go through a miserable period. We *want* to be right and can't make it! We live with an inner guilt – I get off with this sin; I get off with that sin; I can't *make* it. Then I live in a kind of semi-guilt because I think I ought to be different. I ought! NO! I move over to a daring thing! I *am* different! I move over into the "I am"...out of the "I ought to." I am different! I *was* in Satan; now I **am** in Christ...and Christ *is* the **me** in me!!!

That's why I always say at this moment, although it's not in Romans, the most *total* verse is the Gal. 2:20 one. Because Gal. 2:20 says, "I've been crucified with Christ." I have got that, in Christ my human self is no longer dominated by Satan, who was running me. I am out.

Now the *all important* thing is that you get that, first. You reckon yourself **dead** unto sin. Get that! Get that clear. Now you haven't got so clear that you are alive unto God through our Lord Jesus Christ. It is more than that. Alive unto God isn't a complete statement because he had not gotten to Romans 8 yet. This is a relationship. It is not a relationship, it is union. It is replacement. It isn't a relationship unto God through Lord Jesus Christ. It is a replacement. Christ has taken me over. That is a deeper thing. You can't quite get that yet, because you have this false concept, "I'm a person...a kind of independent person," which is a *lie*. And, so Paul seeks to show that to us in Rom. 7 by a statement, "You are dead to the law" because if you are *there*, the law shouts at you, and it shows that you're not there. Because the law is there while I think I'm and independent person...or under Satan. That's the law. It tells you, you shouldn't be that! So while you are under the law you are under a false illusion. It means that you *are* there. If you are *dead* to the law, it means you are not there. Because the law will shout at you, while you think you are independent.

Now I move over. Now this was the complete thing that Paul did. He said, "Not only am I crucified with Christ, yet I live." That is where he's replaced. That's the important point. Gal. 2:20 says, "I am crucified with Christ, yet not I," No, "nevertheless, I live, yet not I," because it isn't me. My living self is not I. Get it? "I am crucified with Christ." I am not in my old relationship. Now I am no longer "I" flapping about here. "I live, no I don't, Christ lives in me." *That's the replacement.* That means my real I now is the Living Deity of Jesus Christ – the Person living in me. Now, you see, if I *get* that, and I have been disillusioned about this false idea of self running itself, if I get that now under my new life, I begin to be free, because I begin to be myself...because I am really not I...I am really Christ in me. *Now* you are coming to a new thing. That's where Paul goes on to say, "I'm crucified with Christ," (**out**) "I live, no I don't live, Christ lives in me." That is the middle change over. You have changed over from wrong self in Satan to no self – not you but Christ. Then you come back to the right self – *I* now live in the flesh...*I **live it**...*by the recognition of that fact. Faith is always substance...by recognition "of the faith of the Son of God, Who loved me and gave Himself for me." Now *I* have come out. Now then what happens? The new free life is – *I am God's precious person. He owns this! Every bit of me is beautiful. It is under new management. My body, my appetites, I am all new.* I begin the "I am" life. That's what I am.

Now in the middle of that, here come these training grounds. In the middle of all that, all the time, there is a certain area of life when we just enjoy ourselves. Everything is wonderful.

But, in the middle, here come things that bug us all the time – family relationships, tiny details, big details, we have got our problems at home, our problems with ourselves, problems pour out, problems in business. Now then, your happy self in Christ doesn't remain so happy. Now here you've got to watch. You have come to this new relationship and you say, "This is settled in me. I *know* now." You live spontaneously. You have the inner consciousness; it is not I, but He. Now then when these strains, any kind of strains or the negative come...being human you start to be negative. Oh I don't like that. You *know*...wait a minute! It may take a little time. "Wait a minute, I'm not running that." Don't fight it. It is not there. You don't take law. "You handle that. God, You replace my worries by Your confidence. You replace my strain by Your release. You are there. I am in Your release."

You see, in place of the temptation which is not sin...the *temptation* to feel worried, feel strain, feel tense, feel insufficient, feel so and so...all that feeling stuff...that is your practicing ground. That's your adventure, your adventure of faith! You say, "Now is my chance to say of course I'm weak, but He's strong. Of course I'm worried, but He has the answer. Of course I'm having problems. He's got solutions." And, you begin to live a new *habit-life* in which your human negative becomes your jumping off point for the positive. In the ordinary life a certain amount of it is just released, you are just enjoying things. All right, that's just an area. That's just God around us, in us. But, in the midst of it is always coming to you things that you don't enjoy...either small or large. I know it for myself. The moment something bugs me (ah that's it!) The moment I'm bugged, I know! It shows that something negative is getting at me, and what it is doing, is trying to pull me out to forget that I'm Christ. I'm "Christ in me." I forget that I am Christ in me (I'm me) and I am back in Rom. 7. Then I'm in trouble at once. So see it is necessary for me to get this practicing ground, when that pull (as if I am a bit elastic) out to be – I fear, I resent, I am worried, I am tense, I can't handle that, what shall I do with this situation. I, I, I, I, I...back where I was! I have to learn the **'new I.'** I am not *I*; I am not *I*. That's bunk! Where have I got it wrong?

Go back to, "Christ, *You* meant that to be because You want to show up *here*. You want to show Your peace through me. You're here." And, so the law is not in it because Christ **is** the law! Because, the law of Christ **is** the law – which is the law of love. So, there is no more law on you at all. Law is only on you *while* you think you are independent. When the temptation comes to be independent, you stop. Oh, you will start by law – "Oh, I ought." Watch! You will start that way, you see. The moment I am independent the law says, "I've got you!" It is a lie. It is an illusion. So Rom. 7 is an illusion. There is no such thing as independent self. It said in the beginning that you *were m*arried; you are dead to the old marriage. Romans 7:1 says "law had dominion over you as long as you live." If the husband is dead she is loosed from the law of her husband. If she marries while he is still alive, she is an adulteress. If the husband is dead, she is free from that law; she can marry again. Now you have become dead to the law by the body of Christ. You're married to another! (v 4) You have a new marriage. So you *were* married...he doesn't make it quite plain we were married to sin and with the sin was the law, so you're not under sin at all; you belong to Me. You're dead to the law which says you shouldn't do that. You are dead in Christ to both sin and law! You're dead to the power of sin and therefore law is not there because you are no longer independent! We're not aware we have moved out of that *whole illusion* of independence...back from a false dependence, to a right dependence. Then we say, "It is *Christ* in me! It is *God* in me! The *Holy Spirit* is in me!"

Now my *self* becomes adventure! A part is positive. I use it actively. I am actively free to be what I like and go to it; it's lovely! I am God's free person – the Spirit operating through me. In the midst of that there is always coming these negative things pouring in, but I know how to deal with them now. It may take time, sometimes.

I was just saying recently to a friend. (I only met her a few months ago and she is young in Christ, but she *had* found this – she'd caught on to Christ in her.) About two weeks ago she was desperate. She said, "What am I to do?

My husband has left me for another woman." She acted full of rage and resentment and revenge. "I'd do *anything*! I'm torn to pieces. You talking about Christ in you means *nothing* to me. Help me out. I am just full of it. I'm torn to pieces. I don't know what to do. What about my children and the rest of it. I say Christ is in me and it doesn't mean a thing." I wrote back and said more or less, "You silly fool...you are not you, you're Christ! It isn't Christ in you, you *are* Christ! It isn't you fighting in Christ. You *are* Christ. The *real you* is Christ in you." Then I said, "Why do you fight your feelings? Of course, you have rage. It isn't wrong, it is right. Of course you want revenge. Of course you feel revenge and hurt. Of course, you feel temptation, who wouldn't...left deserted like that? That is not the point. Because you are under this vast mistake of Rom.7. (You're not *there*!) Then you cry and shout you shouldn't be. You are not there, you're Christ!" Then I said, "You take a position that you live, nevertheless, *Christ* lives in you and He is the Person in you."

You know what happens? You are in for trouble because, of course, Christ loves His enemy...including your husband. It is rather tough on you. See, He wants to get your husband saved if he isn't already, and He wants to get the other woman saved too! So *you* have to begin loving them now. You're for it! You will begin to find with Christ you have got an adventure in which you can *dare* to say, "You can use this, Lord, to give my husband a good 'beat up' en route." You can ask Him for that one because he deserves it. See this? As for your children, if you at this juncture, can show your children *love* for a husband who has done this, you have taught them more than they will ever learn in 13 years of school. If they can see a torn up wife who can still say, "Well he did wrong, but I am loving him and so on," you won't suffer. (I have had a letter from her since. She said, "I've had bursts the other way, but I am getting through.")

But, you see the vast difference? So, Rom. 8 is a **replacement**. And it says, "Then the righteousness of the Lord is fulfilled *in* you." When you have got this replacement, the Spirit in you; the righteousness of the Lord is fulfilled *in* you "who walk not after the flesh but after the Spirit." How is it fulfilled in me? Because the righteousness of the law, of course, is Christ! Christ **is** the law. He is a Person who lives like that. Who does that? Christ, of course. So all that "you ought, you ought, you ought' stuff goes out and you *dare* to say, "I am no longer I, but I am Christ in me. The *real* me is Christ." You can say it *if* you knew once, you were no longer you, you were Satan in you. That is what we didn't know. *If* you get the two in balance...you see you weren't

56

you, you were Satan in you. Satan **is** Mr. Self-centeredness...he may be Mr. Righteous; he might be a very 'nice' fellow, but he is still Mr. Self-righteous. *That's* gone out in Christ. Now Christ is Mr. Self-Giving-Love in you. Now you can begin to make the affirmation that the righteousness of the law is fulfilled in you.

I would like to say here in human ways that the Bible doesn't give it as a crisis. The Bible gives it as a known fact, that in Christ, you, not only in His blood, were cut off from your sins and their consequences, but in your *union* with His body you were cut off from the false deity and were put in the right Deity...and that cut you off from the law which went with the false deity, and then the law is inside you. There is no more 'outer' law. You are governed by Spirit. But the fact is that most of us have met another crisis. Very few of us have moved from Romans 1-5, which is the peace with God and the outer relationship to Romans 6-8, where I have found I am a *replaced* person and my *real self* is not I, but Christ. All that I mean is this – faith is always substance. Now we saw in Romans 5 with that first faith, "Oh I am at peace now, I am accepted by God. And, I am in the love of God." I have moved into "I am Life." I am not trying to get something, but it's got me! The Spirit of God has come into me and caused me to know the situation, and the love of God begins to spread through me and so on and so forth.

"Know you not that those who are baptized in Jesus Christ were baptized in His death?" Now remember Biblical knowledge is always know-how. The Biblical word for "know" means to be mixed with something. The simplest explanation I always know is in the professions. The whole *point* of a profession is to get *you*, isn't it? You are at ease in your profession, where you study a profession. "Oh I know how to do that now." In engineering or secretarial work or at home running a kitchen, the joy of life is when you get to a certain phase of something you have learned and it gets you! "Oh I know how to do that." That is actually how you change your name. We say a person learns carpentry and we becomes a carpenter; he learns medicine and we call him a doctor; he learns teaching and we call him a teacher. You're learning something outside of you which becomes your know-how. You know how to teach. You know how to cook your food. You know how to handle your medicine. Then life is happy and constructive and outgoing, and you can give it to people. That's know-how.

Now that's the Bible know-how. It means a thing has become you, so it becomes the positive. That's why we say in Romans 5, "Oh I *know* I have peace with God. I *know* I am in His grace." And my *tribulations* only give me more of Him. Oh come on, come on! Life's only happy when you know how. Now there is a know-how here. I didn't find that except that I went through a second stage when I was trying to run it by myself. Then God said, "Drop it! **I'm** in you." I had to learn what it is to affirm Him in me, replacing this independent self which was out. Then I have got a know-how. It is as simple for me to know it isn't I but Christ, as it is simple for me to know that my sins are forgiven. Now, of course, the point is you live at ease in your know-how. When your sins are forgiven, "Oh praise God, I know that and I can witness to anybody...that I know what it is to have my sins forgiven."

And, mind you, you can reproduce only what you are. All we are ever able to reproduce is to reproduce ourselves. When I am a redeemed person I can reproduce to other people. I say, "Oh I can help pray for that one. I can show them how to accept Jesus Christ and believe in Him" and so on and so forth because you know how! So, what you *are*, you can now reproduce. Now this reproduction in different ways has happened to you. It happened to me! Happened to you...that *somehow* it was settled into that you are not you, but Christ in you. Now that is when you begin to accept *yourself* back. So, until you know that, while you think that you're independent, you are disgusted with yourself; like Paul, you're wretched. While you think that you are independent there is law and you think you ought to be different – all that stuff that I have gotten while under the illusion.

Well I'm out from that illusion. I'm no longer an independent self; therefore, there is no more law shouting at me. I am a replaced self as Christ in me. Now you accept yourself back. Because, when it dawns on you that Christ accepts you, you accept yourself. It begins to dawn on you that you are an asset. You are God's asset. It is through your appetites, your very being, God comes! And, now you are back as a beautiful person. It is through *your* mind, through *your* will, through *your* initiative, God comes! And, you become thrilled with yourself as an agent of Christ, because you are an agent of God. Now that begins to put the positive and the negative back into better focus. We aren't so much bothered about the negative because we are getting more used to the positive. Now *in* that positive there come temptations, but now even your attitude to temptation changes to *opportunity*!

I always say you change, like when you pray the beginning prayer which is, "Our Father which art in heaven," towards the beginning days, before they had Pentecost. It then says, "Lead us not into temptation deliver us from evil." "Ooooh, deliver me from evil, lead me not into temptation." I am young. You go on to James who was a top man and told you what a top life is...how God really works it out through you! He says, "My brethren, count it *all joy* when you fall into diverse temptations, knowing that the trying of your *faith* works patience." Why? Don't you see? He says, "Your temptations pinpoint a negative to you."

Now it is only through a negative that a positive is known. "Oh I'm hurt, I'm bothered, I'm tempted." I pinpoint something which is causing you to go that way. That *very* thing is this stepping off point. "No, I don't fight that. That is what I am. I accept that. I am meant to be that. You're *meant* to be that because it gives me a chance of proving You!" So you laugh at your temptations. You say, "God *meant* them." God means you to be angry to find out how He can give you something else. So you cease to condemn yourself for your 'sins'; they aren't sins. It is very important to notice that. Sins are when you mean to do it; that is what James says. Temptations are when you'd *like* to do it. Sin is you *do* it. Now we don't always mean things. Mostly our trouble is we jump into things. We don't mean it. Before we know it we have jumped into wrong thoughts or jumped into wrong attitudes. We didn't *mean* to; that is temptation!

Now the very thing that may take us a little time to say, "Wait a minute, God, how foolish I am. You have got that in Your hands." Then God enjoys you, going through a period in which your negative is showing God how you can handle solutions. By the way you handle your provision you begin to *prove* God. Then sin is occasional, but they are forgiven. Even then the danger of sins is not the sins, but the guilt. We redeemed people are not to be bothered by our sins. We are to be bothered by our guilt. We think we should deny it; that is our guilt. That is why there is that great verse in Heb. 9:14, where it says, "How much more shall the blood of Christ purge your *conscience* from dead works?" It isn't the dead works, it's "Why fancy me doing that!" And so, we learn from our sins. Don't take it up again. If we have sinned, admit it and go on. Sin means we have done the thing. Well occasionally we do, only occasionally. We don't *live* doing them. We *do* live tempted. *We don't live sinning. Get it clear!*

Many Christians live a bugged life because they think they are wrong because they are tempted. No! Temptation is your jumping off spot. "Count it all joy when you fall into temptation." It gives you a chance to prove faith! The trial of your faith means it gives you a chance to prove faith, and then faith gives you a settlement in patience.

59

So, Paul comes round to this, very simple. He says when you have *got* this in Rom. 8 you discover you are governed by a new law. A law is principle – the Spirit of life through Christ. Christ is the one Who cut you off from the old law of sin, and He said He condemned sin in the flesh. The fact that the thing shouts at you (it is under bars now) "Come and join me; come and join me" like a prisoner can shout through the bars. A condemned prisoner is not free and so sin can shout at us through temptations. But, the law in the Spirit of Life in Jesus Christ is "I have got a new principle – the Spirit of Life." He goes on to say, "If any man has not the Spirit of Christ he is none of His." And, it says in Verse 10, "If Christ dwells in you (the body is dead because of sin) but the Spirit is life because of righteousness." The Spirit's your life. The Spirit of God dwells in you. If any man has not the Spirit of Christ, you're not His! He is *in* you. Then he says, "You are not in the flesh, but in the Spirit." Romans 8 verse 9...Not in the flesh, but in the Spirit. That is where you are!

Now then, all he says is in *this condition* you walk not after the flesh, but after the Spirit. You live this life *now* under this new settlement. It is settled in you now...surely has settled in you. You are redeemed by the blood of Christ. So it has settled into you, you are unified with Him in His body at His death and resurrection. In His death, out with the old; in His life in with the new. He is the one operating your life. You are really Christ in you. Now, you have settled in that. Now it says you *walk* in that, because you are in the world which shouts flesh at you. The whole world is *bent* on flesh. This is the fallen world! This is our *privilege* to shine as lights in a dark world. So it shouts at us.

Now, if you walk in the flesh...every time you walk in the flesh it cuts you off from God. Result is you are fighting, resenting, hurting and you are in trouble. What does that mean? Walking in the flesh isn't some big thing; it is self-response. Flesh is independent-self. That's what self is; that's what Satan is. It isn't some *vast* sin; it isn't that at all. It merely means that every time I'm tempted, "Oh, what shall I do about that?" I'm in trouble. I am walking straight into, "What shall I do about that, this and the other thing?" You always start that way; that is what life is. Life always starts by a negative pull on me. "What about this; what about this; what about this?" Now walking in the flesh doesn't mean that I'm tempted by the flesh. It means that if I proceed that way I am in trouble. I can't do it, and I am resentful, hurt, worried, burdened. More fool you!!! All that is to give me a little more education to say, "Why am I such a fool? I am not that, Christ is managing me." So walking in the Spirit is to recognize Who it is walking you – the Spirit of God – your flesh is an *asset*! It is through your flesh God comes!

It is only its misuses that are wrong. Its misuse is self, independent-self. That is the flesh, independent-self, which makes you think, "I should do that, I shouldn't do that." You learn to live out of that one and you walk and get tempted all the time. But your temptation becomes your practicing grounds. So, he says you have *no more* debts to pay to the flesh. You are **not** debtors to the flesh to live under the flesh. The flesh has no *call* on you. That independent-self got you, through the fall. You are no longer an independent-self...you are Christ in you, and you begin this new life that's out of debt. In this you mortify the deeds of the body, which God uses, because the body pulls at you. Your body's *precious*! When I'm tempted to misuse my body, "I am dead, Christ, You're right in this and You take over, and You overthrow the temptation or something." Now you've become a Spirit-led person. You get that when you get into Romans 8. He moves away from this flesh/Spirit business. He has left that behind, now. That has been *done* in these Chapters 6 and 7 and the first part of 8.

From Romans 8:14 Paul starts talking about a new thing. He says the Spirit bears *witness* with your spirit, that you are children of God. (That's 16.) So, he said, that's the proof. You see, I am saying – witness is knowing something within you. Now this is this further on witness. You *have* the witness, you are redeemed; you now have the witness you are unified. The Spirit bears witness with your spirit that the *real you* is the Spirit of Christ in you. You are settled into this; this witness comes. You are settled. Witness means something fixed to you.

Now he says, "When you are fixed in that witness you are led by the Spirit of God." What does that mean? Life becomes *easy*. Led isn't pushed; led isn't shouted at; led is just you go that way. And, so you take your way to be His way. You have become a free person. Because, you are not you but He, do what you like. Dare to believe that it is He! So, believe that your ordinary, normal life is His leading, "Yes, come along. We are coming this way, I am leading you."

However, when He isn't leading you, He'll check you. When He doesn't check, go along! Don't wait to be led, take it for granted that you **are** led unless the red light is up. Be free. You *are* a led person now. You are to believe in this new life as a led person and you are a son of God.

This has given you a new concept toward God…He's my Father! He's Daddy. All the bondage is out. **Dare** to believe you are free to be yourself and God operating through you and operating in you! So, Paul says, "He has taken out the spirit of bondage and given you the Spirit of adoption." And, I'm in the family now. I go to the icebox if I want to. God delights in me doing my stuff, and He's really doing it! So, I have got a sense of God's delight behind me, God's pleasure and Spirit leading. This is this new freedom. And, then Paul says a sudden thing, "But, you will have suffering." He says it right in the heart of this…suffering. That is startling, isn't it?

He had just said before, "In this relationship you are now son and heir. If you are children, you are heirs of God, joint heirs with Christ." So, you are now beginning to move from the trivial to the magnificent. You are part of God's universal purpose now. So far, that is our personal need…to get out of this and to get into the other. That is finished. You are led. God is your Daddy. Get on with it. That fear stuff is gone. He is with you all the time. You are free and you know who you are. You have got the positive witness.

Now, he says, you're moving to something far bigger. You are one by whom God is managing the universe. You are going to have a new concept of life…which is that your job is, begins to be, that you are a communicator to others. Naturally, as we have all through life, we learn a profession and we communicate our profession. We get our wages by doing our plumbing, or doing our engineering or doing our teaching. That is the whole point. You are communicating. You have got the know-how. Now this is moving into the communicating area. It starts off later when he says, "You see, you manage the universe!" Out through you, you see you are co-heirs, co-heirs with Christ. You are going to manage the universe and move out from yourselves now. Now, he says in that you are involved with the suffering world; you suffer with it. It says, in Verse 17, "If you are children, you are heirs of God, and joint heirs with Christ, if so be that we suffer with Him." Suffering is the pressure we never get beyond. This life is a mix-up. It is a mix-up of joy and sorrow, of glory and suffering. The glory and the joy overflow, but the other is there always. So we are mingled in the life where we are involved with things, which do hurt and do cause us concern. You can't escape that. That is part of the life you are in.

It says, "If you don't suffer with Him, you aren't glorified together." We **do** suffer. How can we put that? Only that I think there is a drive in life beyond the self. A drive in life. Something inner which causes us to seek to be something. Something in our own area, a contributor to others, involvement with others. And, this is to a suffering world. He even says that we are involved even in the creation this way. He says the creation's suffering; it's under a *tension*. And, they live by fear. The bird has to watch this and keep moving, if the cat's on the corner. Everything in life has a certain *tension* about it. This beautiful world has variable tensions about it, you know, "red in tooth and claw" and all that sort of thing is outside of Him. We are involved in this kind of world. So, we must expect to *share* in the tensions and the problems and our share in the solution of them. Again, he says it's part of this whole negative, positive process. It says He *deliberately subjected* the created world to a tension condition...what we call the condition of corruption...that it may be delivered into glorious liberty. It says, "The creature itself was made subject to vanity" (wrong way of doing things) "not willingly, but by reason of Him Who hath subjected the same in hope."

So, you see we are part of the process here. We had to pass *through* the negative to positive. And, we move into the positive in Christ through *whole areas* of negative. And even now we have to 'walk' in the old life, because of the dangers of the negative, all the time...the self-influences on us.

Paul says the whole world is like that, and there's a sense the *whole world* (we don't fully realize what this means) has been subjected to the negative, in which we have this wonderful creation with this greater image...which is suffering. Animals, one eating the other with teeth and claw, etc. Humanity is fitted with its own teeth and claws and is waiting for the manifestation of the sons of God...sons of God! So you see, it says, "Creation waiteth for the manifestation of the *sons* of God." It is in bondage of corruption to be delivered into the glorious liberty of the children of God. So, this is what we are after in this present time. As far as we are able to transmit the liberty, the glorious liberty we *are*, we do know something about that! We transmit like I transmitted to that lady I told you about.

Like you...you're Christ! You find your liberty, when you know that. You have suffering and tension, but you know your liberty and you know you are Christ in you, which gives you an opportunity to love, etc. So, we *are now* transmitting liberty. We don't do it very much, we don't know what it even means with the material creation, but it's here somewhere. By some sense *we're the agency* by which the whole *world* is going to come into utter corruption...we don't know what that means...into a glorious liberty. But we're now the reproducers of glorious liberty. So that's what we're saying, but we're *involved* in the suffering. So, we *accept* that as the necessary part of our way of life. In a sense, even our *faith* has a suffering life, but you can't prove it. We live by *faith*. You can't *prove* your faith, except only by the change it makes in you. You can't *finally* prove that God is a Spirit and the Spirit makes it in which you belong, and the source is 'it' for you. You can't *prove* it except by an inner spirit-consciousness. So, there is a certain element of suffering even in our faith. It is built on a big question mark. We live in the *consciousness*.

All life has an element of suffering and a question mark, and we're involved in it to share as far as He has given us with this glorious liberty as the children of God. And part of that is your body. See Paul doesn't fool about there. Paul doesn't speak about *everybody* being healed. This is the very 'fix' in the whole chapter...now you have moved into an area where you are not free yet. You are not free in your body, because your body binds you. And, so he says here we *groan* with the world. We know that the whole creation groans and travails in pain together now. Not only they, but we have the first fruits of the Spirit...first fruits...but not completely, but that's wonderful enough...but it is only first-fruits. We groan with ourselves, waiting for the adoption, which is the redemption of our body. It said, "By hope" but hope which is seen is not hope. "What a man seeth, why doth he yet hope for?" So, there is an area in which you are saved 'in hope' and not 'by faith.' Faith means that you have. Hope means you haven't yet got it. So, the Bible says, "Don't kid yourself, be balanced." And, your body is part of that. You do not get total redemption of your body. You may get some temporary healings, but we are in a corrupt body which dies, and we await for the redemption of the body! So Paul is a very *balanced* person, who in time will come through in a word of faith in healing. Sometime it doesn't!

So the whole point though is to be able to be in with God in any situation and to magnify God in any situation. We'll talk about that later when Paul is in prison...being able to magnify the body in prison, and so on. And he says even in this situation you raise questions. There are some questions we can answer and some we cannot wholly answer. So, we have infirmities, not *sins*. We don't know what we should pray for as we ought. Now, as a *whole* I don't think there is very practical praying. Many of us know a good deal about the operation of *faith* – trusting God as we do a lot of that, He operates! There are some areas we don't know what to pray for, what ultimate is going to come and how the world is going to come through, etc.

So, in those areas the Spirit in us shares His groaning within us and makes intercession and God has those groanings and we are able to get the total answer there. But, we settled in the point "that all things work together for good to them that love God and are called according to His purpose." So, that becomes, at least on a temporary condition, our answer to the groanings. We learn this *principle* of (it doesn't come much in this letter here) seeing God is His goodness through *all* evil...all things working together for good.

Then he *finally* establishes us in who we are, how we should regard ourselves, where we can be free to be ourselves. Then comes the whole thing...he says you see we have a destiny to be conformed to His image – on that way in His *perfection*, forms which will be exactly like Him. In the ultimate sense, we shall be this, when "we shall see Him as He is." That is in 1 Jn. 3:2. He has foreknown us. He has predestined us here to be conformed to that image, that He might be the first born among many brethren. Then he goes on...the predestinate has been called, and this is where faith comes in. "Whom He has predestined He called, whom He called He justifies, whom He justified He glorified." This is why we see people as perfect. We see each other *perfect in Christ* now. There are elements in which this is being *fulfilled*, but we see it as such. Verse 30, "whom He has justified He has already glorified." Then Paul says you are stable there. "If God be for you, who can be against you?" He has prepared you and gives you all things that are necessary. Who can condemn you? If God justifies you, who can bring a charge against you? Gain the confidence of a person established in Christ, and we follow One. And we don't take it from other people. We don't take any condemnation. God doesn't condemn. We are in God's peace and light. No one condemns you! You don't take charge. You are doing what God means you to do and you're free! You have all resources at your disposal. If He has given you the Son, He has given **all** to you all things with Him freely. Finally, Paul says, you are in an inseparable condition. He says that no things human or super-human could *ever divide* you. *Nothing* can separate you from the love of Christ. Things down here...tribulations, persecutions...nothing down here.

Then Paul says you'll *suffer*...all day long being killed for His sake...like lambs led to a slaughter. But, you are more than conquerors. This is the combination between joy and suffering. We glory in suffering! We go through tensions, all kinds of things, but you are on top of them. And, you are *so* on top of them that you are helping somebody else. "More than conquerors" means you conquered them and you have something to give other people. So, you are right in the middle of this thing where nothing can separate you, but you are in an area where all these kinds of pressures happen to you. And, then Paul says, nothing eternal, nothing temporal, nothing can separate you, "Neither death, life, angels, things present, things to come, height, depth, nothing can separate us from the love of God, which is in Christ Jesus our Lord."

That's how Paul has settled up a personal relationship. The *key* is a personal relationship! In other chapters, Paul will tell us the kind of person we are, how to live our life outwardly. It is based on how we live it inwardly. It is based on a *positive consciousness* of union, of replacement, of freedom. No, we are not taking what man says, not what the law says. We are guided and led people. We are *positively established* that nothing can separate us. That's what arises here.

Yet, at the same time we are *involved* in the world in situations where we have different kinds of sufferings because now we have learned the process how sufferings can be something through which God is coming. Paul doesn't discuss that here. In other words, we learn how to see the *suffering areas* as stimulants to faith. God *puts* us there because He is coming through certain ways of deliverance.

That's about it as far as the main body of Romans is concerned. There are some very interesting things to follow – tremendous area on the subject of *God*...how He can love Jacob and hate Esau...how predestination works in the free will. He handles that *totally* in Romans 9 and 11. That goes on. That's because that is only for the mature. The 'prepared of God' can only be mature. When you have really finished this business, you begin to see *God only!* Now you are in focus. So it is here he talks of only God. God manages everything totally, evil and good alike. You can't see *total* until you are *free* from the nagging question about yourself – when you *know Who you are*, which is not yourself but He, then you are free! So your whole life – you know how to handle it whatever arises. Now you are *free* to move into a detached way and look at God Himself. That comes in Romans 9 and 11 and on from there.

We make an abrupt change in Rom. 9 because there *is* an abrupt change in the operations of the Spirit in us, at this juncture. As we said, up 'til the present, the purpose is for us to be whom we have been created and predestined and recreated to be – which is ordinary humans who know we are *not* ordinary humans...because we are containers and manifestors of Deity. Because the Bible says the whole **Trinity** is in us! John speaks about

God dwelling in us...and here Paul says *Christ* dwells in you and he also says the *Spirit* dwells in you...remembering that *dwelling* is the old fashioned term for *permanent residence*. Therefore, we have the Permanent Person of Whom we are the means of His expression. It's the whole Deity! Again, we remind ourselves that we see it in this chapter...we are talked about as being vessels, as being the body of Christ.

In John's Gospel He talks about the branch/vine and in I Corinthians Paul talks about us being "the temple of the *Living God*." In any case it can't be *more strongly presented* than in Rom.6. We are presented as being slaves to a master – that we humans are the created and recreated means by which God *Himself* expresses Himself *as He is*, and character that He is, and *purposes* He has. As He is – He is *nothing* but love; therefore, we *are* Love...and whatever the purposes and the *ultimate destiny* holds for us as inheritors of the universe. So, we see this quite plainly the *marvelous* plan of God from the ages to have people made in His image – actually humans. His own Son would come down at the human level; become a human like us, to provide us with the necessary *deliverance* from being humans who had gotten under the power of the *false* deity, expressing the spirit of error in us, instead of the Spirit of truth. Then in Him, as representing us as the last Adam, we are lifted into a brotherhood relationship with Him. We brought that out in the previous chapter that He might be the first-born among many brethren.

That wouldn't be enough to think that meant that we were just *side by side*, as if we were *separate* individuals. We have only in a stronger sense the same relationship that the whole human family has with His progenitor. "As in Adam all die, so in Christ shall all be made alive." And, more so because that is not the sense in which Adam lives in us, but there is the sense in which Christ *is* us, expressed in our human forms! When as we saw, we settled into *that*, we are *liberated*...because a person is liberated according to the *ability*, shall I say, that he has to be himself. And so, you have to pass through the stages of learning the *apparent* inability, although there never *was* such a condition. We really pass from the ability of operating the resources of Satan to the operations of the resources of Christ. *A person is free when you have what it takes to be **yourself**!* When it is settled into us that whatever happens we are no longer ourselves, we are *permanent* expressions of Deity, we certainly have adequacy! This is "The Rest," that is spoken about in Hebrews...that when you enter into this relationship, you enter into His *rest*...because rest isn't inactivity; it is adequacy in action.

Strain is inadequacy in action. All life is action. A human being exists to be in action and it is a strained being when we are operating from inadequacy. We are a *complete* being when we operate from adequacy. When it settles in our consciousness that it actually is so eternally — I am not myself, I'm Deity! I am Christ — God, the Father, Son and Spirit **in** me, **as** me...and I operate from that consciousness, *of course from adequacy,* and I am a free person!

So, I am a free person because I have what it takes to *be myself*, and as I am understanding that I am in this union relationship by which *He* is expressing His Self by *my* self. I act *freely* because it's He! Much the same truth as I said before...a man or woman competent in their profession *act freely* because they know their stuff. They don't have to consult; they just do it because it is part of them to do it this way. They have learned now to do it the right way, so they do it the right way. So, their competency and themselves have become one thing. They function as competent this or competent that. Therefore, we *boldly* function as Deity in expression as Jesus Christ, Father, Son and Spirit expression because we have this basis of competency. So we forget the competency and *function* just the same as when we have a competency. We *forget* the competency. We don't keep saying, "I'm competent, I'm competent." I forget who I am and *be* it. If I'm a teacher I don't keep saying "I'm a teacher, I'm a teacher, I'm a teacher." I teach!

So we have come back to this remarkable life in which we are just ourselves and we are our free selves to think our thoughts, make our decisions, follow our motives and *act* as persons. Yet, we live an inward secret consciousness, which is called the "mystery of Christ." But, it isn't really we; it is He. So, it *does* have the outer effect of us appearing egotistical. As I always say using that term, there is no bigger egotist recorded in history than Jesus Christ. No one used a bigger "I" than He did. "I am the way, I am the truth, I am the door, I am the good shepherd." I, I all the way through. But of course, when He opened up as to Who He was, He always said, "I don't do anything by Myself. I've the Father dwelling in me. And when I'm speaking the words, it's He speaking them through Me; when I'm doing deeds, it's He doing them through me." His hidden secret is the 'hidden mystery'. Paul says in Colossians, "Our life is **hid** in Christ in God." and Christ, our life. We are *hidden* in God in Christ, and if we go a little bit further it says Christ is our life. That's our *hidden secret* — that we operate as if we were *just ourselves*!

There are those who are *bound* to hold us in judgment. They are bound to say that we are proud, or self-sufficient, or holier-than-thou or whatever you like. They can't help it, because we act freely as Who we are, and when necessary, say so. They can *never understand* the *possibility* of a *human* claiming to be an expression of Deity! To them it is blasphemy or absurdity or conceit. That is part of the stigma we have to take and glory in the taking, because we know *actually* that truth always bears its own witness. And, it is actually bearing its witness *in* those who oppose us.

Just as Paul saw in Stephen's death when instead of being concerned with his being stoned to death, he was crying unto God, "Lord, lay not this sin to their charge." And, Paul was responsible for that stoning. He saw a quality, a reality of truth, which met his inner being. Because our inner being comes from God and our inner being is to be for others, not for ourselves. Paul *saw* the contrast between him and his proud defense of his own religion, for his own reputation's sake, compared to Stephen who was concerned not about his own needs, but the needs of his persecutors.

So *that* is a relationship, which we moved into as we saw in Romans 8 has a *witness*, because faith, 1 John 5:10 says, "Has the witness in himself." He that believeth on the Son of God *hath* the witness. Faith includes witness. So when we believe something it may not always be at once. It settles back into a conscious, "That's so; that's so."

Therefore we have entered into faith, which is *our* part of the relationship in which is our freedom. We freely attach ourselves to something. It really is a *gift* of faith because we are drawn by that to which we attach ourselves. But still we attach ourselves to some given fact as a *fact*. That's our side of faith. Back comes *from the fact*, confirmation, that it has attached itself to us, as it were. The same principle, as by faith, we attach ourselves to a chair...because it is available and desirable. As we attach ourselves to it the chair comes back to us and says, "I have attached myself to you, I am holding you up." That is where the substance comes to faith. So in this case we move into the inner know-how. That is the end of Romans 8.

We are *adequate* people now! We have nothing further to do on that level except what I always call the "repetition of recognition." Normally you don't recognize, you just **be**. You don't recognize who you are, you just are. The background is Who you are, but you don't recognize that; you just operate as being. When the multitudinous pressures, the trials, temptations come which pull us out, tempt us out to from being Who we really are...tempts us to operate as if we were on that independent level again, that's when we repeat recognition.

69

And so faith really dissolves and becomes fact. I don't sit in this room by faith; I sit in this room by fact, because faith becomes recognition. I just am. There was a time when I said, "I'll *be* in this room." Now I say, "I *am* in this room." Faith has dissolved and become fact. So when we say we believe a thing, it means that we have not quite got it, because faith dissolves and becomes fact. If I hold this Bible in my hand and say, "I believe I have it," you can be very sure I'm not quite sure. Why do you say you believe, if you have it? There is something that you are not quite sure. I don't say that. I say, "I *have* it" because faith has resolved. So, whenever we have faith, we don't *talk* faith, we talk *fact*. We have this, or this is happening, or this is strengthened, etc. This is the word of faith—this happens. And so, we live at ease, and the only *unease* is, if you like, (they're temporary) but there *are* areas of venture where we have moved into disturbing situations, which appear to call us out to see that we are not He in us. And, that is where we repeat our recognition and move accordingly.

Now the ninth chapter moves us into the necessary effect of this union relationship. If the Being of God, and the delight and fulfillment of God is to give Himself for His creation as being Love, His existence is, His joy is fulfillment that He may be agent, the means, by which His creation has their fulfillment – their happiness, their completion, their activity, and their responsibility (whatever it is) *all* so that they become the *true beings* they are meant to be on all levels. One day the animal creation, as seen by the prophets, will lose its antagonisms, which really are the product of our own self-antagonisms. And somewhere it says, "Harmony on every level of creation"...because God is harmony. Harmony means things work together, live together, cooperate together. And this is God in completion...when He can be the *means* by which His whole universe operates like that. What He gets back is the joy and the love of the whole universe by Whom this has become the fact.

And so, that's the nature of God. If therefore I *boldly* say, "I am no longer I, but I am the Deity which is the Father, the Son, and the Holy Spirit within me," I must be that. I can't be anything else. I don't have to *try* and be; I am! Remembering, as we always say, (It hasn't come up particularly in this Romans letter. It comes out more in the Hebrews letter, and so on.) we have learned the differentiation between the reactions of the outer form and inner self. The outer form as it shows us in Hebrews consists of the soul and body — our emotions, our reason, our bodies. They can deceive us, because they can cause us to think we are what we *feel* we are. And then we may *feel* absent from God, we may *feel* weak, we may *feel* so and so, and of course, that's an illusion.

We, therefore, *cannot be*...whatever we think we are...we cannot be a person, a *replaced* person, in whom my *real* self is, "Not I, but Christ," without being a person who *cannot help* being involved in others. Whatever my situation is, this is in me now. I *cannot* be but a self for God! I cannot be *anything* but somebody which is for others, until others should *have* this secret of eternal release, which is Eternal Life that I have. So I become, *I can't help it*, I am an out-goer. There again I don't go back to this other. There is no such thing in *this Life* as "trying it out." That's the danger of saying, as I say the soul may say, "You don't look like it." That is not the point! Other people may say it. We live on the affirmation that we *are*. If we are, if that is what is...so we are! And if we say, "I don't see it" then He puts that in to order causing us to *know* in what way we *can't help* but being. Of course we know we are.

So our lives in the Bible term become outgoing streams to rivers. It is said in John...first it is like a well of water totally supplying us, springing up into everlasting life, but that same well of water now is *continuously* an outgoing river. And, we don't question it...we *are*. And that is not for us to know *how*, because our outgoing river is He by us. So, we don't question how or we will get back on this self-effort and false self- examination. We just say it is so. And, somewhere or other we each of us know how that is coming out in our lives. Now this is what we might call the sad example of it, because this is the great letter which has taken us through the whole progress of what it is to be a true human.

And, here we move into Romans 9 and say the very *person* who would affirm to us that you can't be separated, which was the last final paean of magnificent glory, he said you *cannot* be separated...neither man nor devil can separate you! No man or devil can accuse you. In God's sight you are His precious perfected person in Christ and you *stand* there. The very person who said, that turns around here in the ninth chapter, after saying he could never be separated said, "I would be glad to be separated from Christ, if that would be the means of my brother's salvation." Now we're moving into "other love." He is speaking here about his *concern* over his brothers...beautiful tenderness...because they were the ones who had persecuted him to the *death*! They stoned him; they beat him up and did every mortal thing a person could do and yet, his *total* concern was, "Oh, I would do *anything* if my brothers could see the true Messiah." We may say, "It is a strange thing."

You would think that Paul would have the depths of prejudice against his people for the persecutions. We all have prejudices in our own types, in our own lives. From this distance, it is all right. Is it possible for a Jew, knowing the product of a Jew had been this *perfect* person...that anybody who does not believe in the Deity of Christ would at *least* see that they can't get away from the perfection of Jesus! There has never been a person who has spoken the kinds of things He has, and done the kinds of things He has, and loved His way, and been as un-blamable as He has. You would think no one could deny that this is so...you can't get a more perfect man...even if they don't believe He's God! You'd think to us this is a *strange* thing – that they wouldn't be proud of this greatest product of their race. It shows the great blindness and it shows how we don't understand what prejudices are. We have our own prejudices, so it is easy for us to judge other peoples' prejudices, because they *don't* [see]. And this blindness as we have seen in these chapters has come upon Israel. And here Paul is speaking about the privileges of the Israelites. They had the adoption of God; they had the glory of the covenants; they had the giving of the law; they were the servants of God...promises *piled* on. God had *piled* Himself on in His grace and glory and beauty and promises to these folk. And then *finally* the Christ Himself had come through them, and they don't see Him. And so in the flesh Christ came. It was God's blessing in Verses 3 and 4. It was *there* that he said in Verse 3, "I could wish myself accursed from Christ"...separated, I could wish. That is a strong thing to say. "I could wish I was separated from Christ," which was his very life, for his brother's sake. "This love in me now has moved in this direction." It is a big thing to say that...even I'd even go to hell.

Two men are known to have said that. Moses said that when he was tested about the golden calf. God has to use negative methods. This is why God disguises Himself. We often see, especially in the Old Testament, God is in disguise, because we can't see any other way. So He has to put Himself, as it were, in a rough character to stir up its opposite in us. That is why it appears to be anger and so on, because His anger really is only His concern for us to get us out of our foolishness and corruption and so on. It *looks* as if He is the angry one.

Now on this occasion, Moses was the leader and prophet of these people in the wilderness. In order to *stir* Moses to what he was God *appeared* so angry when they'd been given the law and then they'd forgotten all about

Moses and they'd gone after the golden calf and they were doing their lewd dances and so on—doing all their idolatrous stuff around the golden calf. He said to Moses, "I'll *destroy* these people; I will make a new nation of you"...as if God had no *use* for His own people. That is His *clever* way in which He stirs the opposite up in us... stirs the reality up in us. So God does deliberately take unpleasant disguises upon Himself to *help us* into reality. That was what helped Moses into his reality. "Oh, You couldn't do that God. Why Your name is linked to these people. If you destroy them, the whole of the Egyptians will say You couldn't keep them, that's why! You can't do that!" Moses saw the people...was fighting for the people as if it was against God. Of course that is what God wanted, *because God must come through humans*.

So He must have His *human* intercessor who would die for the people as did His own Son later on. Then Moses having gone back, as he did, dealt strongly with the people, as he should do. He brought them to repentance and still they came back to God. In order to *fulfill* the thing up on the mount, he said, "God, You can't leave these people." God had said, "My Presence will dwell with you." "I don't want Your Presence, we want You with us." And that's what he said when he said, "Look here, God, these people are guilty. If You can't forgive *their* sins, don't forgive mine. If You turn Your back on them, blot me out too." That's intercession! That's a person who says, "If I am identified with these people and I don't want to go on being what I am now, blot me out with them, if You can't forgive them."

You see God uses negative pressures to bring out of us the *real* Person in us. Of course that was God in Moses, really. That was the Spirit of intercession in Moses. It was God's own character expressed through Moses. So, God has to take us through processes sometimes like that. This is the only other case in the Bible, where a man in actual words says the same kind of thing. "I would renounce my privilege of going to heaven, if by that means I could be the means by which my brethren could go to heaven." Go to heaven...of course we don't use those terms now, because we think of heaven as present Eternal Life. In the future, heaven is going to come, but we are more concerned with the heavenly Spirit now...but, that comes to the same thing...having stated that as the *intensity* of his passion for these very people who chased him and chased him, until they could kill him again and again. But, love does not see its enemy. Love *has no* enemies. God's love sees everybody as God's person. So when you see right through, you see *every person* as a form of God, even if they don't know it...even the

73

redeemed form of God, if they knew it, but, mind you, you can reject being the redeemed form of God. You can't see enemies, because they are just those who miss the way, and I missed the way, too. So, this transferred to how you can *help* the person even though the person may be the one who is wronging you, antagonizing you, etc.

Then Paul goes into a phase which is very interesting. That is to say that whether the Israelites appear to reject Christ or accept Him, God's will takes place anyhow. Paul now moves into the *total* sovereignty of God. He stops in Verse 6 where he suddenly says, "I said that about the children of Israel who reject Christ and so their backs are turned to the Messiah and the Redeemer when He comes." Then he says, "Not as though the Word of God hasn't taken effect." He will defend the perfect way of God on *every* level. So, he says the reason that we say *that* is that in actual fact all Israel are not just all the physical Israel. That part of Israel, as the Israel-nation which has moved into a relationship of grace and salvation with God, which of course is true today. I would say of our own churches that the church is those who have entered into what we speak of as the new birth, a new creature relationship. There may be many who use the name and title of being Christian in different ways. We know the difference, we who have been that way ourselves. Paul's defending that by what appears to be a strange way. He says some appear predestined and others don't appear so. It works out that way. Then he goes back and says...You can see it in Abraham's children. Isaac was the seed through whom God's purposes were fulfilled. Ishmael was the one who left the family and went out into the desert and became the progenitor of the Arab race.

That incidentally is why it is so interesting to find in Isaiah, that great prophecy, where it says the days are going to come, when Assyria and Egypt would be back again in brotherhood with Israel, and the three together, the people of God. But, in this chapter it appears as if there are those whom God had appointed and those whom God had rejected. That is a tough saying. That isn't actually said of Isaac and Ishmael, but it is said of Jacob and Esau. And, it is *distinctly* said here, before they had done good or evil, while they were still in Rebecca's womb. In Verses 11 and 12: "For the children being not yet born, neither having done good or evil that the purpose of God, according to election might stand, not of works, but of Him that calleth. It was said unto her, "The elder shall serve the younger." Now watch that! That didn't say they were rejected. It only said that it will work out in that relationship. Well, they *had* relationships.

Of course, when you are in Christ, places don't matter. When you are a love-servant of Christ, you are a love-servant of the people; it doesn't matter to you whether you are the top or the bottom, because *all* you will do is fulfill your love-service. So the apparent superiority or inferiority in the operations of life don't matter when you are really in grace. All Paul said was, that this was *going to work out*...that the elder would serve the younger. As a matter of fact, that is true of all the world. The flesh world is the elder and we are the younger and the world serves us, not we the world!

If you watch through history you will find the world has been serving the growth and progress of the people of God. It might look the other way around. It's good to remember that. The flesh world is only the servant of the spirit world. And, the flesh world crucified Jesus Christ. No! They remade Jesus Christ. He has become world conqueror *because* they crucified Him and He's now winning back thousands of the world and "leading captivity captive." And so, it always is so. As we read before, it is God in people. People who have God *reign* in Christ. They are on top of their reigning and what's happening is only bringing out more of the reign of Christ in them...more of the manifestation of Christ and His love. They are *really* the people who are the leaders of the world, which is the reverse of what it looks like.

This is what took place in the case of Esau. Notice it doesn't say that Jacob would be accepted and Esau would be rejected. He didn't say that. He said "The elder shall *serve* the younger." Then he goes on to say, quoting from the last Prophet, Malachi, "As it is written afterwards, 'Jacob have I loved, Esau have I hated.'" Now *something else* has come in there. That first prophecy before birth didn't say that. It just said that they would have a certain relationship. One would serve the other. But, *here* it says long afterwards, it says this, "Jacob have I loved, Esau have I *hated*." You see hate is only love in reverse. Every opposite is only the thing in reverse. "No" is 'yes' in reverse. It's just saying "yes" turned around, that's all. Hate is reversed love. If Love loves one way, it must *hate* its opposite! If Love identifies with self-giving-love, it must hate self-loving-love. Of course it must! So hate and love are one thing.

It's said of Jesus in Hebrews 1:9 "Thou hast loved righteousness and hated iniquity, therefore God, even thy God hath anointed Thee with the oil of gladness above Thy fellows." That is a statement about the Lord Jesus Christ in Hebrews 1. If you love in the right way you must hate the wrong ways. Of course we do! The seriousness *is* our identification with the right or the wrong. When we as persons identify, then we are of course in the Love-dimension. If we *identify* with the wrong, that hate is on *us*. As we see later on, it's a hate that can be reversed. The reason it can be reversed is *all* of us are Esaus. We don't start as Jacobs. Jacob is the one whose heart was set on God and who moved into the new birth, and bought the birthright promises...and remained all the way, God's precious person.

We all start as Esaus; of course we do! Esau representing people who are for self, against God, and mind you, this is a person hate mocks. Mind you if a person is born the elder and has the elder's birthright privileges and he is taught by his parents what the *real* privileges are that God is *your* God and God has eternal destiny, eternal purposes for you, eternal operations...and then you wipe God out and disturb it, despise Him, and sell Him for a bunch of lentils, that is pretty good contempt. See, that person was *contemptuous* of God. He wouldn't sell his birthright for a bowl of lentils if he had any *thought* of the wonder. He had no *wonder*! He was a man of the flesh. He had no wonder of God and His promises...and all that nonsense. That is what the world *despises*. Well, you see you are then in the hate realm. As you see later on, that doesn't mean that you can't be love, because everybody starts out hating, really. We have all been Esaus; we *all* start in life rejecting God in our own way, turning our back on Him, and being bound to the flesh and to the world and to the devil. We have all *been* Esaus.

There is a certain subtle truth that we come to here: Esaus don't remain Esaus, but become Jacobs if they want to. But, at the moment Paul is not saying that. What he's saying, a very strong thing, he is saying that you *have* to face the *total sovereignty* of God – that God does what He likes and it takes place. Until you see the other side of it, it *looks* as if God is a ruthless Person, who would *save* some people and damn others! It looks like that because, again, it is difficult for us humans to accept the *character* of God. He is totally sovereign! What He says goes and nothing else goes, and He alone is the last word. The reason it's said thus is that we humans *have* to come to this place where we *bow down* to God even if we don't understand Him...because *God will never be understood by reason*. He can only be understood by faith. So this is an area where you have to take Him as He stands. Knowledge doesn't precede faith. Knowledge follows faith. The Bible says, "I know Whom I have believed." You know when you *believe*. Reason can't find it. Faith is an apparent absurdity. You've *leapt* into some truth which for certain reasons, you *boldly* take, because it is given you and as you take it, you say, "Oh I see!" And, the seeing only follows the faith. "I know

Whom I have believed." *Not* I believe Whom I have known. You *believe*...then you know. *That* the world can't take. That's why the world *must* reject us. They say, "You know then you believe." No! You believe then you know, because belief is the attitude of *obedience* to the One higher than yourself. When you accept that He is higher than yourself and greater than yourself, you say, "Well, I may not understand it, but I'll believe it because He is the great One and I'm the small one. I will believe Him." And, then as you take the *right* relationship as a human to the Deity you will find, "Oh, I understand now. I can see what He means." So the world cannot *take* that because the world is not going to start by yielding themselves to God. The whole point is they've become rebels. They don't want to yield to God. They are enemies! They won't yield to God! So, they *claim* to be able to rationalize themselves into God and despise those who say certain things, as if they're certain, because we *know*, because we've believed and they can't say that.

Therefore, the "works-Christian" is *bound* to despise you. The Christian whose basis to life is "my own self effort" is *bound* to think we're crazy. Because they think you can know without having to come this way...and you can't *do* it! You only know when you have found the end of yourself and been replaced by Christ. So, we've got to realize what the great Kierkegaard called "the absurdity of faith." We live in the foolishness of faith. He has a great book on the agonies of Abraham's faith, when he had to sacrifice Isaac. To *sacrifice* Isaac...even now the liberals laugh at it...is to burn your son as a burnt offering. He wasn't just going to kill him. He was going to burn him! He took him up with wood and the knife to burn him...his own precious son. Who is going to do that? He describes in that marvelous book called "Fear and Trembling"...the agonies that lie between "Is it murder or is it guidance?" He has a *very striking* instance there. He uses a lot of long terms. What he calls that is the *anti-logical suspension of the ethical*. The thing he means is *this* – ethics can still be self. "Oh *I* do a *thing*; I do so and so."

Suddenly God comes and calls you to do something which is unethical. "Oh?" How can you do something which is sometimes called unethical? I'll tell you eligible means ultimate. In the ultimate purposes of God you can be *led* to do something that goes against human morality. Now that's awkward. This was the case. *Was* Abraham called to be a murderer? Was it murder or was it guidance? That is a pretty stiff decision to make before it happens. It is all right to look back now and know what happened; it wasn't *then*.

You get the same illustration, which is clearer one of the highest places given women in the Bible, is the harlot, Rahab. There in Jericho she alone had *heard* about God and *believed* in this God of Israel...that *this* was the true God, and that these were God's people. All the people of Jericho were trembling and wanted to escape, but she believed! So when the spies came to her house and then the King of Jericho found these spies that came in – "Let's get them!" The crisis came to her house and what did she do? She was spinning flax, laying flax out I suppose to dry or something on her roof. And when the emissaries of the king came she told them, "Oh, they've gone up the mountain. They left here two days ago. Chase them." That was a *lie*. And, those wretched men went up into the mountains to chase the two spies up the mountain. As soon as they had gone, Rahab said, "Hurry and slip out and get back across the Jordan to Joshua." And, that lie is presented as a great act of faith by a harlot. That harlot *actually* was a progenitor of Jesus. She moved and she married, and she became one of those who lined up in the generations of Mary.

So in both cases God justified a lie and a murder. What Kierkegaard is saying on that point of faith is that faith will not be understood. In this book he talks about it. He says you can be a knight of faith or a knight of consecration...a knight is an important person who is going to give himself to war. Anybody can admire a knight of consecration. "Oh, you are going to fight a crusade and you are going to kill people for Jesus and you're going to the altar." You know that famous picture of a man presenting his sword...a young knight before the altar. "Ooooh, that's magnificent! He is going out." But, that's still self-effort, of course. It is *self* which is going to do something which they think is for God! But, a knight of faith is crazy. A knight of faith is saying God's going to do something, which the world can't take at all. There is no admiration in that. You walk a path which makes you a fool. And, the world says, "You are a fool." And you are a **knight of faith**...and the world *despises* you. You are moving along the line which the world says, "Nonsense!" That's faith. Faith is *always* in that dimension. It's in the absurd dimension. That is part of that suffering we talked of. That is what Kierkegaard calls great faith..."the *absurdity* of faith." So there is an area to understand that this is the point of this chapter. We *never know* God.

"It doesn't seem just; it doesn't seem right to me; I can't see that." You have *got* to believe first and then you fit in afterwards. And so, you have it presented in the *boldest* way...presented to us in, "Jacob have I loved, Esau have I hated." Then he says in Verse 14, "Is there unrighteousness with God?

God forbid." There is a question. And then Paul's strong word – forbid! Ridiculous! A strong word, get out, impossible! Then he says, "God says, 'I will have mercy on whom I will have mercy and I will have compassion on whom I will have compassion.'" Paul says, "It has nothing to do with you willing and you running. It is on whom God has mercy." So this is the first presentation of a God of mercy. "I will have mercy on whom I will have mercy," meaning there may be some whom He will not have mercy on. And, "I will have compassion on whom I will have compassion." It is not a question of you running and seeking. It is God's free choice.

Then he goes *stronger* and says, "That's why I hardened Pharaoh." Ohhh! The scripture says, "For this same purpose," God said to Pharaoh, "I'll raise you up" to show My power on you to destroy you. He destroyed Pharaoh, who was swallowed up by the Red Sea when he was chasing the Israelites with his chariots. Remember? Destroyed him! So the comment he makes is, "Therefore He *will* have mercy on whom He will have mercy, and *harden* whom He will harden."

Now here is a double standard! Am I to take that? Now he says, "You take it first." You've *got* to get the fact that God is *always perfect*. Now that's a very great thing for us to learn, because that's very difficult for us to learn sometimes — that God is behind *everything* that happens...and it's *always perfect*. That's a very great lesson for us to learn because that is what *tears* us apart. "Oh, I *can't* take that! That can't be God. What kind of a God would do that?" And you are torn up inside, and then you live in your hell until you can say, "What God does, I may not be able to relate it to love at the moment, but what God does is perfect." And therefore I am able to say what God does is perfect.

And then he goes further...the world says, "Well, why does He find fault, if He hardened Pharaoh and had mercy on others? Why does He find fault with a person?" Then, again, Paul comes back and says, "Don't say that! Who are you to reply against God?" Steady now, don't you reply against God. God will explain Himself sometime, but don't you reply against Him. Accept what He says. Even we Christians don't like that too well. Paul takes the common example of the potter. He says, "Shall the thing that is formed say to Him that formed it, 'Why did You make me like thus? Has not the potter power over the clay, of the *same* lump to make one vessel unto honor and another unto dishonor?'" Some for useful purposes. Dishonor, you see, is more than just a humble kitchen pot or something. Dishonor is the implication for *unpleasant purposes*. Heb.9:22 and 23. "What if God, desiring to show His wrath and to make known His power, has endured with much patience the vessels of wrath made for destruction, in order to make known the riches of His glory for the vessels of mercy, which He has prepared beforehand for glory?" That is where we get that we are *all* vessels. This is one that proves that humanity always contains a deity. Which deity? Vessels of wrath express the satanic deity; *Vessels* of wrath...the same *humanity* as vessels expressing Jesus Christ through Whom mercy comes.

Then he begins to change. He says, "Look, (now he slips in something) because now, you see, it *looks* like that. You have got to get it! God **means** what it is to be to be. That is what it is. Because, there is a hidden trick in this thing...there's a hidden trick in this thing. He says it's like this: God is prepared to have mercy, even to us who He has called, not to the Jews only, but also to the Gentiles." Oh! Gentiles are mixed up in this. We know He came to the Jews and the Gentiles now! Then Paul says, "God has said a strange thing, 'I will call those people who are not, My people.'" This is from Hosea, "Now I will call those people (those Gentiles) who are not my people...I will call them My people. I will call them beloved who are not beloved." (the Gentiles) And, in the place where it says, "You are not my people; they will be called sons of the Living God." Which is another lovely expression – the children of the Living God. Then Paul says He always had mercy. Israel was so rebellious. However, there was always a remnant there. There has always been this remnant all through history – the saved Jews. Isaiah said that – "The remnant shall be saved." He said He left us a seed even though we behaved like Sodom and Gomorrah. He has left Himself a seed.

Now then, "What shall we say then? The Gentiles, which have followed not after righteousness, have attained to righteousness, even the righteousness which is of faith." The Gentiles who followed not after righteousness are declared righteous by God. They received the righteousness through Jesus Christ. We talked about justification through faith. "But Israel, which followed the law of righteousness hath not attained to this true law of righteousness. Wherefore, **because** *they sought it not by faith*." Now we are getting something. "But as it were by the *works* of the law for they stumbled at that stumbling stone, the Rock of Offense."

Then Paul goes on in the next chapter and says you see this was the trouble. He says "My prayer to *God* is for Israel that they might be saved. I bear the record that they have a certain zeal for God, but not according to knowledge. For they being ignorant of *God's* righteousness they went about to establish their *own* righteousness." And not as that *submitted* to the righteousness of God. *There's* the key. He says there's a self in this matter and here's God's grace; here's God's mercy offered, and if you have built up your own righteousness you do not submit yourself to being a sinner needing justification by faith. The Gentiles did. That's faith! The Gentiles said, "We are sinners. We submit ourselves to God and we accept with thankfulness, as sinners, justification by faith." Israel said, "We don't want that stuff. We have the law, the covenants; we are the people of God; Abraham is our Father, and we don't want that thing of yielding ourselves to Christ" – because Christ was a terrible person to follow. You see, self was so built up in the Israelites, they *loved* that temple. That's the danger of modern churches...the whole danger of our modern churches...we love the form of form. Ohhh...we are proud of our churches because they are magnificent temples! You see they are full of self. "*My* temple." "*My* God." It is still self. "Oh, look at that! That's where God dwells." It's a lie!

Jesus was terrible. He said, "Destroy this temple, I'll build it again!" Woooo! He walked on the Sabbath and said, "The Sabbath was made for man and not man for the Sabbath." It isn't that we are made to fit with some laws of keeping the Sabbath. The Sabbath is made for us to do what is necessary and we are in the Sabbath Day of Mercy. He healed on the Sabbath – "I don't care about the Sabbath. I don't care about laws. Should I eat this or should I not? If on the Sabbath there is an opportunity of me showing the mercy of God I show it even if they slay me"...which they did in the end!

Now then he says – the fact *is* that the grace of God has *always* been operative in response to faith. It has to have that. He *has* to meet humans on the basis of 'they love themselves.' That's the Fall. While you love yourself, you are *hardened.* So, the hardness is not really in God. God has to *say* it that way to make it plain God *means* it. But, the hardness of Pharaoh wasn't something – "*I'll* make him hard." Of course, it wasn't! Pharaoh was a human being, but he was only *God's* human being. All human beings are God's human beings. They live and move and have their being in God. So what was his basic excuse in his humanity as God's human being? "I won't to do that. I don't want to give in to Moses. I am going to keep the people." Step by step he hardened himself...not for the offer of grace; not for the promises; not for the threats. He nearly came through at one time when he saw the miracles of Moses. He wouldn't come; he hardened *himself.* Because he was a form of God and because God *means* us to be what we are and God is *sovereign*, so it works out in us...as God's hell or God's

81

heaven. But, it is all God! But, when you get down to the inner circle, it acts according to my response. Now that's the hidden secret. So you see he *has* to present to the world that this is where you can only take the ALLNESS of God...when you are mature enough to do it.

This is the *allness* of God. God is total! Everything that happens is of God. Now *there's* our great key in life! Everything that happened God **meant** it. Now it may have come through Communist hate or something...God *meant* it...and has produced certain products. God *meant* it. This is the part of God's purpose that the hardened should be hardened and those who should receive mercy should receive mercy. So He has got to seek us, to see a God to whom we relate everything. It is very important for *us*; for when you do that then you take the shocks of life...God *meant* that. It can change your attitude. That's why our attitude *cannot be judgmental* towards a person going wrong...even a person doing wrong to us! The neighbors in our neighborhood or whatever you like. "Oh, I can't stand them!" God *meant* that! God meant that to be so. Because the moment that I do that, I am released! I can say, "Well God meant that." Then of course, I, knowing grace, can say, "But God's got grace around the corner for that person. God's letting that person... means that person...to be tough or so and so, because that is where he is going to find his hell. He is going to find his hell in his toughness. But God is around the corner with His grace." And I am a person of prayer – a prayer of *faith* that God is going to put *grace* into that person. So this gives a *whole release* on our outlook on life...where I can take *any* circumstance that is rotten..."God *meant* it."

God meant it to come through, what you like, maybe through some person of responsibility or it may just come through the mix-up of this world...mixed up with tragedy and disaster and disease in this world. And so, Ok...God *meant* it; God meant it. But *then* you say, "Wait a minute, God *meant* that to happen to bring this condition, but God is *always* around the corner with His grace. Jesus Christ redeemed the whole world. I'm going to take by faith that God means that hardness, as a loud voice, "Get out of it now. Come back to Me; come back to Me."

So, we go to the end of this chapter about the rejection of Israel. Paul talked a little more about faith. The last thing he says here to Israel, "All day long I have stretched forth my hand unto a disobedient and gainsaying people." Can you imagine *God*...this Authority...of God stretching forth His hands for mercy? Paul speaks later on about God *beseeching* us. Can you get that? *Almighty God* saying, "Oh I do *beg* you to come?" That's God! That's God!

But, that can't be the first thing you have to learn. The first thing you have to learn is that God is God and hell is hell; heaven is heaven and products are products. Then it doesn't turn out that God predestines a person to hell. It means that we are all predestined to hell *and* to heaven. We all have a double predestination. We are *all* Jacobs. And, the end of Jacob is a lost eternity. But, the very same Person who says, "That's My law and that's My rule...if you follow in the way of self, you go the way of spirits in prison." Now you get it; that is it. That is the wrath.

That's the God Who says that, because that's a fact. He said, "I predestined My Son before the foundation of the world to shed His precious blood for you. My own *Son*, God in Christ, Who reconciled the world unto Himself by the *death* of His Son. That's Me! And, I will *save* you who'll be saved." But, that is the hidden secret which has to fit into the fact that you get what you are meant to get. But, God is *always* merciful. All day long He held out His hand through Jeremiah, Ezekiel, to this disobedient gainsaying people and *some*...some found Him. You get at the end a classic verse...underlined (that the great Karl Barth made a great deal of) beautiful verse in the eleventh chapter, the 32nd verse. "For God hath concluded them all in unbelief, that He might have mercy upon all." Conclude is an old fashioned word for "shutting up". In other words God *means* us to be in unbelief! "You have gone your way. Okay! Be unbelieving.**"**

That's why when a person comes to me and says, "I believe that I'm an atheist," I say, "All right then...you *be* an atheist. (I won't fight them) Be an atheist. Get all you can out of being an atheist." One day they'll come to me and want a solution. Don't fight them. Let them *be* an atheist. Be what God's made you! If you are a rotten person, be a rotten person. But, I warn you, "You'll have to learn the hard way, because that is God's mercy." He *shuts* us up in unbelief that He may have mercy...not that He may have judgment. That's God!

So we have a *beautiful balance* in this scripture. There is one other thing that Paul said, and that is, "The *possibility* of faith is always within all men." It was in Adam and Eve because Able found that in the *seed* of the woman was the implication that in humanity, there's a Christ. Now how can we make it out? Of course, the seed of the woman was the term used which was Jesus Christ. God said in the Garden of Eden, "I will put enmity between thy seed (Satan) in which he has impregnated us with his spirit of error and her seed, which is us." There **is** hidden away in the human race, a Redeemer. Abraham saw it..."Rejoice to see my day." Moses saw it..."There is a prophet coming like unto me." Micah saw it..."One whose ways are everlasting." Jacob saw it..."The star arises in Jacob." Even Balak saw it. They were always seeing it. Implicit in the human race is the One who would come. But, *because* there is no *time* factor in God He always was there.

I am pretty *certain* Adam and Eve did...for He clothed them in skins was the first idea that a sacrifice...a sacrifice was made for you. He clothed them in skins. It was Abel who made the sacrifice. I think that the two go together. They were able to see that by that, the mercies of God applied to them. So, Abel we are told was the first redeemed person definitely recorded in Bible history. And, so you see the remarkable thing that Paul does, he takes quotes from Deuteronomy! They were the days of the law! He said, "In the law it is said this: Don't say in your heart who shall ascend into heaven to find the way. Don't say in your heart look over *there*. The word is 'nigh you in your mouth, in your heart!'"

That comes in Deuteronomy, said by Moses. It is picked up and interpreted here by Paul a thousand years afterwards and saying, "Don't go saying who shall bring Christ down from *there* or say who shall bring Christ up from here." See in your heart the **word** *of faith*, the ability to say, "Christ, I accept You. God, I come to You for Your mercy." Anybody can say that; therefore, any Israelite can say that. So, that **word** *of faith*...Moses knew it!

It's very interesting. That's the very chapter in Deuteronomy where it also says strikingly, "Circumcision is of the spirit, not the flesh." Well you hardly think they knew that in those days! But, Moses knew it and said so. In the same chapter Moses said this..."For this commandment which I command thee this day, it is not hidden from thee, neither is it far off." This is Moses to the children of Israel thousands of years before Jesus Christ. "It is not in heaven that thou should'st say, who shall go up for us to heaven? Or bring down to us that we may hear it and do it. Neither is it beyond the sea that thou should say, who shall go over the sea for us and bring it unto us that we may hear it and see it? The word is neigh thee, even in thy mouth and in thy heart that thou mayest do it."

That's what Paul picked up in this other phrase. In that very same chapter Moses said this, "The Lord thy God will circumcise thy *heart*." But, they thought that they were talking about the physical. No, that is only the "outer". The real sense of Jesus, the Spirit of God *way* back in Moses' day, knew it was in the Spirit and not in the heart, if they were willing to see...and some did, all the way through. And, so all these years afterwards,

Paul picks it up. And, so you see what that means. It means there's a capacity in *all* of us...our heart and our mouth. He puts mouth first because mouth is the finalizing of the thing. The word *finalizes*; the heart *settles* it. But, it is finalized by the word – word being, "That's what I will do!" It may not be verbalized, but it means it. And so, the heart is, "I desire something and I choose something." Then the mouth says, "I am doing that."

We desire to meet here this weekend. Okay, we'll go! That's the word. On that word you move. So he is saying here, you see, it has always been in everybody's heart. In your *heart* you can say, "Well, God, I accept You. I believe in You for mercy and righteousness." And, with your mouth you say it. And so, he says, "The word is nigh thee, even in thy mouth and in thy heart, the word of faith." Faith is my free ability to relate myself to something. I *relate* myself to that, and my heart confirms my mouth. Anyone can do that at any time when the thing is available...and what's available because of Jesus Christ to us. Then he makes the comment..."If thou shalt confess with thy mouth the Lord Jesus Christ and shalt believe in thine heart that God hath raised Him from the dead, thou shalt be saved. For with the *heart* man believeth unto righteousness and with the *mouth* confession is made unto salvation." In other words, the heart is the inner center, and you have done it in your heart (believed God) He says, "In *My* sight you are righteous." But the experience hasn't come to us; the *mouth* makes the experience. You see you say a thing in your heart. When you say it out loud, it becomes experience. You say, "Oh, I will do that now." That's the value of the word of faith. *Confession* makes the thing public. So, he says with the heart you will say, "Oh all right, God, I have accepted Jesus." God says, "Okay, in My sight you are righteous." Well, that doesn't give me much excitement. It puts me in the right relationship in God's sight, but it gives me excitement when I come out and say, "I belong to Jesus Christ!" Then that comes back into me; there you are! *That* makes salvation. Salvation is God *experienced*, grace *experienced*.

So you see here, right in this place here and that's what he goes on to say – see it was always there. So Paul says that the scriptures say, "Whosoever believes on Me shall not be ashamed." Whosoever! *Now* you've got that. The same Person who said, "Whom He will hardeneth. I will have mercy on whom I will have mercy. I'll accept those whom I will." That doesn't come of you; doesn't come from you running, it comes from God. Quite right, quite right. But, when you get *down* behind it to the nitty-gritty, "Whosoever believeth on Him." "Whosoever believeth." There is no predestination to

85

heaven or hell. Predestination is through hell to heaven! The first predestination we sought and lost. The second predestination is Jesus Christ when He predestines them to heaven. "*Whosoever* shall call on the Name of the Lord." First he says, "Whosoever, *believeth* shall not be ashamed." Whosoever. Then he gives that beautiful phrase, "There is no difference between the Jew or the Greek...the *same* Lord is Lord over all of us and bestows His riches upon all who call upon Him." That's a magnificent universal phrase – same Lord over all bestowed upon *all* who call upon Him. Then he adds "Whosoever shall **call** upon the name of the Lord shall be saved." It's a new thought. Whosoever *believeth* on Him shall be saved. He's reached to all. Whosoever shall **call** upon Him.

It seemed he suddenly called unto Paul – "Wait a minute! "How can they call, if they haven't heard?" This is the great missionary area. This is the few missionary verses in the Romans chapter. He says...Stop! Wait a minute. "How can you call on Whom you haven't believed? How can they believe on Him, unless they have heard? How can they hear without a preacher?" See how he goes back? To call they must have heard of Him. How can they believe without a preacher? And how can they preach unless they have been sent? And, then he says, "How beautiful are the feet of them that preach the gospel of peace, and bring glad tidings of good things."

So it comes back to *all* of us. There is a place for all of us to preach the good news. Some of us have the actual privilege of being missionary preachers. I thank God that missionary preachers today are often Indian preachers in India and Japanese in Indonesia, and the *whole world* has become preachers of the gospel! This is a wonderful *day* and the gospel is going *from* the whole world *to* the whole world. There are over 125 Eastern missionary societies run by Japanese and Indians and Indonesians...not ours, not ours! They have 3000 from India, Indonesia, Japan, Taiwan...out to the world! So we have a marching army going out as preachers of the gospel from *all countries* to all countries. What a *marvelous day* it is that we are saying! And, there is a *'sentness'* here...somewhere we are all sent. I think that we all know that there is an area in which we are all sent. And, somewhere, all of us see "how beautiful are the feet of them that preach the Gospel of peace."

So then Paul makes the final statement – "Faith comes by *hearing* and hearing by the word of God." So let's get the word sent. To have faith you must *hear* and to hear you must have the thing which to hear. So we must *hear* the word of God. Hear it! Oh, I believe it! That is how faith comes. So you see, he made a beautiful 'round' here presenting to us the *immutability* of His counsel. You cannot change God. What He says is negative is negative; what is positive is positive, and *they* come to pass. And, that is what it is. But *behind* it, we find there has always been for the human race, the breakthrough by grace. We are free to turn from the building of our own righteousness to brining ourselves the righteousness of God and come through. In the *end*...saved are those by faith, and the lost are those who reject.

In Chapter 11, he gives what I think is remarkable. I think it is the foresight of faith. I think he had the agonies. Agonies get foresight. I think that his agonies were weeping over his own people who had beat him up, that they should receive. And, so he finally said, "Wait a minute, don't you believe God deserted His own people." Therefore there is a sense in which we have to have a special respect for the Israelite nation. He says, "Don't you believe God's deserted His people; God **did** choose Abraham. He did go out through Abraham to the people. He did choose the people to be given the law and the promises, and if they'd *known* the Gospel...and he says, "God still works within His purposes."

The gifts and calling of God are without repentance. On the way He always *has* had people. Then he quotes from Elijah, in a very bad day of apostasy, when Ahab, who had *grabbed* the nation, and Jezebel who had destroyed the 400 prophets. She had destroyed *all* the prophets of the Lord except for certain prophets who were hidden in a cave by Obadiah. He had hidden fifty prophets in a cave, otherwise they would have been destroyed. So, the Israelite faith was destroyed and replaced by Baal. Then Elijah stepped in...that *magnificent man*...who brought the fire of heaven down and word of God in. But, after that *tremendous* event he was swept over by a **soul** reaction of feeling that he was alone. He ran alone from Jezebel and hid in the wilderness for forty days. He was forty days alone! A strange thing happened which is very interesting. God spoke to him by "the still small voice." It is very interesting because that's how God speaks...not by wind or by thunder or by earthquake or by fire. All those experiences in this cave...though the *still, small voice*...the still, small voice means nothing! After all, His voice is not still; it's noisy! So, he really means a **non-existent** voice. *That's how God speaks.* "A *still* small voice" means more than small; it's still. And, if it is still, it isn't speaking. So you see, *God speaking* is something deeper than we know. It is *inside* us. *How do I know?* That is **it**! Somehow I know *that's* God speaking.

So, *way* back then Elijah had that, and that's where He said to Elijah, "No, no. Elijah, No, No!" Elijah had said to Him make intercession, "Lord, they have killed Your prophets and dug and torn down Your altars. I only alone am left and they seek my life." God's answer to him was, "I have reserved to Myself seven thousand men (it doesn't say women) who have not bowed their knees to the images of Baal." So in that apostate day there were seven thousand, which probably means with the women...it came to twenty-one thousand all told...who had been faithful to God. So, even in **that** *day*, God had His faithful ones. *Thousands* of Israelites have been faithful through the ages!

So there's that, but then he goes on to say, as by grace, "Even so God has not forgotten His people." Now this is where the prophecy comes in. It is to be an example to you the *strange* way, the remarkable way God uses the negative for positive ends. That was what I was saying to some of you today. "Communism is a *great blessing* in the world." I tell you truthfully communism is done. It has *forced us back* to believing God! The first time in history a whole nation has **mocked** God...thrown Him out, despised Him and destroyed Him as a whole nation...and proclaimed atheism. It has been a remarkable reflex action. To do that, they had to destroy the institutions...the Orthodox Church. They destroyed that because there was too much form and too little reality. This has had...I have seen for years that this is so...a reflex action on the world – the *shock* of Communism. They have *shocked* us back into: "Is there a Living God?" There is an amazing new age of response to the Living God, through Jesus Christ. The second area of Communism is this – with all their wrong, they have certain rights. They *did* establish the rights of man. Of course, they didn't know how to do it, because flesh doesn't know how to do it, so they made an awful slavery of their claim of the rights of men...because flesh does that kind of thing. They had an element of right in itself and that's had a *profound* effect in the world of shaking up Colonialism. Now we British know that. You see in our days nations couldn't be themselves. Indian churches couldn't be Indian churches, because we were the Sahibs. We white people were the Sahibs...*we're the people*...they're just our slaves and servants – despised. They couldn't be real people because we kept them down.

I was in the Congo, where we weren't *allowed* to make Congolese first class citizens. They gave us a government. It wasn't a bad government; it was Belgian Government. They gave us stations, an area of maybe 30 or 40 acres or something, where we built our centers. We could not keep it, if we gave it to Africans...only if we whites held it. Africans were kept in their place, so we weren't *allowed* to let the Africans rise up and be people of God. They had to be underlings to us. Well of course, that is a hindrance to the spread of the Gospel. Now the challenge, which has come as a reaction to Communism, is that we have given people back their rights. They have *claimed* this freedom and thus have got it! It has had an *amazing* effect, as we missionaries know. All over the place now, the *churches* which God used us to start have come into their own. "We are true churches of Christ. We have the Holy Spirit. We are really God's people, now. We are *free people* and we will line up with the Westerners and share with them the taking the Gospel around the world." So you've got this marching tide of people moving around the world...all nations bringing the gospel to other people besides getting it themselves!

I am only saying that God *used* a *blatant attack* on the Being of God to replace the Being of God as never before in the free world, and indeed to the whole world...*and* the spread of Him!

Now in the same way, Paul is saying a remarkable thing. "He shut up Israel to loosen the gospel for you." If Israel hadn't got *shut up* and *persecuted* and turned the gospel out, it may never have gotten out. It may have stuck as just an *improved* Jewish faith. But, casting out by Israel of Paul the Apostle to us, has *spread the gospel* to the world! So, Paul says, "Through their blindness that it comes to you." That is the wonder of God that He used the Israelite's blindness! And he said *God meant it.* Of course, it was done by their own freedom, as sin is! That's the *strange* fact of sin. Out of their position of blindness has come the sweep of the gospel to the whole Gentile world. But, he says...remember the original olive tree started back with Abraham. God's olive tree with the oil in it was **God's** tree and a sign to Abraham. He says, "Therefore, if the first fruit is holy, the lump is holy. If the root is holy, the branch is." For certain reasons the old branch had been cut off and you have been grafted in. Don't boast about that! All you have is the same oil of life coming through you. You have joined in the oil of grace which came to us through Abraham in the absence of Jesus Christ. So, we are merely sharing the oil which first came into this world through the nation of the Jews. "Don't boast against the branches which were cast out. But, if thou boast, thou bearest not the root, but the root thee." You stand by faith. They were broken off because they were without faith. So, mind you, keep the walk of faith. Then he ends up by saying there's going to be a reverse. "I would not have you ignorant of the mystery lest you should be wise in your own conceits, but blindness *in part* has happened to Israel, until the fullness of the Gentiles comes in." Verse 26: "And so all Israel shall be saved; as it is written, 'There shall come out of Zion the Deliverer and shall turn away ungodliness from Jacob, for this is my covenant unto thee, when I shall take away their sins.'"

Now that is a *very strong* word. I can't answer that, but to me it is impossible for me to think "all Israel" means that. This happened in 2000 A.D. Just the A.D. 2000 Jews were saved? I can't believe that! But, some way the whole nation (I can't understand that) will be saved. All Israel must mean more than just the people who happen to be alive when this happens. That is the word used..."*All* Israel shall be saved" and there are no strings attached to that. So, he says: "Concerning the Gospel they are enemies for *our* sake." In the election they are beloved for the Father's sake. They are enemies that we may have the Gospel, but in God's sight, for the Father's sake, they are precious; they're the election. "For the gifts and calling of God are without repentance." So he says this last thing he says, "As ye in times past have not believed God, yet have now obtained mercy through their unbelief, even so have these also now not believed that through your mercy they also may obtain mercy." There's a reverse there. *We* obtained mercy through their unbelief; through their *rejection* we got mercy. Now this should be turned around; through our *mercy* they have obtained mercy.

There is some way in which we Gentile believers are to contribute back, not in unbelief or opposition, but in compassion and in love...the mercy of Christ back to the Jews. And, that's where he makes this great statement, "For God has concluded them all in unbelief (shut them up) *that* He might have mercy upon all." He has another great paean of praise. "Oh, the depth of the riches both of the wisdom and knowledge of God! How unsearchable are His judgments, and His ways past finding out! For, who has known the mind of the Lord? For *of* Him and *through* Him and *to* Him are all things, to whom be glory forever. Amen."

There is this paean of praise by which God turns each thing round for His own purpose. So, He's turned this concern that Paul had for Israel into a very remarkable outstanding facet which is very greatly misunderstood. The 'mind of the flesh' thinks it means God chooses some and damns others...as predestination. It doesn't understand the depths; the weak move into the depths...the *total rightness* of God is presented, and yet, geared to mercy, geared to mercy, because it's geared in the end to our freedom...to our faith or rejection. Well, that's the end to that! That's the important part of those chapters.

Norman begins a new session...

> "We don't pray, Lord, we're just talking with You, that's all...that's all we do together for You to talk with us as You talked with us yesterday through Your living Word. You talked through Your servant, Paul. What great, liberating light You gave through him...what strong mind, strong spirit in Yourself expressed through his humanity and even today, Lord, we have become re-interpreters. That is what You make us each, so we are able to take the world, given through You through a man, and put it again through our own words...because only our own words are really living to us. And so, we repeat again, and we go on now in this group together. Now we are again going to be repeaters and interpreters of Your living Word, a thousand different words...just this precious book of Your Word and all the other ways in which You give us to interpret Your living Self. So, it is You speaking through human forms, and manifested by human forms through human forms...become the same who have become manifestors of Yourself. This is the purpose of the Universe. Marvelous Lord, Your vast family of those who are You in human Son form, expressing Yourself to a bound up world, as we read yesterday, who are in the bondage of corruption. But, somehow or other You fulfil it through us that they'll move into liberation...into the glorious liberty of the children of God. So, we thank You...thank You, Who brought us together in the fellowship to laugh, and the joy in the freedom and the fun we have when it's in You and with You... altogether a little touch of the joy of heaven. So, thank You, in Jesus name. Amen."

Well, now we've finished, briefly, those last chapters of Romans. We see that we move right out of the "inner" to the "outer" now. Because the whole purpose of God is that we might be in an "inner" relationship by which He communicates Himself out *from* us to others. We've *seen* that. So we are in this third stage, which we call the Fatherhood stage, the Priesthood stage, the Ascended stage...when it is *He*, as a Spirit coming through us...reproducing Himself in others, so that others become expressions of Christ... even as by infinite grace, we have become. So we are moving on from that.

We saw, first of all, Paul's heart-concern with his own people...and that's where ours starts, beginning at home, beginning at 'Jerusalem'. So, we will start with a heart-concern and a purpose, which has a *burden* in it until we can replace the burden by the assurances of God for those with whom we are personally connected. That is where this outflow begins. It begins in the ninth chapter, when Paul says he would give up his own hope of heaven through grace, if by *that means* he could be the agent by which his *own people* could find their hopes in the grace of God. Then it turns his intercession into an inner assurance. He had to find a stabilization to it, so he went through this *magnificent presentation* of the *total* sovereignty of God, which could only be accepted by faith, not by reason...which shows that we have to give up our own opinions, and accept God's **totality** in evil and good – that God is meaning evil as He is meaning good. And, then as we *move in* by faith we can understand and explain it. We can see how the *meaning* of evil is only this *negative necessity* which prepares us to find the positive – the positive being the free grace of God.

Therefore we see in the end that we're all hated Esaus in fact if we remain in our fallen condition and that conditions us to find that we are in need of the grace of God. Therefore, we see in the end that we are all hated Esaus in *fact*, if we remain in our fallen condition. But, that's not the realness. It is hate because it had to be hate in that condition...the *real* underneath this other sort of surface hate. The real underneath is *always* the eternal love of God. The *condition* is to find the **need** of the grace of God.

Then we find that grace has always been a free fact. So that, through Jesus Christ every human being can *be* a Jacob, who is God's precious person, through faith. We see that His determined purposes are fulfilled our conditions...both in our lost condition and our saved condition...but in between as free people we move in by faith, which means that we transfer ourselves from our own false self affirmations, and do what Paul did. "What things were gain to me, those I counted loss for Christ." And then we move into faith; then we *change* from being Esaus to being Jacobs. Paul traced that through and finally says that there is something special about those people through whom *we* knew Jesus Christ. There couldn't have come a Jesus Christ unless there was a Living God Who had certain holy standards presented by laws, so that we understand that we are sinners...by the law is known sin. By the law is the knowledge of sin so we had to come...had to be a people who had the law of God, and by the law find the 'law of sinning' in their self-righteousness, although certain ones didn't. But, it's prepared the way and the necessity and the possibility of a Savior.

When the Savior came, He was a Jew. So among the Jews came our Jew-Messiah. Then He had fulfilled His course through this strange, obstinate way in which they themselves slew their own Messiah for our sakes, as it were, that the world of the Gentiles might have a Savior...and yet the Gentiles are only saved through the Jews.

Paul was a Jew. *All* the Apostles were Jews. So, the whole out-birth of this church of Jesus Christ has a Jewish basis, an Israelite its basis. So, it is right that we should have a respect, a thankfulness, a special love for the people who humanly we wouldn't love. Humanly the world despises the Jews for many reasons, but we don't see it. We see them as God's Chosen People. And so, Paul in intercession is able to see through. Probably we couldn't see through unless we have this intercessory burden that he was able to see through to the finality. God's gifts and calling are without repentance (Num. 23:19)...that He has *ultimate purpose* for the Jewish race! Though in another sense they're not fulfilled yet; they *have* been special agents of God. And so he moves into a thing which we can't fully explain yet – then he said, "All Israel will be saved." But its linked first with the completion of the work of grace among the Gentiles...until the *fullness* of the Gentiles is come...then the fullness of the purpose of God into His living church...then Israel will move back, and in some way or other our mercy will bring mercy to them. And the word will be fulfilled..."He shut them all up in unbelief that He might have mercy..."

Then Paul gives this great paean of glory and praise to God..."Oh, the unsearchable riches of God! His wisdom is past finding out." "For of Him and through Him and to Him are all things...of Him and through Him and to Him are all things." That closes this revelation that came about through his intercessory burden for his own people. And we interpret that in the sense that we ourselves have an intercessory burden for those among whom we are put. He then moves on final chapters into some touches of our outward relationships as members of the body of Christ. He starts off in the twelfth

chapter with that famous scripture which is sometimes misused, as if a beginning scripture where it says, "I beseech you brethren by the mercies of God, that you present your bodies a living sacrifice, holy acceptable unto God." It's really misused, but that is all right. God uses it that way, as if it was kind of a *beginning* commitment. We preach that as we're beginning to *know* that it's a *mature* commitment. This is the *body* to be the agency for the salvation to others...for the *will of God* to be fulfilled through it. This isn't the body committed to Jesus that we might be right with God. That is way back in Romans 6 to 8 where we found that we died with Him and rose with Him. All that's out!

So, we passed through those growing, *mature* stages. As a *mature* people this is the word to the mature. *Now* your body will be a living sacrifice because there will be a price you will be privileged to pay in your 'outer' life...that by a laid down 'outer' life, Life may come to others. We shall be among those who fill up in our bodies, in our flesh, the sufferings of Christ. Afflictions is the word, "the afflictions of Christ for His body."

So, Paul is saying this is our ultimate privilege. *You* are now on the altar of sacrifice. He says now by *your* body Christ may be reproduced in other bodies. You're way off considering this need is for you. You are now in this relationship for what the world needs. So he says that's your living sacrifice. Always remember the basis of all is the inactivity of the mind. The body is the "outer" agent. The inner agency to whom God speaks is the mind. The mind's not the reason. The mind is seeing as God sees. The reason is in the soul level...you think things through. The *mind* of Christ – you're seeing as God sees. You are seeing as Christ *sees*. The Bible says in Corinthians we have the mind of Christ and it says here "by the renewing of your mind"...that behind *all* is a transformation of the way you see things. You don't see things as the world does. "Be not conformed to the world." He isn't talking about silly little self-indulgences. It is talking about *seeing* – having the world-outlook or the God-outlook. And, the God-outlook causes you to see God in everything...like we've talked about.

You begin to move into a God Who perfects things *through evil and good alike*. So, we have a new outlook. When we see evil things (they *are* evil) we see them from a different angle. We see them as "Yes". We read in Rom. 9 God *means* them to be. And because God means them to be, God has a purpose of redemption and grace coming through the thing which appears to be evil. And so, our renewed mind sees the will of God being operated through the negative. We always start there; we start by seeing the negative, and that is our jumping off point – saying we see it now with a renewed mind, which sees God in operation. And, in *that* you find where you fit. There, when you are seeing things in the positive, it says you approve God's acceptable will, because we are the will of God. You don't *find* the will of God. We are the will of God! So, we *being* now in the will of

God, we find some who are part of the will of God as operating where we are...and that is good, acceptable and perfect to us. So, we relax back now to being an expression of God. We are not fussed because we are this or that or the other, because it's not the 'outer' position which matters. It's the 'inner' attitude that matters. And, it is God coming through us in any situation.

Then he says that is where you relax because he says now, "Don't think more highly of yourself than you ought to be." Accept yourself you *are* Christ in human form. If you've got the 'are-ing' you don't get fussed. That is one of the great secrets we learn about the Bible. When you begin to read it as a bunch of 'oughts' – you ought to do this, you should do that, you ought to love, oh I shouldn't do that. That's baby stuff. When you're there, you say, "I *am* that!" Well it says, "Don't lie." Well, I don't lie! It says that you ought to love. I *do* love! So, read the Bible as one who is there, as an 'are-er' not an 'ought-er'...an 'ought be-er.' And even when he says, "ought to," you say "Yes, that is just to remind me that is what I *am*, not what I ought to be." Cut that word "ought to" out except as a reminder – that's what I am! You drive a car...well, you may say you ought to drive to the right of the road. You say, "I am!" You can say, "ought to" if you like, but you just *are* driving on the right of the road. So we are God expressed in human form.

That's made a *great* difference in the whole outlook on the Bible. If you don't see that you will always be nagging, "Why am I not that; I should be that; I shouldn't do that." Then you are always as if you are apart from God and you have got to become something. That is self again. That is walking in the flesh, really. When you walk in the Spirit, you say, "Praise the Lord that is what I am because it is He in me! So, if He loves, I love. If He is true, I am true." That's all. Paul says accept what you are. Don't think more highly than you ought to think, just be what you *are*. "Think soberly according as you have the measure of faith." All right, don't get fussed.

There is a great book, which has been a blessing to many, which I had the privilege of writing on the life of Rees Howells. Now that was a dynamic life! It's an unusual life and He tests people that way. If you are in the 'ought to' level you say, "Oh dear, I feel such a worm, when I read that because he had such understanding of God, and did such remarkable things and certain miracles took place." That shows you are only a baby. If you are mature you say, "Oh, praise God." That is how the Holy Spirit revealed Himself through Rees Howells. He can reveal Himself through me in *my* way. The same Spirit is in both of us. So, I line up and say, "I am interested in learning some of the principles of faith he had." I began to get something from that. I am not going to imitate Him. Those principles of faith operate on *my* level as they operated on his level. We have the same Spirit. That is what he means here..."a certain measure of faith."

All right, if you are to have a larger faith, He will do the expanding, but all faith is just operating on what you see. You attach yourself to Christ as you know Him. When you were saved you attached yourself to Him as Savior; when you grow up you attach yourself to Him as the One Who has replaced you and so on. Then you attach yourself to the Priest Who is operating His purposes to others through you. Well, according to your faith; don't try to get any more. Be content with Him as He is, because He is the operator in you. He is no secret Person; He operates. Leave Him to be the operator in you. So, that's what he's saying. But then he says, "Look out...we're members." This is the first reference in Romans to the body of Christ. Not His body to which we identified to have sin removed from us, but now we're talking about where we come in as the whole Body, of which He is the head. This is the first time he mentions it...that we're many members in one body. So, Paul says there is plenty of variety. We have gifts differing according to the grace given us. So, operate your gift as far as you know it.

I am never quite certain whether it is good to know your gifts, because it might tend to pride or to think you might operate something. So I prefer not to look and see if I have got a gift or not, because we all have gifts. In 1 Corinthians 12:11, "Dividing to every man severally as He will." To every man! So we all have gifts. And, if you understand them, operate them. And so, he gave a list of the very simple gifts. There is the other list where we have the more dramatic gifts—and God bless those who have them—like tongues, miracles, or healings. God bless those that have got them. Most of us are not on that level. Paul said, "Do *all* speak in tongues; do *all* do miracles of healing?" No! Accept your measure of faith. But he says there are a whole heap of God's gifts which are beautiful through which God does come, so we are given here the gift of prophecy. Prophecy means speaking out. Some are given the gift of speaking out the word of God. There are some that are good at teaching. There are some who are good at proclaiming the Word of God, like a Dick Halverson or a Billy Graham, but they can't teach. But, we can teach. There is the gift of teaching here, you are able to teach. Maybe that is your ministry. Well, that is all right.

There are things listed here, that are so simple that you wouldn't think of them as gifts of God. One is giving. One man we know, who sees that in himself says, "My gift is giving." And, he gives illustrations from his life. There is the gift of managing. "He that ruleth let him do it with diligence." Managing things...running a home, running a business. This is a gift of *God*. So, it comes very beautifully. This is just an *ordinary* life...just ordinary expressions of our lives. One is a generous giver. One is an executor or manager. Then in the other list in I Cor. 14, he says "helps." One is a helper. What could I do without my two precious ones here, Pricilla and Susie? It'd be a mess! They are helpers. They all fit together with Pauline, when she was in bed, always said, "I go with you in spirit." So, she's helping us in the sense that she was in the spirit of faith with me...helps. Showing mercy and compassion, visiting, concerned in helping people in their spiritual needs. "He that shows mercy with cheerfulness; he that rules with diligence; he that gives with simplicity." There is a whole *bunch* of what we would hardly call gifts *are God coming through* in gift-form. So, it is made beautiful for us...just relax and be yourself. That's you...and God's coming out in *His form* in each of us.

Then Paul follows up with just a list of little touches on practical living. If you are a business man, put your heart in it, he says. Do it well. Don't be slothful in business; be fervent in your spirit. If you are a home maker, be hospitable. All of you—have an attitude of acceptance toward everybody. Don't know any more class distinctions. And what is a curious old fashioned statement...don't condescend to men of low estate. We don't recognize low estates in Christ. All are wonderful sons of God! So everybody is welcome...we are hospitable; our doors and hearts are open. We are honest; we do things and provide things honest in the sight of all men. We are sympathetic either way...empathetic shall we say. So when people rejoice, we rejoice with them. When they weep, we can help them in their weeping or help them *out* of their weeping. So, we rejoice with those who rejoice, and weep with those who weep. And then one *special* thing he always puts in...he says as best as you can live as best live in peace with everybody. "As far as lieth in you" is interesting. You realize that some people you won't be linked with. "As far as lieth *in you*, live peaceably."

And, then he adds...you do get enemies en route. Now is your chance! *Find* the ways you can express practical love. That may be to our neighbors. Some of us can be very antagonistic. If your enemy hungers, feed him; if he is thirsty, give him a drink. It is *practical*. This is a practical daily life. Find some way in which you can show some practical love to a person who resents you, and maybe lets you know that they resent you. This is then what is called "heaping coals of fire." Fire is, of course, rightful discomfort till they realize what a wrong attitude they have towards you. Leave God to avenge. But, of course our vengeance for people is that God will give them the negative and make a positive. Our vengeance is we *hope* that what happens to them will turn out to lead them to where it led us—to the true heavenly life, which is Christ in us. Paul ends that whole sentence with that total positive. "Don't be overcome by evil, but overcome evil by good." Find out how you respond to evil with good believing, good attitudes, good actions. So, your response to evil is not evil to evil, but good to evil. That is *all* some way in which God is going to come! That is a beautiful phrase. That ends the chapter. "Be not overcome by evil, but overcome evil with good."

Then he moves over to our practical relationships...our official relationships. This is another revelation as members of society. Paul says, "Show your appreciation and obedience to the leaders of your country and to the laws of your country." He says remember that's been the point of God. That is pretty strong speaking. Some of those men around were Herod, who killed James...Nero and so on. They were the nemesis of God. Yet, you are to respect the men who God puts over you. You are to fulfill the laws of your country and pay your taxes. So, then you are acting as a citizen in right relationship, and in a country like ours an appreciative relationship. We have an enormous amount to be thankful for that we *are* in a country like this. And so, we have a sense of loyalty or we may be in one sense critics, but beyond any criticism we have there is loyalty to our leaders...therefore, fulfilling whatever laws that are there to make us work as a harmonious society.

Then he mentions the word neighbors. We had been talking more about brothers in the previous chapter. Now he says neighbors. Neighbors are anyone next to you. Then he says the way to handle your neighbors is always love...because, love does no harm to your neighbor. "Love works no harm to your neighbor." It says here in verse 10. So, it means that if you always fulfill the law of love, you always do what is best for your neighbor. That is the safe way of life. You fulfill the law, if you are doing that, because you don't steal, kill, commit adultery or you're not saying malicious things about them, bearing false witness, or covet. You don't do those things because you are operating by the law of love. You are for them, not for yourself. So, that is simple isn't it? So, you *owe* no man anything except to love them. Our marvelous indebtedness is the new attitude that we have. We have a debt to pay, which is – we are here to help other people. So, in that sense we are always debtors to need. We pay our debt by whatever forms of love there are.

Then he adds: "Watch your social habits. Live as one who puts on the Lord Jesus Christ." That is putting on our clothing. Here he isn't talking about our inner person. He says, "Put ye on the Lord Jesus Christ and make no provision for the flesh to satisfy its lusts." Meaning that our life should have a *tone* of what it is to be a Christ-person. Probably, a certain humor we enter into which feeds the flesh. Maybe certain social activities we wouldn't enter into where we obviously feed the flesh. Don't do anything which feeds the flesh. Therefore, don't live like the world does in its talk about sex, drunkenness and hating that's mentioned here. Don't live in that. So live in a social life, enjoying your social life, yet have that amount of restraint of a way of living that you are seen as a person of God, a person of Christ. There are certain things that maybe you don't enter into which would merely make provision for the flesh. So, that is what he is speaking about, our national and social relationships...your government and your neighbors.

In Chapter 14, he comes back to brotherhood again. Paul speaks about our essential liberties, our freedom to be what we understand to be the right thing to be, and yet, what our relationship should be to our brother Christians in so doing. He says, "When *you* are free, *all things* are pure." You should decide which you shouldn't do. You're free. Mind in your freedom you give this freedom to the other person. That's the important point. So, it says, "If you are free, let your brother be free too. And, if one will eat this and the other won't eat it; the other will do this and won't do it...well, all right. Don't judge them!" You accept your freedom and you eat what you like and don't eat what you like or go where you like or don't go where you like even so far as the very Sabbath day. That's why he says here, "One may regard the day; I must keep the day; I must go to church and do so." Ok. He abides by the law. Another doesn't regard the day. Well, OK, he doesn't regard the day, but he's doing it unto the Lord. The *point* is count on Christ in each other; see Christ in each other and therefore, don't judge. Say, "Well, he is the Lord's and the Lord needs a person to do something like that or not do something like that. That's between him and the Lord. When I free my neighbor, I free myself; when I bind a person I bind myself. If I judge my neighbor, I'm really judging myself. So, giving him freedom allows me to be free equally.

There is essential freedom in our habits, actions and activities. We will live our lives on whatever level of outer activity or outer habits that we think is what God would have for us. There is one point to watch. Don't practice those things which you feel *hurt* your fellow Christian. This is written for the mature, of course. This is at the *end* of the Romans letter. If you are moving with someone who hasn't got their maturity yet, you need to 'climb up' too. And so you might consider that...and there may be some things that you wouldn't do, not because they're wrong to do them, but because you feel the example may encourage those who are not strong, who cannot do a thing or drop it in freedom...and they may be bound by a thing or come under condemnation if they do it. Because you do it, they'd do it and be thick with guilt. Where you are free, they are not free. So, for *their* sakes there may be things you feel you shouldn't do. We each have our own way.

When I started life as a young Christian, I went into World War I. I had only first found Jesus and did become a witness. An older Christian told me, "Mix with the world all you can and you win them better." So I took up drinking with them. I never had trouble drinking...and I smoked. I enjoyed smoking, particularly a pipe. I still would. So, I smoked and drank and I was a witness...an almost absurd combination! On a free afternoon with my men (I was a young officer among them) I'd take a packet of cigarettes with me and hand cigarettes and then give the gospel to them. So I'd be like them and preach at the same time! I had certain responses through those five years, but more and more I felt they don't remain. I knew where I was. I went through with God, but it seems as if many accepted and then didn't live it through. And, then it came to me in the end...I may be wrong...at least for *my* way of life. I was a missionary. I'd better cut out those things which were not necessary. The very last day of the War, the day of Armistice in 1919, I remember throwing my tobacco pouch in a plowed field. That wasn't any credit to me. I had come to see in my type of life it was better that I not do it. That is OK; others do. We just do what we are free to do.

Just now there is one who is very much one with us in Charlotte. She has really come to *see* and know, but apparently she had a problem with smoking. I was staying with her. In a group, she said, "I'll tell you, Norman, I do have a battle. Really I do like to smoke, but I know I shouldn't, so I don't. Then I give in to smoking and then I am guilty. Then I don't smoke." I said, "Olive, drop it. Get on with smoking. Don't be guilty. Guilt is far worse than smoking. Go on smoking and then say to God, 'God if I really shouldn't, You have got Your ways, You cut it out for me. You make me stop.'" "Oh," she said, "that is fine." So, we went to a drug store, I thought for food, and she came out with a package of cigarettes. So I helped my friend become a smoker again. That's OK. Free. She should not be under guilt. Let *God* stop her. A sin is a sin. Guilt is a far bigger problem than smoking. That doesn't matter; we *don't* judge each other. Let the Lord settle each of our problems, because they never will be settled by self effort.

But there may be a point as a mature person (I am a missionary) that it isn't suitable to do certain things which I might do if I wasn't a missionary. I personally haven't for a long time...I don't drink alcohol. However, there are one or two friends I go to who have a sherry and I have a sherry with them. I am not against drinking, but *normally* speaking it wouldn't be good to be running about as a missionary with a whiskey bottle in my hand. So, we are just free and we don't judge others. That is the secret! But at the same time, I do *watch* that I am a person who has certain responsibilities to my brothers...my Christian brothers. There may be some things I feel I am better without for example's sake. Because he says, "Whatsoever *is not* of faith is sin." That is how he ends this chapter in the twenty-third verse.

Now faith means you are settled. That is OK. Now remember faith swallows up doubt. All life is doubt. Doubt is on the soul level. "Should I do this, should I do that?" Now if you are *mature* you will say, "I will do it until God shows me. I won't go by niggling doubts. I won't go because *man* says I shouldn't do it. All right, if I shouldn't do this thing, You'll tell me, God." Now that's faith. You're settled in your faith and go on doing something, maybe. You say, "If I'm to stop it, You tell me, God." Because, when God tells you, He has a way of doing it, doesn't He... which is an easy way. It isn't condemning and destructive; it up-builds you. It is something..."Oh, I shouldn't do it." And then, it is *easy* not to do it. That is all right then.

But you see, if you haven't got *that* faith, you may say you believe God, but you're doing something which you think you shouldn't do. Then you really condemned and get under bondage and condemnation, and perhaps even throw out Christianity by saying it doesn't work. You haven't discerned between soul and spirit. You are taking doubts that you could say, "I'm not taking those until God gives them." But, you are grabbed by them and other people set the example to you until you slip away. I wonder how many in our churches were disillusioned because they fought and failed. They haven't known how to fight. They have had their guilt. "It hasn't worked," so they have thrown it out.

It could be because they haven't seen any...first example and then teaching...to help them into this faith, which doesn't accept doubt. If he accepts doubt, which is not of faith, it is sin. Then we are free of sin, if we do not accept doubt. We only accept conviction. Condemnation comes from Satan. Conviction, we accept from the Holy Spirit. Conviction isn't a bad word. "Oh, I see that!" (I mean, like I did. I saw that I shouldn't go with it for my calling. Okay, then it was quite easy for me.) Then the conviction will fit right in. So, faith can include conviction, but it does not include condemnation. When you're *young* you may mix up faith and condemnation. Then you get guilty, and you struggle and fail, and perchance throw the business up.

Paul says, "For meat destroy not the work of God." We can destroy people, you see. "Let us therefore follow after things which make for peace, things which edify one and other." "For meat destroy not one and other." In other words you say *I will*. In those days they had a problem with eating meat which had been offered to idols. That's a problem we don't have today in the same sense. We have other problems. Don't stick to this thing..."I'll *do* this thing"...and destroy your brother. Destroy is a strong word! He accepted drinking, but he says don't do anything if it causes your brother to stumble. He says to me all things are pure. It isn't wrong for me to drink my wine or eat this special kind of meat offered to idols. Nothing bothers me. It doesn't occur to be because I have this faith, but don't do a thing to stumble a brother.

So, there is a beautiful balance here between affirming freedom, and being free, and taking no conviction except what God gives. And yet, in turn not judging my brother if he does a thing and he is convinced. Okay, bless him. The scripture given in this same chapter is, "Why dost thou judge thy brother? Who are thou that judgest another man's servant? To his own master he standeth or falleth. Yea, he shall be holden up, for God is able to make him stand." So don't be judging your brother. He is God's servant and God will deal with him. Who are you to judge another man's servant? To his master he is responsible. And that beautiful word – "And he'll be kept up." Yea, he will be held up; God will uphold him for God is able to make him stand. So, we can have *faith* for our brothers like that and be free. Yet, at the same time be sensitive and not do things which we can freely do, and yet we feel on the whole are not helpful in the fellowship to which we are linked.

Then he goes into his final chapter. He says a little more there and the first few verses really belong to the chapter 14...the first few verses 1-7 where he's saying because you're strong you should support the weak. You live to please your neighbor; we do not live to please ourselves." Now don't take that as bondage and say, "I'll do that." It is saying here—we ought to bear the infirmities of the weak and not please ourselves. Even Christ did not please Himself, but it is written, "The reproaches of them that reproaches fell on Him." Now the danger when you read that..."Oh, I *should* please them." Don't say that! I am *not* pleasing myself. *God* is in me and I live like that. I am only saying that self-pleasing business needs putting into focus. You *do* please yourself. You can't be yourself and not please yourself. Life consists of pleasing yourself. Love *must* satisfy itself. Love must have full satisfaction in you. This was the *first* point which challenged me as a young man...the first touch I really had of repentance. The first touch was that I was self-centered. I was in a football accident and was in the hospital...our English football we call rugby...and I had a surgery. While I was there it *suddenly* occurred to me, "Is the whole world selfish?" Because I was selfish.

There was something wrong with me. My *father was for me;* my *mother* was for *me;* everything was for *me.* There was something wrong here. I had been reading a book. I'd been reading John Stuart Mill's *Utilitarianism,* which is *all* is done for self ends and that began to disturb me. (This came from some of my school reading.) I got out of it for a time by saying, "Oh wait a minute. The Bible says "For *Thy* pleasure we are created." So, God pleases Himself. Oh, I'm in a good line then! Why shouldn't I please myself if God pleased Himself? "For Thy pleasure we are all created." I got down to the scripture about Jesus in Hebrews 12. It said, "For the joy set before Him, He endured the Cross." For His own joy He endured the Cross. So, I traced back that in God Himself is Self-pleasing, so why shouldn't I be self-pleasing? I hadn't seen the point! Our form of self pleasing is to get just what we want for ourselves. Our *redeemed* self-pleasing is to get what other people need. We find our pleasure in *other* people's needs. So we please ourselves by blessing *others.* Or, you please yourself by blessing yourself. So that's the difference.

In the *new life* there is always this pleasing. I must enjoy myself! But, in the new life my self-enjoyment is secondary to my other-loving. In my old life my self-enjoyment was primary. It's for myself. That's the difference. Your self-enjoyment is what you live for...for ourselves. In the new life you still have self-enjoyment, still enjoy this and that, but the *underground stream,* the *basis,* really is that I may be the means by which others will find their enjoyment in God. That is the difference! When you find that you do not come to condemnation. "I shouldn't be self-pleasing." You are *not* self-pleasing.

Then Paul adds a word on scripture which is good. It is the one place in the whole letter where he says scriptures are valuable to you...keep reading your scriptures. That's Verse 4. He is referring you to learning what kind of a person Jesus was. He didn't come to please Himself. So, he's saying, "Through patience and comfort of the scriptures you might hope." He is reminding the Romans that they have this feeding on the scriptures to build them up in the faith of God. Then he is saying, "Have this mutual fellowship with one mind and one mouth glorify God and receive each other" so that you are operating in fellowship. That about ends it.

Then he turns back to one final, great message. He says I want to remind you that I've had a very great privilege of being a *minister of Christ* to the Gentiles and this was fore-spoken in the bible. And he suddenly turns away and says Jesus Christ came to be a minister of truth to the circumcision, to confirm God's promise to Israel. But then he says the *real* reason was that through Israel the world might have the gospel. Israel rejected that, so it came out in *spite* of Israel. God had originally said to Abraham, "Abraham, if you go through with Me, not only will I make you a blessing, but in you *all* the families of the earth shall be blessed." So, there was a *universal blessing* right in the very first revelation which came to mankind in the purposes of God, which was the universal purpose. *All* families of earth will be blessed. That's God! Jesus Christ *did come* first to bring truth to His own people. They rejected it except for some special ones...then through those special ones, out to the world.

Now he says, "*I* have the privilege of being the mainline minister to the Gentiles" and then he gives three quotations that always *had* been in God's purposes. He says, referring back to the scriptures, "Rejoice ye Gentiles with His people" and again "Praise the Lord for ye Gentiles" and Isiah said, "There shall be a root of Jesse, and He shall the Gentiles trust." So, he picked out these wonderful foreseeing phrases that come in the prophets that the gospel was for the whole world. These supposedly outside people were without God and without hope...this world outside of Jewry, Israel. Then he says, "That's why I have a joy in you. Actually you are *not* my harvest field." He speaks of his harvest field much. The Roman church *wasn't* his harvest field; we don't know much about the Roman church, or called the church at Rome. He said this beautiful word, "I am *persuaded* my brethren you are full of goodness and knowledge and so on." I like that. He had the *positive attitude* towards the church of Christ. He didn't pick up niggling little things. He said, "The God of hope fill you with joy and peace. I am persuaded you are full of goodness and, with all knowledge, able to admonish one another."

So, I *confirm* you. Christ in you is your goodness, we would say. We have already said that, and you have the knowledge so you can build one another up. He spoke positively to this church to whom he was writing whom he hadn't yet visited. Then he went on and said, "I write this to you because I have had this special privilege that the grace was given me of God. I write boldly to you, God's grace has been given me to be a minister to the Gentiles that the offering up of the Gentiles might be acceptable, being sanctified by the Holy Ghost. My *privilege* always has been to go to people who have never heard. This is his last great word, "I don't speak about Jews as my harvest field. I won't speak of things which Christ has not wrought *by* me."

We have an individual ministry. This is the purpose of God. *Each* of us should be able to say, "This is my individual ministry; this has happened through *me*." There's a place where we can say that. That's God's purpose. All of us in a certain situation should be able to say, "Yes, this happened through me!" So, I am not working on another man's foundation. Of course, he's making a very *special* point that people never had Christ at all! That is God's purpose for all of us. Paul says, "I won't dare speak of the ministry of Christ wrought by others." Then he gives that wonderful phrase..."Through mighty signs and wonders, through the power and Spirit of God from Jerusalem round about to Illyricum I have fully preached the gospel of Christ. I have striven to preach the Gospel, *not* where Christ was named, lest I build on another's foundation." Beyond that!

And then this *precious man* towards the end of his life saying, "Now I do want to come to you in Rome for *one* purpose. It would be a joy to be with you, I could confirm you in the faith and you could bless me. I have been hindered." Because he had to fulfill his commission in Jerusalem—again, the negative turned to positive. He said, "I've got to go to Jerusalem because I am responsible to get this gift to the precious Mother Church. I have been busy collecting gifts from the Corinthians and the Macedonians and the Philippians, etc., which will be a *bountiful* gift to the 'mother' church. I want to *fulfill* that! He says that blocked my time for the time being. I'm so keen on coming to see *you*. He didn't see himself there as it really turned out. God did it. He *had* to *go*. Remember they tried to stop him. Even prophets told him that he shouldn't go. He said, "Don't break my heart, I have laid my life down for Jesus Christ; I have *got* to go." And, that is what he did.

He laid his life down in a sense. The Jews turned on him and seized him and made him a prisoner to the Romans. And then his way of escape under God's guidance...practical way...he said, "If you're going to judge me I appeal to Caesar. I am a Roman." And they had this great respect for Romans. "I'm a Roman" and they wouldn't touch him. "Very well, you appeal to Caesar" and they took him to Rome. So, they took him to prison. While in prison he wrote the prison epistles. Out of that came these marvelous Ephesians, Philippians, Colossians from the prison epistles. They sent him to Rome that way and came as we see...the work of God in Caesar's household! So, right in the *heart* of that, we would say flesh-given people, (we are all flesh-given people)...Nero's household, Augustus household...he *boldly* preached the Gospel and then came this harvest in the Praetorian Guard in the household.

Then he said, "*Why* I come to you." (This is marvelous!) I've got to go to Spain. Here was *this man* beaten about, shipwrecked three times, a night and a day in the deep, frozen and starved, his body covered with the scars from a half a dozen beatings, imprisoned, stoned. Every time it was the Jews doing it. It wasn't the heathen, usually. It was the Jews stirring up the heathen to do it. He said, "I must *still go*, for Spain hasn't heard the Gospel." I don't know what they knew about Spain in those day**s."** And then he got them into it...this is where we missionaries get them into it! I want you to *help* me on that way. Wherefore I take my journey to Spain, and I trust you wherefore I am brought on my way by you. Maybe you'll give me a team to go with me." A job as a team to go to Spain. So it's the *last* thing he's saying. "Oh, I live for the people who haven't heard. I live for the next place that hasn't heard." Isn't that marvelous? *That's* the man who wrote this letter! He asked for prayer that he should be delivered from the Jews who were persecuting him in Jerusalem. He *was* to go to Rome as a prisoner that the gospel may be taken to Rome...and he wrote those final precious epistles.

Then the *father-heart* turned back in that *extraordinary* last chapter full of names, all sorts of twists and turns of Latin and Greek names of precious people. He named, named, named. He *carried in his heart* so many people. It is very interesting the care he had of women. I always liked that because people 'go' for him. He knew how to organize churches. We mustn't mistake local conditions for eternal principles. We missionaries know that.

Usually as a Congo Missionary you subdivided the men and women. They didn't sit together. The women were on one side and the men on the other. There are customs that you grow into and there are certain relationships in certain countries, so you *fit* the gospel to the customs of the country. Of course, this is rather a joke. C.T. Studd was a joker. He liked a good joke. In the Congo no women wear hats. In the old days they had bound their heads as children and made longer heads. It was sort of a beauty custom. It didn't affect the brain apparently. Women never wore them because they had that short curly hair. Men always had little hats on the back of their heads. So, only men wore hats and women in those days wore nothing except a little cloth on their waists. That's all they had. A godly man from England said, "Dear Brother Studd, I hope you're fulfilling the law of commands in Africa and your women come to church veiled and having a hat." Tell you what his answer was...he was a joker. He said, "Dear brother, I've got a little problem. In our country women don't wear hats; only men wear hats. The only way women could wear their hats would be to take the garment off their waist and wear it on their head. Should I have the women do that?" He got no answer on that one! He got silence to that one!

See how we can be silly about customs. Customs are just part of it. So we don't 'go' for Paul. Paul knew the conditions and he knew there were conditions in those days where there was some moderation of need... some freedom that we don't have. But, this is the real Paul. And, the very first thing he says in this list of commendations..."I commend unto you, Phoebe, our sister, a servant of the church. She has been the succorer of many...a helper of many. I entreat you yokefellow to help those women who helped me in the Gospel." He also beseeches two women who have had a quarrel..."I beseech Euodias and Syntyche to be in the same mind in the Lord." So, he has a great deal to say to women. After all, what was the first church in the western world? Lydia, the seller of purple, was the one whose heart God opened in Philippi when he crossed over to Macedonia. Lydia said, "Come live in our home." They had a little group of worshippers at the seaside. This is the birth of the church in the women. The same as in the resurrection...it was the women who first saw Jesus. It was women who brought the news to the disciples that Jesus was alive. So, I am with women's lib a long way. We have *room* to give women their rightful place. I tell you, God help the mission field, if we hadn't got many of them.

In fact we have some famous occasions in our own Worldwide Evangelization Crusade to which I belong, where one famous country was opened up to the gospel. We were the only mission in it. Twenty years ago, we had three young men who went out and one young woman. It was a West African pastor of independence. It used to be called Portuguese Guinea, but it now called Guinea Bissau. It's a small land in the bend of West Africa. The three young men were landed in the country. You couldn't send a single woman in with three young men. So, she remained on an island, called Cape Verdi about a week's journey out from the mainland in the Atlantic. The three young men became frightened when the war broke out and they thought the Germans might come because the Germans were fighting for West Africa to take it over. So, they went back to England, left that precious calling they had...left one woman. I was in charge of the mission at home in those days, so I sent this young woman fare to come home. She was only a slum girl. I had picked her up in the slum area. They called her a nipy. A nipy was a servant in the East End Café in the slums of London. She had *caught* the vision and *gave herself* to the Lord and said, "Can I be a missionary?" I said, "The Holy Ghost makes the missionary, Bessie, not education." She was so sharp that she learned Greek and Hebrew...she trained herself! She had the Holy Spirit and this was the girl who went out.

When she was on this island and these three young men deserted to the mainland I did everything I *could* do. I cabled her, "Bessie in this condition the only thing you can do is come home. The fare is ready for you to come home." The answer I got from her was, "Dear Mr. Grubb, I write to you with respect, but I have to remind you that it wasn't you who sent me out. It was the Lord Who sent me out. I am waiting to hear what the Lord has to say." And then, three weeks later, I got a letter saying, "The Lord said to me despite fears and despite absurdities I am to go alone in this land." So, she went and she expounded the work of the gospel. The gospel work in Portuguese Guinea today is traced to her all over the place. She remained there several years and then came home on furlough and married one of our missionaries. Then the two of them went back together there. So, that's where we have got the motto in our mission, "The woman is the man to do it." So, we give plenty respect for women. And here he is here.

And so, he passed on the little different words to say to different precious ones that we never heard of...one called Epaenetus, the first fruits of Achaia unto Christ, the first convert in Greece. It is a name we never hear otherwise. He speaks of Priscilla and Aquila, a husband and wife who risked their lives for Paul, "Who for my life laid down their own necks." So, he is appreciative all the way through. He spoke of some kinsman, which was interesting. He had kinsmen who were fellow prisoners, who were chief among the apostles. Then he said this person a helper, this person beloved in the Lord. Salute these different...salute, salute, salute. Sometimes he puts the whole lot together in Verse 14, Asyncritus, Phlegon, Hermas, Patrobas, Hermes and the brethren which are with them. He *piles* the names on. Salute Philologus and Julia and Nereus and his sister and Olympas. Isn't that beautiful? Naming these precious people who were precious to him, giving them his greetings. So, he went down the list.

And he warned them about false people coming in. He was warning the early church of people who pretended to have the truth, but hadn't. Then he finally says, "The grace of our Lord Jesus Christ be with you." Then he sends greetings from those who were with him...Timothy and Tertius and the chamberlain of the city. That's remarkable! So the chamberlain, a kind of mayor, I suppose, of the city of Rome salute you. So the Holy Spirit had really worked in Rome. Gaius, my host... Gaius was famous for hospitality. He mentioned many different people. So he says...there it is. "I commend you to the Person Who caused me to preach the gospel which has been a mystery hidden 'til Jesus Christ came. That revelation of the mystery which has been hidden now made manifest by the scriptures of the prophets according to the commandment of the *everlasting* God unto all nations for the *obedience* of faith." That's the last words he speaks.

That *isn't* the obedience of works. It isn't...go and *do* this. It's...go and *believe* this. Well, they won't believe. Anyone can believe. Believing simply means my freedom. I attach myself by what to me is real. I will relate myself to what is real. I attach myself to the Word of God; I relate myself to it. I *confirm* it, and then faith brings substance and the confirmation comes back to me. So, the *last* thing that I call for is the **obedience of faith**, not the obedience of works. "To God only wise, be glory through Jesus Christ forever. Amen." That's the closing of this *wonderful masterpiece*, which has always been the foundation stone to the believing church, and being built up into what God really has given us and revealed to us in Jesus Christ. So that is it!

II CORINTHIANS

I believe God gives dark moments, and apparent clouds (**II Cor. 12:7**), so as to teach us that these things are an illusion and a mere outward appearance, and thus to teach us to live where we really are - with Christ joined to us within, Spirit with spirit. I believe the great lesson of life is with the outward eye to see and feel evil and dark and lonely appearances around us, but for us to learn not to believe in them (for we experience what we believe), but to transfer our faith to the Unchanging One with whom we are in union within. That is where we really live, right in the midst of outward darkness.

Knight of Faith Volume I

In **II Corinthians 4:17** Paul calls that death "our light affliction". Some lightness! "For our light affliction, which is but for a moment (some moment!), worketh for us a far more exceeding . . ." Worketh: one builds the other up, doesn't it? They're connected. The suffering works unto glory: "Our light affliction . . . worketh for us a far more exceeding and eternal weight of glory." So we call it light. It doesn't feel light down here at the start. But the outcome is a "weight of glory".

Suffering...Its Secret
Think on These Things

That is a total revolution and it destroys the emphasis on the outer so that in **II Corinthians**, we find Paul went all the way saying, "I don't know any man after the flesh. I don't even know Christ after the flesh. I'm not interested in the historic Christ." That was a very strong thing for him to say! He was saying he was not interested in any Christ who had outer form. He was only interested in the Person who is **the** Person with whom he had died and is now risen. *Paul knew that he existed only that the world might find that the only true life is one in union with Christ so that all self would be an expression of His Self.* The outer doesn't matter.

Old Testament Journeys of Faith

111

II CORINTHIANS

This sharing is from 3 double-sided tapes comprising 6 sessions so you will find a bit of lead-in as Norman recaps a bit for his listener who may have missed a previous session.

Prayer....

Finally, You...we and in Your purposes for the world...tell us in another session this afternoon that You will again say what You want to say to us by Your Word in this talk. Amen?

I will attempt some of II Corinthians, a letter with *vast* riches in it, and I don't know how far we will get...but at least we can start. It's one of Paul's *intimate* letters – love letters. He wrote one love letter as a *brother* in Christ to Philippians, and one letter as a loving *shepherd* to his flock – which is II Corinthians. They are the two most heart-opening and most intimate of his letters. So it is really a *love* letter! His purpose always was to...well, he had to minister and it *had* to be disciplined...had to be done through love. So what they caught was love – that he *loved* them! The cost of loving them was to have to say this or do that, but the love was paramount, and it comes out through this letter.

It's the intercessor's letter because it totally is *for them*. He says again and again that whatever happened, it was for them. He would *say* it was for them. He was very glad to spend and be spent for them. He said that kind of thing several times over. They had been through this very *grave* crisis in the greatly blessed church – the Corinthian church. It came behind the new gifts and was very much a Spirit-filled church, and a problem had arisen that he had to deal with. He visits them twice. He had written them two letters. This was the third; the middle letter is missing.

His first letter had been more of going into details of how a church functioned. It is the standard letter in the Bible on that – its activities, its message; its basis in the beginning is the Cross. Then heading up in the end is the resurrection....the two great chapters and with a letter, with a visit, there was no further need to go into the outer problems. But there had arisen considerable *personal* assaults on him...attacks on him as an unreliable apostle...to divert their attention to others, who claimed equally to have their ears as representatives even of Christ. So his personal position with the Corinthian church was considerably under fire.

That wasn't bothering him, because an intercessor is only bothered with those in need of being saved. It only bothered him so *far* as it affected them in being established in the truth that had come to them through him. What it did to *him* wasn't the point. His *hurts* were because they were hurt. If they were hurt, he was hurt. So he pours out this letter from his heart to them....runs from one point to another without any of it being a *prepared* letter...just put out in paragraphs and that sort of thing. More a letter from the heart. The next thing that would turn up would be the next thing he was thinking about...next expanding.

So he starts on a personal note – leveling himself up or down with them in what he was going through in his ministry. In all he is saying he is always on top! He's always speaking from the *glory* point of view. Whatever happened to him was the *background* to the glory in his soul. So he starts by saying the *total sufficiency* he has in God in the many sufferings through which he was going...speaking of God as the God of all comfort, and the certainty and security he had in God in these things he went through. And he was thanking God for that fact right from the start...saying whatever peace and release he got from his sufferings in Christ Himself...that if the comfort overflowed the sufferings, it was for their sake...so that they could experience the same release and comfort and strengthening when they went through the same kind of things.

That's the *only* way we *can* transmit reality. As far as we *know* reality, we can transmit it. Those to whom we transmit it must themselves *find* the same reality. We can only be the agent, or the midwife, that can bring it into reality in them, because if we knew how ourselves (the fullness of comfort and release and sufficiency in troubled situations) *then* we are able to explain to others how that *is*...and it can be for them also.

The *human* Paul comes out a great deal through the letter in which again he levels up with them in *their* humanity. Thus he says here that he is *comforted* in his sufferings, and how he had to have a restoration of faith in some situations (probably for emphasis) where he is pressed so hard he spared of life...not unlike Elijah and these other men. And then he said he saw that he had the sentence of death in himself and there was no way out for himself that he might not trust in himself, but in God who raises the dead...and so his period of inner distress and despair. He uses the word despair here as the *necessary background* to every restoration of God he has to deal with.

So he gave that preliminary start to his letter coming to them, and therefore is a fellow human – needy person, fellow sufferer with them. And he expressed then, too, the need of prayer – that they could *help* by praying for him...so as deliverance came and as many as prayed, so many could praise! Simple, *identifying* sharings, which would make a bridge in heart with them for his own speaking about means by which his own needs are supplied...rather than theirs. So he wasn't approaching them with any spirit of superiority.

He then went on to a personal explanation of why he hadn't come to see them when he said he would, and was being attacked for inconsistency and insincerity, because he *said* he would come from Macedonia to them and didn't. Here he stands *firm* to the reality of his walk *in* God and *with* God...and all he was doing was what he understood to be God's will. There was no question of some human scheming in his change of direction. But there's a basic type of simplicity and sincerity which is a beautiful description of his walk...*simple*...isn't *we*; it's He...*sincere*. All we want to get is that he would *say* and do that! That is why this is a childlike life; it is an *easy* life, because we see if he had sufferings, they only made the way for the abounding of the consolation in Christ – His way for them and so the same here.

And he took (slipped in when he said that) the word about the total positiveness of God. There is no nay in God, only yea that God is true in our word toward you...*not* nay and yea...the Son of God, Jesus Christ, Who's preached among you even by Sylvanus and Timothias. He never took all to himself; he shared his ministry and mentioned the men with whom he shared his ministry. He was comprehensive in his fellowship; this one who preached to them, by them, was not nay-yea; only yea. All the promises by Him are yea and in Him amen, and to the glory of God by us!

So, as I say, we never *see* the negative. It *looks* like a negative, but still *say* it is a positive. What looks like a negative, we still say it has a *positive purpose* – *God* fulfilling by what looks like a negative process. So there are no "Nos" in God. There *is* no negative! The negative is basically the product of our fallen condition. When we've said, "No" to God then we live in a no. But God doesn't see that. God is in process of using our negative as the background to His positive in Jesus Christ...and His restoration of us. So he says, therefore, it wasn't in me a "Yes" and a "No". I just, I didn't go – wasn't a "Yes" because I wasn't to go...God saying, "You'll do this; you'll do that." And he used words to underline our *settlement* and *stability* in Christ through God.

He says that *God* sent the letter; he directs always back through Christ to God. So he says the One who *established* us with you in Christ and anointed us is God and *sealed* us – always put in this reality...*us* with you. You are the interest; we are just along with you. With you we have been established and sealed and anointed. And this anointing is earnestness of the Spirit in our hearts. And so we have a stable basis; and upon this stable basis we will move along as God takes us along. Whether it looks to you yea or nay, it is always yea!

He gives the reasons why he *didn't* come to them at that time. Their faith stood in God. He had no claim or control over their faith. They'd moved on from anything they had known from Paul to Christ, and upon Him they were founded. But he was a co-operator with them in their joy. And the relationship should be one of joy, freedom, oneness; and he didn't come for that reason. He wasn't going to come if there were causes, unsettled causes which would shatter the joy. So instead, at that moment, he is writing that letter to them. He referred back then to the letter he had written previously over the man who had fallen into sin, the man involved in the case of incest that hadn't been judged at the time. And he tells them how he wrote with great anguish and tears that they might know his *love*; not first for judgment, but that he loved them and wanted them to do what was the *right* thing for them...and they should know through his letter what his love to them was.

So far as that matter was concerned to them it could not be settled. The man involved had been disciplined. There had been a period of excommunication with now evidence, that he referred to later, which Titus found when he visited them on behalf of Paul, that there was a *real* concern of turning back of the people from the casualness about allowing loosened standards in the church and putting the things right, and that *now* had come the time when they should welcome back this brother. That's good. Presumably, he himself, by that time has known just what is wrong in his life. They should comfort him and forgive him, so that the end of it should be love, not discipline. Discipline is only so that mutual love can be on its true basis in Christ with sin dealt with...so you are exempt to it. Accept him back with forgiveness.

So far as can be said that he was hurt, you have to admit it was a concern. This was the first church! This is the founder of everything. If *this* went wrong, the whole future of Christ's church was at stake. No *wonder* he was concerned. This was a man who couldn't produce any written word of God to them. He couldn't give them the kind of background that we can give to people. Here the whole Gentile church hung on a string – on what God had given them through Paul, how far they still accepted what God gave them through Paul, and how far they were faithful to what God *had* given them.

These different discords had arisen. It was of great concern to him; and therefore he said well, I had to advise you to take this stand, as he did in the first letter towards this man who had gone into sin, but I *assure* you if you can forgive him I forgive him with you, and I hold nothing back from being one with you. The one thing that Satan wants to attack – it isn't oneness in this thing he wants to attack, he wants to bring about a dissention between us. We're not ignorant of his devises.

So he explained to them in a simple family fashion...shared a little of what he had been going through himself – how he'd had revived and renewed faith, and how he'd found God is His sufficiency in the storms that blew around him...and now how he was with them in heart and there had been God-lead purpose in not coming to them, and he wanted to explain that (took the trouble to explain) share himself with them...share with them any explanation they should have. And as far as that matter was concerned, because of what he heard from Titus, they could surely say now the man is welcomed back and loved...and there was a renewal of the bond of fellowship in which there could be a throne of joy.

The healthy relationship in the company of God's people is *joy*...freedom to be *ourselves*. Freedom to love each another and be ourselves, centered around the One Who is the real One Whom we are expressing. So there's this quality unknown to the world the world calls *gaiety*, which is itself trying to build something up which hasn't got a foundation to it. Joy comes from a foundation – this is the *real* thing! This is what *really* life is! *This is true life* – being a part of God, with God in His love adventures in the world and to find *my own* peace and wholeness in being an expression of the living God. *This is joy!* It may or may not come out in expressed happiness, it probably does among ourselves. It may not always look so to the world, because happiness is external. And we can build it on the false foundation. The world tries it's best to do that; world *can't* have joy. "My joy I give unto you, not as the world giveth unto you, but *My joy...*".

So he wasn't willing to pay another visit to the church, which wouldn't have its joy-basis. And therefore he held back in order to write this further letter to them. This time, especially concerning the attacks made on *him*, which might cause them not to be hearing the voice of the Lord through him who was their *father* in faith.

And then he stretches a bit on the glory level when he says, "Whatever we do we are presenting the triumph of Christ." We are always presenting the triumph of Christ. We like one of those carried in the Triumph of a Roman General. Our presence is displaying His triumph...so we're *displaying* the triumph of Christ wherever we go. That *never* changes.

It may have two *effects*. It is a sweet savor to God. As I say, it all centers on God; what is God's purpose; what God's purpose is to produce through Christ; what it means to God. So this is a sweet savor, but we are to God a sweet savor of Christ. And the savor may have the savor of salvation or the savor of damnation. It is the savor to those who respond of the savor of Christ coming into their lives. It is the savor of lostness in those who are rejecting, but their lostness may be the background to *their* salvation, too. It may be that they go the 'rejection way' first to prepare them for the 'acceptance way'. Anyhow, it's *all* in triumph! There is a triumph because we just give what we know is true; that's our release; that's our blessing.

He was beginning to touch now on those who are attacking him. It appears corrupt to the Word of God...we give you what we know to be this amazing truth, completeness of restoration *to* God, *into* God and *as* God, into the completeness and purpose which He had ever destined He would have His company of His loved sons, loved cooperators. It is that simple. I just keep giving what I know to be truth. So I do not have to corrupt...sincerity and simplicity. He said I speak with sincerity; I speak as of God, in sight of God. I speak in Christ, because Christ is the way we come to God. So I'm walking simply and plainly in the light wherever I go, giving the light...of what I know to be truth.

That ends his first delivery of love-approaches to them, renewing his love bond with them by these different things he shared with them. As I say, these things are easier for you to follow when following the scriptures. I do not think they can mean much to you if you are not, because if I am just dodging around picking up here and there, it does not mean too much really unless you are following through to some extent with what he is saying, so I can't have that, so I suppose he is speaking to this, I suppose. So I have not read the scriptures through, I am just quoting here and there as I go along...commenting.

So now in the third chapter, he begins to address himself in seriousness to the attacks being made which could *cloud* their own faith if it affected their faith in him, because through him they had the living word. And if these others could poison their faith in relationship to him, they could quite likely poison their relationship to God to Whom they had come through him. So he began to address himself to that, and he said now let us start at the beginning. I don't need words of commendation to you. I don't need letters to commend myself to you; others may, these others who have come to Jerusalem who have wormed their way in by some letters of commendation that people should accept them in their more legalistic approaches. I don't need them. Why don't I? Because *you* are my letter!

Now he touches the truth. The truth is the Spirit. The truth isn't outer form, outer gospel, outer scripture; it's Spirit! The truth is that *you're* the epistle. You're the epistle written by the Spirit of the *living* God; Christ's epistle written in your hearts by the Spirit of the living God. *This* is truth! So the gospel is *people* who have the Spirit. That is all! People have the Spirit, or people have Christ because the Spirit comes to confirm Christ to us. If Christ is confirmed to us, the Father is confirmed to us. We have been brought into union with the Trinity...by the Spirit in us. The Spirit *is* the unity; He is the unifying Person, the Spirit Who establishes the unity in us. That's all it is. You are a people of the Spirit.

And the fruit of the Spirit, therefore, is the expression of the Spirit that comes out through your life because that's what you are now...a means of God's Self-manifestation. So he says that is quite simple. And he says this is the ministry that God has compelled through me. He says we *have* sufficiency; we are *able* to fulfill our calling. A number of times in this letter, because they had attacked him as a human self he would bring in"...not of ourselves, not of ourselves." It is obvious, as he had said before, that we trust not in ourselves in the previous chapter. Here he says, "We are not sufficient in ourselves; there is not anything in ourselves." But he had to put that in because they had been bringing these attacks on him. But our sufficiency in God had made us able ministers, by what? By the New Testament.

The New Testament is a covenant of the Spirit, not a covenant of words, of letter. So he says...I am able to be a transmitter of eternal truth to people, because it would seem to me they have the Living Spirit – the Spirit of the Living God transmitted to them, and through the Spirit, Jesus, and the new creation. So he is underlining – the only *reality* in the church of Christ is *people*...people who are born of the Spirit, and filled with the Spirit, and bearing fruit of the Spirit. That is the same as saying that we are expressing Christ. *This is the only gospel there is, the only truth there is.* It is inner, not outer. So he is saying I am a minister, a testament, which is not of letter, but of Spirit. It is not an outer form; it is an *inner* reality. So he is underlining the fact that nothing outer can ever be real to us. All we ever have is what is inside us in our inner consciousness. That is what we are, that is our spirit.

Now we are only real in so far as we are what we are in our spirit. If our spirit is in tune with His Spirit, in union with His Spirit, then we are in the eternal truth. And the letter can only be a *means* to introduce us **to** the living Person in living relationship. By itself, the letter and everything outward...it **kills.** It can only speak to the outer in us. Then in underlining the reality of the ministry of the Spirit, he says in the *previous* letter...it came in a stone presented from Mt. Sinai. That had glory, because that is the *first step* back to God. It was through the written letter that they found their lostness, not their foundness...but that was glory. Their lostness *exposed* to them was glory.

So Moses had the ministry of glory in bringing to them a covenant with conditions. Conditions, of course, to expose self, because self *cannot fulfill* those conditions. That was the meaning of it. So there had to be this presentation of the written law and the covenant with conditions which you couldn't fulfill. This is the first step into the ultimate glory to find out what they're *not*, before they found out what we *are* through Christ. So he says that's a touch of glory in Moses that his face shone and had a veil put over it.

Moses' glory was because Moses saw right the way through. It says Moses had a veil over his face because the Jews *could not stand to see the* **end** *of that which was to be abolished.* So Moses knew this was only a stepping stone into the final act of baptism. There cometh One Who baptizes you with *not with water, but with His Holy Spirit.* Moses knew that! So Moses had a preview of the glory. That's why the Bible says it was an angel who gave the law to Moses, because Moses' own relationship was face to face with God. He had two visits to God. One was through an angel who gave the commandments and the law – that first covenant. Later on, he went back and had a face to face time, probably at the tabernacle, because the tabernacle was the pattern. And he would see through the pattern to the Eternal One coming, the eternal tabernacle of which we participate. But that was a glory he couldn't share, so he had to have a veil over his face.

The veil wasn't really over Moses; it was over their hearts. Because the *veil* is self-centered self...self-righteous self; that's the veil. It is when disillusionment has finally come concerning our self-righteous self and we *turn* to the Lord...and then the veil is taken away. And the Lord is that Spirit. So it is *very* remarkable how Paul is bringing the Spirit to center here, that our basic relationship with the living God is a spirit relationship. It is His Spirit with our spirit...the Third Person Trinity...that with Him is the *whole* Trinity, because He came to reveal Himself. The point of the Spirit is – He is inner.

If you do not know any better, you may say God is far away somewhere. You would say Jesus Christ came in history and rose again. Spiritually, this is what he is getting at, that the real truth is *inner* truth. And even evangelicals fight that today and try to say we must keep up the outer relationship with the historic Christ. Paul did not do that. Actually, in his letter he turned his back on the historic Christ *right out* when we follow on. He says the only truth is my inner self in union with His inner Self...in inner relationship...which is foolishness to the world and meaningless to the world – comes out, as James shows us, in new forms of activity...love activity. This is *all* reality is...it is Spirit reality. So he goes right through it. He says when they do turn to the Lord (he *does not say they turn to Jesus;* he says the *Lord* is that Spirit!) When he does turn to the Lord, that veil is taken away. Now the Lord *is* that Spirit!

Paul's second letter to the Corinthians is the personal explanation of how God revealed Himself to man through men. This is the letter of Paul as the minister of Christ, in this case, to the Corinthians (sparked up by a lot of underground opposition in the Corinthian church) and attempts to downgrade him and his authority in his ministry – he wasn't an intercessor; he was interested in himself. *He* is interested in what he is for *others.* If what he is to others damages what *their* life in Christ is (because of the standards of the one by whom they had been ministered to, because his standards had been attacked) he will seek to explain himself for their sakes...because the intercessor is on the *third* grade of God's ways by which He expresses Himself through humanity.

The first is that He gets into us as a personal Saviour. Then He establishes us as being He in human forms. He incarnates Himself *again* through His body to express Himself *through* His body. When that has become a settled question, the interest ceases to be around ourselves, because *our* needs have been met. And having got what *we* need to be *people* now, we can be what we were meant to be – what God is. God's a Person for others. He is interested in His universe. We, now as forms of God, expressions of God, exist for the same purpose – to move in towards the ultimate reconciliation of the universe to Himself. So the stress of our life is outside ourselves. What happens *to* us is outside ourselves, and what happens to us is not for ourselves...it's for others. That is the *third* level. That's what the Bible speaks of as the fatherhood level, the cooperative level...from justification to unification to cooperation; salvation to sanctification to service and so on. This is this one; this is Paul...the outgoer, the intercessor.

The word intercessor *doesn't mean* saying a few prayers. It is a *whole life laid down in the person* – it's a precarious relationship; a Jesus relationship. You lay down your life *for* others. As you lay down your life, life comes to others. You take their position upon yourself that they may come into their rightful place in Christ. That's what we are talking about here.

We have gone so far as to see when they were challenging what right he had to present himself as a minister of Christ, who had been a minister of Christ to the Corinthian church. What right did he have to come back as if *he's* the one to whom they should listen and by whom they received their benefits? So he started off with some personal explanations in this third chapter by saying that our commendation, our recommendation, explains *you* – because all the meaning of being a *person* **is** that in our inner self we should be in union with the Divine Self, the human spirit with the Divine Spirit with God Himself. It is God expressing the kind of Person *He* is. He expresses love by us. And so we are in our normal life, living normal lives – expressions of Christ...of God, or Christ – the Trinity in self-giving love. So the basis is a *spirit* relationship because our real self is spirit. The

121

rest is just forms of expression – our soul and body express our spirits...ourselves. The true meaning of the self is the human spirit in union with the Divine Spirit, and is an expression of that Divine Spirit.

The Divine Spirit is the Universal Person Who expresses Himself in the *whole* universe. The whole universe is an expression of Him in interesting forms of love and wonder and power. That is *all* He is! He is a Person for others. That is why God is love. We become persons for others. And He says my recommendation is *you*! By preaching Christ to you and your receiving Christ, the Spirit comes into you, and you are people of the Spirit now. The Spirit of the *living* God is in you, and the Spirit is the One Who confirms to you...makes real to you, your relationship in God. The Spirit is the inner Person Who confirms to us and makes real to us our relationship with God. The Spirit is the inner Person Who confirms to you our relationship with the living Christ and the living Father as **one** (not a separate people up here somewhere) as one unity. Jesus' prayer – that we are one – "I in You and You in them, they in Us" as one. Actually the whole universe is one. That is the ultimate discovery we come to where the whole universe is one expression of One Person. We are the privileged people to be (having found the unity ourselves) as conscious people, like God, to be able to transmit the unity to others of the family who He purposes to have as His eternal sons. And His eternal sons, His eternal heirs...saving His whole universe, manage His whole universe...*destined* to manage God's universe. And so he says, this is my recommendation – you are now sons of God because *you* have the Spirit of God in you! The Spirit of the Son has come into you and you *know* it, and you know your intimate relationship with Him. You are alive to Him. He is the Spirit of the *Living* God. He is living to you, and it has come out in the fruits of your life. So that is the only recommendation I have – that I have been a minister of the Spirit, *not of the letter*, because nothing outer could ever be real to us.

We are inner people; all we ever have is what we inwardly know. We only operate by what we inwardly *are* and what we inwardly have. So any form of outward religion or outer code, outer book is nothing to us *unless* it becomes inner reality. When it's ours then we operate spontaneously by what is to us...by what is knowledge. Knowledge is inner knowing, is inner union with something in there so it is part of us. This is what it is to be this *new* kind of person, a *real* person...as a human expression of God. And he says that produces something for which he used the word glory – THIS IS IT! I am what I am *meant* to be; I have got it! This is reality...*glory*!

Glory is the word – all that is, all that it can be! *This* is what we are to be on earth. We have *got* all we can have! We may need an enlarged understanding of Who we have. So he is saying here that when the Spirit has taken up His abiding place in union with us, He reveals Jesus to us in an ever-enlarging sense. So we are open-faced now because there is nothing hidden. This is the truth – **this truth** – *the sin life has been put away* in Christ...bought it out in the blood in Christ in crucifixion with Him, and opened His new life. And now, with open face, we *see* more of the *totality* of what God is – His love and His power and His presence. It is the *only reality* because the whole universe is One Person. It is beginning to *dawn* on us, and he says we begin to be changed because we reflect this Person. What you see, you *are*. We always see what we really are. We reflect...we begin to reflect. So, it says, we are changed into the same image, we reflecting this Person in us in a very enlarged sense, from glory to glory, by the Spirit of the Lord he says. So the Spirit is causing us to be *more and more thrilled*, and *filled* and *adequate*...apparently normal people and yet living on top! Life is always on top; underneath, nothing.

We are crazy to be God's gods...is what Satan said. We are created gods; God is on top, never underneath. God is adequate; we are adequate...because our adequacy cannot be a higher adequacy...it's the adequacy of God expressed in me. I am adequate – I am adequate because **I am**! So *this* is glory. This is it! Only, of course, it isn't 'it'; this is **He** *really*. He and I are one Person in an ever-enlarging sense.

So we look to the world like egoists. The world thinks it is clever *not* to have. They say, "Well, I am nothing." and then, "Oh, no." The world tries to hide...wants to be something, but it hides it behind a façade – "Oh, I'm nothing; I haven't got it." That is baby stuff. We *have* got it! But the world doesn't like that, because you *have* got it if only you've got Him. You *haven't* got it in yourself. It is true in ourselves we haven't got it, but we don't like to admit that. That is where we have got to start; we have not got it; we have failed; we are *wrong*. And we would all like to stay like that, because it's an excuse for our deviations and so on. So we tend to like to downgrade ourselves; not really, underneath we upgrade ourselves, and we pretend we have a self-pathos...downgrade ourselves.

So, when a person says, "I've got it all," we say, "Hey, what are you talking about?" You're a conceited fellow." The flesh doesn't like people of the Spirit, because people of the Spirit boldly say, "I *have* all." Well, *if* my human, little self has become the dwelling place of His divine Self, *I have all!* I have to find that I am nothing, the nobody, but I do not mind being nobody when it contains Somebody. That Somebody is *God*! So I rise up, and that's how Paul is saying...I am adequate! In this very chapter, Paul reasons I am adequate to transfer the Spirit to you. He says, "My adequacy is of *God*." Not that we are sufficient in ourselves...to think anything of ourselves...our sufficiency is of God, Who hath made us able ministers. So we are not unable people; we are not insufficient. We *are* sufficient people. We *are* adequate people! We *have* got what it takes! We *have* the wisdom needed. That is a pretty conceited word until we know the secret!

While we think life is myself built up – that is conceit. If I say it's my down-break not build-up...out of my down-break...I have not been what I should be; I have not been what I should be, but God through Jesus Christ has accepted me back...not only accepted me back, but given me what I came for – renewal, which is Himself – making **me** His body, *His* form of *His* expression, the branch of *His* vine. Well, then I *am* adequate...but so far as I *am* adequate, not in myself! He says my sufficiency is of God. So we say the same.

So this was Paul's first reminder to the Corinthians that he *had* produced the goods...because 'the goods' was the Spirit of God in them, and they knew it! 'The goods' wasn't something; he was. It wasn't something he preached, except as an agency. But through his preaching, as he explained to them how he received Jesus, and the Spirit is in you, as a revelation of Jesus you receive Jesus – He said you *know*. That's my commendation – you're the commendation, because you know you are being indwelt by the Spirit of the living God. That's a lovely phrase that's not used *anywhere else* – Spirit of the living God! And he says that moves *you* unto glory, unto glory, unto glory!

Now, he says, I will talk to you a little about this question of how you minister. I'll tell you a little of what it means to be a minister of the gospel. My authority and my validity has been *challenged*. So, not for my sake, I don't mind, but that you may not have any hesitation, because you got your truth through me, and therefore if I am unreliable, my truth's unreliable. So it's probably good that I should show you how we are ministers of Christ, and what it means to be ministers of Christ. The word we usually use is intercessor, because intercessor is a person for others. The word intercessor comes from the Old Testament when you pour out your life unto death and make intercession. Intercessor, used in the Bible, as God has given a person a *special* commission that there are *gaps* to fill, *needs* to be met, and an infinite variety of us to meet infinite needs. We have a sense of a *specific* need. And when we get a specific need, we say "God, this is my honor, what happens to me is the law of death which produces life; what happens to me is not the point. Here I am; I put myself in the place of those to whom I minister, in any way which I can be the means of bringing You to them." That's an intercessor. He is not interested in what happens to him except to do something for others.

So he starts by saying, in the fourth chapter, that in outer form what he does is quite simple. He has not played any games; he had been quite honest. He had not had to trick or twist things because he manifests the truth – the truth is Jesus the Saviour. And because we're sinners and God met us in His love by taking upon Himself our sins in the body of His Own Son on the tree, and by which He becomes reconciled to us, and we come back to be children of God by faith in Jesus Christ and all that follows. So he says this is a simple truth. He says all I give is the simple truth and commends to yourself your consciences, because you say that fits! That's a fact. I *am* a person who has messed up my life. I *am* wrong, but I can't take it if God is like *that*. God isn't an avenger Who comes to destroy me. He is a person Who so loves that He took the destruction upon Himself, and goes to hell on my behalf. That appeals to me – a God like that!

So it does commend ourselves to a conscience open to recognize we are sinners. Then he said, of course, the gospel only hits some because it is written to sinners – a sinner means you have failed. Then he says there is *another* god. There are those that the god of this world has blinded. That is why they don't believe. That is another god – the one who claims to be the god of this world, which is the god of self-centeredness.

A god is the originator of something. So he is called a god because he originated the dimension of self-centeredness. God is the dimension of self-giving love. Satan is the dimension of self-centeredness. So he is the god of this world and he afflicted this world with his philosophy – the glory of life; be for yourself; get what you can; fight for it, get what you can, the hell with the rest, more or less. That's the chaos of our world, of course; that is the god of this world. Now, *if* you are still finding

125

satisfaction that way, you are blinded. You do not want to believe. You believe what you want. Belief isn't technical, believing doctrine; it is *moving into* something you *want*.

The word "faith", we talked about this morning, is moving in something – I want that; I will take it. That's faith! The mind only conveys to you the thing you need...parts of the means, the conveyance. I want that; I'll do that; I'll go here – that's faith! You have involved *yourself*. Well, you have involved yourself in something you want. So people can't believe in Jesus Christ, who find that in the god of this world they are seeking to find their adequacy. They have *got* to come to this viewpoint first.

So he says there *are* some, and when they are like that, they are blind. Because the devil is busy trying to make them be satisfied in what they are in themselves and what they get *by* themselves. Thank God, He breaks it up! Thank God, His first work in us is the breaking of us up before the remaking of us. But there are those who don't appear to take that. So they cannot see glory. They're like the glorious gospel of Christ. They do not see glory in being an expression of God in self-giving love.

They have to find glory in being in the world of self-loving love. Self-loving love doesn't like self-giving love. They're two enemies. One is light, and the other is darkness. So until you are disillusioned with the self-getting love...it's a no-thing. The whole universe is a Person Who is Love...which is God. The other is a no-thing; it is a nothing; it is death, not life. We call it life instead of death. It is living for ourselves. Until you find that it grates on you and it has left you empty...it doesn't meet your need...and while you still find glory there, but of course, you don't want the other...you don't see the glory in the gospel of Christ expressing a *God of love* to you. So he says *all this* like that.

He says then...we preach that, and the indication we preach it is you follow up in it in yourselves. You catch on to that, you say, well we aren't pushing ourselves. We are pushing the Living Person, Who is everything to us. So he says – one of the indications of this truth is the agent will be a servant. That's something that has often gotten lost in our churches. That is why I do not like this ministry business; I am partly anti-church, because I don't like some sort of boss-man, unless he is a *real* servant. And there are some today here and there...real servants. I wish they were not paid; the fact that they're paid makes you feel they are getting something out of it. The original gospel was unpaid. Paul in this gospel would not take pay – "I won't take pay. Other people can provide my need if they like. I may be paid by you; I will not give indication." That is the difference between himself and a false apostle. They were getting something good out of it. I would like to rebuild the whole church with nobody getting any good out of it...let them starve. Why not?

I belong to a mission where God supplies the needs. We have got 1300 scattered around the world, and somebody said to us, "Couldn't one of your missionaries starve?" Well, we said, they would starve gaily anyhow...starve for Jesus! One of them said, "When I was in Africa, in the early days, we had very little money come." He had heard a rumor that one of our missionaries in the Belgian Congo in the early days had starved! We had a leader who had a sense of humor. So he sent around to different stations. We had about eight stations. "Have any of you got a skeleton there, a missionary who starved for Jesus?" And so when he got the answer back, "No", he wrote back to the fellow and said, "Dear friend, I am *very regretful* to say I have not yet found anyone who has had the honor to starve for Jesus." So this is the way it *is* coming. There *are* pastors today, I am afraid they are paid, which is a pity, but who **do** show this new servant spirit. Thank God! Both priests...Catholic...and it *is* happening today.

But this is the standard – Jesus was a *servant*, not a priest! He was a common carpenter. Common in the sense that He was a *common man*...walked about the streets. He loved people – *that's all*. They couldn't *stand* Him! Their idea of religion was to make a great big noise. They couldn't *stand* this man who destroyed their concept of what God is! God is just a common servant running about, loving people. We do not want a God like that! We want a something that is really a projection of *our own* superiority. We want a superior God because we want to pretend to be superior. So we project to have an idol or something of God in the big temple, because we like superiority...because we love superiority!

But when we, ourselves, have the spirit of serving, we love the Person of the Spirit serving; we love a God which is a servant. We love the fact, it says the One He highly exalts through eternity, is the One Who became a servant to the point He died and took on the shame of the Cross. And *that's* the One God exalts! So God *delights* in the spirit of serving. That is what He is; He is – a servant. That is why we love Him. So Paul says in *this* sense you can test the genuineness of an apostle of Jesus Christ, because

He has a genuine spirit. He is serving. Really, you know he is for you...he is not out to get a good thing out of it. He is not preaching *at* you. He is speaking to show you this Person who changed him and will change you. In other words – expose *you* in your failures, in your sins, to be replaced by the grace of God. And he says, as we do that, because that's what we are, we present you this fact – you can *know* what God is by Jesus Christ – the glory of God in the *face* of Jesus Christ. He says this is marvelous! How, in other words, can we know God is like that? Our whole *concept* of God is some superior, vengeful, terrible being.

That sense of worship is (I don't go to church to worship – *everything* is worship to me!) It is God in His beauty and love to me. That's worship to me. Everything is worship, because worship is a Person, expressing Himself in *all* forms of love. That's worship! Jesus said you worship in Spirit...not by going to church...in Spirit and in Truth. Truth is what He really is; Worship is what He really is. This is the amazing thing; *this* is God. Who could believe that!

If Jesus Christ hadn't come...and He *had* to do certain outward things, because in that day, there was no other way of giving some demonstration of Who He was so He performed miracles. We do not need that *kind* of miracle today. The miracle today is I am a changed person...and you are! Where I didn't love myself, there is a *new* motivation. That is the miracle! That is the only miracle needed in the world. The world needs lovers – not people for themselves, but people for others. But who could believe that? With all the idea of the buildup of this *vast* Person, and you are told this *common person* walking about Palestine is God. Who would ever take that? And *all* that Person knew was to love. And all He rebuked was anything which militated against self-giving love. If anything in the name of God militated against love He was after it! Rightly! But nothing else...He was after nothing else. He *served* everybody, healed and so on. But this is God; that's *all* God is. If I want to know what God is – *that's* what God is. Wonderful!

But of course, He had to give sufficient evidence that you could fit that this *was* God. So to do that He did perform things we do not see too much today...some kinds of miracles...because in those days, they were given *some* impression He is the kind of Person Who did miracles of mercy, not miracles of self-glorification. He refused to jump off the temple and do things that would magnify Him as a special kind of person. But He would do miracles of mercy! Actually, that is the One we preach. We preach, of course, far deeper than that, we preach, of course, His *cost* and *resurrection*. And that is all part. But here He is trying to show what God is in the face of Jesus Christ. He referred to the face of Moses, which held the glory, and even that had to be veiled in the Old Testament days. *This* One has an open face and a common face; God has not got some mystical glory. Glory is a Person. Isn't that wonderful? Our faces are too − same thing! Something becomes a *quality* − that is Spirit. Spirit's a quality. It's not some weird halo stuff...something mystical. It's common sense. It's *common people*. A *quality*...and that *quality* is the Spirit of Love. That's all.

But he says there *is* a way in which this has to come to you...come to you, not by some powerful minister, not by some magnificent preacher, but a person who is a real 'dier' − who is weak, and goes through the process of death. And there is a quality of him in his death − a person who goes through distresses and persecutions. *This* is a minister, not a great big reverend with a half dozen degrees and preachments and things like that.

He says − the *agency* by which He comes is a person in whom you see a new quality of life in which they will take all kinds of confrontations and distortions of life, and yet *somehow* pours out as a victory and peace and love in them. Somehow they are able to show in their *ordinary* life an extraordinary Spirit − peace and love and light, and purpose. So he says...a minister is a person who is just an earthen vessel. Earthen is not a *bad* word. It means made of common clay. We're the common clay, and this common clay possesses a *treasure*! And the treasure is the living God, expressed in Jesus Christ. So the *power* is seen not to be in the earthen vessel, but in the living God. How does that power come out? We see it in faith somehow. We don't need a great big, tremendous, dramatic presentation, in common situations of trouble and perplexity and sometimes persecution and smash-up...and yet, *somehow*, in that situation you're not smashed up. *Somehow* you are not in despair. You are *perplexed* and *troubled*, but you have a quality of peace that through the trouble something good is going to come! So you have a quality that man has not got. This, of course, is God! We *have* that quality when God is our sufficiency. So in these situations we say, "Yes, I am perplexed, but God's my wisdom...so I am cool."

You say, "I don't know; I don't know what to do." So I say, "Alright, I *will* know what to do. *God* will show me. I am persecuted; well, it is an *honor* to be persecuted for Jesus!" So you are finding a praise and glory in something by which most people are offended. Or you're *troubled*...all the troubles of life...lack of this or need of that. Okay! But that is not the point. A person who really is *here* expresses the Living God in His sufficiency. No need to be *my* sufficiency. So there is a poise and a peace and a praise in tight spots...so nothing crashes! Cast down, but not destroyed...knocked down, but not knocked out. So there's a kind of *bounce* in the Spirit!

There is a *bounce* in a Christian. Something comes up all the time. Now people won't see that, because you are not responding as we usually respond. This is the ordinary manifestation. A minister of the gospel isn't some *amazing* person, some *amazing* preacher; in fact, Paul perhaps was a poor preacher – good writer, poor preacher. But there was a quality of glory and peace and victory, friendliness and love and freedom, which wasn't found in most people going through that kind of thing he went through. Now, what that *really* is...is bearing about the *dying* of the Lord Jesus, that the life of Jesus might be seen in the body, in the mortal body, seen here. Always bearing about the *dying* of the Lord Jesus in the body...the *dying* of Lord Jesus...that the life of the Lord Jesus might be manifest in our body. What does that mean? It meant that Jesus died to His own human reactions. It says when He went to Gethsemane – "If I could get out, I would. I'm a human. If I could escape, I would. But no; I mustn't. I must take what God's got, because God's way is the right way." So He took the dying. Right to the very bottom of dying, and then of course, He had a rising.

That is repeated in His body...He is the head...it is repeated in His body. And the dying, in that case, means that underneath, the Cross is mainly hidden. You do not make a big fuss about the Cross. You hide the Cross to show the glory! That man I was talking about that I lived with in Africa had a little word he would say, "Take my life; let it be a *hidden* cross, revealing Thee." What he went through, what others went through was really all right, but it *appeared* to be really roughing it in the Heart of Africa. You *hide* the Cross because the intensity and the joy and the fulfillment of being able to see Jesus Christ in the people. You show them resurrection *life*!

So he says there is a hidden dying, and the hidden dying is – I am again and again accepting things I do not like. I say, "Wait a minute. I do not like that person treating me like that. I don't like not having my needs met. I don't like to have problems I cannot solve. I don't like being knocked out." *I don't like* – dying *is* that – dying to something *I don't like*! It's always something I don't like. I am here for them...this is *God's* way for me and I accept it.

Now when you accept it, what happens is...in *you* there is a reviving Spirit of God...it is God! Now *God's* life! So out of this death come 'hints' of God. God is my sufficiency. That comes out. It comes in your body. Something about the quality, which people can see, just something that's not normal to an ordinary person in a distressing situation. This is how the intercession for others is fulfilled.

Now there is that *difference*. In our *earlier* days, we have to go through tests and trials (we talked about that in James) to find out ourselves...our need. We have to find out that we don't fight our own battles. We have to move into – It is not I, but Christ. That is the earlier stage...when you go through trials for *your* sake...settling you into the fact. This life is not you, but Christ. When that is *settled*, you will go through another *realm* of trials. Your *whole life* is for others! That is what our life is, whether we think it or not. When we get through that, in some way, it is something by which God can express Himself to others through us. So that is an intercessor's life.

So it is not to do with Paul's own needs. It is to do with how he can be involved in situations in which he can meet the needs of other people. So he says we're delivered unto death for Jesus sake. So we accept it if it comes from God. We accept these situations. Then he says, "*This* remarkable thing happens, as death works in me (and the resurrection life is Him) life comes in to you...presumably, mainly by osmosis – you *catching* on. Because *we* cannot give life to others. The Spirit of Christ gives life, and the Spirit of Christ gives life by causing them to see their need, and themselves "receiving Him Whom I have received". So the way it works out, as they see simple people, ordinary situations, walking in this quality of free, loving, helpful, considerate life; not some big bossy, noisy lives, but a life that has this quality. You catch on! I like that...I like that! Then you begin to find you have the same Jesus I have. Come on now...begin to find you have the same Person. Now then, life is worked in you. So through Paul life came into these Corinthians. And sometimes in big scales; sometimes the Holy Spirit works in many people at the same time...as in preaching and so on, they catch on.

So death works in us. That is the intercession life in you – death in us, life in you. And he says, part of it is we have the spirit of faith...I'm saying that now. He is saying that now because they attacked him. I say *we* have the spirit of faith. And he quoted the Psalmist: "I believe, therefore, I spoke." He said I believe...that's why I speak. I see it right to the end. He raised up Jesus Christ; He is going to raise you up. We are going to rise up together. You see the humility. This was the father of them! He said He raised me up with *you*, not you up with *me*. You see, he was always putting himself down. He says *you're* the people that matter. You will be raised up on the resurrection day, and I will be with you! You would think he would say you will be with me. He didn't say that. "In that day" He will present us with you...present *you*...and I will be along with you. That is the Spirit. I am delighted in *you* are what you should be and I get to identify with that. So he saying here *all* things are for your sakes.

Now we understand that's not a thing we put on. The life we are talking about is not a put on life – I *ought* to be like that; I'm not. No! I daren't say it, because God does it by me. This is what we were talking about the other day. Do not say you haven't – say you *are*! So say, well, Jesus is in me. Do not take false condemnation and false accusation, and false sort of self-assessment. Drop all that stuff. Dare to believe that what He has taken He will take me on. He, in His Own way, *causes me* to be a father. Do not try to be, just dare to accept that situation. I accept that situation. This is the new meaning of being. I'm an expression of being who is for others. So all things are for your sake. I take that! So if it doesn't appear to work out, you still believe it, because He said believe it. And more than we know, He is working out through us. We know it! Sometimes we know it. Sometimes we don't need to know.

And then he says, yes, and he didn't hide. Of course, in those days, we know what Paul went through...he gives a fantastic list later on. But what physically, besides spiritually he went through in those days – the pioneering days of the gospel. That is why he says we do not faint. Though the outer man perish, the inner man is renewed. He didn't make a big fuss of the body. One of the ways today (I suppose God uses it)...Oh something good will come to you. The Bible never says that! The Bible says that the *highest* thing is – good *doesn't* come to you...so that others may have the good.

The Bible *doesn't* say that! The Bible doesn't say, "Oh, you will have a perfect body with lots of healing." The Bible doesn't say that! It is a *dangerous* gospel, because it's misinterpreting the *glory* of this life. It is not – *I* get something, but I'm something for others...and that will cost! So it is dangerous to build people up for – 'something good comes to you'. So bypass the 'day' of the whole healing ministry – *you* will get healed. That is not the point. I am for others. I may or may not be healed. You see Paul is not interested in his body. "My outer man is perishing." (*Shouldn't* say he was a good victory man today – *should* say, "I am perfectly healthy." It does not say that. It does not say that!) He said I am withering up, but my inner man is renewed and comes through my old, withered self. So you see it is another concept of truth. It *will* cost; it *will* drain me out. It will cost me physically, and mentally, and psychologically; but that's not the point. The *inner man* is renewed. That's the Spirit. That's where God is. That is renewed, because that is eternal. That's renewed!

Then he puts it in a simple way, "*my light affliction*." That is all you *see* because when you see the glory it is light! Because what he sees is this: That this light affliction (there is a law...a law of intercession...a law of death and resurrection) it's the law of the harvest. It is a law that Jesus enunciated when He said a corn of wheat has to die, that one corn of wheat produces many heads of corn. The world eats those; the corn is to be eaten. So His *dying* produces a whole crop of good grain, and the world gets the grain – and that's a law. That is the same as the law of nature. So Paul says my "light affliction"...in a way I count it as light... "works an *exceeding weight of glory*." My light affliction, which for a moment...a few years...works a *far* more *exceeding* eternal weight of glory. What words! Works. You see there is a law there. One is producing another. It isn't a mistake. It's not guess work. It's a law! As there is this *involvement* in what *costs*. It's working...it's producing a *far more exceeding*, eternal weight of glory. Now that's not working **in** us.

In another place he says your sufferings work something **in** you. Your tribulation worketh patience in *you*. James..."The trial of your faith worketh patience in *you*." This is working not *in* him, but *for* him. Works for him means out from *you*...is going to come into a tremendous harvest. Only in eternity do you see it is a tremendous harvest for those coming into eternal glory – the eternal life, the eternal purposes of God – because you went this way that causes *light for me* for a moment. Not so light in one point of view, but I see what it is working. We take that.

And because he says that settles us, and helps us to see we are not looking at things we *are* seeing; we're looking at things we are *not* seeing, because the things which are seen are temporal. The things that are not seen are eternal. He is not saying that the things that are seen are

133

illusions...it's not far off...they are temporal forms. And we are learning...we have to practice...everything is in a temporal form. Temporary, not temporal – temporary forms! Reality is the Spirit behind the form. And so he says, "Don't look at the things that are seen, which are temporary forms, but look at that which is not seen, the eternal secret. This is the eternal purpose coming through the forms...operating with eternal purpose...who may renew the forms and so on.

You are living an *ordinary* life in tune...in union...with the One Who is *All*, the Spirit, which of course, to the world makes you a fool. You are just a hair-brained person. And yet this is the *most realistic* thing! You can't get a more *practical* life than a God-governed life. When God's *got* the lot, and *is* the lot, it is the most *practical* thing! In *all* these things that tear a life up, I have got the *practical* answer. It is on the gamble of faith, if you like. Only faith doesn't remain a gamble. It becomes an inner certainty! Faith is the inner consciousness (on the inside) not outwardly by the letter...inwardly by the Spirit. It is *true* to me that God's like that, and loves me like that, and lives here. And so it is a *practical* life, because on *that* level, I *have* what it takes to release Him.

I have learned to see *through*. We talk about being see-throughers – seeing through the *visible*, which are only forms...not illusionary forms, but temporary forms. The forms are forms of God, but they often come misused...messed up...mixed up forms. That's what Paul's saying. But I am seeing through to the eternal *reality*...through it all.

Next we'll say...one stage further into the final glory. Now to some extent among us here we find *joy* and *glory* in the midst of problems and tribulations in what we talk about in this union life...where it's settled in to us by *infinite* grace. It *is* He expressed in our human forms that we tend not to be too much occupied with the future and the ultimate resurrection. It may be because we do not get the kind of persecutions that they got. We do not live with the kind of pressures they lived. They lived dangerous days, more like the Christians would be in Russia, and so on. It *may be* that! So perhaps it doesn't impress on us as strongly as it did in the days of the Bible. This is only peanuts. This is only peanut glory. This is just fiddling things, light things.

We are moving into *inconceivable* glory...into inconceivable completion and *total* satisfaction and *total* ability based in the total love to be a self-giving love. It will not be a satisfaction for me. It will be a satisfaction that

I am what I am meant to be – a form of God for others. We will be part of that *total* completion of who knows...what that glory means? It is apparently to include the whole universe, because it speaks about the reconciliation of the whole universe. "He gathered together in one *all* things in Christ." What does that mean? "Things in heaven and things on earth He gathers together in **One**." So you see it *is* a unity. So now when we see it (we just don't see it because we see false illusionary diversity.) Now we *are* unity; we are all each other when we really see it as we said this morning. So here is given us in Ephesians – He is going to gather into one, *all* things the whole universe into One Person – and we are that Person! That is the fantastic thing! Christ is head and body...until we all come to *a* perfect man, he says in Ephesians...not many men...that Perfect Man is head *and* body, of course. We are Christ!

Ephesians 4 says until we all come into the unity of faith and the knowledge of the Son of God, into *a* perfect man. And then he says one other thing, I like in his first Corinthian letter when he says "as the body is *one* and hath many members" (in verse twelve) "and all the members of that being One Body, so also is Christ." So he's calling Christ the body, you see. So Christ is the Body here. The Body is one having many members, all those are one Body, so also is Christ. So he includes in Christ the whole body. Now we're saying this *inconceivable* something we're going into, when we are Christ, forms of which One Person expresses Himself in many forms, like a head expresses through His body through eternity, involving some *vast* purposes.

When you see, it says we are co-heirs with Christ, and then in Hebrews I it tells us what He is heir of. If we're co-heirs we are heirs of His co-inheritance – what's He the inheritor of? And it says in Hebrews I, "whom He hath appointed heir, whom He hath *appointed* heir of all things." Hebrews 1:2 So fantastic! We are *involved* in the owner-development of the whole universe. What's happening; who knows? But God's not a fool! God doesn't bring vast numbers of these conglomerations of stars we have today...these great 'families' of millions of stars we have today. If they are in being, they are in being for purposes. We're heir to all!

So he's only saying here...he says I'm looking for something *greater*. I'm looking for a better body. Again, if any of us are afflicted, we may feel that more. We're all *really* constrained; we're confined. Of course we are. We can't *go* where we want; we can't *reach* who we want. Our bodies are wonderful, but they're confining bodies, and they are weak bodies in their senses and so on. And so, Paul with all he'd been through, felt that very much. He said "I'm looking at my new tabernacle." He said I'm not looking to renew the old; I'm looking to a transformed one! But he said something happens that the corruptible becomes the incorruptible. We can't understand that. It's like a season to an oak. Your present body is like an acorn...your future body is like an oak. The whole thing...same body development, of course...that doesn't mean much to us. Those are things we have to leave unexplained. But He means we are going to a *total* efficacy...I presume universal.

After all, it's God's universe; He's *everywhere*. So are we! If we are part of the universe of God, there'd be no time-space. There's no time-space in the 4th dimension...something we don't understand. Only Paul thought of it as an infinite greater glory we're moving in and he said "I'd like to move *in*." And he said, too (that's a kind of paradox there) he said, "I shall be meeting my Savior face to face." Now that's a paradox because in one sense we *have* the Savior. In one sense we have an inner union of consciousness, but it is a *consciousness* that has a certain veil.

All my life I've been a great reader of the mystics, and they would talk about the oneness "as dark with excessive light," whatever that means. Light so excessive we can't catch it – it's almost like dark to us, we can't catch it, we can't catch the excessive light we're going into. There's a certain shadow. Paul puts it when he says "we now see through a glass darkly; then face to face." There is that. We have this marvelous union, yet it's a union indescribable; it's an inner relationship – who is He, where is He? We just know *inside* somehow, that He and we are one. There's a certain level of knowing; there's a certain level of *not* knowing it! Again my great friend Kierkegaard, he would always say, "Faith has a base of suffering; all faith is based in doubt. All faith is walking on sixty thousand fathoms of water." You never know where it will leave you.

Well that's true; you can't *prove* it in the end. We *are* walking on something indefinable. It's true to our consciousness...that's what we've got. We agree that's truth, but we're certain we believe *in* it. So there's an element that we can't prove what we're talking about. There's that element of question mark underneath it which is in a sense suffering. So there's a paradox here, because in one sense we say how can we be closer – when it's not I but Christ; we're one! On the other hand Paul says "I long to meet Him face to face." And then he says you see, "We walk by faith, not by sight." "While we're at home in the body, we're absent from the Lord." "We walk by faith, not by sight" in 5:7 – willing rather to absent from the body and present with the Lord. So there *is* another sense which will be yet more infinitely glory, and we can't put that in human terms; we can't perceive of eternity, when we occasionally can see Jesus Christ by some human sense which you occasionally see a prism or something. So obviously that doesn't work. You can't *interpret* what that means – what the eternal face to face may mean – something adequate in the person to person relationship like we have person to person relationships here. Yet it's got to be combined with eternal reality. That we can't say. That's one these paradoxes we have to leave.

But evidently Paul *had* that. And so he was glorying in some *greater* relationship, some *greater* reality into which he was to move. And so he says, I'm laboring with that an end and that's the end. Again, be careful, it doesn't mean – Am I doing right? Don't do that. He can't *help* laboring. We've talked all along, when you're in the union relationship, you can't help it! This isn't a forced relationship – I ought to be this; I ought to have come out. You can't *help* it! *Be yourself*...but you're *driven* we're just driven, but since you were born-again you *had* to be 'something' for Jesus...something *different's* happened. Gone is the strain...beautiful.

That's why I've always made so much of that verse in Ezekiel 36 when it talks about the Spirit being in us. Ezekiel was a prophet of the Spirit. Isaiah was a prophet of the Cross and the Savior. But Ezekiel unto the Spirit, and he talked here about the Spirit. He said "I'll put My Spirit within you and *cause* you to walk in My statues." I like that 'cause'. Get walking and don't slip. You can't help it! It's a *natural* life. Just take it, accept it; *dare* to believe it! If it's a mess-up, tell God to improve the mess-up...it's His fault not yours! If He's running the *show*, let Him run the show, that's all. It's the *easy* life...He *causes*. So when he says labor, don't say, oh I'd better get doing it. No! God's *causing* you to be. If you want to...say, "Lord, if You want me to be some 'more' *You* get on with it!" It's *easy*. You *have* to do it! You *have* to do it. That's the blessing of this life.

So he says we labor to be accepted of Him and we appear before the judgment seat of Christ. We mustn't be afraid of judgment; judgment's healthy. Judgment will fix us as we ought. It may be few things have got to drop off. Well, I want to have dropped off what shouldn't be there, anyhow, don't you? I want to have all the perfection there is, so why would I be afraid to have God say, "Well, this bit wasn't too good about you." Well, okay, I'm moving on! I can't accept an eternity which is static. Because the only thing we understand in life is dynamic! To be static is atrophy. If you don't use a limb, it atrophies. So we can't *imagine* a life which isn't growth. I take it that we should find out who we really *are,* and rejoice in so far that God would be thankful in so far as we have been restored as Christ. If there are certain areas that will be lopped off, and they are lopped off – we *want* that. We want all the ultimate perfection there is!

So all judgment is – is to assess you – sets you in to what you *are.* And remember if it's eternal joy, it has no weeping. You *can't* weep at whatever you are. It's a curious thing down here...if you are settled in what you are (and you're *meant* to be) that's the whole meaning of life! That's why a lost person can *try* to satisfy where they are; that's a danger of course. But if you are saved up to the level – "Oh, I've got it". When you've got it, you aren't thinking about much anymore at the moment. At the moment – "Oh, I've got it! As it seems you've got the *whole world*...you've got Jesus Christ! You've only *really* got babyhood. You don't even know that then. So you see how clever it is. In each area of experience we're satisfied and complete in what we've got. We don't say..."Oh I wish I had *that.*" It is wonderful!

Heaven *must* be like that. You can't imagine heaven with some deprived people saying, "Oh how miserable I missed the way." What kind of heaven is that? If it's a heaven with no tears and all songs and joy and servants, each on the adequate level, must be *just* what they were meant to be. C.S. Lewis went on a bit in his somewhat – fantasies – his clever books talking about the future. You only see yourself as you are. That doesn't mean you don't go...then you go on a little more. Come on...we move *on* further in the adventure! So I take it to be like that.

We need not be afraid of judgment. We *welcome* judgment when *God* is in it...when Jesus Christ is delighting in us! It says every man hath praise of God (I Cor 4) that judgment day when we don't judge before the time...when God brings light into the heart of life. He says I stand before Him – let every man be of praise! God's going to be *delighted* with the manifestations of the grace of God through us. And where it's needed, that will come along. That's what he talks about now.

Therefore, knowing the *seriousness* of it...there's a mistaken word here – the *terror* of the Lord. The terror is only reverence, fear. Fear in the right sense...respect. He *cries* for you to know how great this life is and move in as God enables you to see the greatness of it and participate, and catch on a little more to the greatness of it. That's what he means...until we persuade men. And he says this really is to give you a touch of the glory on my behalf.

I'm telling you this, he says, not that I may commend myself, but that you may *catch on* to what's God's *done* by me and through me to you. He was trying to *show* them the reality of the glory of what happened in him, through him, to them...to give them a chance that they could answer. In verse 12 are these words...they were despising Paul because he was not much of man physically and so on, and making him contemptible and judging him by outward things. He wasn't supposed to be such a good speaker, and so on. And so he says, I will show you *real* glory and they answered, "Oh he isn't much of a man, isn't much of a speaker."

He says we live a kind of two-fold life – we're both crazy and sane. We're crazy, but we just follow Jesus, and somebody said that looks like we *are* crazy. The natural man thinks we're crazy, and sometimes our fellow-Christians think we're crazy. Sometimes we think we are ourselves. So he says if I'm crazy, it's for God. He says here "if I'm beside myself, it's for God." I *must* go, I *must go* with Him. If it ends like it did with Jesus, with the humiliation of the Cross, then it *ends* like that...okay. So there's a sense in which *I'm* a fool for Christ. There's another sense in which I'm sober for your sake. In other words – I'm sane – I'm able to give you rational explanations for what I'm doing...not flying high for nothing. So I'm both crazy and sane. Of course he says, "This love of Christ constrains us." The love of Christ, of course, is His love imparted to us, not our love for Him. The love of Christ is His love imparted to us (which, of course, is other-love) which causes us to come into the constraint of other-love.

And he then gives the intercessor's interpretation of our relationship to Christ – how an intercessor would see it who is on the top level... *all* for Jesus they can. He said it's like this, "If one died for all, *all* are dead." I'm far beyond just *I* be dead; the whole lot's dead. So you see the *whole world*, if only they knew it, have *died* in Christ of the old thing which grabbed them and sent them to Hell. The whole lot, they're *all* dead. An intercessor sees widely. I have to be able to get people to see that this deliverance is *already theirs*, but that's the negative side we're living. The positive, of course, is to replace with the fullness of Christ, when you're ready for it...so he says that. We judge if One died for all, then are *all* dead. And then He said "they which live". Now he limits that – "they which live". He says all died...which they must find out. Then out of those who receive the death..."they which live" don't live unto themselves, should not live for themselves because the human died and are OK...can they *help* it?

So you move in *now* into the death and resurrection in which the Spirit of Christ is yours! Part of living unto Christ means living unto Him in the world, because He then fulfilled the word. You're caught up by a *new drive*...this new consent. You can't help it! This new Spirit of Love has taken hold of you and you begin to love! The first proof of new birth is the love of God shed abroad in your hearts. What happens? Not your love. When you discover you've been a lost sinner, and you see that He took my sins away, I begin to love! If I don't go to hell and He *died* for me...and because therefore God's my Father...I begin to love! In my youth, in any elementary outer outlook, I think it's *me* loving, but the Bible says, "No". The Bible says that's *God's* love shed abroad in your heart by the Holy Spirit that gives the Spirit. In other words, *now* by taking the Spirit of God you've got the Spirit of God Himself in you and He's *love*! He is causing you to *enjoy loving* somebody else, not yourself...that's the first time!

After you've been born-again, that's the first time. Up until that time you've been a self-lover. You've *begun* to love somebody else...how'd it happen! This One who died for you – now you and the Father are one. You've *begun* to be constrained by Other Love. You don't live unto yourselves, but unto Christ. And then you begin to find, of course, when you're constrained by Other-Love and it includes everybody, you want everybody to know this is the truth! And you begin to be a world-lover.

So he says this is what simply happens as you move in this direction. And then he says that has a *big* result – because he's now talking *universals*. It's the intercessory outlook on redemption. It isn't *I'm* just saved...the whole lot! He says *I don't see men again after the flesh*. My that's strong!!! I don't any longer just see men a bunch of lost people. They are God's precious few and don't know it! They're all redeemed and don't know it. They're *all* God's expression and don't know it. Everybody's a form of God and don't know it! The Bible says *every* human being has their *being* in God – not speaking *saved* – in the *whole* human family...Acts 17..."In Him they live and move and have their being." If you have your being in God you are a part of God! If you move in God, if you live in God, you are part of God...you don't know it!

That's our royal freedom! We must be free people so we can choose, and we can choose it totally. We can reject it totally, but that's what we *are*. Now Paul says, "So I don't see (tremendous!) I don't see anybody else in the flesh again." My! "Wherefore, henceforth knowing no man after the flesh." We see everybody as really in the reality of the Spirit, a person, a living person...redeemed if they knew it...one of God's persons they just don't know it. They are messing about because they just don't know it. They have to come to the place where they choose who they are. I don't *see* men. That's a *big* thing! I'm very slowly learning to look at that. Not to see just outer man. This man's a *form of God*; he's an expression of love. I say he's made of love. He wants to love and be loved, he's trying to find it by flesh ways maybe, maybe not...trying to find other ways, because we're *made* of love and to be loved. That's God! And this is a precious, eternal person, part of God and God's after getting him. And I begin to *look* at people like that!

He goes *very* far. He says we don't know men after the flesh. He says, "We've known *Christ* after the flesh, but we henceforth know Him no more." That's strong! I'm not interested in the Christ of history he says – that's strong! I'm interested about the eternal, universal Christ – the new Christ – the Christ who *had* to come in history to be my Savior; to be a man. I don't know Him *like that* now. That's what He *was*! I see Him now as this Universal Person *operating through the world by me*.

Then he says, "If any man be in Christ he's a new creature, old *things* are passed away, all *things* become new. So self is new; others are new; things are new...what's left? We've become new, if we're dead with Him and henceforth don't live unto ourselves. Then he said I don't know any other man after the flesh. All men are really spirits in whom God is operating, *including Jesus Christ Himself,* in history. He says they're new *things.* He says as new creatures old *things* are passed away; all things are new! I have a new outlook of which *everything* is just some form of this wonderful God.

We begin to get this *whole inner spirit* scene, in the place of being dominated by the flesh. Now we're human so we've got to start with the flesh always...because we're part *of* the flesh. We've got to *start* seeing our bodies (seeing things) and we learn gradually to replace the seeing of things, and seeing what they *really* are – just forms of this One. And if we see what's there we know they're forms of repetition increased. And we're not limited to things, because things are only little peanut forms of the Universal Person.

So we're moving into this new concept. Now he says in that concept, *all is God*, yes all is God...the *whole* thing...*all things* are of God. You can't get higher than that, can you? All things are God - well then they are *all things of God*, which reconciled us to Himself by Jesus Christ. Now *this* is the purpose of this intercessor interpretation. I am to be a reconciler as given unto me in the ministry of reconciliation. It's – *we're* enemies to God...not God enemies to *us*...and He *seeks* to reconcile His enemies. There's nothing on *His* side. He said 'reconcile *us* to Himself'. He seeks that so He can get us back. We had to go this way, as we always will; because we had to find out we were wrong before we were right. We had to go this necessary way. But to get us back – this is the purpose – to get us *back into* this ultimate reconciliation. He said the day will come when He will reconcile all things unto Himself. And He's given us the *ministry* of reconciliation – and this was that *God* was in Christ.

Now that's not been said very often before. This is the depth. This isn't God sending Christ – "For God so loved the world that He sent His only Son." In John...said God's *sent* Him – God gave Him. God was **in** Him. This is the depth of the intercessory life! This is the depth that the intercessor can see. This wasn't Christ *was* God - this was God in Christ. He wasn't God saying "Now I'll stop here and *You* go do it". I can only come as You in forms. The Universal can only come in a particular form. I came in this particular form. It is *I* here in Christ doing what's necessary to reconcile the world unto Himself.

What He *did* was to take the whole 'sin system' upon Himself, not *bore* our sins. This is what it says in the final verse, "He was **made** sin." Now sin is the whole system of self-centeredness – sins are products...the judgment of the fall. Sin's the whole system, the whole *sin system*, the whole *sin dimension* – He was made that! This was the final place, Jesus Christ, as God became the whole sin system, which involved us and everything else that's gone wrong. As He became the *sin system*, we became the righteousness *system*. Now we don't *get* righteousness; we *are* the righteousness *system*. We are gods! We are god-forms of God in His righteousness. It says He made Him to be sin, who knew no sin, that we may be *made* the righteousness...not *have* the righteousness...not *get* justification. Be made the righteousness. We are now the right people! We are now as He became the wrong person in all its implications, so we're now the *right* people with all its implications! So we boldly say we're the right people...we're God's righteousness; we're God's rightness now. Not *made* right...*are* right!

And He says therefore it's given to us to bring this message, reconciling to others not imputing their trespasses unto them. In the final way when after trespasses have begun to cease taking their *sins* away by removing their trespasses from them, but He went the *whole* way and was **made** the whole *sin principle* and removed the whole thing out of the self. And we have this *word* given us. We have the Word of the Father to give it. And in the final word he says this is such an *incredible* thought "He beseeches us." This is *God* beseeching us! This is the *eternal God*...bossing us? Beseeching us! Come now, come *back*, I *want* you. Beseeches – come. That's what God's doing – beseeching people to come back. Fancy the love of God beseeching us! *This* he says is the intercessor in his message. *This* is the intercessor in his commission; *that's* the intercessor in his quality of life in his vessel, and *this* is the intercessor in the message...the totality of the message.

A law means it has an *inevitable fulfillment*. It's something which comes to pass. So an intercession is something which comes to pass. Its fulfillment will be there. So there isn't a 'may' about it, there is a 'must' about it. In it somewhere is a death, the death of the intercessor – whatever form it may take – out of his death comes life to others. So it's the same principle which was fulfilled by **The** Intercessor – by Jesus.

We may say that Paul's intercession was the Gentile world...a very big one. He was the apostle to the Gentiles. He laid down his life – his life was poured out, and finally literally taken in establishing the gospel all over the Gentile world. Again, he was the apostle to the Gentiles. It's not time now to go into various contemporary local examples that can be given of an accepted and a fulfilled intercession. It's what we speak of – you *gain* an intercession. There's a death and you *gain* it, and you *know* it's there and it's going to be fulfilled...and you've *gained* it. It's the Cross taken up for others. It's the third meaning of the operation of the Cross – the same as it's the third 'grade' of our relationship with Him who is living His life by us.

We come **to** the Cross for redemption, receiving the benefit of what He did *for* us in His shed blood. We get **on** the Cross, receiving the benefit of what He did by His body in dying and rising into which we identified. It says we were crucified with Him, buried with Him, risen with Him, seated with Him. His *blood* removed the consequences of our sins, which was judgment, wrath and eternal destiny. He went that way – right to hell and out of hell again, and closed the door to hell behind us. Being the last Adam, did it for the whole race. That's why He's called "the last Adam"...what He did for the whole human race (what the first Adam did on the natural level) The Last Adam did for the whole human race to raise them into the spiritual eternal dimension – for those who have been freed persons, *who received* what had been provided for them.

In the death and resurrection of His *body*, to which we were identified, He delivered us from the spirit of error – the *producer*. His *blood* delivered us from the *products* – the sins and the wrath and judgements and guilt and the destiny in hell. They are the *products* of the *producer*. The producer is the spirit of sin which captured humanity that we read about today. It said, "In whom the god of this world works hath blinded the minds". He's *in* the unbelievers...in *all* of us, **in** us; he's an inner god, inner spirit.

And that's *the relation* that He received for us from His Father when His Father made Him to be sin; God made Him to be *sin* for us, not sins – **sin**. Sin is the *nature* of the sin spirit. Love is the *nature* of the Holy Spirit. Sin is self-centeredness.

He therefore *became*...representing us...*a body*, because our body has the sin spirit in it. And when He died our *body* died to the spirit. There's no spirit in the body that's in a tomb. That's why it's buried...an indication there's no spirit in the body. When He rose it says He rose being put to death in the flesh...*quickened* by the Spirit. It's a quickening within His own spirit – the Spirit of God raising Him up again. In this *we* participated. So that's the second relationship to the Cross. The first one is we come *to* the Cross, and He did something we don't touch. He shed His own blood, went by Himself as representing the world to the consequences of our life of sins...to hell...to death in hell and rose again. That took away sins and its consequences of the wrath and the guilt and the judgment and condemnation...and the whole thing. But that's just what comes from the *products* of sin.

The *producer* is the one who is the real problem. It's not the effects...it's the **cause** that's the real problem. So there couldn't be redemption if He hadn't removed the cause from us, as well as the effects.

And the *cause* is – we become *captives* through the fall to the spirit of error, the god of this world that works in the children of disobedience. How could we be delivered from *that* one? Only when One who *could* represent us, the last Adam who Himself was never occupied by that spirit could become us...could be made *as us,* which He could do because He was our Author, our Creator, and He could represent us, which He did. So in this case we identify with Him because joined to His body, as that body represented us, where He died, then if One died for all, then we are all *dead*. That's not our sins...that's **sin**! Dead to, cut off therefore from the spirit of error. That's the second phase. If He died, we died. Now a dead person is cut off from his spirit. That's why the Bible says we are dead to sin! We're *delivered* from sin and its consequences in the precious blood. We are *dead* to sin in His body, which means we are cut off from *any* of that spirit of error and anything he can do to control us. He may attack us and influence us and stain us for a moment, as it were, but he cannot possess us again. He can be an *invader*; he *cannot be a possessor*. That's the efficacy of the dead *body* of Christ. That's why we celebrate the two at the Lord's Supper...body and blood.

In this case, it's a faith identification – we see ourselves *as* He; we came *to* the Cross and saw Him do something *for* us, which was went to hell for us and took away the judgement and wrath. We see *ourselves* now *as* He in Spirit representing us, going through a fate, which we therefore in Him we've gone through which has cut us off, so we've no longer that control. That's what we say, we move in by faith there. And in the place of the spirit of error, His own Spirit; the Spirit of God, the Spirit of Love – occupied that Body...occupies *our body*. And this is the second phase. We come *to* the Cross; we're *on* the Cross, and *in* the resurrection. And when we fully learned our lessons on *that* level, we've come into a **realized union**.

The *importance* of the union is because we're so used to our independence...even though we *are* a redeemed people, and we're no longer hell-going people, and no longer under God's wrath and judgement, condemnation...we're God's precious children. We're *so* used to the life as operators of independent self that we still retain that separation. We haven't moved into that third dimension of unity – spirit is union – *all is One*. We're there today! We're coming to the day, which is there *now*, when He'll gather *all* things in Christ. Obviously, this is what really **is** – *all* things in One Person. It's unity! **God all in all**. And we don't get that easily, so we go through the fighting, failing area where we **are** the Lord's and we think we must somehow become 'better' people.

We're redeemed people now, but we haven't got the unity. We've 'got' redeemed, and cleansed and justified – delivered from the consequences of our sins...and *really* from the sin spirit! We're new creatures, but being ourselves we think we're in a condition that we should be improved selves, and we shouldn't be giving way to these assaults to the flesh – our hates, our fears, our lusts, our reactions, our lack of peace, our lack of rest in God and power...whatever you like.

This is the *second negative necessity*, which can be replaced by positive, because positive can only operate on its negative. It's only an entity when it has the negative which it operates on. That's why we couldn't have

145

redemption until we knew our sins. When we totally knew the sins – the negative – then redemption could replace the sins. *Then* we could become the entity of redeemed sinners. One swallowed up on the other. You must have the negative for the positive to manifest itself and swallow the negative up. That word of "swallowing up" comes again in the chapter we read today of II Corinthians when it says "Life swallows up death". Put in this way mortality is swallowed up of life. Life swallows death. The positive swallows up the negative. It gets its basic *hidden* power from the fact that there *is* a negative. It's a *reality* that is negative which is swallowed up and that makes an entity. Truth has swallowed up error. Redemption which has swallowed up lost condition and so on. So in each case there has to be a negative for the positive to swallow up.

And the *second* negative has to be our despair at our inability to manage ourselves, which gives us in our redeemed life a guilt and a condemnation...our sense of failure. So our consciousness in our *redeemed* life is more a failure than of victory in Christ. *We're more guilty self-centered than happily Christ-centered.* We *have* Christ, but not in that *free* sense of self in which the attention is Christ operating His life. I don't *know* that yet. So we have to have the negative of the discovery. And the final discovery comes when...we're not *meant* to! It's an illusion – the 'concept' of an independent self is an illusion! The union with Christ in His death and resurrection – the way *we* become One Person – symbolized/typified for us best of all by the vine and branch...vine and branch make one tree, and the *branch has the sap flowing through*...the real branch – just the sap *covered with* the branch. So the main part isn't the branch; it's the sap coming through, producing the flower and fruit...and the branch is just a part of the vine system through which the sap flows. That's unity. That's the simplest symbol of the illustration given us.

So that the idea that we are separate functioning – got to call on something as if we're separate from the vine...got to call on Somebody to help us is a false thing! It's calling on God to help that which was a form of *independent* self which was the Fall-problem. Independence went its own way. So we're still *saved* to going our own way, while we conceive ourselves independent. Well, it's an illusion. We conceived ourselves as that. We are slaves at once, because that's the *whole point* of the Fall – *independence*! Independence in the end follows its own way. So down we fall on our faces. We *can't achieve* the holiness and the victory and the peace and the power we should have. At *last* this negative has come into focus.

146

The first negative – *I* am a lost sinner. I don't try and do it with my own righteousness; that's the first negative. Then I'm conditioned for the positive to swallow up the negative...I've got Christ blotting out my sin. And when some moment comes when I recognize that I'm not *meant* to be an improved self. *I'm not really an independent self at all!* I'm a self, *but* this idea of an *independent* self – that I run my own self is false; it's an illusion. When I recognize that, which I've explained as I have so often done – I learned I'm just a vessel. Well, you are *more* than a vessel; you're a person...but just forget you are a person for the time being and become a vessel.

So in reality you go through a phase from the *wrong self,* to a *no-self* to a *right self.* The wrong self of course, is the self-centered self; you've got *almost* to cease to be a self – reckons I'm just a part of a vessel. Well, I'm *more,* but I have to go through that to get into to me the pot *doesn't change.* The pot isn't improving the pot. The pot is there for the purpose of holding the liquid...and the liquid is the living God! Then that can dawn on me; I *cease* trying to improve the pot. I give up being pot-minded. I move into what is a *fact,* but has to become faith – based a thing on experience.

Faith only can make it experience when you're on the level you want the thing, and it's *real* to you. Until then you can't take a thing that isn't real to you. If it's not, you don't see it. We only see a thing that is real to us. No telling how many different ways a person can see a tree. A carpenter sees it one way, and a horticulturist sees it another, and an artist sees it another; you only relate to the tree in the way you *see* it! The other way is meaningless to you. So you only relate to a thing, which is faith, in the way you see a thing. You can't relate to the fact that I'm in the union until I've seen this is the truth...then I move in. *That* is the settlement of the **second relationship to the Cross**. When I'm *on* the Cross, which means I'm 'off' in the *resurrection.* I'm on the Cross means I *cease* to be an independent person. I'm crucified from that which may be independent. I'm not my self - it's a lie! My *self* has been through a second Cross, which is, of course, meaning the independent spirit's *out* from me.

In the place of the *independent* spirit, I have the New Spirit. If you like, I am a *dependent* spirit to the New Spirit, the Holy Spirit – I'm one! When *that* can settle into me, now faith becomes a recognition. Faith becomes a sight. Faith is knowledge. Faith is substance. You move **into** a thing and there it is! You take a food and here it is. You take a chair and there it is. Faith is substance. It's completion. It's the thing you've related to has become a thing to you. Faith is not reaching to something; it's identifying something by which the thing identifies itself to you, with you.

So in this second case, there comes into our consciousness...this *is* a fact! Now we begin to be positive...*this is a fact*. **I'm not I...I'm He**. Something in me witnesses that this is what the truth is. Now I begin to be free from self-fussing. I'm no longer *afraid* of myself...I'm a human! I'm not fussing about my *humanity*...and the fact that I get moved in anger and fears and hurts and lusts. I don't bother about that. I'm that, but that's not the *main issue* any longer. So I *cease* to be self-suspicious, which most of my temptation is the sparking of suspicion because I'm *suspicious* of myself...sensitive to myself...I very quickly 'catch' the temptation; the temptation *gets* me!

When I cease to be suspicious, and *forget* self, it doesn't bother me so much. It *does*, but not so much, because I begin to move into the positive. I begin to accept God *in myself*. That's the new one. Now I've begun to be a new self. From wrong self to no self to *right* self. I'm a self now, because the whole recorded mystery of humanity, mystery of deity is that deity is only expressed through humanity...because a positive is only manifested through its form of manifestation. You cannot *see* electricity unless it has a light to manifest itself by. You can't *see* an atom unless you have things that are forms of atoms...that which you say, "These are forms of atoms". You can't *see* the universe except by its particular forms, so you can't see the universe of God except by a particular form...and so God's never *seen* except by Jesus Christ! That's the only way we have that reading about Jesus Christ today...can't be *seen* any other way...and it can't be seen by Christ, as it were. He is the Creator; we are the created *forms* of Christ.

So the *tremendous* significance to be a person is that I'm forever a *forefront* person. *If God is the background...I'm the foreground. That's why it's necessary for me to find out and move into what it is to be a real self.*

So we move now into the asset level. I'm not a liability...I'm God's precious asset! In the last book of the Old Testament when He makes up His *jewels*...that one of the terms used of us. Most precious treasures to Him. That's we! That's we! That's we! So He accepts us *precisely* as we are. Then we get off our tensions and trying to be religious and trying to put on the face. It's precisely as I am...just the funny face I have and funny everything. Yes, I always say life's a permanent joke to me...thinking God can live in this. [Pointing to listeners] It's a much bigger joke to me that He lives in this!

[Pointing to himself] It's a life like a joke, but it's *His* joke, not mine...because He chose me; I didn't choose Him. He chose me!

Now we're coming to a fun life, a free life...because we're *dead*. Say, "I *am* this person...*I am* Christ in human flesh! I *am* this Person operating." Deep down you *know*. If you've been through your brokenness you don't take glory to yourself. If a person tries this out who *hasn't* been through his brokenness, he might really mean *his* humanity is Christ. But if you've been broken you're *not* going to be fooled again. You *know* you're the human, and He's the deity...and yet the mystery is that you *are* one, and so you are *He* in form...in human form...because your *emphasis* has gone over from *your* self to He Himself *in* yourself, or by *your* self.

It's what the Bible calls a mystery – Christ in *you*. The mystery is *not* Christ; the mystery is *Christ in you*! That's Colossians 1:27. That's Paul's great mystery; that's Christ in you...the two together. That's *bound* not only to be foolishness; it's bound to be fanaticism, nonsense, blasphemy, ridiculous...even to Christians! *How can you say that?* Those who are still hanging around the separation of self, and don't know this basis. So you become the free person...you just *be yourself* – that's Christ! And you *don't fuss too much* about the deviations.

We read today that the build-*up* of life is temptation. You *must* have a negative to build a positive. Trials are that which *press* us into Christ. Because you're *tried* – "I'm not going to hang around my fears and impatience." No, it *pressed* me to say "I'm Christ having this thing." That's Paul – perplexed, but not in despair; cast down, not knocked out; persecuted, not forsaken. You move over...your trials press you, confirm you into reality, which is the real entity. All through our life, we shall always be tried, be tempted people to the very *pressure* point and the necessary. It works the other – it *works* settling in to the recognition of Who we are.

So we'll always be tempted...occasionally slip, but don't bother! Don't *mistake* the two – temptation isn't slipping. Jesus had it. Don't mistake the two! If you do mistake the two, it's forgiven. Get up. God doesn't even **see** sin! He only sees the blood which blotted it out. So just get up and thank God and go on.

So we've begun to live this free, liberated life to be ourselves, because deep down we have this consciousness – it isn't we, it looks like we but it isn't we...and yet we function as if it *is* we! And so again we are continually

149

moving into certain, shall we say paradoxes, which lie in the basis of life. You can call it paradox...or it's just the way life lives. That is – to have a profession means somebody's *got* you inside. Profession is some subject you've studied until it becomes you. You study medicine until you *know* how to practice it. You study carpentry until you know how to use your tool. You study cooking until you know how to cook. And you're only a liberated person, not by studying cooking, but by being able to cook. Not by studying carpentry, but by being able to use your tools, or whatever line of life we have.

So life is based on an inner-consciousness being at ease - that's what we call a competent person! We say a person who knows carpentry...becomes a carpenter; a person who knows plumbing...becomes a plumber. If he knows medicine...becomes a doctor. If he knows teaching...becomes a teacher. We use a term meaning they've *got* it.

Now the significance when we *are* in that situation is we skip the 'got it', and *be* it. We don't keep saying I'm a carpenter, I'm a teacher, I'm a lawyer...I just practice. So there's a *hidden* background. So in the new phase of free life, you forget you're Jesus Christ! You forget Him and be yourself. 'That's me'...at last means you're functioning as He and that's the background. That's this new free life. Except most of the time you're not thinking about Him, you're thinking about your job, your interests. Underneath there's like a flow going on! Underneath you're very confident that it isn't you...that it's *He* thinking about that. So life isn't constantly trying to *think* of Jesus Christ; it's *being* Jesus Christ. It's being yourself, which is He. There's this new liberation! This is the unified life we talk about.

Now the third and **final revealed phase** in relationship to the Cross is *taking up* our cross. You've gone *to* the cross; you're *on* the cross; you *take up* the Cross. That's for others! That's for others. You're now taking up the same in which other *people* can move into their cross, and resurrection, and redemption relationship. Now *this* is the highest, because this is what God *is*! God is a self-given Person for His universe. That's why that *strange* title is given to Him - given to Him in the Person of His Son, if you like. Twenty-one times, I think, in Revelation He's called the Lamb on the Throne. That's a very remarkable thing to call almighty God a lamb. There's some gap between God's almightiness and the weakness of a lamb...that's the whole point! The whole *difference* between the symbol of natural lamb and the Divine Lamb is natural lamb can't help it. He's *helplessly* available – do what you like. He's defenseless...do what you like with him. Use him any way you like.

The Heavenly Lamb is *purposely* available. He *means* to be for us. He *means* to be identified with us. And in *this age*, it means to be identified into death that we may have life. The day will come when the death level is finished forever, I presume. And that identification will be wholly on the life level. We're not there yet. So the point of God is the Lamb moves in...so we're lambs. Paul says we're lead "as sheep to the slaughter". That's Roman's 8. We're *slain* for the world. *This* is the intercession. The intercession is when having been released from ourselves we're not bothered with ourselves. We can be what? Be somebody for others. And we can't help it! Nothing was ever 'put on'...it's motivated from within. It's not *our* motivation. It's not put on by us...not "I've *got* to be". Drop that whole idea. That's out!

You're a motivated person, you *naturally* move in new motivation...and in the new motivation – you can't *help* yourself! It's when you've got the key to life and know what life is...and you can't *help* wanting others to know the same thing! You become like the identification with the One who reconciled the *world* unto Himself, so there comes this basic drive of life that somehow it'll be something that other people find is missing. The old life is nothing – wood, hay and stubble. It's just *rubbish* unless it becomes this we're talking about – what a *new* creature is, what the *whole* man is. So we get this *new drive* of life! This is the third.

Now we're on the intercessor level...on the *cooperating* level. This is the delight of God! The other two levels are *dependent* levels. This is a **co-**level...equalizing us...a fellowship *with* God. So it isn't hanging onto God; it's being with God for others. In fact, Paul puts it in the highest term when he says it's God hanging onto us. Because Paul says the highest honor I know in I Timothy, "For He had known me; for He counted *me* faithful...putting me in the ministry." I can rely on *that* person, God said. Now that's His delight. When He has people cease fussing about their own, because that's *fixed*...the whole situation is *fixed*. If it's fixed they won't come back. They *know* living on that level. And now they can be "co" with God. Co-workers...*co*-god's the word is because we're gods...*co*-gods! With God.

And this is His 'food' when He has *co*-workers – *co*-laborers with Him, so He's consulting with them and showing *them* how to do the job. And He can count on them to fulfill their part; *that's* intercession! Intercession means, shall we say again (as far as we *see* it) maybe it's more automatic in our lives... maybe when we haven't understood that principle necessarily, and that is a sense of purpose – a sense I'm set somewhere for purpose. My life isn't just a doing job in a business, in a home, in a profession. There's a *purpose* in it. And somehow you can *catch* the purpose – the purpose may vary through life, but something which just *grabs* me for the time being.

So a commission is something that grabs *you*. You don't grab it...it grabs you. Somehow this becomes of interest to you. You put *yourself* into that; you're going to *do* it! That's it! That means it's something that's identified with bringing Christ to other people...somewhere for others; some relationship, something for others. It may be part of a cooperative operation or an individual operation. That's intercession when it's accepted as such.

The *law of the intercessor* is you're like the extended body of Christ. As Christ's body went into death and resurrection, so *we* as His body, go into death and resurrection. "We *fill up* that which is left behind of the sufferings of Christ for His body sake." And still in an inert situation, when life comes out of death, it symbolized by everything...by what we eat...by everything. Life comes out of death. This is the *phase* we're in now in this world. So we become the agent of it – through our death life comes to others. And that means in whatever way we are *available* now...in whatever way He *calls* us to be identified. Now, there will be a thousand different ways...in which somehow it takes time, maybe, and God says it takes our inner interest. It takes time; it takes sacrifice...may affect our home, may affect our business. We've got something *higher* in life...beyond what we're doing there's this *higher* end and we're identifying with it. No *pressure*...no fanaticism in the sense of *trying* to do something; we don't *try* to do anything. In fact you run away from it in a sense, but He *makes* you...and you move in.

And usually *somewhere* there's a death in it...where there's a *purpose* in it...something comes along that is like a *death* – where the intercession is gained – somewhere where it's *cost* you something. Don't make it up! It may be your reputation...may be your position...it may be a thousand ways. Don't for goodness sake make it up...that's *God's* business! If somebody's fulfilled, when God *pushes* to do something, and there *has* been a laying down of your life at some level...then out comes that product! That's the law. The intercession is gained. And this is Paul's products we're talking about.

Now, here Paul illustrates to them what lay behind the products. The product was the *great* Corinthian church going through certain phases of difficulty, and therefore he was *still* in that sense an intercessor for them. But he was showing how he'd *poured* his life out. They were only *one* of the churches in which he *poured* his life out. They were already the visible fruit. He was now more in the phase of keeping and tending the fruit, and so on...but it was all part of the *permanent* intercession.

So that's what we've been reading today, a letter where his *only* concern was the people to whom he was an intercessor. He loves them and lives for them. They're *his*; everything he does is *love*...however much it may be a firmness or a rebuke or a check-up, it's clothed in something which shows how he *loves* them! An intercessor is a lover. And at the same time, as we read about today how you go through different experiences of the general principle - death working in us - involving you in all kinds of things, pressure, afflictions, persecutions, losses, death, so and so. Out of that as he walked in life in action, you *see* the Cross...you can see the glory! As he walked in life in praise and victory in these situations, this life will be transmitted to others. Whether it is that they catch it from him, or whether somewhere the Spirit imparts it to them and *they* become co-saved, co-redeemed...and we come up. We hope to be co-intercessors with Him in their faith for other people.

And in the way that the Lord so often works He uses the negative for His own conveniences, and He used the negative of their attacks on Paul to bring out this *marvelous* presentation of what an intercessor is and how he operates. We should not have *known* Paul would have been forced to explain how he operates as an intercessor, what happened to him as an intercessor, if he hadn't been *forced* into it because of this dangerous moment, in which these false prophets (even false-Christs it says, who were like angels of light) who could win the gullible Corinthians over, and implied that Paul was just a poor thing and put him out.

Now he *may* have started them off...but *put* they him out now and put in some new ways, which would be back on self-indulgent ways of course – building up self and the law and attachment to man...but we aren't told in what ways. This is a *highly dangerous invasion* from among the Judaizers and it forced him to explain to them *how* they come into birth through the intercessor now – not what their birth was. He discussed that in others – the Cross in 1 Corinthians 1...and resurrection in 1 Corinthians 15...and so on and other things. This is how the intercessor is the *agency* by which this came to pass. That's the II Corinthians letter.

Let's explore and see if there is in any way a *helpful* addition we can make to what we read when he explained what is the operation of the *law* of death and life, which is intercession, and we underlined this afternoon – don't get on to this foolish idea that life is *always* fun, that it's a thrill. But it's a hilarity which is at the heart of *great intensity*. So it's a combination of hilarity and intensity. And the intensity is the main line and the ending of intensity is hilarity. Hilarity is a Bible word. It says they ought to give hilariously. When giving your gift, give hilariously.

Therefore this stage of presentation, which is a *childhood* presentation – that something good will come to you...be careful! The highest good is to *lose* your 'good' for Jesus and other people. The highest good is the Cross for other people. Not that you make a big deal of the Cross; you make a big deal of the resurrection, but *behind* the resurrection is the Cross. *This* is the highest! So we want to keep that in the foreground. It's very attractive, the other. You get your thousands who say, "Oh, I like that...I get something good out of that! I get – there's always healing for me and all recognition...well, all right, if you lay it down for others...if the *purpose* isn't for you (but mainly, of course, it *is* for us)...if the purpose is – I *have this* for others!

I was with my friend, Bill Volkman, who's doing this Union Life Magazine and he shook them up when he went among the business men in Bermuda where we were looking at the expansions of the Willowbank, because we were going to write something on the guest house in Bermuda. He told them (of course they were men, finance barons, folks with big supermarkets...probably multi-millionaires and others of that type....*very fine* people...government people and so on...men of that type!

Bill was telling them that as a *young man* he was always saying he was going to be a millionaire to give it for God! Well, people talk like that, of course. And then he became a lawyer and a CPA and a building and land developer and so on and so forth, and he told them how he *did give* his first million away. He literally *did give it* away, and now he got another million and giving that away. That's fun! He'd given his million away. Now he's on his second one! The only point is that a point like that can sometimes reach certain people. It isn't just talk. It isn't just idle boasting. Anyone who knows Bill knows he's not just an idle boaster.

So we proceed through this heart outpouring of Paul and we've passed through the major explanations he gave. He passes on to certain personal appeals, which we needn't go too far in. And into one final aspect we'll look at for a moment. The personal appeals are – he *had* his concerns and he used them. It was evidently not a *free* fellowship. It was a mixed fellowship. You *can't* have a mixed fellowship. At the end of this presentation of this immense information is intercession.

He gives a *marvelous* description of the kind of person a minister of the gospel is in his outer life. He gives a whole list of the type of person the minister *is*. That's in the first part of the sixth chapter, after he finished about being an ambassador for Christ and Godly teaching and all that. He says in the *public* aspect, one other thing – he says "present" is a *'now'* word. He says we know it...a present word. You're that *now* and he moves into it in chapter 6. He says a minister, of course, must give an outer defense. He must not only have the inner Cross, and being outpoured in the inner way and having the time of the victory of his life being seen in him, but his life must bear out what he is living and preaching. So he goes through this whole tremendous list of what he goes through in Chapter 6...necessities and patience, frictions, distresses, persecutions, labors, fastings...*tremendous!* Outpoured in intensity! And any ministry should have that. Any of us should have that in our way. Well, yes, there *is* that – an outpouring of intensity at whatever level my calling it is!

And then he talks about the type of person he was in relationship to his people. *Pure* in his relationship to them and knowledgeable...knew what he was talking about...and gentle, patient, long-suffering, kind, a genuine love. You can catch genuine love pretty soon. And pretty soon you'll know whether it's phony love or a genuine love. And this was the impression he would make with the people he was ministering to. His life would be involved in all these persecutions and these fussings, and so on, in different levels – something of an outpoured life...which is a costly life according to the level on which we live...and in Paul's relationship to other people there'd be this presentation of a loving, faithful, pure, reliable and knowledgeable man. And then he'd be bold in his message; he'd *know* the truth and *give* it! He'd give the word, the truth, and the power of God, and there'd be something about his conduct...they wouldn't get at him! His conduct would be such that they couldn't *attack* him on his conduct or on the righteousness – the right type of man on the right hand and on the left.

And then this curious *dichotomy* operating two opposites – to some people you are despicable; to some people you are honorable. To some people you are a heretic; to some people you speak the truth. To some people you are insignificant, unknown; to others you are very well-known. This mixture, he says, you get here. To some people your work's nothing to it; it will *collapse* as dying, but then it doesn't die...it goes on. Some people think that's a *miserable* business...why do you have to live a life like *that*! Sorrowful...yet, really we're the people *filled* with joy! So he says here, in this *marvelous contrast* happens, which each of us has are these two wayward lines. To the world we are poor...maybe not materially poor, but we're *making* many rich...not are rich. I like that! He twists it there. He doesn't say they think I'm poor...I'm really rich. No, I make *others* rich – that's my riches! That's wonderful! My riches are others. I like that.

I'm poor...maybe I'm made poor. That's not the point. Poverty is of course how you *use* a thing...it's not what you've got. But the point is, whatever I have, I'm *making* others rich. And having nothing...but possessing *all* things! You are apparently not holding anything; what you have, you use! You don't necessarily have a lot, but what you've got, you use it. But your life is you're not really holding anything...possess *all* things, because you possess the universe! So I guess this is the *marvelous presentation* of the opposites in which a servant of God, or anybody...any of us live...if we are keen agents for Christ.

It's after that then he then turns to them. This is the first time he began to move into a little bit...up until this time he'd been showing his love, forgiveness, acceptance...for reasons why he didn't come to them and explaining the background of the proof that they are the evidence – people of the Spirit and his work and so on, and all those things we went into. Now he does tell them...he says, "Your fellowship isn't healthy. You must have a healthy fellowship." He says, "If you had a healthy fellowship, you'd be *free*." He says when you're healthy you're free, because if it's just God...you're *free*, of course. You just do what God tells you...you're free. He says I'm free to you; you're free to me, you see. That's a sign! He says you're not 'straightened' in *me*. Alas, you are straight in *your own* bowels. The only thing that will ever straighten you is yourself. There's *something* tying you up, he says. "I'm *poured out* to you. You're not poured out back to me as a whole lot." He says, "I *suspect* some mixture in your fellowship."

Now he isn't talking about the world. Of course you're to mix in the world! That's what we're here for...to mix in the world. That's what we're here for to mix in the world! And our family...of course, we're going to mix. But there's the *other circle* which is the Lord's people...you don't mix. Now there's a place where we *should have* in ourselves, unmixed fellowships. Now that's awful mixed up now. It makes you feel much better that way when it happens. You'll find we have about nine hundred churches in Africa where there was nothing out there when I went out there about fifty years ago. It was primitive Africa...dark forests, that's all there was. And what it's *worth* today...due to my friend, C.T. Studd, and those of us with him...so there's these lovely 'harvest fields'. They're pretty hard, these simple Africans. They won't even keep a young man in the church if he's engaged to an unsaved girl, or vice-versa. They wouldn't even allow an unsaved engagement, much less an unsaved marriage. They're hard!

Well, they're beginners, but they want to keep the thing *afire* for Christ! And of course you're in a problem – you're in a church where there isn't *near* this. Many are in churches where new birth isn't even given...or these silly 'operations' like bowing at crosses and holy communions taking its place...which are nothing, just nothing. You can have *all* the communions and your baptisms and your bowings and have **nothing**! Because *all* you have is what's inside.

I'm so glad that in our mission we cut out Holy Communion and the like for about ten years. We had about five thousand for Christ then and we began to find...and we figured, "Oh, I'm going to eat the body of Christ." (No Catholics around...maybe, who knows, they picked that up from Catholics; I don't know.) Now baptism..."Oh, *now* I'm saved" won't do. We had a fiery leader in C.T. Studd and he decided we'd have no more communion and no more baptism for ten years! They just mounted in the thousands...but they had the *inner*. They had the inner baptism. They had the inner feeding. We learned how *nonsense* outer things are. If you want them, have them...but for goodness sake *don't mistake them* for the **real** thing! And you know, many of you, you are in churches where they *are* mistaken. There are mighty few churches today where the standard is – you *really* need to be born-again. Mighty few!

This is what he was getting at. He said, "You're of mixed fellowship." You're mixing on the *fellowship* level. You can mix on the business level or on the family level, but you shouldn't mix on the fellowship level. You're mixing with those who haven't got the Christ you've got! They don't talk of Christ the way you do, and you can't have accord that way.

So there *is* a place for inner separation. Of course, it may be easier in a mission like ours, but we would not *take* it and we're 1300. We *wouldn't* take a person who was not only born-again, but dedicated, Spirit-filled and *all* for God! Wouldn't! We put standards up, saying you should run away if they come near us anyhow. We only want the ones on fire! Of course, that's easier to talk about in the mission field, but the missionary body shouldn't be different from the home church. That doesn't mean you don't have unborn-again people there. You bless them. But the *real* family circle should be the born-again. There should be something going on there where the real family circle is born-again, Spirit-filled. It isn't in most cases...you know that. So He gets us in here...there's something going on. "Come out and be separate", He says. "Touch not that unclean thing." Whether there were 'things' mixed up in their lives, as well as people...I don't know.

And then he gives that *beautiful word*. He says, "*You* are the temple of God." It's a beautiful statement – he says *you* are the temple of the *living* God! And that's the second time in this letter he has spoken about the *living* God...the Spirit of the *living God*! As God said, "I will dwell in them and walk in them." I've always liked that. (That's the King James Version.) **God's** walking in us...that's it! It isn't *we* walking. He says, "*You* are the temple of the living God. I will dwell in them and walk in them." That's life......*God walking in us*. So He says come out and be separate, and I'll be to you a Father and you'll be to Me a son. So he spoke like that, and he appeals to them – all filth is in flesh and spirit. You've got filth in the spirit if you've got pride, if you're in unbelief, and so on in the flesh. You're *perfect* in *wholeness* in the fear of God, he says.

And so he ends there and then he goes on into personal details, which I think we needn't now. He told how he was concerned. He was a human and he was *tremendously burdened*. Well, he was a pioneer...and *remember* it's alright for us to talk, but there was no New Testament to build them on; no other people on whom they could rely; no other Christians about the place. We're alike on the mission field. We get the feeling of lonely souls, but at least we're given the Word of God! He had *nothing* except himself, so it was a *serious* time! If corruption had come into the early church and there was no representative of Jesus Christ to which they could turn...no New Testament – nothing – well he knew, of course, what the costs involved...and he did have costs involved...and he had a very *real* concern. He talked about how he had fightings without and fears within. So there's that! Of course, you know how to handle it...the fightings 'out', the fears.

Then he told of his joy when he heard that there had been a *real* repentance over the previous problem about the incestuous man...and when there's a tremendous repentance, there's a great hope. He'd sent Titus and he'd brought back that news from them. And then he spent two chapters – we needn't go into that now – when he was telling them about how to take their share in this special gift which we give the 'mother church'...this is special on his heart to give the 'mother church' in Jerusalem...some great gift. I suppose, they're often in poverty in the intensity of the situation in Jerusalem. And he talks to them about that, and inspires them to have tremendous discretion in the Macedonian churches, who were in persecution and poverty, but they were *so full of joy and love* that they sacrificed themselves beyond what they ought to sacrifice. They weren't going to stop the chance to give something to the 'mother church'...so that moved his heart, he says. He says to them – *you* (the Corinthians) were the first to propose this, not the Macedonian churches. It was *you* who proposed this!

Now he spoke – Come on, boys. Come on when we come down to pick up the gift let it be a *big* thing. I made a boast of you. I told the others the kind of church you *are*...because he *loved* his Corinthians. He said...you are washed; you're sanctified; you're justified. He says here, you've got all the gifts. Well then express the other gift. Seeing as you have all the gifts, show this one also. "As you *abound* in *everything* in faith and utterance and knowledge" (7th verse, 8th chapter)...*in all of Jesus* see that you abound in grace also."

So he set them up. I'm sure they responded, and he sent Titus there to help correct what they had already spoken about. And he puts it in his own down-to-earth manner. He said – Now I'm not fooling about this. I'll not have anyone saying that I'm making a good thing out of this. He said, I'm not handling this; Titus is handling this, and he is a man you can trust. There are several other brethren who are known and relied on in the church. They are going to come down and pick this thing up. "We sent with Titus the brother *whose praise is in the gospel* throughout all the churches" – that's a *lovely* phrase. "Not only he, but others too," he says "I've chosen to travel with us." So it must have been a pretty large gift. "So no man shall blame us in this abundance providing things honest." That's good, isn't it? Right in the middle. I want to provide things honest so no one can point fingers.

So he pressed this on them, and he just mentioned toward the end the great statement of the principle of giving...and he says remember it's a law that if you sow sparingly, you reap sparingly; if you sow bountifully, you reap bountifully. So again, it's the outer expression of this *strange* law that life is giving. When you give, you get. You don't do it for that *purpose*, but it works like that! God's the Great Giver; God gets back the whole!

So it's the *opposite* principle to what they are used to. Of course, many of us here can signify it by our lives here...you give bountifully, you get bountifully; you reap bountifully. You give sparingly, you reap sparingly. He says don't do a thing by *law*. Don't listen to me and say, "I ought to"...don't do that! Don't do that! Give to the glory of God, if God *moves* you to give. So he says "every man as he purposes in his heart, so let him give." Not grudgingly, not out of necessity, not...ooooh I *suppose* I've got to give...or I *must* give to be with other people. (That's verse 7 chapter 9) But God loves...*that's* where we get the word hilarious – the word cheerful is hilarious in the Greek. Oh, this is great to have a chance! Well, we do know that you are giving. Jesus *did* say it's right. It's one of the things that's quoted He said, "It's more blessed to give than to receive." Well, we know...somehow, it is...there's great joy in giving. So it's God loves a hilarious giver. Then he adds this. Now this is in relation to giving – God makes *all* grace abound to you. It isn't in the relationship of just 'general' grace. You see when you *are* on that level God makes *all* grace abound to you. "You may have sufficiency and all grace may abound to you in every good work."

So this isn't grace...you're talking on the level of your *need* now. He's saying if you *are* on this level, God makes grace *abound* to you...and so it gives you the all-sufficiency in all things so you are able to go on giving – abounding in every good work! And he says he is a ministry of 'seed for the sower', both the minister of *bread for your food* and multiply your seed sown – both recipient and giver so that you have sufficient for your own needs...bread for your food, and yet seed...so that you have the *more* to give to others. That's the principle of giving that he mentions in those few verses in Chapter 9...ending of course with thanks be to God for His *unspeakable gift* which is Jesus Christ.

He now turns to the last section of this letter. I only want to go into it in one way in a moment. Here is the apostle...the intercessor...who when necessary, is *firm*. He's not going to give into error...not going to have that! So he begins this 10th chapter...he says, "I beseech you by the meekness and gentleness of Christ". I'll just not be a servant of myself, but as a servant of *you*. I'll be gentle, but if necessary I can be firm. I'll not be you, and I'll not

160

talk about *myself*. He was now *turning* on these people who were corrupting the church. And he said we won't have any nonsense with them, nor nonsense with those who involve themselves with them! I hear this...so I come. I hear some of you are murmuring and backsliding and going into adulteries and so on. He said, "I shan't spare!"

He said when they began to talk about him as if he was just a self-operator, and that he walked by the flesh and for his own ends and so on. He said I'll *show* when I am there that I do not operate in the flesh! I operate in the power of the Light; I speak the word in the *power* of God! He wouldn't give in *one inch* in the ministry of the Spirit he had! He said they'll find the weapons of my warfare – not gone – they're *mighty through God* to pull down *anything* which moves from Christ. That's the key! When you got *down* to it, they were not, of course...obviously weren't centered in Christ or they would be *with him*! They were putting some form – some diverting Christ with *legal* conditions. Something was coming of it. He'd *wipe* it out! Everything that wasn't captive to every thought of *being* is Christ...that doesn't mean that every thought we think is the being of Christ; it means that the whole *principle* of what you're operating is related to what *is* the will of God in Christ in situations. So he talked with them like that! And discussed with them some of the things they said – his writing was strong; his presence was weak and so on.

And he added one or two things – he said now they're great self-comparers; they compare with each other. We don't do that, he says. That's a *good word* – don't compare yourself with other people. Don't be among those who measure themselves by themselves, compare themselves with themselves. Don't do that! Stand on your own feet! Just be yourself. When you read a book about some great person, don't say, "Why aren't I like that person? You aren't *meant* to be! Thank God that's God's expression coming through that person and say, "Thank God His expression comes through me too!" Don't go down...act like what you *are*! You are *also* His means of expression, and accept that He expresses Himself the way He wants through you, as He does through that person. So don't compare yourself with other people. He says, "I don't do that. I have a *right* to come to you, because I came to you first of all." He says, "My measure stretches to you, because you are my harvest; you're my fruit." And even then he says...he always had this urge on him. He says, "I want to come to you again, not to remain *with* you, but that I might preach the gospel in regions *beyond you*. I only want to come to you for *that* purpose."

161

Alas, after saying certain things along these lines, and also making defense that he wouldn't take money from them; he wasn't going to move from that. He wasn't going to be one of those who they could say he was getting an advance from them. He wouldn't take it! "I've been in *need* sometimes," he said, "but when I was present from you and *wanted*; I was charged by no man. I was in need! In a wonderful way the churches supplied my needs," but he says, "I *never* was in a position where I was making a gain out of you."

There he stood, and there he warned them against these who would be like a thief...and compared to ministers of righteousness...*be* like an angel of light and *appear* to be apostles of Christ. We aren't told any more detail about them except that they were Judaizers.

And that brought him to his *last* phase of his self-sharing which completes this letter...or nearly completes it. Again, the challenge forced him! He'd given them general principles of what in a sense it is, but he said it was like making boast of himself. He said, "Well, I must make a boast of myself...seeing many glory after the flesh, I'll glory also." Sometimes there's a *good* reason for glorying after the flesh. What he meant by that he says, "I think on this I should explain to you in my own *personal* experience what it meant to *me* to be an apostle...what it's meant to *me* to be an intercessor." So *here* he puts his personal in. He talked in general terms; now he talks in particular terms – and he shared what he had gone through *for* God – *for* them *as* God, and what God had taken him through in three separate forms as a basis to his apostleship.

One of those is this *almost unspeakable* list of what he went through in the physical, which is *so* well known – the actual outer afflictions that came to him – labors more abundantly, stripes above measure, in prison more frequently, deaths often. And the Jews – *five* times he received forty stripes save one! *Five* times he says – thirty nine stripes! Three times beaten with rods – that was the Roman lictor. That was pretty fierce! That was the Roman punishment. The lictors carried these rods, and at certain times they used them severely. *Three times* he had been beaten by the Roman lictors. We're not told these things, so we have *no* idea what he went through in between what we *are* told. Once stoned...we know about that. Thrice ship wrecked...we know of *one* when he went to Malta...a night and a day and the deep...seeing some demon or something. "The night and the day and the deep"...never heard of that. And then this extreme pouring out – journeys often, dangers in the waters, dangers from robbers, dangers by his own countrymen who persecuted him, dangers among the non-Christians, dangers in cities, dangers in the deserts, dangers at sea, dangers through false brethren. Living in this *'atmosphere'*! And then what it cost him personally – weariness and painfulness and watching with hunger, thirst, fasting, cold, nakedness. *My, my!!! Besides* all those things that were without that were cast on him daily – the *care* of the churches! I *shout* with the churches! If a church is weak, I was weak with them. If they were offended, then I'm burdened. So if I must *bleed* for them, I will glory in my infirmities. Isn't that *tremendous*?!!

This man's *glory* wasn't in opening churches in Macedonia and opening in Philippi and opening them in Galatia...not a word of the harvest! Only a word of what he'd gone through. His weakness and his dangers and his sufferings – what it meant for him to be this poured out instrument of God. And he gives a final illustration, which evidently remained with him as almost like a sense of *shame* showing how weak he was. He said in the early days to escape the soldiers in Damascus...they sent out soldiers to capture him and "they had to let me down the wall in a basket." Here was the *great Paul* being let down secretly through the wall in a basket and escaping...a really weak man. It had come to *that* for him to go to Arabia. It turned out again to be one of his greatest moments. From there he went to Arabia. *That's* where he learned about the *unified life* in Galatians 2:20. So again, the Lord always turns these things into benefit. So he said, "I'm only glorying in the *human* distresses and weaknesses and sufferings and they're at the back...not that to glory at the *suffering*"...except that's what it meant.

Then what he *had* with that also was a *great inner* revelation. *Every* intercessor has some inner revelation somewhere. This was unusual! It's what we speak of as a mystical experience. There have been those through history who sometimes called it a cosmic consciousness – something that breaks open the whole. You are *out* of this flesh...out of this realm...it breaks *open* reality! I've not had that so I don't know.

He wouldn't even call it by name. "Fourteen years ago"...so it *stuck* with him as a memorable event. Here and there...very rarely...I meet people who have something like this. They don't forget it! Usually they've moved into a sense of the universal. They've seen oneness of everything – the love of God streaming out to them. They don't *see* anything but that! *I'm* only talking theory. In Paul's case he didn't *know* if he was in the body or not. That, I also understand, is what happens. You don't know if you're in the body or not. Something happened to him...he was *lifted up* into what he called "the third heaven"...and he also calls it Paradise.

So there are *some* stages of heaven we don't know. If there's a third heaven, there's a first, second, third and maybe more. He *heard* unspeakable words – something he heard which wasn't wise or lawful for him to share. We can put whatever speculation we like on that one. There was something he *saw* and *heard* – some revelation which it wasn't suitable to share with the church of Christ on earth. He said I'm saying that because I want you to *know* that God *has met* with me in unusual ways. I hope in much weaker ways...any of us through Jesus Christ can say that. There's some specialized ways in which God has been very *special* to us. We've had special forms of revelation, which we can share. I think that *should be* so and different ways with each of us. *This* is the way God's made Himself very special *to me!* That's become the *main* line of our messages, probably. A few have had *actual* experiences like this.

But he says he didn't give his own name to that. You'll just have to know he meant it...as "a man in Christ." He said, "I'm not going to glory in that; I'm going to glory in my infirmities." His final form of glory was that he had some *constant* physical trouble. It was mostly considered blindness, because we know in Galatians he said, "I know you would give your eyes for me if you could." There are indications here and there that he was either weak-sighted or possibly blind. Some people imply that it came out of revelation when he was blind for three days on the road to Damascus, and this is the instance when he prayed three times...persistently prayed for deliverance. And he got the answer, but it wasn't an 'eye job'! He got a bigger answer.

Here's the answer! God gave him the answer – "I'm not going to deliver you, but I'm going to *show* the world how My strength is made *perfect* in weakness." Therefore, there came out of that a testimony, which if the other, would have meant nothing! If he'd been healed, who'd have remembered it? Haven't others been healed? Hasn't he healed others? It's interesting that he healed others on occasions, but it wasn't the point! Physical healing...we've talked about that before...wasn't the point. No it isn't! He had been the one used here and there for healing. *Here* he wasn't healed...but if he *had* been healed, who would have remembered it...but the *other,* remembered!

I learned a *great* secret – "When I'm weak, then am I strong." God said, "Now you are to *remain* in weak physical disabilities, because My strength is made perfect in weakness." And Paul then took that all the way and said......"Oh well, if that's so, if His strength is made perfect in weakness, I *welcome* the whole list of infirmities and necessities. Necessities may be material needs, persecutions, distresses, reproaches, infirmities; these things *pour* from *me*. I welcome, because when I'm in *that* condition...when I am weak than am I strong." And the point of *that* remark, of course isn't – he doesn't say what God says, "My strength is made perfect in weakness." I *am* strong...you see union? He says, "When I'm weak, then am *I* strong." Because I'm not I; I'm He. So he comes right out there! It isn't God expresses His strength when I'm weak – it's when I'm weak, then *am I* strong. I'm worthy; I'm now in sync with the Lord! I operate *by* the strength of the Lord *in my outer* distress. So he says *that* is his personal testimony!

That's the only thing he'd say about his great Gentile ministry, of which we're all a part. Nothing about his fruits and his products...everything about the glory of the privileges – intense sufferings and difficult times he had to get the gospel to us, and a touch showing how the Lord *did* meet with him...even private revelation. But in the end he remains just a *weak* man...but through his weakness comes strength, as of course, as he says the Philippians will find *now* he'll be strong when he goes up there and he finds things out of order.

So his last word is "Examine yourself as to whether you are in the flesh and whether Jesus Christ be *in* you." Isn't that interesting? That's the *last* test he gives them in the end of the thirteenth chapter. Now he says examine yourself because I'm going to come to you and *test* you in faith. And the faith is *this* – not did He *die* for you..."Know ye not your own *self* that Jesus Christ is *in* you...should you be reprimanded, castaway, disapproved." Very interesting? *This* is the gospel...he said you are a people with the Spirit in you. Now you test how well you can say – "Yes! Jesus Christ is *in* me." Of course, that's *all* we **can** say when we're walking by faith. That's proof! And that your life will be up to that – that you'll be strong and be perfect. And the last word – be perfect and be of one mind and at peace and the *whole* Trinity will be your blessing. And the grace of our Lord, Jesus Christ. This is where that final blessing comes...the love of God and fellowship of the Holy Spirit *is* with you, really not **be** with you...*is* with you all!

GALATIANS

But when I joined "CT" and with Pauline was beginning our ministry to our black brethren, I sensed in CT a greater depth and indeed *completeness of liberation* in his own life and his one objective which he named as seeing "Jesus Christ running about inside black bodies" – not just coming to them as Saviour and Lord, but taking over so completely that it would be He expressing Himself in and as them! That is what set Pauline and me seeking for what Paul said he travailed for the Galatians to have – "Christ FORMED in them" – **Gal.4:19**, which was a big stride on from just having a saved relationship with Him. Pauline and I sought and found after further digging into the full meaning of Paul's own search beyond his Rom 5, first step of "justification", to his "total" of Christ in him as him in Rom.6-8.

Knight of Faith Volume II

So I think, as I saw it myself, that many of us may come into some relationship in which it's "not I, but Christ." It was just a *middle* relationship. That's wonderful! It's no longer a self-relying self. I've got that clear. I accept myself and all of that; I know where I fit. It's not I, but Christ. But the third area is – "Now it's I again." Paul says in **Galatians 2:20**, "I am crucified with Christ." That's the old one out; now, that's the regeneration. Now the middle one, the union, is "I live, no I don't live, Christ lives in me." Now the third, the reproductive element, is "now I live by the faith of the Son of God." God's operating by me, "by the faith of the Son of God," *God's operating* His faith purposes *by me*. Now I'm out living again. *I've* come back again and it's Christ in *my form*...not just Christ. So it isn't "I can't, *He* can." It's "*I* can." That's the third one.

Old Testament Journeys of Faith

But as we move in by the bold choice of faith (as by the affirmation of **Galatians 2:20**), the Spirit will bring us that same light of revelation which Paul had. Inwardly we will "see" our wonderful God-made human selves as solely expressers of His Spirit of Truth in place of that false spirit of error. And we will settle into our true God-ordained condition, as out from us flows the river of the Spirit, as in John 7:37, 38. Nothing then can stop us from joining what Peter calls "the royal priesthood" of intercessors with, as Paul said, "...death working in us, but life in you."

Think on These Things

GALATIANS

We're taking a look at Paul's Galatian letter. It was written for a very specific and fundamentally important purpose at this period of the birth of progress of the early Church. So it's *standard background* to what God was bringing into reality through Christ and human lives in the final fulfillment to His purpose – a vast multitude will be the church of Christ and sons of the Son through eternity. The point was that this was written to the *redeemed*, not the unredeemed. It's written to those who *had* entered into what, I suppose, we would call a saving experience of Christ, but they hadn't got it into focus...and therefore they were not able to live the *liberated* sonship life for which Christ had fulfilled His redeeming work to make *actual*. And it's centered in such a, I suppose we would say, *startling* revelation that the Apostle Paul hung *his very authenticity* around it...as he did of *nothing else* when he said...*this is a revelation to me...such a fundamental revelation of truth...that if I preach anything else I should be false, and if anybody else preaches anything else it shall be false!* He starts off the first chapter with those *very strong* statements. If it's an angel from heaven, or he himself, preaching **any** other gospel he'd be an anathema or accursed. They already *had* the gospel. He was preaching to those of who he was going to say in the third chapter, "Having begun in the spirit..." They'd begun in the spirit so he was not writing the gospel to the unsaved. He was writing to the saved and his purpose was that his God-self should be his *free*-self – as liberated sons in *perfect freedom* as liberated sons! What is it to be *liberated* sons...not just a redeemed or saved son, but a *freed* person as his liberated self! What's it mean to be that?

His revelation shows him replacing the truth from objective to subjective...from *external* to *internal*. Gospel truth...that at that period of the church of Christ (even the Apostle Peter apparently had not *really seen* the true implications of the gospel) which are that we're *inner* selves...what a true inner self is – that all we are is an inner self, and what a *true* inner self is! The reason being is that through the Fall, we'd fallen into an *external* interpretation of life and life had become to us a relationship to outer things as if *they* were the real!

Paul's letter to the Galatians is a tackling of a solution to the basic problem of us humans...the problem of what I'd commonly call our self-life – ourselves – to put us back into focus, because we have gotten *radically* out of focus as human beings. Because the lost secret of the universe is unity! The whole universe is one because the whole universe is One Living Person, who is Love, expressed in all His manifestations...including us! But whereas He can only manifest Himself *to a point* through a thing (a Person cannot manifest Himself as a Person through a *thing*), He manifests Himself as a Person through persons. That's why He came and manifested Himself through His own Son...the only way in which He can be known...and then through the Son, to sons.

And so His manifestation to us is leveled up to our being what He is (in union) as we're gods with God...different from His manifestation through things. And our *destiny* is to be God manifested in the universe, because a Universal is meaningless except by the way it comes out by its manifested forms. Otherwise it can't be known. It's there to manifest itself through its forms. Electricity is only manifested through its power, light and heat. Or the atom is only manifested through things. You don't see an atom, you don't see electricity, you don't see the Living God...the universal One. You see Him in the Trinity, through His own manifested Son. That's the Trinity! So the Trinity is God manifested, because He couldn't be known unless He's manifested.

Through the manifestation, you come back to the Manifestor. So the Son manifests to us Who the Father is. He says, "If you've seen Me, you've seen the Father." So that's how we know the Father is the love, the Universal Lover, because the Son's manifested Him as such. Now that also means that through the Son, we come into being, to be co-sons...our destiny. Our present situation is the same. We're God's manifestors; God only can be known by us! Through eternity it will be so. The *means* of manifestation is in the foreground, and what it manifests comes out through it. That's why we call that a light. Turn the light on. It's not a light, it's a lamp. But the lamp is the manifestation of the light. So it just means to us that the conveyance has disappeared and we just see the light. We say, "Turn that light on; there's that light!"

So for that reason, it's been necessary for us as persons to *find* ourselves as persons...for we're to be real functioning persons through eternity. That's why there had to be this background human history in which we had to *appear* separate from God, to find ourselves. Because we're to *be* ourselves forever! But a real self, in its *real* relationship, is in a *hidden union-self* – as a real lamp is a lamp because it's a light *expression*.

So we had to start by being unreal selves – as if we're *separate*. That was our temptation in the Fall. That's why Satan, in a sense, was a necessity; somebody had to come out to be *opposite* to God – because you only know a thing by its opposite. You can only know the light in opposite to darkness, or sweet in opposite to bitter, or anything else in life. So Satan became the originator of the opposite – a person apparently apart from God. He, himself, is a form of God, so he is just God's agent. And in this case, God uses him to start the human family on the *wrong* foot...by which we have to *find* ourselves, as if we're separate from God. So the temptation was – get something for yourself. And that's how Adam and Eve found themselves to *be* selves. They found they had *appetites* and *eyes* to see with and *want* things...and eyes could develop by being tempted to want things for themselves. They had to be!

Equally, they had to find that you only know a thing by its alternative. We had to enter into the opposite alternative to God...which is not really real...the alternative of being a self-loving self, instead of being a self-giving self. That's why it says of God in that striking statement where it talks about God as everything. God's almighty. God's limitless – unlimited! Then the bible says He *isn't* unlimited. He's limited because the bible says that one thing God can't do – He can't lie! Which is one of the most unlikely statements in the bible; He can't lie! Not 'didn't'...He can't lie! Why? *Because that's the opposite type of self.* A liar is a self-lover; a liar lies to get his own ends. God *can't* be a person to exist for His own ends. So He's only positive self-giving love, because the opposite possibility has been swallowed up – being a person of self-loving love. That's been settled in God. So really, the negative isn't there. It's just *appearance*!

The negative is a self-loving appearance we're in. Now, we fell into that. We *had* to do so because until we discovered that until we confronted the opposites, and discovered the wrong opposite and be delivered *from* it, we can't *safely* resettle in the right opposite...or we might go back to the other one. Same as we're always saying, there's no competent professional at any level, who is competent, unless he's first known how **not** to do what he's doing – how *not* to use his tools, how *not* to teach this, or whatever it may be. Only then can he know the right way to do it.

But that has left our humanity under a *great illusion*...and that is the illusion of separation. So we see *everything* as it *appears* to be in its outer form – here's a chair, here's a piano, here's a person; everything appears to us as separate entities. They *are* separate, but when we're back with the true seeing...we're seeing with *God's* eyes in union with God...we shall always be seeing every separate thing as only an external form of the One. And we shall always see the One Living Person manifesting Himself in some form of love through these things. In other words, we become see-throughers rather than see-atters, which is what we become when we move into this reality of union with Him.

Through the fallen condition, in which we had to *find* ourselves, we've lost sight of that because self-loving-self has turned us into those who are here to grab and get and hold for ourselves – things. So we've fragmented the world up, as if it's just a whole lot of different things we ought to have or discard or handle or so on. We come to see life in its fragmented form...including ourselves and including God! Everything is a separate entity to us. This is the lost condition, this is the illusionary condition we *had* to be, to prepare us for the true one.

It always *had been* God's eternal fixed purpose that the *true* family would be the spirit family joined to His Son. That's why He's called the last Adam. The first Adam brought us into being as flesh persons...through which we become a flesh family. That's of great value! It's *through flesh* that God manifests Himself! So first of all, we came into being on the level of what's called living souls – where we have our emotions, our reasons, our abilities, our faculties; that's what's made us real people. But that's based on self-interest, and self-interest is *self*.

Now the *real* Adam, predestined from eternity, has been the eternal Son...the last Adam. He's the *true* progenitor of the race. He's progenitor of the fourth dimension – spirit, the heavenly family – the universal family which operates on the universal level. Now in order to *bring us* to that fact, He came as one of us – as if He was a lost person along with us under the law. He was confronted by everything that could divert him to be like us (a self-centered person), but the spirit of error could never get *inside* him. He lived His life in union with His own Father, although He had all the pressures of ordinary human living upon Him. And then He went the *whole* way we go, the end of our condition if we remain in a lost condition. We are eternally separate. *Apparently* separate. (Even hell is in God.) We appear to be separate; we live out of a separate consciousness...a self-centered consciousness. That's what hell is: self-seeking, self-gratifying consciousness, which is when we know the hell of it *here* in the shadow form. If we pass out through death into the outer destiny, we should know it in an eternal form.

171

Jesus, the Son, as representing us, as the Progenitor of the new race, representing the whole family, being the Author of the family, went that whole way. He went through physical death, which has enormous importance in it – separating body and spirit. He went there representing us, the human race. And a dead body hasn't a spirit in it. And that's where He, on our behalf, made a *fact* for us – as we relate unto Him, we're cut off from the old spirit. In the death of His body, which represented us, in which in God's sight was made sin (sin is the spirit of error in us), dying like that; He died to sin, and He cut off our human race from our *self* being indwelt by the false spirit.

The physical death is only a passing temporary form – the leading on to the destiny. That's the seriousness...the *destiny* to which it leads. And if we die in Satan, we go to Satan's dwelling place, whatever we call that using human terms. If we die in Christ, we go to the New Jerusalem, as it says. And Jesus dying *as us* went to the lost destiny. So that's why the bible says "Thou would not leave my soul in hell." If the bible says His *body* died and His soul...representing us was there...means He went to hell, but it couldn't retain Him, so He came up and that *closed down* the *destiny* of the fallen race. It closed the door on it, *finished it* for us! And He became the...He's *announced* as God's Son in the resurrection! "Thou art my Son. This day have I begotten Thee." That refers to the resurrection. It says it in Heb. 1 and in Acts 13. So this was the beginning of the new dimension, which is Jesus raised by the Spirit, the outer Jesus raised from death, raised from hell by the Spirit...back where He eternally was and is. The manifested form of the Trinity – God.

Now that opened the door for the human family destined to be sons with His Son, and the eternal means by which God is seen by persons to enter into this relationship. We enter *in* because being lost people, we lost our way...but a lost person knows there *is* a way...and although we were *lost* people, we were all forms of the being of God, because everything is a being of God, and that's why, basically, we always knew what we ought to be. So thank God, there's always been that guilt and discomfort, basically, in the human race that we're not what we *ought* to be. That's why all our politics and philosophies, and everything else have as their ideal – brotherly love. We *ought* to love. Communism was supposed to be brotherly love. Capitalism, everything's supposed to be brotherly love. Different political parties always talk about love, but of course we don't know how to get there! The significance is the whole human race says, "We *ought* to be that." So we know we're wrong. If we didn't *know* we were wrong, there wouldn't be any possibility of becoming right.

And this conditions us by the preaching of the Word (and first of all by the coming of Christ, and the presentation of the coming of Christ to us through the scripture) to find the way back to the right. Because there's *that in* us, to be a god, which confirms to us that there's truth in this – a god like that who loves like that – His Son becomes our sin-bearer and dies on our behalf...and what the destiny is of those who are lost...and then what is offered us in the gospel – forgiveness and eternal life and sonship. These things register within as *truth* because basically in our being, we can know what truth is.

And that *leads* us by our free choice (it's possible for us *not* to make the choice) so we want to move out of this wrong life we have, geared to our self-interests and our self-centeredness, and move **in** to the relationship we *should* have with God. And that is where we use our 'royal faculty' (which is the faculty of choice, which we call *faith*) for its true purpose. We've *always* lived by faith because faith is not mental acceptance (it *includes* understanding something, believing something), but faith is my inner self relating myself to something. That's why it's the *word* of faith – I'll do this; I'll go there; I'll say that". We've inwardly moved to something. In this outer world we then fulfill our inward movement by outer action. We say, "I'll go there"...we take our car and go there. "I'll eat this"...we take our hands and eat it. This is the only way by which humans ever experience something...because then we experience the thing we take. We experience the place we go to, and the faith becomes dissolved in the fact. When we say we'll come here this morning – that's my faith; I'll come here. Now I say that by believing through the invitation there's a house to come to. I can't prove it. I believe it. But belief isn't enough; I say, "I'll come." That's faith. Faith isn't just the invitation's there, but faith says, "I'll come."

Now humanly, in this case, I'm able to do it. I'll use my feet or my car – I come. They're just conveying my faith here. Now when I *get* here, I don't *believe* I am. I'm in the place; it's become a *fact* to me! Here's the house. I'm in it. So faith dissolves and becomes fact. It disappears and becomes experience. You take food; you believe it...take it. It becomes you. So faith is the only way in which we operate in any situation – because we've moved into it by faith, it's become a *fact* to us; we operate in it.

173

Now the moment we've become sufficiently disillusioned about our lost condition (see it to be a wrong condition, because we have these inner influences on us from the word of God and through our own inner responses) and we'd like to have the wrong condition replaced by the right and be brought back into right relationship with God (and Jesus Christ came to *get* us into that right relationship) then we take that *greatest* step we've ever taken through our eternal history, I suppose, when we transfer our believing capacity – our faith capacity – from relating to things and things around us, to Him. But the great step is we are here relating ourselves to things which are materially reachable, visible to us...we just move into them. *Now* we are relating ourselves to Someone who doesn't belong to the material realm at all!

For the first time in our human history, we're saying the *real* is spirit – because when we relate ourselves to Him, we're not relating ourselves to just a *crucified* Christ, because crucified Christ is history. You believe that, and that's history – into the tomb. The *risen* Christ is beyond history. Reason can never give you resurrection. What is it? Lots of people believe a crucified Christ who *never believe* a resurrection...because resurrection is someone who has gone beyond history into either reality or unreality. Which is it? Is it just something phony, or is it real?

Now we've come to the point in our need where we're prepared to say, "This One is risen...Who is a living Person in a spirit dimension – the fourth dimension – the spirit dimension is the real Person!" And we *accept* His offer. We can be related to Him as the Savior. So we take the step, and somewhere along the line, we express that word of faith...which means we have now accepted Him – receiving Him as a Savior.

I was talking to someone who came to see me where I'd just been to Memphis, and a woman about 45, and she wanted God, always wanted God, and we talked about certain things and I could *see* she was trying to run her problems from her own reason. And it occurred to me she had never come into the living relationship with God. And I asked her, and she said, "No, I haven't." I said, "Would you like to?" "Oh yes; yes, I'd like to!" she said. "Well, that's quite easy then...like to do it now?" "Yes." And being a very religious person, she wished to kneel to do it, so I bowed my knees (for about the first time in 30 years) with her and we knelt there. And I said, "Now *you say* it. You are saying that you're receiving this offer of Jesus Christ to be your Savior and Lord and so on, and so she kept saying, "Now Lord, I want You to be this to me, and I want You to take my life, and want

174

You to be my Savior." So I said to her, "I don't want to waste my time or yours; you're only wasting time. And not only that, you're being very rude because when someone offers you something and you say, 'Please give it to me', you're implying they haven't offered it to you. If a person offers you a plate of cookies, you don't say, 'Please give me cookies'. You're implying the cookies aren't very nice or you don't believe the offer. You're insulting the person. If it's offered to you, all you do is say, 'Thanks, I'll take it.'" So I said, "You best start again and you'd better thank Him that you've taken Him and He's taken you."

"Oh, that's it!" she said. "That's it!" So I said, "What's it?" "Oh, I'm God's now; God's got my life now." So it's the *word* of faith, isn't it? And by the same principle of faith, faith is a means of experiencing – faith dissolves and *becomes*. You're *in* it! You say you'll come into this room and you're in the room. You don't say, "I *believe* I'm in the room. I *am* in the room." Faith dissolved. "I believe" is faith. "I *believe* I'll go there." I *go* there. That is faith. Fact! I don't *believe* that, I'm here! So faith dissolves and becomes fact...and so in this case. But in *this* case, the greatest moment in our human history has come, which is into our inner consciousness...what the bible calls a witness is born to us – conveys to us a recognition, "Well, He *is* my Savior. God *does* love me. He *has* forgiven me. I *am* God's." That's the spiritual substance.

You come here; the home is your material substance...I'm *here*. We move our faith onto the level of the Spirit in receiving the risen Jesus Christ; now back comes to our inner self – consciousness - He's your Savior. "He's my Savior," and so on. And we start to discover *The Life* as my *inner* self. I don't know it yet, but it's actual fact in *union* with the Spirit of the universe – Spirit. And I have received a consciousness which is so real to me that you can take the world and leave me Jesus. He's the real One to me, and the rest can go! And so I've entered into this new Reality.

It has had two effects on me...inward effects on me, which are part of the evidence of the reality. One is a sense of peace – sense of coming into harmony acceptance and welcome with God. The other is a new motivation of love. I can't *help* now beginning to love. I can't help beginning to love He who has been revealed to me as One who loved me like that...and died for me like that...and the Father accepts me like that. This is the *substance* of my being now a son of God. Because the being of God is love; the basis of His being is He exists for His universe. He is love. His purpose is having a Son Who has sons who are what He is – basically lovers. The basis of their being will be to complete, and to perfect, and to fulfill any for whom they're responsible. Not — they benefit us and we benefit them; we're for them! That's love. We've had the first evidence of that in the new birth, because we finally just can't help loving God, and then wanting my neighbors to know and have what I've got. What we *haven't found*, is what is the *true* working basis to this new love life...Lover-life. I've got to experience this. I have the peace, and I express the love, and I know that is the consequence of my relationship with Christ, the Spirit witnessing to — we are in this *relationship* which has introduced me through Christ to the Father. So I'm in the family. I know that much, but I have not got yet what it is to be a *person* in full working focus.

The reason is quite simple. The only life I've ever known is the life geared to a separated outlook, which I've been saying from the beginning. Things are things...and people are people...and I'm I...and God's God. That's the only interpretation of life we had — I'm a person, you're a person, here's a thing. That's our whole relationship with life and with God too. So that, of course, has become a habit of life to us. Now it's a revelation for it to become the reality to me, that this outer concept of what I am and what you are — the separate concept — is only an illusion. And the truth is a union. And the first form of that union is *my inner self and God's inner self as one*.

That's incomprehensible to me! Because I've been so used to the other, that's the *lost truth*. We've been living in the illusion — separation — because we've lost the truth of our basic union, the unity of the universe. So we're trying to make the new life in Christ operate on an *impossible* basis — of me, as a separated self, functioning as a new self, a new creation in Christ, under the motivation of His Spirit...but thinking that the way it works is that He'll make me as an independent sort of person, a better kind of person...and that I should become an effective representative of Christ — expressing His character and being like Him, and so on. That is impossible, but I don't know it's impossible. It's impossible because the whole meaning of a *separated* self is a self-affirming self, a self-loving self. That's what the Fall was. We entered into what appears separation — individual life — because we chose to go our own way and be ourselves, we were lost to any *true* union for which we were created (to be expressions of God Who is self-giving love), and we entered instead into the way of life which we were peoples of self-loving love.

Now self-loving love can't conquer self-loving love. So I seek to be myself, even with God's help, and combat all the solicitations of the flesh around me, because I'm in a *whole world* here which exists to please itself, to gratify itself, to affirm itself, to get what it wants. That's the whole atmosphere we're in. So it *continually* streams something into us through our flesh. Our flesh is used to responding to that. It responds to self-gratification, it's pride, it's inquisitiveness and so on. So it's *impossible* now for I, who's regarded as a person for myself, my independence is – I'm for myself.

That's why I got the consciousness of independence. Now is it possible for me to combat that? I've got a new motivation and spirit, but He can't help *me* to conquer my fears or my hates or my lusts or my reactions. So I'm in a bind. I want to. I should like the law of God after the inner man. To will is present with me. I want to because I'm a new creature, I've got the new motivating spirit...but I can't! Because I think I'm just myself doing it, and independent self is a self-loving self, self-seeking self at its basis...and self can't conquer self. When I'm pulled that way, I can't conquer wanting to go that way; that's the way I want to go! So I'm in a dichotomy. I want to and don't want to. My flesh wants to and my spirit doesn't want to.

Now this was where Paul brought in his revelation through the letter to the Galatians of the fact that we're spirit people (inner people), not matter people (external people). As our relationship to Christ crucified – Christ risen. We're not an *outer* relationship, because we didn't die physically with Christ; we weren't risen physically with Christ. It's a spiritual relationship. That's another entire dimension... *spiritually*, we're crucified with Christ; *spiritually* we're risen with Him, and *spiritually* we ascended. That's largely an unknown relationship to even us redeemed people in our first steps. We haven't reached into being Holy Spirit people. We're earth people under Spirit influences, Spirit's control. But *mainly,* we're our separated human selves.

Paul said he got this revelation, which was really the *whole* gospel, that humans are spirit-people joined to Spirit, only in outer form. Our *real* self is our inner self joined to The Inner Self of the universe. The rest is just clothing. In Arabia he escaped from Damascus, let down from the wall by a basket. It could possibly be that disturbed him, because he brought that up among the list of sufferings he had years after to the Corinthians. The last suffering he mentioned, or last incident he mentioned...he'd been beaten so many times, been shipwrecked and so on...once they let me down by a wall in a basket. I *wonder* whether at that time there was a mixture there between self-effort and God.

And this was the way they planned to get him out. The governor of Damascus wanted to arrest him, surrounding the town with soldiers to arrest him. And they planned this, letting him down by a rather humiliating method, in a basket through the wall he escaped. And that disturbed him. It didn't seem like a very miraculous deliverance from *God*. He had a miraculous conversion, and he had come into a kind of a living Jesus. Didn't *seem* much like the living Jesus, running away...being packed away in a basket and running. It could be...I couldn't *prove* that, except that he mentioned it twice over. It's remained...this disturbing characteristic. And of course, the negative is always the way to the positive and so determines our blessings. They *condition* us to find the answer to our disturbance. That's why *all* our negatives in life are our blessings; they condition us to find deliverances! Anyhow, it took him to Arabia...the desert. So much *now* present goings on in the world. And in this same letter, he brought out the illustration from Mt. Sinai as the place where the law was presented...as *against the New Jerusalem of grace*. It may have been *there* that he went to Sinai, and there to *face out* this *whole question* of the law...which is one of the issues of this letter.

The meaning and value of *law* is to confirm to us what we are or ought to be. The whole world is *law*...but when it's *right*, you're part of it to enjoy it. We made *sure* those men would never try to go to the moon if they weren't quite sure of certain scientific laws which to the millionth of an inch were not changeable...or you wouldn't risk the moon! So the law's a pleasant thing – it's how a thing works when you work *with* it. Law is valuable when you don't work with it to warn you that you better *get* with it. If not, you're in trouble. That's why we have laws by which a *nation* runs – to get some harmonious living on a national and social level. So the value of law after we've found the final secret...law's only *part* of it. That's its value. It's troublesome when you're not part of it. It's a healthy trouble-some, healthy trouble. Taken on a physical level, I enjoy my bodily laws. I don't think of them...my eyes seeing, and my tongue is obviously speaking, and my tummy's working, and my legs are moving, and I've got a whole marvelous mass of laws working...marvelous, marvelous! I enjoy; I'm a *part* of them until I get a pain.

Now a pain's saying, "You're out of touch here. Something's gone wrong here. Get it right." So the pain is painful, but valuable, because it says, "Hurry, get that right." That's why I thank God we feel pain when we touch a hot thing. Otherwise, you'd get burned to death. I worked among leprosy people, and the problem among them is their burns, because they all sleep in huts with their fires. We all do in Africa, on the floor. But they have no feeling, and they wake up to find they've been sleeping with their head in the fire and are all burned up! Never *know*. So pain's most valuable! It makes you jump, but it also says, "Get it right." So the law sets you to work to get a thing right. "Get the doctor or get your faith." You've got faith better than the doctor...and get it right!

So the law came along (most carefully and helpfully) to get us right. We're *so* blind that we try to justify sin. I mean you take one thing: you take our sweetness to each other. It's mostly pure sentiment, not love. See, love is a readiness to give yourself, no matter how you *feel* at all. You're just *there* for people. You're there as a basic harmony in which you're there to contribute to other people's needs. That's love! Has nothing to do with sentiment. And most of our sweetness is mere sentiment, and we mistake it for love until we get scratched, and then we don't love the person we're sweet to. That's the point!

See, love's the person who *isn't* sweet to you. But the human love only loves the people who are sweet to you. That's why God's love is - when we *didn't* love Him, He bore our sins. That's the proof. So in other words, we fool ourselves, and we're under all sorts of 'nicenesses' in a nice, harmonious civilization...nice kindnesses. It's mostly convenient sweetness...it isn't love...because we shouldn't be so nice to a person unless he's first nice to us. Now *that* means revelation. It's *radical*. The bible's *radical*. That was the value of law coming along; that's why there was a Decalogue. The Decalogue was the 10 commandments. Because the *very thing* happened!

We *so fool* ourselves...they become God's people! They *knew* they were God's people. They'd been redeemed Israel from Egypt through the Passover lamb, and all the miracles of the plagues, and come through the Red Sea. They are God's people...but mediated by Moses. They were baptized under Moses, because Moses was almost like a savior to them, and they came through and they were God's people. Oh! They were God's and God said to them, "I've got great promises for you, My precious people. I liken you to an eagle carrying his little ones on his wings; I bore you like eagles...beautiful...out here to talk to you (to Mt. Sinai) and I'm going to talk to you, because you're *precious* people. You're My people; you're a peculiar people.

Of course, they didn't know then that the whole world could be. It was too early for that to come out yet. Because *all* people...the Egyptians were just as much God's people as Israel. They didn't know that, and we don't know that too well *yet*; we're *just* knowing it. So this was the early days, of course, but it was very precious.

Then He had to put it: "Alright," He says. "You don't know what. I'm going to make you what you really *are* when you find yourself – a kingdom of priests. Now priests are for others; priesthood is you lay your life down for *others*; you're here to relate *others* to God. Having been related yourself, you want to *share* that relationship with others. Then they find their true relationship! A priest is for others...a high priest for others – intercession. So He said, "You're going to be a whole *kingdom of priests*. Not a high priest, but *all of you* – priests. All of you are going to be a bunch of other-lovers. That's what the church is, of course. A bunch of other-lovers – priests. All beautiful. Now that *suits* us, because underneath, we know exactly what we ought to be. We know we ought to love and be loved, and in some sense want to; at least we want to *be* loved, and don't mind giving a little love now and then maybe. So that appeals to us, and it appealed to them. Now watch! In order to expose it *has* to be exposed. He quietly said on this occasion, and this was Moses speaking to the Jews at Sinai. This was *before* the law, before the fire was burning there and all that, because that only came when *self* couldn't take it...before the tabernacle. It's the first quiet word. He said, "I'm going to have a covenant with you...this is My covenant. You're *that* to Me, *if* you fulfill My covenant...if you go along with Me. Now you see – exposure? They were all gaily, "We'll do it. **All** that God says to us, we'll do!" You see? Deceived! They *thought* they were other-lovers. They were not other-lovers. Nor are you and I! They weren't other-lovers; they were self-lovers. They were there for their convenience. They weren't there to die for the Egyptians. Not at all. They didn't know. You see their blindness? We think we are, and the sweet world thinks it's sweet, and it isn't at all.

So God in His mercy – *that's* why God brought the Ten Commandments. Now it's always *been* there. A very significant fact is – how did Joseph know he should be pure? How did he know when everything was against him? He'd been *horribly* treated. He was a slave and a prisoner...and he was given an opportunity to express his lusts – to have a secret affair with Potiphar's wife. Why didn't he do it? How did he know he *shouldn't*? There was no law. Law is in here [indicating within]. It was hundreds of years before the law was given. He said, "Oh, before God, I can't do that. My Boss trusts me. I can't sin against my Boss like that."

So you see, the consciousness of right or wrong is there deep down, but it's very much hidden. That's why Paul said, "By the law did I have the knowledge of sin." And you're only direct condemnation when the law is *said* to you. Now the law says what you ought to be. So there the Ten Commandments came down to show you what you ought to *be*. This was to show up they were *not* that of course. All of us! That's the value of law.

Now here comes law in to redeem. This is a bit awkward! This is law for the redeemed...not the unredeemed. Now we understand that law brought the condemnation and the curse for those who didn't fulfill it...and when we come to see...put the whole world under condemnation. That's how we found *our* condemnation – through the law. And then we found that Christ had *taken* the curse of the law. That's in Galatians...and wiped out the guilt and judgement and damnation which has come to us as lost people...wiped the whole thing out. The law's out, isn't it? We're free from the law, aren't we? And Paul actually says here and in Romans, "We're *dead* to the law." In 2:19, "I through the law am dead to the law." And he says this in Romans 7... "I'm *dead* to the law." But they weren't...he's talking about the law. The *whole issue* is – you're caught up by the law. This is what Galatians *is*. Don't get caught up by the law!

But they were redeemed people; they'd all left the law behind, hadn't they? Apparently they hadn't. Why not? Because the **final sin is – I run my life**. I can run my life – that's my final sin. It isn't *how* I run it. I know it arouses our hates and all, but those are its *products*. It may produce hates and fears and lusts, and so on...they're products – I'll have my own way; I'm myself; I'll run my own life.

Now the *highest* subtle form is I run my life well. I'll be a good person, not a bad person. That's a higher self; that's a higher form of sin. I'll be a good person. Of course, I turn out to be a bad person anyhow, but I'll at least *think* I'll be a good person. Now, *this* was the final issue. In this *partial* understanding of my relationship to God, I still carried with me what I'd been *used to* all my human history – I'm a person and I had to be fine there. I told you, we've got to be this sort of human *forever*. We have to be responsible people, thinking, willing, acting persons. We don't *lose* our personality, we gain it! So it's right I find my person. I had to find that in the Garden of Eden – I'm a person! And somehow I've got to retain that. So I'm retaining it! Now *surely*, I'll be the kind of person I ought to be. Now I've got Christ...I'm redeemed now. I've got the Holy Spirit witnessing to me I'm a child of God. I can call on God. I'm alive unto *God*...not yet God's alive in me. There's a *difference*. I'm alive unto God, but it's still separate. I'm alive unto God "...reckoning ourselves dead to sin, *alive unto God* through our Lord Jesus Christ."

Now that's where Romans 6 doesn't take you into union. Romans 6 takes you into union on the *negative* level...cut off from the old...doesn't take you into union on the *positive* level, which is Rom. 8. So we have to go through this second phase of disillusionment...when *somewhere* my heart is set right; I delight in the law of God in the inward man; I'm a new creature in Christ; I'm motivated by the Spirit; or I *want* to be — like Jesus. You can't be 'like' Jesus, you can only *be* Jesus...but you haven't known that. You can't be *like* Jesus. You can only *be* Jesus. That's *too deep* for the separated person. That's blasphemy to the separated person! "You say you're Jesus? You say you're God? Who are you?" It's blasphemy! To an unsaved person, it's even blasphemy to say you're saved...God's accepted you. That's blasphemy to them! We have a *higher* blasphemy. The unsaved people say, "Who are you to say God's forgiven you? How are you going to say that! Taking God for granted that He accepts y*ou*. How do you think that God accepts *you*? *That's* blasphemy. You shouldn't *say* things like that."

We say we *do* say things like that and there's a *higher* blasphemy. We don't say, "I'm like Jesus. I *am* Jesus." Oh, wow! It's your bible people who will attack you then. But there's a hidden secret here. There's a gap *filled* here...a bridge has crossed here. This is what he crosses!

So he says, "I had to find this final truth, which is the fact of my innerness...our inwardness...our spirit-self is the *real* self." A spirit's a union, whereas we've lived in this other separated life he says, "I've found that out." He said, "It's not *really* a new thing. You all know it." Actually, when he *wrote* this, he'd already taught this. It was a familiar teaching, but they hadn't grabbed it. They heard it but had not grabbed it. For certain reasons, it hadn't become a fact to them. So he was telling them what he'd always taught, but it had to come home to them now. That's how he put it in the Galatians letter. And he said, "I'm going to tell you what that new truth is — you know light. You'd die for it, (we're doing I John now). He said, "Light is inner inspiration. To the outer senses, light is this, which only affects your life everything is light, everything is just radiation waves of light...E=mc squared, as Einstein found for us. Everything is light! All these things are light in a variety of forms. And so light comes as a sound, the speed of light...sound! So the speed of light is sight. So the speed of light is sense. You touch things. That's *outer* light. They're the outer forms in which light is expressed, because you can never know a thing *outwardly* except by its contrast. So you only know light if there's darkness. I can only know sweet through bitter...electricity – positive/negative.

So outer light is only known because it isn't darkness. And sound is certain noise against silence...against its opposite. Sight. Everything is known by its opposite. That's outer. That's the fallen sense life. Inner life is being light. God is light. These are lights. He gives lights. Light is separation. Light comes through light and dark. Sweet and bitter. It's only known by its opposite. And it brings itself out in different forms like that. That's the outer manifestation. But God *is* light. Now you can't *know* that, you can only *be* that. You can't know a *single* thing...you only know it by its opposite.

Now God has no opposite. God has no darkness! So you can't *know*, as we know outwardly. That's the sense world. That's the fallen world. We all know light by sound. We call it sound; it's really light...and we all know light by sight. We all know light by touch. We just call it those things. They're all just that. We know they're all just atomic science and all. We all know that. That's outer. We *think* that's knowledge. That's knowledge *about*. It isn't knowledge; we think it is. All science is knowledge *about*...it isn't knowledge. It's just knowledge *about* things.

Knowledge is being. Knowledge is – in you something *is*. When we come to Christ, what happens? There's something *inside* you. A light! A light! Oooh, *that's it*! Light is inner knowledge. That's light. Call it inspiration. It's a spark. Light is inspiration and ecstasy. Ahhh, that's *it*. Life's ecstasy! Inspiration's ecstasy!

Now, outer light isn't that. Outer light's interesting. I *hear*, and I *see*, and it's helpful; it doesn't give me inspiration and ecstasy. It's just that I have those effects and use them. Inside, I know. Now that's what God is; that's what we are. That's why you've got to *be* God. You can't know Him. You know outer light. You and He, you don't know yourself. You only are; you don't know yourself. You only *are*. I am...that's all. This is what I am. Its effect *on* us inside is this, "*Oh, this is it. This is reality.*" The inner faith has become inner consciousness.

This is what Paul had. That's why he says, "I had a revelation!" He says, "If I preach any other gospel, I'll be accursed. I'll be misusing you and myself." That's to be accursed. "If another angel.....Nooo, I *know* this. It's come to me what *is*." So do we! You live in the end not by a bible; you live what you are inside yourself. Abraham was a pretty good father to us all, and he had no bible. So he had God with no bible. So don't say the bible is the way. It's a means to an end. The end is *He*. The book merely brings us to a Person. It's the Person through the book, not the book...and Abraham found that Person with no book...and he's our father, the father of the faithful. It's sight in the *beyond*. And you in the end don't live by the bible. It may be to help you in the end...because 'that' to me is *real*. That to me is real. That's it! That's light – that *inner* inspiration, conviction. Ecstasy – *that's it!* And you would *die* for that one. We may have some fun in outer things (we do), we make that fun, but it isn't real fun. In reality it isn't real fun. It misses the final note. You know what that is. Unfortunately, sometimes it happens in our partnerships. That's why, of course, the Lord says if you marry in time, marry in the Lord. I talked to a family yesterday who has come for the Lord...has a good husband and a good home, but not *real* because he doesn't know the Lord. See he *misses* the final point. She said sometimes I'm up against my husband. I said you're bound to be because the final isn't an outer relationship. You lose a 'good' relationship into a *new* relationship. You see, an outer relationship can *never* give you it, because we're not outer people...not when you've got the inner. Because, you see, the inner is the truth. And this is what Paul had. So he said this in a strong way. He said, "I did confirm it." He said, "I'm one, the least of the apostles, the last of the apostles." He said, "I did go to Jerusalem after three years; I did consult with them. I'd come very free of man. They're nothing to me; whatsoever they are, means nothing to me. They aren't 'big boys' to me, because I'm one of the 'big boys' myself, if we're sons. Why should they be 'big boys'? We're all 'big boys'. We're all God's! It means nothing to me that they're Peter, James and John. I didn't go because they're big people, but I *did* go because they were the originators – the agents of the light to me. I want to make sure that my light agrees with their light. That's fair; they were there before me. They were Jesus' own chosen people." He was in the church like "one born out of due time", he said – Paul was. So he did go that much.

Then he said, "We had a crisis." A very remarkable crisis...right with the human founder of the church. That's why he wouldn't follow man. The human founder of the church was Peter. Now "upon this rock", and he's the man of Pentecost. He was the mouthpiece of Pentecost...the speaker! The first great speech of Pentecost – Peter! So he was the head of the human [church]...leading man. He said, "We met a *crisis*." Perhaps from further on...his final crises in the history of the church of Christ.

Peter, of course...Peter *knew!* But mind you, it's one thing to have had the experience; it's another thing to know what you've *got*. Peter had Pentecost. He was the first to *have* Pentecost...tongues and everything. He didn't wholly *know* what he'd got! It proves it now. So there is something more than experience. It's the knowledge of what you've got. That's why the bible tells you, you're only safe when you *understand* what's working...what's *happening*! That's the value of what I'm talking about...the value of the bible and so on.

Peter didn't. This great Peter! He *did* know a great deal. He'd had the vision from heaven with the great sheet of different animals, and what God has chosen don't you call common. And that's prepared him to go to the Gentiles, to go to Cornelius to take the gospel to the Gentiles. So he was a great pioneer and broke away. But he still *didn't know* the whole works. Why? Because there was a strong influence, a very dangerous influence, in Jerusalem which was a mixture of "We've got Christ, but *we're Jews*...and we're *Godly Jews*...and there are certain things we should do to keep our faith and to build ourselves up." and certain conformities you have...outer conformities that are the right kind of things Christians should do – go to church on Sunday and silly nonsense like that, or Wednesday (if I were you, I wouldn't go at all again. That's up to you. I haven't for 30 yrs.). Or you must do this; you must do that. Now there's this *business*. You see we're independent people; we've got Christ, but now there are certain ways which we must conform our lives, build ourselves up, improve ourselves etc.

And so it mentions in this book about 'keeping the Sabbath, holy days, religious observance'...it comes here in the 4th chapter, "You would turn to weak and beggarly elements; you observe days and months and times and years (4:9-10). So Peter had this influence on him, although he'd broken through. And he broke through to the point that he'd come to Antioch, which was the great thriving Pentecost, first Gentile church, under which Peter, Paul and Barnabas went to preach, to take the gospel to us all. This was this great church and he visited them. And he had broken through a great deal on the question of customs – you should eat this; you shouldn't eat that, all these inhibitions. Instead he ate with the Gentiles. They'd broken up the idea that Jews shouldn't eat with the Gentiles and that special kosher food Jews have...and all that stuff.

185

Then, whenever the pressure came on in Jerusalem, and James was the elected head apostle...head elder, I suppose by election. That's James the brother of the Lord. The other James had been martyred...the Apostle James. And he sent a group of obviously aggressive Jews, redeemed Jews, saved people, up from Jerusalem to say something about all these laws you should keep – to tie up their liberty. They were too *free* to *do* what they like; too much rejoicing in the Lord and praying, anyhow. I suspect they did all sorts of funny things in their services – speaking in tongues and all sorts of things they shouldn't do...and set these people up. Peter was there eating with them. And they had these *certain* laws...one of them was who you eat with or what you eat, I suppose. And it says that Peter feared them and separated himself from the Gentiles with whom he was having living fellowship when they'd all eaten. And even tender-hearted Barnabas, who was a very precious person, tried to throw Paul *out*...we owe Paul to Barnabas...defended them likewise. He withdrew and separated himself, *fearing* those who were of the circumcision. See the point – if you sacrificed was part of it. You must have certain outer forms to outwardly show you belong to Christ now. You must still have outer forms showing you belong...certain laws you keep. Circumcision's *one* of them. Therefore, I said they appeared dead...doesn't say they were redeemed people. I assume they *were*. At least they came from James! Well, James was the one who wrote the letter, so I assume they were redeemed people.

They separated themselves and other Jews disassembled likewise, and even *Barnabas* was carried away by their dissimilation! And *there* Paul came out, because Paul *had* the basic revelation...and you *stand* by what you've got. He had an understanding that Peter hadn't got. As usual, a crisis. A negative situation is the very thing where the positive, where the light shines out. Light shines out of darkness. And this is the moment when this thing was established...and Paul *came out* with it.

Now you see what had happened! Peter was in the union, but didn't know it. He didn't know what union meant...he was just now a redeemed spirit with the Holy Spirit...One. And that's all he was. He walked freely with this person or what this person said to him or did. That's all. And *knowing I'm a man* standing up so right...in this *new* dimension of simply – walk as God, with God, and doing everything God says to you. That's all. Free as can be...no other laws on you...because you are the law, because the law is love. Now love is an asset when you're in it. And when you come into Christ you are the law because the law is love. The only law of the universe is...God is love. That's the only law there is! And you are that love because you are the law. So it's no longer this outer law shouting at you. That's why we're dead to the law.

But while you think you're yourself and God will make you something, then God says, "Be that!" because you've still got the false idea that your self can *become* that. Your self in itself is a self-loving self, not a self-giving self. You're only a self-giving self if you're *one* with The Self-giver! When you *find* truth that you must be *joined* to the Divine Spirit, you've found *the truth*! Do you know that *by yourself,* you're still a self *for* yourself? You've cut yourself off! You're *really*...underneath...the spirit of error! Although he doesn't live in you now that you're redeemed...it's the flesh he comes through, and so on.

Now Peter didn't *know* that! He *was* that, but didn't know it! How do you prove it? Why? Peter had these two opposites we all have. He was *very* fearful...and *very* bold. The two go together. They're two sides of the same thing. If you're a fearful person, you're a bold person. And we know his fear; we know how he denied Jesus, but this is after Pentecost and after this and this and this, "You crucified Jesus Christ." He was the boldest of the bold at Pentecost, and after Pentecost. He headed them all in boldness. They put him in prison, you know, and all that. So on one side he was a coward and on the other, a man of total courage. Same thing. *All* negative and *all* positive are the same thing...in different ways. Love is hate, and hate is love. It just depends on which side you're on of it. Everything is only one thing...in the two are different sides, that's all.

Now you see if Peter had *known* – settled where Paul had..."I'm not I, I'm Christ in me." Now the human in him (the flesh) remained wrought with fear. Here it was! Now if he'd *known union* when this hit..."Ohhhh, will this cause division or something...*Oh, whatsoever*...what's the Lord saying?" Of course the Lord would say "Oh, you walk on with people." He would have walked on and dissolved the fears. Because he *didn't* know that he was in human fears and showed it. So it showed, he didn't know union. If he'd *known* union, he wouldn't have gone like that. He would have replaced his human fear by God's courage, and stood where he *knew* he should have stood, of course...in this union with the Gentiles. And that's where Paul brought out his great statement.

He said, "Now I want to tell you something else; I want to remind you of it. You know that we Jews and Gentiles were not just found by works of the

187

law, but by the faith of Christ. You Jews by nature (vs 16), you *know* a man's not justified by the works of the law, but by the faith of Jesus Christ, and so *we Jews,* who know Jesus Christ, are justified by faith in Christ, not by the works of the law. By the works of the law shall no flesh be justified."

Now that's the *external*, you see. Now yes, we know that by the works of the law, I'm not justified because I'm a Jew, because I've done good works...because I haven't done good works. I've kept the temple laws. He knew that. That's the old self-righteousness...about building up their righteousness. Peter knew that! He knew that his day as a Jew, a sinner, and justified in the grace of God. He knew that outwardly. So he knew an outer Cross.

Now here's the difference! There's an outer Cross in history. There's an inner Cross where you are...where **I'm** in the Cross. That's a different one. That's a spirit-Cross. The other's a body-Cross; that's a spirit-Cross. That's the difference!

Therefore, as he went on now to speak to the Galatians in the next verse he said, "Didn't you know, oh foolish Galatians, who has bewitched you before whose eyes Jesus Christ has evidently been set forth crucified?" Their eyes out *here*! [indicating to the external] So they knew more; they knew an outer Christ. Outer Christ was in history and took away my outer sins and saved me from death and from hell. That's wonderful! So I'm accepted by God. I'm in God's righteousness. I'm in God's sight righteous as Christ is. I'm in God's family...but it still has outer connotations. Jesus Christ was set before me crucified. You've got the same in Roman's 3 where it says – "Whom God has set forth to be a propitiation" (verse 25, Romans 3). You are *justified* by faith which is in Christ Jesus whom God has set forth"...outside you, outside you.

Now you see we *do know* more than that or you can't be born again. You do know the Spirit or you can't be born again. You're born again *by* inner knowledge. You *have* come to know it isn't an outer Christ only. You know that. It is an inner Jesus to you or the inner Spirit. And really the Spirit dimension is open to you, but you haven't quite got the final step, which is – you're wholly that and that's all you are! Now *that* is when my *real* self has been crucified with Christ; my real self is risen with Christ and steady with Christ and we're *one* there. I'm spirit joined with Spirit and my flesh is just outer form.

Now that's why Paul advises and says, "Peter, listen to this. We're dead to the law. Now, you again are caught up by this law as if you're an independent person running life. Then do it; do it! Be that. And you've got the idea; you *should* keep the circumcisions and some things. You should do it...be a good outer Christian with outer conformities. You got afraid and mixed up with that thing, and you're under the law while you think you ought to be. You're shown up by the law because what you *ought* to be you *can't* be, of course! Won't work! It just comes out in self-effort. See? So there's the 'law to'. He says, "Peter, you're dead to the law." Why am I dead to the law? He says, "I, through the law...the law got me wrong and Jesus Christ got me right. I am dead to the law and alive unto God." Now...then he says, "Unto God...no that's not enough! It isn't unto God." I am crucified with Christ. "*I* am crucified with Christ: nevertheless I live. No! *Not I, but Christ lives in me.*" Now he says, "The life I now live, I live by the faith of the Son of God"...which is faith.

Faith is recognition. Faith is having. I told you faith disappears and becomes fact. So it isn't believing Jesus Christ, it's *recognizing* that's what *I am*! I'm in this relationship...some of the fun – I'm one! He lives in me. I'm one with Him and more than one – *He's the real me!* Because I live, I don't live; Christ lives in me...He's the Real Person living in me. It's Christ, not *I*. Now *that's* a leap in!

Now that, Peter...you live this but didn't know it, because you haven't settled into the *fact*, you get shaken. You see, you're no longer a Peter an Apostle. You're Peter Christ...Christ in Peter's form! You're crucified as a Peter with your fears and doubts and courage and all that stuff. God will *use* your humanity, but that's another matter. What you really are is a crucified Peter, a risen Peter, and the real risen Peter is Christ in Peter. It isn't you at all. You're in union; you're replaced with the union and you're Christ in Peter form...and you live by that recognition now. Now **that's** the revelation!

And he *then* said to the Galatians they'd taken up the same problem...they hadn't understood. "Having begun in the Spirit are you made perfect by the flesh? Are you so foolish?" They *knew* the Spirit. "This only would I learn of you (Galatians 3:2). Received ye the Spirit by the works of the law or by the hearing of faith? Are you so foolish having begun in the Spirit, are you made perfect by the flesh?" So you see, you can have experience without knowledge. "You've *begun* in the Spirit" but they didn't quite *know* because they'd run back to the other – thinking they're back to themselves with the

Spirit motivating them or something. No they're not! They're *Christ* in total! *That's* the jump over.

Now to jump over...*very few* bible-believers *take* it. It's too far. I've been having a very thrilling two or three days writing the story that's coming out about this, and this friend is helping me type it, of this man who's launched this *tremendous* outer launch of faith in Memphis. It's the largest Christian school in the country with 4,000 students – a magnificent place. And he's built the whole thing by faith...moved to sixty-five million dollars when he had nothing! He's a man about thirty-five. I've been with him. Now this man, he caught it through us. He listened to us and *caught* this law of faith. He caught more than it; he caught the inner Jesus. Of course he'd been redeemed, but he lived by the strain and stress and long praying. "I don't pray anymore, I just enjoy the Lord," he says. He's a great pastor of a great church of thousands. He says, "I don't even preach the gospel; I preach Christ in you and they get saved. Ohhh, they *get* stuff!" He's taken on new things. He's caught it! He's taken on new things about faith values.

He went to the Presidential Prayer Breakfast and he wandered in (I don't know how he got a seat as you're usually appointed to seats) and he saw a table with only two men on it...two Naval men...and he sat down and they said, "You're welcome; come join us." They introduced themselves to him, and he to them, and he has some service interest. I thought he'd been in the Navy, but someone told me he'd been in the Air Force. He had a *concern* for service men and particularly for the naval people. He has a TV thing himself and talked about his audio visual stuff, and he said I've got a great burden to get out cassettes with *real* bible teaching for remote Navy stations here and there and where the men are these days who are hungry for God and so on. I'd like to have some system where we can get all the original stuff scattered out through the services in remote areas. This man turned out to be (sitting at the table) the Chief Chaplain, Admiral Connor, of the Navy! "Ohhh!" He said, "I'd been looking for somebody to do this long ago! All you people are so denominational minded. When I go to a denomination they say that it is not denominational enough. If it wouldn't just be Baptist, our people wouldn't want to spend the money like that. You mean to say you as one church would do that?" He said, "Oh yes, we will do that; we won't have to take it up." One man! So their whole denominations refused it, but he found one man. It cost him about half a million to start it. But this is interesting...he's *caught* the fact that he isn't he. He's the expression of the *God of the universal resources*! And his case...He's coming out *this* way!

Life is to operate universal resources. That's what we have to know...that He's an infinite Being! We're all big in our area. We're *all* big because we have a big God...so we see where our 'bigness' comes out, that's all. I'm only saying I delight in him because it isn't just outer bigness. We have great fun in The Life. He knows the Real Life and lives with ease. That's what attracted me in all this magnificent place. There's such beautiful equipment and every pupil being taught in the high school has his own electric typewriter. They all have their own microscope. It's top equipment, and they say the state schools envy this equipment they have in this high school. Because they say what God does well puts meaning into it.

What I like is that he reminds me of Rees Howells a bit...lord of all he surveys, yet got nothing. "Oh," I said, "I like this man. He isn't a big, puffy, important pastor." Now we had dinner with the man who is the best known preacher in the South (in Memphis), very well known...a very dear fellow. His wife was very interesting. She had some books and stuff. What a contrast! Now he's a *dear* fellow, but he *couldn't take it*. He *must* have burdens. He could not see what my friend's talking about...he couldn't see it! He's a preacher of the "Word". He can't see union...oh, it's too dangerous. He must carry burdens. He said, "Oh I'm a rotten old carnal thing." He's *not* a rotten old carnal thing, he's a precious man! Self-condemnation – mixing up temptation and sin. Wouldn't let himself be a *man*. And you could even see his face – be a man! But there was *freedom* in Wayne's [pastor friend] face. You could *see* it! He couldn't take it.

It came out rather interesting in this way I thought. These preachers...we were there three hours having this dinner and they kept sort of exchanging what they were going to preach about on Sunday and stuff. But this dear man, all his preaching was extracting scripture. He was going to speak on filling of the Spirit. He'd found seven references in Acts – when you're filled with the Spirit you do *that*; when you're filled with the Spirit you do *that*. His mind's around presenting scripture. Now Wayne's mind was around people. You saw what he's into – how you get the people, not what scripture said. That's the difference! One is blessed, but basically letter-minded; the other's people-minded. That's the difference! I am only giving that by way of illustration.

So you see these Galatians got caught up in the same way, because they had the experience but they hadn't moved into this tremendous fact that I'm never 'myself' again...a tremendous fact! It is experience by faith that everything else is. He goes on to say, "You Galatians, you're geared to the faith of Abraham, not to the law. I told you the law came four hundred years after Abraham. It says here in Galatians...it wasn't even given by God, but given by angels. Very interesting. It says, "The law was ordained by angels in the hands of a mediation", verse 19. Why? Because God isn't – Thou shalt. Thou shalt not. God is *being*. God isn't shouting – Thou shalt not. Thou shalt not. That's not God at all. That's something that comes from outside to show us up for what we're not. I don't know of any other way to put it. It is really a projection of our lost condition which needs to have a standard presented to us...not that we *are* that, but we ought to be and can't be, of course. That's the law.

Now he says that came four hundred years later because it showed that the people of Israel thought they had it when they hadn't got it. "I can do it" when they can't do it. They had to have the law to show they hadn't done it...to prepare them that only Christ in them could do it! And he says, "You go back to Abraham and Abraham *believed* God." That's *all* he did – *believed* God!

Now he didn't believe very much, you know. He didn't know about all we know about Christ dying and rising and so on. He knew Christ's day! Jesus said, "Abraham rejoiced to see My day." My days are quite 'me' – like some of the 'light' I live in. It isn't quite me. He couldn't quite...because Christ hadn't come in Abraham's day. He had a sense because it's the same light. Now all that Abraham did was, he believed that God, Who said to him, "Now Abraham, I'm going to bless you. You come along with Me. I'm the real Person and I'll make you a blessing to the world. You'll both be blessed and you'll pass that news to the world."

And he relates himself to God in the sense that he just accepted this to be a fact...attuned his inner being to – This is a fact! And he never built a home, but lived in tents as proof. "My real home isn't Canaan. My home is God's City, Spiritual City, which looks as a city without foundations, it says. "Abraham looked for a city without foundations which Builder and Maker is *God*." A city of God's people, of course! The rest of it doesn't matter. We're not interested in gold; we're interested in the Lord. So Abraham *had* this, you see. Now that's *all he had*. He said, "That's all. You believe *God*!"

What's 'believing God' mean? Believing God is you *move in* to what a thing is to you. That is how you see it...or who a person is to you. I mean I'm always thankful to say with the AAs...when they fall, they give themselves to a power higher than themselves for that time. Amen to that, anyhow! They may not mention that, but better *that* than looking to your own power. They commit themselves to a power beyond themselves. Well thank God...it can be a first step in finding Jesus Christ!

Now this is what faith is — as far as you *see* a thing to be, or a person to be, or a statement to be, or a fact to be...they are free. If you *want* it you'll say, "OK, that's available to me. I take that." I say, "That's mine." I go there. I kept telling you before some of these others came in — faith *has in it* a mental understanding, but faith is not a mental understanding, not mental believing or something. It's — "Yes, I see that. I'm for that thing. I'm giving myself to it." Faith is my inner self joining myself...my inner will by which I *join* myself to something.

I interchanged you when you came in, because you came here by faith. You can't prove there's a place here; you *believe* it! Now your mind believed you'd go at a point, not that you said, "I believe I'll go." Now materially speaking, you've come in your car. Your car brings your faith *here*. Now what happens? Your faith to get here becomes fact! You don't say, "I *believe* I'm here." I **am** here! You don't say, "I believe." I believe has disappeared. You're in the room! So faith has dissolved and become fact. It's been replaced by fact. So faith is *always* replaced by fact. That's what I tell you...when you take Jesus it's replaced by consciousness — Oh He's mine! Faith has disappeared and in its place is fact. Now that's what faith is.

So in this case he went on to say to the Galatians, "now stand fast in the liberty wherewith Christ has made you free." That's chapter 5 verse 1. He'd said one thing before — Replace the negative by the positive. Replacing the negative by the positive (I told you he had his mind on Sinai and Hagar and Abraham and Ishmael and so on and Isaac) and he picks it up in what's called allegory. Towards the end of the fourth chapter he says, "I want to show you about allegory. Abraham has a son — Abraham by self-effort has a son, Ishmael. This is his natural son and it was natural to have pride...of course, anybody would have, and rather particular pride because he was the son of a slave, Hagar, and yet, here he was the only son of the household — like I said, he'd got the heir you see. Self — ohhh, I'm somebody!

193

Then came the promise – the word of faith – You'll have a son when you're a hundred years old. You'll have a son by faith, and we get the victory of faith the way Abraham and Sarah had this son in their old age who was called "Laughter"...the joy of faith...Isaac! He was the son of promise. He was the son of the product of the Spirit of God. Now there came *controversy* in that family, because the other son was just proud of himself...wanted his own way; wanted their own *rights* and so on. And they fought – made controversies, Sarah and the new son, Isaac...under God's guidance, because guidance changes. Previously, God told Abraham to take Hagar back, when out of jealousy, out of resentment, Sarah put her out before the child was born.

Now it's the other way around! Sarah stood up and said, "Cast out the woman and her son. Put her out because this is now God's family starting. It's *God's* person here, and those who are on another wavelength, a self-wavelength, they mustn't be here. Cast him out." That doesn't mean God left him, because God blessed Hagar and looked after her. God's for everybody! But in *that* condition had to be cast out of disturbing this growing new family, which was God's family...out of which is going to come Jesus Christ one day. So there's a 'cast out'.

What he's saying in Galatians is – kick out this business of 'you yourself' have got laws and then the law can 'talk' to you. Cast out this self business. You are no longer an independent self; cast it out! Recognize...put it that way. You're no longer an independent self to which law can say this and that to. And then he goes on in the next verse..."Stand fast in the *liberty* for which Christ has made you free!" In other words, stand fast in what we just read in Galatians 2:20...the liberty by which Christ has made you free is that Christ in you is your freedom! You are *really* Christ, not yourself. Your real I...I live, no I don't, *Christ lives in me*. Now *that's* freedom because Christ is everything! When Christ operates *all* resources, *all liberty* is mine...or the fullness of the Being; I'm part of the Being of the universe! I'm God; I'm God in human form! Now he says, "Stand fast in that liberty", and *that* is freedom.

In other words, the way in which this union becomes knowledgeable to us, is the same way of faith. I had to do it *years* ago, and I think *most* of us do. Most of us don't *know* it at our redemption, and not even at the baptism of the Holy Spirit, apparently, because Peter didn't know it and he was baptized in the Spirit...and some of these others baptized in the Spirit. They didn't know it. So the experience of baptism in the Spirit hadn't done it. It was blessed and liberated and wonderful, but it wasn't the *final settling* into the *ultimate* of truth. And this came through the Apostle Paul.

Now he says the ultimate of truth is this – to settle into the fact that you're no longer (it's an illusion) an independent self. That's been *cut off* in Christ's death. Your independence was your *self* under the dominion of the spirit of error. You're no longer an independent self. In Christ's death you're also in Christ's resurrection, which now you're a union, and your new self is you, but it's this paradox – it's you, but it's really Christ in you and you're just the way in which Christ expresses Himself.

Now for most of us that takes a second step by a step of faith. Back again...the first step of faith was in my lost condition. I had to take it as a fact that there is a risen Person, Who doesn't belong to this dimension; He was crucified, was alive. He belongs up here...can't see Him...can't feel Him...can't know Him, know anything about Him except the bible says so. To me the bible makes Him a wonderful Person...I'm giving myself to You; I'm believing in You; I'm receiving You. Back comes to you – *Oh you have*! Oh, OK...a confirmation. Faith disappears – *Yeah, I know Him*! Spirit! Oh yes, faith has disappeared and has become knowledge. Yes, He does love me...I am saved!

Now, you've settled into a self-contained position. You *don't* get saved again. You don't question *that*. That's a settled matter. You act from that as a basis. Now he's saying this is the second one. For most of us (I don't know whether Peter had to do it...don't know) it's a sense of confirmation of what is already *there*. What's the use if you don't *know* it? It's no good having things tucked away in a bank and you don't know it's there to cash. You've got to know it's *there*.

The second strain of trying is when you move right in, because you see it in God's Word and say, "I'm saying this thing now...that through Your grace I'm in eternal union – the unity symbolized by vine and branch. Vine and branch make one tree. A vine and branch is one tree; you don't talk about the branch, you talk about the vine. So it's neither branch nor the vine in branch form. So when I see a tree I don't say, "Look at those branches." I just say, "Look at the tree." A tree is the branches, isn't it? It's trunk and branches – the whole of the tree. So the whole of me is Christ! If He is the vine and you are the branches, the branches are on the vine...and you're merely Christ in your human form...so am I! We're Christ. And **this** is the union. And this is a little too far for most people to go, and the reason is

195

that you still hang on to fear of self. You haven't got it, because like Peter, you're afraid and say, "Oh, I'm awfully *weak*. I'd *dash* into that temptation and *dash* into that one. I'm afraid of *myself* and any old thing I'll go into. I'm not safe! And that's why we *like some laws* until we know the other way. That's why we like our churches and our systems...come on Sunday and keep praying; read the bible and keep close. If you don't, you'll go bang on your face. We think we're *kept* by certain things, and we love that because we're afraid. Most of us have a *deep fear* in our Christian life – Oh I'm afraid of myself. I must have supports in bibles and prayers and stuff to support me. Unh uh...they are inspirations by which you can know a bit more about Him, but they aren't supports. Not supports!

Therefore, you see, it's a step over. I don't think you *get* it until *somewhere* it comes into you that your self can't – isn't meant to. I get through on that. Your human self isn't *meant* to. See, while I think I *ought* to...that's still law. The law will be there while I think I ought to. If I think I ought to and *don't*...and am *meant* to, then I'm condemned. Why I'm afraid of myself. I meant to and don't. I shall go and do it again! And I live dragged under by condemnation and guilts and sense of my weakness.

When it somehow dawns, apart from this revelation Paul had, that my humanity is an illusion...I'm not meant to because I'm no longer really...I'm the illusion of being a separate human. I'm a united human; I don't know that...haven't seen that. It's no longer that I'm *meant* to, it's a question of recognizing – my flesh shall remain the same! And my flesh shall shout at me. I shall always be stirred up to hates and fears and lusts. They're under there, but I no longer say that I oughtn't to have that. I'm saying that in my flesh...BUT I'm not my flesh! That's my outer form. My *self* is Christ in me. Now *that's it*. When I take that *that's the faith* that will say, "Alright, I may not understand it, but I'm herewith saying (because You're a Self) it's no longer I...*You* are living this life; You're living it!"

Now if you'll *say* that *word of faith* – produces substance. Same as you have said, "Jesus, You're my Saviour", sure enough He was in! You already *are* in the union, if you know it. In case you don't know it, you *are*! Every redeemed person is in the union, because that's what redemption is. You are this; you just don't know what you *are*. So there is a point where, by the word of faith, you say, "I'm *here*." I did it years ago sided up with my bible and said, "Now this is a *fixed* thing. It isn't I; it's Christ." Now the *confirmation* comes from Him. Faith dissolves when you get to the *fact*. You come here to the room. "I'm here!" You don't say, "I believe I'm here."

The same thing...when you say, "You and I is a settled matter. I've cast out the bond woman; I reject the fact that I'm a human meant to do it by myself. That's a lie; I'm not that! My flesh will get at me, but I'm not just myself asking; it's Christ. Christ, You're the Real Person in me." Now you take that word of faith, then the Spirit somewhere along the line, sometimes at once, says, "That's it; that's it!" It should normally be immediately, because I've said, "Oh, *that's* it!" Now that's the new life.

There are other things he says here. One other we'll say. That doesn't mean you'll be free of temptation. You will have lusts. Lusts are any strong desire. Lust isn't just sex; it's *any* strong desire. We have pride, hate, fears, reactions...anything you like. He says you'll have them...now I'm showing how to handle them. That's when he talks in the fifth chapter when he says, "You're to walk in the Spirit and you shall not fulfill the lusts of the flesh." Walk is spontaneous. It isn't a big effort to me to put my next foot forward, is it? I just continue to do it! If I'm walking, there's something about our balance. It's a law that causes you to step, doesn't it? You fall over if you don't (I don't understand it). You're always falling over, aren't you...and your next step is a compensation for falling over. What I mean is, we don't make a great stress about the next step, we just make it. Walking is being on your walking or on your inner life...next thing, next thing, next thing. See? No sweat. You're *in* the Spirit because you *are* the Spirit. He's got you; you've got Him. You are the inner Triune. That's just the background, a fact!

And then he says, "You won't fulfill the lusts of the flesh." Oh? So the lusts of the flesh are there? And then he says this, "For the flesh lusteth against the Spirit, and the Spirit against the flesh." Now you see he takes on this side here. He doesn't take on so much the other side, thus he explains to us that flesh is asset not liability. Flesh is the asset through which *God* comes! If I hadn't got a voice...and a body...and a mind...and an emotion, how would *God* express Himself through me? My *flesh* tackles this...my reasons and emotions and body are very precious. I mustn't downgrade my flesh. They're *God manifest* in the *flesh*!

He manages our flesh. So flesh is precious *real*, but because of this world, it gets very much diverted. We are *used* to being diverted. We are *very quick* to respond to our hates and our fears and our lusts. They're around the corner all the time. That's what he says here. "Flesh lusteth against Spirit." In other words things appeal to me – I want to do this; I want to do that; I resent that. All that stuff comes in all the time. So *here's* the flesh, which isn't me, but coming through my outer covering – my soul, my reasoning

197

and so on. Coming at me...coming at me...against the Spirit of course. The Spirit is the new "I" in me.

Now he says (very substantive in the middle), "These are contrary, the one to the other." Christ is here to manifest *through* the negative. That's what we're here to do. We're the negative world. Christ comes *through* the negative, and through my fear, brings His courage; through my impatience, brings His patience. So we *live* in the world where they're contrary one to another. One is there to dissolve the other...manifest through the other!

But then he says this (it finally comes out)..."Ye cannot do the things ye would." Now watch that! That's back on our old self. You *can't*, no you can't! We are *so* used to think we ought to. You *can't* do the things you would! No you *can't*; you weren't *meant* to. Self *can't do* it! Self can't do it. That's the whole of Romans 7...is that *one* statement! But you see how subtle it is? Well, what's wrong? The flesh doesn't get to Spirit. Sure! I've got this disturbance or anger or something else. I've got it! The Spirit in me doesn't want to do it; *I* don't want to do it, and the thing that I *would* do is what the Spirit's doing. I *would* do that, but I can't do it...*can't and never will*! See we're back on the old slip-up – I can do it. You never will, because by yourself, you're a slave.

But then it says, "If you are led of the Spirit, you're not under law." They law says while I'm under law I'm beaten up. You ought to; you ought not. Look at you, you're back again. You ought to have done that and haven't, then you're condemned! You're fighting and erupting and don't feel so good, because you've mistaken yourself as an *independent* self to the law, who says, "Go do it." But when you say, "I can't do it. I'm not there. Of course I'm disturbed and all that, lead of the Spirit – leader of me. I'm going on with the Leader. I'm going on with Him and He's had me in this." He handles it! You transfer your attention from this false idea you ought not to do that. Of course, that's all I do. I like that! I'll give way to that, but that's not Who I am. You're in me, Lord, and with You, Your courage will overcome my fears. So he says, you see, we *have* that.

Therefore, in this unified life, your attention has changed. We live by *attention*. We live by recognition. Now before I know the unified life, my recognition is myself. I've *got* Christ, but I've got a very good recognition of my human self, and I'm a real self and I've got all these things bothering me. I tend to be self-minded and suspicious-minded. My mind is: all I do is so weak; all I do is this. I've seen the 'I do, I do, I do' side. But I don't know the union. You *live* where your attention is. When you've moved into union, there has come into you a consciousness of Christ, and your *attention* has changed. You don't live fussing around the flesh in the *wrong* way. You live being a *free* person...I'm Christ's person! You're just yourself...and *be* yourself and you accept your *self!* You're operated. Don't fulfil yourself. Use yourself; be yourself! You're God's asset! Because you know *underneath* it isn't you.

That whole *basis* of consciousness is to forget the consciousness and operate! That's the final phase of this thing. All through life it's this. That's why you study a profession. The profession gets *you* and you forget it and practice it. A doctor may spend seven years studying medicine that he may forget that he knows it, and *do* it! Nothing is...what do I do? What do I do? What do I do? You know *what* to do...do it! You're trained as a technician or carpenter or builder to learn *how* to build *not*...how do I build? How do I build? How do I build? All I know is, I have a set of plans to build the house or make the thing. You go 'up' to your inner consciousness into operation. That's life. *This* is life too. Your 'up' to inner consciousness is "Not I, but Christ". That's your hidden background. You go 'up' as a person...just as a free person. *Be perfectly free. Dare* to be exactly as you are! *Dare* to be as God operates through your mind.

You see that pastor couldn't have that without seeing Wayne. He said, "How do you know the Mind...there's my mind and His mind." "No there is not" said Wayne, "There's only *one mind* and I've got Jesus' mind." He was quite like that! He was excited about that. (I've now written to ask him to write a Foreword to the book!) So you see what I mean? You don't say, "Whose mind?" You've got the mind of Christ! Believe your mind! Whose will? God's will. Well, use your will. Don't be afraid! Be yourself! *This is liberation...perfectly free!*

And where self stuff comes up, the point to realize, as I've said before, you'll always be in the foreground. The whole meaning of this is it's not electricity in the foreground; it's *light* in the foreground. It isn't atoms in the foreground; it's *things* in the foreground. They express the atom. We express God, so we are in the foreground. So *always* be yourself. Think your thoughts, be *free* to be yourself............but you have a *big wink!* It isn't you at all, and you *know* it isn't you, it's He! And that's the hidden secret. That's *your* hidden secret. The bible says in Colossians, "Your life is **hid** with Christ in God." You are hid in Christ. You're as hidden with Christ in God...as Christ your life he goes on to say. Hidden with Christ and Christ your life...a *hidden* mystery. There is a hidden side. You can't throw it out to everybody. You can and cannot. So underneath, you live as it's just you.

And that's how we become *pride egotists*! The biggest egotist ever was Jesus Christ. No one has ever had as big an **'I'** as He. I am the door; I am the shepherd; I am I am the light...ooh...ooh...ooh. Ooh as a person! And this Person, when they challenged him said, "I don't do anything by Myself. I do what I see the Father do. I have no peace in Myself. As I hear I judge. I've got an *inner Person* whose voice I hear...an inner Person operating. It looks like Me operating, but it's He operating, but it is Me!" The paradox – you come back as a real self. Don't be afraid to *be* yourself. *Be yourself!*

I told you that one about that husband who has a good relationship, but the wife says he doesn't really want us to go to church. I said to her, "Well, church isn't really *everything*, but church is some fellowship to you. You're not first a wife; you're first a woman of God. First off, find what God will do. Only go as far as God will tell you to. I don't think that God means for your husband to just manage all your time like that. You may have to say you are going to have what God has given me to do. Otherwise...you keep free. You're an egotist – I'll do what God shows me to do. That's this life!

This liberty we live in Christ, and yet there's an area of temptation. Then it says, "Watch. There are *works* of the flesh and fruit of the Spirit." Now "works" is a hard word. Self's always *hard*. When you're hating, it's always *hard*. Scheming, worrying is *hard*. Just decide whenever you're feeling it, you're off. Whenever you feel that *self*...watch. That's the "works" of hard work. Flesh means – Ohhh what do I do? Watch...watch. You've stepped back for the moment into the false condition that you're 'by yourself'. You get *plenty* of it...plenty temptation! The fruit of the Spirit – fruit is *spontaneous*. Fruit just happens. Don't look for the fruit...just *be* the fruit. Just be the vine. Fruit comes as *yours*. Light never sees itself. Other people see the light. Don't try to see your light. Just *be* light and other people see it. *That's* this life.

He then goes on to a few outside things. He says that if you learn to accept yourself, you accept other people. He said – Have pity on those who slip, because you're a slipper yourself. When you're not a law person trying to be good and pretending you are, and you're just by yourself a human. But that's gone. You are Christ in you. You know in yourself you haven't got anything. You don't mind when the other fellow slips. It says here, "Have sympathy with those who are overtaken with fault, because you're tempted yourself" (Vs 6:1). "Restore each other in meekness; consider yourself less you be tempted." You see when you free yourself, you free other people. You don't condemn them because you know how quickly you could be off, but for Jesus. Then it says, "Bear other people's burdens, but bear your own; be responsible. There's a place where we bear other peoples' burdens – move in with them. But you bear your own. In other words, each of us are our own selves. Let every man bear his own burden. You rejoice yourself, not in others. In other words, *you're responsible. Rejoice* in being a person; God's something to do by *you*! Don't hang onto other people; be yourself! God's got something to do by you. In the meanwhile, you can help other people with their burdens. Be sure you're also carrying your *own life* through. He says there is a *law* that if you sew to the flesh, you get corruption. It doesn't mean hell. It means this life, or so to speak, in eternal life.

And then *finally* he says – he was somewhat on the side of cutting them *off* from the old. So he made mention of the Cross in Galatians..."I am *crucified* with Christ." Therefore, with Christ I have *crucified* the flesh. He ends by saying, "Now God forbid that I should glory in anything but the cross of our Lord Jesus Christ whereby I am crucified unto the world and the world unto me." I said, "Understand...the world looks upon you as out. Accept that. They regard you as 'on the Cross'. They're running their own show; you're off on the Cross. Accept that! The world will have *that* viewpoint – 'you are out'. Accept that...and the world's out to you. You're crucified to the world. The world sees you as on the Cross – you're not on our show any longer. We're not here; you left us. Quite right? And the other way? The world's crucified to me, I've left you too. You're off for me. I'm not following you...man. Imagine this...I'm free. That's the Cross which *cuts me off*. He talks about that because that was their need at the time being – crucified with Christ. Of course he goes on the risen life and so on.

Now leave me that I bear in my body the *marks* of the Lord Jesus. That's the highest honor! The marks are sufferings. Now we're moving on. He doesn't touch that much in this book...moving into sufferings of others – bear the *marks* of the Lord Jesus. And then he says, "Mercy shall be on the *Israel* of God." *We're* the true Israel! I'm not sure about all this 'fuss business' with the Jews at all, because we're the true Israel already. There is only one nation in God's sight – THE nation...the holy nation. Here he says *we're the Israel*. But these days we've been talking so much about Late Great Planet

Earth and things you have all sorts of weird ideas about what's happening. I like to be part of the Israel myself!

PHILIPPIANS

"Great is the mystery of suffering: yet this much we know; suffering is in the very warp and woof of the slow progress of mankind from the vanity of time to the riches of eternity, so deeply interwoven into the stuff of things that the very Captain of our salvation, in order to be "made like unto His brethren" had to be made perfect through suffering. Borne rebelliously it "works death"; born courageously it unifies; borne vicariously it helps to redeem.

All men taste of it, the innocent with the guilty; but not until the Creator was crucified was there placed within reach of a groaning and groping humanity, not indeed the full explanation of suffering, but at least the key to its transmutation: we have to learn that faith transforms the messenger of Satan into the means of grace: that believers are to glory in tribulations, count trials all joy, because all things work together for good to them that love God; and that God-soldiers are to see in their crosses the mystery of the birth-process, whereby death works in us, but life in others for only the corn of wheat which falls into the ground and dies bears 'much fruit.'"

Alfred Buxton of the Congo and Abyssinia

When Moses was forty years old, he came to the moment of *radical* decision in his life...and *totally* turned his back on all the world could offer him. *That* is when God can begin to utilize a life! It may take varied forms, but there is a *total turning*. There is *nothing* left of what this world can offer you...which has *any* further interest to you. It *actually* becomes offensive to you. That's what Paul said in his self-dedication...which can be compared in some sense with Moses' great self-dedication. In **Philippians 3**, Paul says that he *suffered the loss* of all things when he *saw* the Lordship of Christ; what things *were* gain to him in self-righteousness were *lost* in Christ. There is a *certain* element in which it cost him to give up his position as one of the *topmost* young Jews, but then, he said, "I count them but dung that I might be identified with Christ." Things which 'smelled' a little nice when I gave them up smell offensive to me *today*. *That's* how God takes you! That *old* life becomes offensive to you. You don't hanker after it any longer...and it becomes something you *can't* touch because you've got something *far more* glorious.

Old Testament Journeys of Faith

PHILIPPIANS

Galatians is the *true* interpretation of the new birth. Of course the new birth *includes* the identification; Colossians is the *risen* life – the Resurrection. Galatians is the Cross – process of resurrection. "If we then be risen with Christ, keep seeking things above." Christ *is* our life. Christ *is* all, in all. And Ephesians is, of course you know, is the ascended life – when we've left our Cross-identification, our Resurrection-identification behind, and therefore the basis of this "seated" which means something's been settled – finished – and not seated in the sense of inactivity. There's not a thing such as inactivity. God's totally active and so are we! That's taken in the sense of a certain *understanding* of who I am that's settled...crucified, risen and the seating is the evidence that has been completed.

Having left that behind, we move into a new level of action. Therefore the soul life is the *outgoing* life...the *reproducing* life. It's from the soul the Holy Ghost goes out as a Third Person. He's been a Third Person *in* us; now He's a Third Person *by* us! So I said what is He also when He came up on high..."He led captivity captive." That's the previous one (the devil's captives become His captives...that's the Cross and Resurrection)...and gave gifts unto men. That's the Holy Spirit equipping us for action! That's what the gifts are. All the gifts come in there...the forms in which the Holy Spirit moves into action by us...it's the same reaction!

So I take it those four letters present us with the total truth first in a general completed form in Romans and then broken up into detail in Galatians, followed by Colossians, followed by Ephesians – how we relate to the Cross; how we relate to the Resurrection; how we relate to the Ascension...or where we are in them.

Philippians is a letter of the permanent *personal* condition of this one person, which is joy. It's a *personal* letter. It tells a great deal about himself and a 'joy experience' in his *ascended life*. His ascended life is intercessory life! I don't know what more to say......

Question from audience...

People often come quote to me "I press forward in order to attain" as striving to accomplish something. It really helped me, when in a private conversation you told me it was Paul's intercessory life. This is not a pressing forward to show how grateful you are in being saved or to pay back as a merit kind of thing people always quote these passages of scripture which imply self-effort, but he is pressing forward as an intercessor. Would you comment on that? Would you amplify that?

Perfection is the completion of God's purposes *by* us, not *in* us. He says, "Not that I am already perfect..." That's not referring to inner perfection. It refers to the completed outer product – what God does *by* me. That's what it says in Hebrews...that Christ's perfection was that "having learned obedience through the things He suffered, *being made perfect*." He was able to bring all others to that same relationship out *from* Him. That's what that perfection is. "Though He were a Son, He learned obedience through the things He suffered *being made perfect* became the Author (that's the perfection) of salvation unto all those who obey Him." His perfection was to bring other people into what He'd got!

That's an incomplete perfection. That only is as far as the universe is concerned when our human life finishes. That's what he is referring to in Philippians when he uses that as the whole scripture does...the three-fold levels. And he said he had been a lost person...for of course his lostness is self-ward, self-centeredness – "I might have confidence in the flesh. If any man might think he might trust the flesh; I more." That's self-centered self. All is vanity with himself concerning – "Circumcised the eighth day, Tribe of Benjamin, Hebrew of the Hebrews; touching the Law, a Pharisee; concerning zeal, persecuting the church; touching righteousness which is in the Law, blameless"...*a perfect devil!* A perfect devil – a perfect self-sufficient self! In all his level of perfection was a perfect self-righteousness. That's a perfect devil.

So the first step is "What was *gain* to me I counted as loss for Christ. He saw the *devilishness* of that false perfection by contrast with Stephen. That's why our lives convict other people...because when he headed up the stoning of Stephen, and when Stephen had these stones poured on him, and he was a dying man he looked to heaven and said, "I see Christ standing by the right hand of God"...and so on. The last thing he said was, "Lord, lay not this sin to their charge." *That* got him! His love was to *destroy* Stephen; God's love in Stephen was to *save* his enemies...got him! *Other* love. He didn't want his enemies to go to hell. Paul *wanted* his enemies to go to hell. He saw this!

That's the goad...the prodder (You kick against the pricks, kick against the goad all those years inside Paul, all those months)...that *got* him! Because he was an *intense* man, he *intensely* reacted! Intense reaction is very healthy. It's a good sign. Intense reaction is what lured him to Christians...to escape this inner goad – you're wrong; you're wrong, you're off beam. This self-loving self; this self-elevating self...making much out of your Jewishness and your temple. That's our self-interested self...this is a lie!

The treasure of the love of Christ – what things were *gain* to me I count it as loss for Christ. When he got a vision of the love of Christ (It'd come to *him*...same as it came to Peter from the heavens) and this Voice said to him, "Saul, Saul, why persecutest thou Me?" And he *caught* the meaning of love. He caught Eternal Love – thru Stephen "in Christ"...*that* was his gain...to be accepted and received as a redeemed son by Christ.

But then he had to move on from being an 'accepted self' to finding Who he truly was – a Christ-self. Not Christ *for* him, but Christ *as* he....being he...and for that he had to go through a painful process, which he had to *experience* the Cross. He received a bit of Christ's Cross...what things had been gain to me I lost for Christ...justification through Christ's Cross. Now he had to *experience* the Cross. And he said, "Yea doubtless, and I count *all* things as but loss..." Not just my self-righteousness – *all* I am, *all* I have...*all* things as loss...not just my own ego-hood, as in the sense of my pride and all that...for the *exceeding* excellency of the knowledge, *exceeding* inner knowledge, *exceeding* realization of Christ, my Lord – meaning Christ has taken me over. *He's the me!* He's the One 'running' inside...not *I*, my Lord – Christ, my Lord!

That *exceeding* new stage that *he* was this Person...that his whole *being* was this Person! And that cost him all things. "...who must suffer the loss of all things." So it cost him! There was a *hurt* there in that dying in whatever forms it took – being cast out from his own people and any other thing it cost him. There was *personal hurt* there. He suffered...the loss of all things, so it *cost* him to lose! That's the next stage when you've found the total 'treasure of life' – precious is my being He. He being you. Christ is my Lord...my Lord...not just my Savior. My Lord has the implication that it's He running this show now. He's the I. Instead of I being 'my own lord' or Satan being 'my lord' – Jesus Christ is not just my Savior, He's my Lord!

Question...

Is this 'cost' a cost you are real conscious of or is it other people who see the cost more than you do? I don't think that you sense that your life has had this tremendous cost. You've done what you had to do, what you wanted to do, and I suppose objectively there might have been a cost, but do you as yourself really see it was a great price that you paid giving all to Jesus, or is it that other people see the cost about ten times as much as you do?

I would think in saying that, I am confusing the price I paid as an intercessor and the price I paid to discover union. This is the preliminary price he paid. I think He paid it in those three days when he learned he must "suffer many things for My sake"...before the Holy Ghost...I don't know. *This* price I'm not talking about, this *costly* price isn't, of course – "having lost all things"...now you're burned out – you become a living sacrifice! That's another kind of suffering. That's II Corinthians suffering; that's an intercessory suffering. That's what he calls "my *light* affliction." That's a light thing; this *wasn't* a light thing! There's an *inner place* where it costs us to die...or to find we've died. (Isn't that right?) And it costs! That's *all*.

What I'm going on to say is this: the *whole point* of this is....he turns right around and he *loathes* the thought of what he has much loved. *This* is the third. Because where he'd said here "I count all things but loss for the excellent knowing of Christ Jesus, my Lord, for Whom I've *suffered* the loss of all things...and do count them as dung." Now dung is offensive. Dung is manure! Not a very pleasant 'space' – where things weren't very pleasant, where the very presence those things are very present...where there is a 'smell' of things apparent – I don't want to *lose* my reputation; I don't want to *lose* my everything. I don't want to *lose* them! I'm losing things that have a pleasant smell to me. They've turned now and have an offensive smell! That's a radical change there!

So the *values* of life have changed. Now this is the third one...that's not the second one. The second is the discovery that He *is* my life...my 'me'...my all....which has had a *cost* in it, and then that cost is gone. I *grieve*; then it's gone! I've been there. And when you've moved into this life, this new life, you are *sold out* to others having it! Anything else is *dung* to you. You can't be *bothered* with it; it's offensive to you. That's to waste your life. Not our daily duties, that's part of the way God comes through. My interests and values in life have changed.

So everything I have becomes part of something for others. Like *your* life, Bill. Like John and Linda's home is for *others*. It would be hateful for them just to run a big show and have a nice home or for you to accumulate your money. You can't do it! It's become dung to you. There *was* a time you liked doing it, and that's what had to die. And once it has died...somewhere that costs. "If you hate not." There *is* a place where you hate not father and mother, wife, houses, land...yea, even my life also...forsake not *all* he had. Unless he'd forsaken *all* that he had, he cannot be My son. What you *really hate* is that self-love...it's the *completion* of that area of that 'self-love'...in Christ...but that love which is still attached to things and people – father, mother, wife, children, houses, land and things. Well, they're not my salvation now, but they're things, and to some extent I am still attached. So *that's* the detachment! That's the middle detachment. *So radical*...because Jesus uses *radical* terms. We wouldn't say "hate". We'd just say "dislike."

Jesus saw in 'total' terms. He was a 'total' Person. To say you *hate* your father and your mother and your wife and your children, your houses...yet, really we do. Actually, we've done it. When the chips are down, we do it! When the chips are down, we'll sacrifice *anything* for Jesus. We won't if we can help it...but if the chips are down, we'll do it...which is – we 'hate'. It's the same hate that Jesus had when His mother and brethren tried to get Him out of all the crowds around Him, because He was getting fanatical. They were afraid for Him.

He said, "Ahhh...I don't see you. You're all My mother and My brethren who do the will of God! I reject My mother. I 'hate' them! His own mother, the same mother whom He commended to John's care on the Cross, was the mother who a few years earlier He'd said, "Ahhh...you're not my mother!" These people are My mother! That's strong language. That's *Jesus*! That's *radical!*

And so, basically, there is a hate...for love *is* hate, of course. It *has* to hate that which combats love. So I've tried to say....I think it's the second one...I *hope* something we've gone *through* and passed *out* of, but as we look back there's a certain area which was a costly business. But now the very things, which might at that time have felt costly to us, we laugh at keeping....now we laugh. We don't want them! They're offensive to us. They're annoying...*wrong* to us...a hindrance to us. We don't want them; we want *everything* for Jesus.

The curious thing is, of course, when we give everything, He gives everything back! That's the paradox! You come *back* into Paul's I Corinthians 3 when he says...when you *are* Christ (in other words you are Christ now the way He's taken you over) for *all* things are yours. Whether Paul, Apollos or Peter or all the world...*all ours*...all life, all death, all things present, all things to come; all are yours twice over! Not all are *not* yours...all are yours! It's an extraordinary paradox – you hate them; you get rid of them. Then you get them all back...*because* you are their brothers! It's the main theme behind all *persons* is that there may be some means to reach others. That's proved...that's what union-life is!

We're moving *into*...Dan and I were saying last night it's a *radical* basis. Not many of us sort of say well I'm related to this union-life or something. What we're saying is you *can't* be a person who *'you're not you, but Christ'* without being a person for others. You can't make it, so you'll make it so. You are so! It's *got* to come out...and you say you'll renounce your home or you'll renounce your business. You can't hold back; life's for others. That's what the world can't see – you get everything back for others! You get the whole lot back – not for you! There's something *in* you which released you and you know you're not for *you* – and you know if you begin to *be* so, you know you'll say again, "I'm not taking that. **You** *take* it...remind me of that." Now that's the beginning of the Third.

Question...

Is this an experience of the unification period you said, "This is in the second level; is this death in the experience of 'I live; yet not I, but Christ'?"

Yes, and there's a cross in it. I *suffer*...and I don't like it. It's really hurt. That's a baby...an adolescent. We look back now and tell others, "Aye, that cost me something!" We describe *how* it costs us in different ways. That's the value of our testimony, isn't it? Sure, it cost me something, but "Thank God" now....I couldn't say "Thank God" then. I "Thank God" *now*! Out! But that's only settling me in. It's putting the 'me' out to settle the real me, which of course, is Christ in me.

This "for others" becomes the third. *Because* you are this free person, this free position, you're no longer interested in having your home to yourself.

Have a nice home if you like, but not for yourself! You're not interested in having more money....have all you can get, but not for yourself. He turns it right around and becomes a paradox. If you *can*, be a wealthy man or a well to do man....well OK, be all you can because you have a wink. It's not for you; the world may think it is, but it isn't! This new drive's got you.

Now in this new drive, there'll be other forms of death. This is another death. This is His death that Paul "coveted" – participating in. He now said I've counted as dung...this thing has turned around in me so things I once liked...ugh! Now my ***will*** is in Christ; my attitude has changed; my interests changed. My interests *totally* changed...making money, doing this or doing that as an end unto itself. I've changed....I mean we're *Christ*! Now Christ is the Deity for others! The whole Deity is for others.

I may *win* being Christ. Win means 'be like'...you've won the prize. It's *your* prize now...not now a prize of a person, say 'to you'. It's out...that stuff's gone. We always say in an ***outer*** position – we're 'depending' on God. You've become a co-god! He's your *permanent* bread...and all that stuff – that's out! That's why we don't always pray and stuff...that's out! That had a form of dependence in it.

Now you're *winning* Christ! You've won the prize. You've won it now! The prize is Christ! Not something He gives you, but Himself! Christ a Savior...Christ a Savior. He's *totally* others. His Deity, not just a Deity for eternity, but to be us! Now if I'm not mistaken He never gets it back again. If I'm not mistaken there's a sense in which the Deity itself is unique and can't be understood...because He can only understand by its opposite. There is an opposite to His Deity. So the Original One – Father, Son Spirit – we don't know; we don't know. This was the Eternal Original One. When you come out to *be* something, you limit yourself. You come out to be other people...You limit Yourself.

Now it says that Jesus counted it not robbery to be *equal* with God. And then it says He made Himself of no reputation to the degree He emptied Himself, and took upon Himself the form of servant. Now, "the form of servant" – that's the Philippian one...in not serving us, it means 'general service' because it comes before He became a man. It doesn't say He became a man to become a form of servant...before He became a man. He made Him of no reputation and thought it not robbery to be equal with God. He was God! Was...is...was...in a certain unique sense! In the eternal Deity He was not that.

Now He emptied Himself, made Himself of no reputation (Phil 2:7) and took upon Himself the form of servant. That's His permanent form! And *then* was made like unto men. So He was a *self* before He was a man. He took upon His whole – His expression of God – the servants expression in which He identified with those...so He's a paradox...the Lord as a servant to those whom He serves.

I'm seeking to *say* something happened to Jesus before He *was* Jesus...when He was the Word...and then became the Son – Jesus on earth to fulfill, apparently, an eternal purpose – that He was *forever* to be 'man number One'. He became a *man* because forever the Deity is manifested by His many agents, and the first man-agent is His Son. And so often in the Scriptures you get little things tucked in, don't you? A great phrase will have a great revelation in it...that one little phrase in 1 Timothy is not said quite like anywhere else...where it says "There's one God and one mediator between man and God – the *man* Christ Jesus." So there is a *risen* Person called 'the man', not The Crucified, not the human person. He's the risen One...the mediator, the *man*, Christ Jesus.

So, of course, He's the Eternal Man. Now I'm going to get into this in a little bit to show how His life, therefore, has a *hidden basis* of renunciation. I say hidden because we shouldn't say too much about renunciation. Renunciation is for us an unpleasant word. We don't easily see the glory in renunciation...the *hidden* basis of it. My mentor, Studd, he used to make these little poems. He had one..."Take my life and let it be, a hidden cross revealing Thee." Tisn't a cross up in the front..."Take my life and let it be a *hidden* cross." Great union mixed up in there..."revealing Thee."

I'm saying, therefore, Christ has *permanently* become that. He's become like the 'Top Man' in the universe, and in *that* sense remains second to His Father. Now that doesn't fit unless you make room for these things. It said He counted it not robbery to be equal with God...and yet in the final word given us in 1 Cor 15 – "For He hath put all things under His feet"...the Last Adam (he must reign – Jesus)...until He put all things under His feet. "The last thing that shall be destroyed is death, for He hath put all things under His feet." When He says *all things are put under Him*, it has manifest that He has accepted which He'd put *all* things under Him. "And when all things shall be subdued under Him then shall the Son also Himself be subject unto Him who put all things under Him that God may be all in all." So we're left with the equal Son becomes the subject! There may be that.

I'm only trying to say to you something of the involvement in a Life which is involved...that other people live. This is the Third Order. And therefore I'm saying winning Christ means that. Winning a *Person* means you're now what that Person is. That Person's a *Savior*...not just a convenient Savior for me, but He's a world Savior. That's "that I may win Christ"...and be found **in** Him. He beautifully preserves it's all in He...it keeps off the law. It's not going to become *found* in him – not having my own righteousness...not having something built outside myself, which is the law.

I'm not back there in that self-effort stuff...but that which is *through* the faith of Christ – the righteousness which is of God by faith...I am what I am in Christ, because Christ is that, I'm *that*. It has *nothing* to do with my *becoming something.* I'm that because Christ is that; therefore I'm that. Be very careful that we rightly center the Third here. So we don't run back in the Third and say, "Now I must become better. Now I must be used." We don't run back and say, "Now I must get going." We must be *very careful* we're preserved from being law and law-effort...to it all being Christ...right in the heart of this Third development. And that's where he says, "That I may win Christ and be *found* in Him...not in my righteousness...that I may *know* Him and the power of His resurrection."

So that's what we're always doing – a *permanent involvement* in fresh discovering! Always fresh discovering – who we are...what He is...how we operate. It's a daily fresh discovery –knowing Him in that sense...knowing Him and being Him. It's not now knowing Him as Savior or Lord or all that. It's knowing Him in His *eternal purposes*. Moving into what it says of the father – "I write unto you, fathers, that you *know Him* which is from the beginning."

"And the *power* of His resurrection"...now I've got to learn how to operate by this *wholly new* **Power**. Now it's all part of knowing how to *operate*. This is a safe business – we're taught how to see *nothing* except as an expression of God! I learned that by Lanyon. That's why I was so keen for us all to have Lanyon. This is the kind of thing Lanyon will talk about.

"The power of the resurrection"...in every situation you move back into what He is. You move back from the first appearances...first outer appearances...meaning this stuff up here. (Indicating the temporal) We're operating on this 'safe level' which is *that* level. (Indicating the unseen) We say, "That's *so*; that's *here*; that's *here*." We're dropping the word faith out of it and replacing by fact. The fact level. That's it! That's what the word of faith is – *a fact is a fact!* We're all learning that, aren't we?

Now that's *part* of this thing. To know Him is to know *how* to be He on earth...*to walk this Spirit life **in** matter form!*

"And the fellowship of His sufferings." Now here is a new type of suffering. This is in the book form...the letter form...where II Corinthians comes in. II Corinthians is the opening up of what it *really means* to be an intercessor – your inner attitude, your outer actions, your relation to others, the price you pay. The whole business is there! So it's a great deal of suffering...a great deal of pressure. Paul doesn't block it. He comes out on the other side...so it's a letter of *glory* in sufferings. A great deal of suffering; a great deal of glory!

And so there is a point in II Corinthians where it changes to "from glory to glory." It's a glory letter. But he doesn't block the *fact* – you're pressed on every side; all that list of suffering through and through; fightings without, fears within; as a vessel...persecuted but not forsaken; perplexed but not in despair; cast down, but not destroyed...*always* bearing about in our bodies the *dying* of the Lord Jesus. I'm seeking to *see* it in something, which is I'm replacing my negative responses I *must have* when something's costing – something hurts to the positive, which is Christ in me. Even my *body* shows it. Christ is manifest in my *body*. "Always bearing about in the body the dying of the Lord Jesus that Christ may be manifest in my *flesh*." Your body shows it...shows the glory I mean, shows the victory. "Always bearing about in the body the dying of the Lord Jesus" – he's talking about the physical sufferings now..."that the life of Jesus may now also be manifest in my body for we are always delivered unto death, that the life also of Jesus might be made manifest in our mortal flesh. So then death worketh in us, but life in you."

Now that's the power of resurrection. That's the fellowship of suffering. That's what we are put into. That's why we always say, *"Recognize that!"* This intimately involved life. That's our glory! It *will cost* us. This is the intercessory life now. For the intercession, which is this Third area, is a sense of commission. We always say it's a *specific* commission...something negative...now *this* is what I'm in; I accept it...God by me operating out *from me* into others. It's on that level we put in those premises – those two when Paul said "Not I live, but Christ liveth in me. And then in that same place – mighty in me towards others.

He's *mighty* – so *He's* doing the job. It's in *me*....so it's expressed in *me* towards the Gentiles. It's not what's happened here (indicating himself); it's what happens there. (indicating outwards) And I always say, we say, "That's a fact!" Don't try and get it. It's a fact! That is happening in you. Don't ask, *how*? That's God's business; don't look around. So it is a given fact because God says it's so, and because He's living in me. He's mighty in me toward others. And somehow it's *happening*...somehow it's *happening*! This is the same faith business. Now we always take that same Scripture in John 7 where it says, "If you believe out of *your* belly rivers shall flow." Now that's saying the attitude of faith by which you got saved; you know the union; you know the supply – *out!* Take it and operate on *that* level of faith. *How* it happens has nothing to do with you. But it *does involve* the next part of the commission – *I'll do it by you.* The body, the body...intercessor's body. Faith is spirit. Intercession is body. The intercession is in the body, and that means in the outer circumstances. And suddenly I am materially involved, as well as spiritually. It's *all* I can say!

That's why I am so objecting to my own mission now. That's all I hear. They've inserted the word "retirement." But I said there's no such thing...there's redirection! Cut the word out! Even a word can hurt people. One of these ridiculous people...I talk to him all the time...they've put retirement at sixty-five. What's sixty-five I said! If you take that you'll ruin this mission. One of the first lessons I learned in the mission – we had no fallow period. If you do, you crumble it. When you go out for two years and say, "In two years I'll go home"...instead of being *immersed* an extra two years, and asking *what* shall I do when I go home? So don't have...I'll have this fallow five years! Don't have it! Don't say a thing about that. What then comes after five years? Because we're human and you come up to what you *see*! Oh you're retiring...I'm coming up sixty-five now!

I'm afraid we have some precious workers who really have done nothing for fifteen years. They live in a retirement home, they're good people...of course they're my age now. That doesn't matter now by lots, but we put a wrong quotation on them, which is why they've changed now. If they kept another tone – put it *redirection*. Life's to be redirection! Maybe it can be at 70 years of age...not to tramp out to Africa. Maybe it's how we do it. When we retire we get *redirected*! So we don't know that, do we?

All our life now is to be permanent redirection. That's a person who suffers...and someplace death. That does mean outwardly. *Choose* that you'll be finished off for Jesus...be conformed unto His death. He *chose* it for Himself! He said "No one took My life from Me." Part of this *whole* intercession is you *claim*, not only that the Lord shows through you, but that you yourself will be intimate...that your life may finish you off in the Person of Jesus. And that's what he's attaining.

I never *have* understood what he means by the next one..."That I might attain the resurrection from the dead." I've not had that which conveys *total* light to me, not yet. It isn't the resurrection all have. It's obviously something more. Because you know what we all have is resurrection which happens after salvation. So you don't attain to that, do you? I think there is a certain element and a truth in the Bible that there are those the Bible says are "overcomers" who will pay with a certain area of their life really being operative for God. I think it must *mean* that.

Question...

Might the word realized resurrection help? With the suffering etc., etc. there's a greater and greater realization that the Kingdom has come, and we stop looking to the hills from whence cometh our help and we don't look forward to Maranatha, but we know Maranatha has come as a realized thing.

It takes away from the power of development...from cutting down to winning him, to power...resurrection power, sufferings, death. There's something more to realize than what I've got. I'm *sure* there's something there. He's after attaining it. It doesn't matter; we'll leave it.

Back to the original...that pressure on now. Now then – Not that I've already attained, or that I've been made perfect. I'm not 'trying to be' savior. My perfection is Christ in me; my life – Christ as me. The Savior – that has been perfected through the years. That which I'm apprehending; to be an intercessor and so on...the press to the mark. That's all. So I understand the high calling of God to be that – to be among those who are co-saviors...intercessors. The prize...the **high** calling of God...and the highest is to be co-savior. We know!

Question...

Not pressing on to, but pressing on in?

Press on toward the mark of the prize...I think what Paul says also in Philippians 1..."According to my earnest expectation and my hope that in nothing I shall be ashamed, but that with all boldness, as always, so now also Christ shall be magnified in my body, whether it be by life, or by death." Bang!

Question...

Do you think maybe he's got a little bit of what the psychologists would call a 'martyr complex'...that he would look forward to die for Christ?

It's a good martyrdom! I say, "Let's have it!" It's a martyrdom for the world. Christ is a martyr. Yes. The false martyrdom is – I'm getting something out of it. The martyr *for God* in the world, that's the high calling, I think! That's it! So Philippians is kind of a first explanation; II Corinthians is an intimate revealing light on what it means to be an intercessor. James and John are other levels and polish off what Paul says. There's a flash in which Peter is the beginner; Paul's the middle and John and James, the end.

Peter began where we were yesterday on the new birth...on the milk of the word – born again and all that. Then into Paul into union life; Paul opens up what a true being is – union life, and settles into union life, and explains the other and so on as he goes into it. John simply tells you what you *are* as such. As I said yesterday you don't find the word faith in John, except in the last chapter where he explains *faith is fact*. All John..."I know, I know, I know...you know, you know, you know," because faith is *knowing* and knowing is *being*. What you know you *are*. So the whole of John is – you *know* you're walking in the Light. You *know* you're righteous as He is righteous...you know this; you know that and you operate out of that, but we're not going into that now. And James is saying when you are a knower then you're a doer, and here are the doings...and explains the conflicts that arise when you *don't know* who you are! If you don't know who you are, you're double.

James is a *double* letter because he's challenging – you've got two minds; you've got two tongues; you've got two motives; you've got two attitudes to other people...and even in your self-image, you've got two ideas of self-image. *All that* you read is double! Fortunately we realize Who we are that's not who you are. You're not double; you're single! Then you *act* on the single level – the single eye, the single tongue, the single mind, the single motive, the single operation...as you saw. Those put us on the top. So...different ways.

216

HEBREWS

There is no other way. In all life we are not sure first, and then believe afterwards. No, we believe first (and act as believing), and then we become sure. **Hebrews 11.3**, "By faith we understand…", not we understand and then have faith.

Knight of Faith Volume I

The writer to the Hebrews made that distinct differentiation between those soul-reactions and my true self, which is spirit. (Heb. 4:12) But, of course, I must also have those soul-reactions as a living human. So now we see that, in Bible terms, we have a God-created humanity with both its body-drives and soul-expressions, by which we operate as humans…that is, therefore, evidently right and not wrong, as my basic humanity.

Think on These Things

To put it briefly, soul is the seat of emotions and of reason; spirit is the seat of ego. Spirit is the ego; God is spirit and He is the first Ego; we are spirits, of whom He is the father (Hebrews 12:9). Down in the center, the spirit, is where you know and love. Knowledge and love, mind and heart, are the real self – the real person. That's where you irrevocably live, but your soul is more external. It is how you express your spirit. Your mind (your knowledge) expresses itself in reasons, but reasons can vary for they can be influenced by all sorts of things. The heart expresses itself through the affections, the emotions. That is where we feel, but our feelings can vary quite apart from the set purposes of our heart… We have to learn how to discern between soul and spirit, and refuse in our spirit (our real self) to be dominated by the reactions of the emotions or the reasons – our souls. When we have learned to discern and to discipline the reactions of the soul, then through our reasons and our emotions we channel Christ, and are not moved by the reflex action of the world coming back at us.

Think on These Things

217

HEBREWS

Foreword

Dear Reader,

My attempt at interpreting the glories of this Hebrews letter is not meant to be verse by verse. I have always been led through the years in reading the Scriptures, whether in the lives of some of the great men and women of faith or in these New Testament epistles, to seek to catch the essence of what the Spirit is saying to us by them, which may then be applicable to our own lives. So I have sought to do this here with this wonderful letter which I attribute to Paul as the writer as did the translators of the King James Version of the Scriptures.

I find the main purpose of the Spirit by this letter is to introduce the Hebrews recipients, and thus us also, to the *total adequacy of our life in Christ*, entering into God's rest from His works...and so we from ours. Also, in the completion of the ministry of "Jesus the Son of God" as our Great High Priest in the perfection of our salvation, how we, as sons with The Son, know how to *complete our priesthood ministry* in meeting the needs of the human family of our generation. What a letter!

Lovingly,

Norman Grubb

P.S. There are a few repetitions on some of the most vital parts of the letter.

This is a letter written by the apostle Paul to some of God's people who were scattered and going through tough times, and its aim is to give a *revelation* of God's plan through the ages which are centered in His own Son...and with the Son, the sons – ourselves!

He starts by the revelation of His Son, from eternity to eternity, as the express image of the Father, the brightness of His glory. By His Son He made all things, upholds all things, and has appointed Him heir of all things. So the whole plan of God in His universe centers for eternity in His manifested Son; and right at the heart of all this, Paul wrote, we come into relationship with the Father through His Son, for "when He had by Himself purged our sins, He sat down at the right hand of the majesty on high."

Such is God's grace that right in the midst of His eternal glory is the purging of our sins, the means by which, through the Son, we become sons – and function as sons. He purged our sins because it has always been God's purpose to manage His universe through His vast family of sons who would be co-heirs. He appointed His Son to be heir of all things and His sons to be co-heirs with Him, and they're to be the living persons by whom He is going to manage His universe. So they have to be real people and they have to start by *finding themselves*. That's what the creation of man is for, and the fall of man.

Through being ourselves down here, being confronted with being ourselves, we find ourselves, and the means by which we find ourselves is to be first fallen self-for-self selves. Therefore we start by being the opposite kind of persons to what God is. His only nature is self-giving love. He lives for His universe. This is His fulfillment, His completion, His life – to exist for the perfection of His universe in His self-giving love. Now we, in order to find ourselves, had to become *self-loving* love – which is death. God, who is Life, is *self-giving* love. Persons who are under the control of the god of self-loving love are in a non-life...in a death. That's what we are, in this fallen condition. But by that means we find ourselves as real people, and His own Son was to identify Himself with us so that we might become a family of brothers with Him, and the co-sons of the Father. That is this chapter one.

The second chapter tells us how His own Son became a man among us...and to be one with us suffered all we suffer. It was said that He came on earth to taste death for every man. He had to experience what we experience. So He became a human person with persons...and the purpose was to bring many sons to glory. He became linked with us on earth and all we go through, and He finally took upon Himself the destiny we all have – the destiny of death. But physical death isn't the issue. It is that when we have a physical death we go to our eternal destiny; the self, the inner spirit, goes to its eternal destiny in its lost condition, the Satanic condition of self-centeredness. And Jesus took that death upon Himself and it says that He destroyed him who had the power of death because He died representing us...and Satan never got any sin-control over him. So, as representing lost humanity, He went to hell in our behalf, but hell couldn't hold Him because He didn't belong there. He arose representing us all and so broke the control of Satan over us. He delivered us through death from him who had the power of death. So by that means He could be both the Pioneer of our salvation and raise us up even to be His brothers. So it says here in this second chapter that He is not ashamed to call us brothers. He "declares God's name among His brethren; in the midst of the church He sings praises." As the Son, He is leveled down to us and levels us up to Him. Indeed, in a sense He gave up His position as the unique Son of God (Phil. 2:6, 7) in order to become man and then lift us up to be sons with Himself.

He was also destined, not only the Savior and the Pioneer of our salvation, but the High Priest – the One who would be responsible for the upholding and the keeping of God's people like the high priest of the old covenant days. He identified Himself with us so He can be that among us and is presented in this way in this letter.

Paul (taking him to be the author) then leads the ones to whom he writes through the stages of our different relationships we have with Him, so that we find out who we are, where we are, and how we function. First of all, in chapter three, he likens Jesus to our Moses – the one who delivered the people from Egypt and took them into the wilderness on the way to the Promised Land. He says that Jesus is to us what Moses was to the children of Israel, only with this difference: Moses was a servant in the house and he could only link us up with God on the level of being servants in the house. Jesus was the Son of the house. So if we come into link with Jesus, we come into something more than a servant relationship. We come into being members of the household, of which He is the head. That is when we first come into a *living, saved relationship* with Christ by our new birth in the Spirit.

He then goes on to show how not only is Jesus to us like Moses was to the children of Israel in getting them out of Egypt, but also like Joshua in getting them into the Promised Land, and getting us into the land of which that was a type – the land of fullness and rest. This he speaks of in the fourth chapter as resting from our own works.

That was the second stage in finding out what it is to be a co-son with Christ, a brother with Christ, because to enter into His rest it says that we have to cease from our own works even as He did from His. What the Fall has done for us is to delude us with Satan's lie of being *independent* selves running our own lives, doing our own things, into a life under the dominion of sin, the god of self-for-self, *as though* self-relying independent selves.

Now we have to learn that when we've been saved we've entered into a new relationship, and it's not that of self-relying-self, which is Satan's nature in us. The children of Israel learned it because of their inability to handle the difficulties they met with in the wilderness and they were continually getting into the sin of unbelief and murmuring and rebelling because they couldn't obtain what they needed. They were accusing Moses for not delivering them. The reason was that they hadn't faith, and it says that we are to take heed that we aren't like the children of Israel in the wilderness, "lest there be in any of you an evil heart of unbelief in departing from the living God." Now faith is being linked to something to which you have joined yourself which has become real to you. All life consists of living by faith in which we join ourselves by our inner choices to something and it becomes real to us and we live in that relationship to it. For instance, we come into this room by faith. We choose to come...and now we're linked to the room and are at home and comfortable in the room because the room has become an outer reality to us through faith, the faith which brought us into it.

Now, because we've fallen from God and become people geared to self-relying-self, even though we are born again, we only appear to know God in an outer relationship, as if He were some distant person. But the truth is that we're not outer persons at all; we're inner persons. We're spirits – my real self is my spirit. That's the I AM in me. That's what God is – Spirit. He's *the* Person in the universe – the I Am. He has manifested Himself

in all outer forms. Everything is an outer form of God...love expressing itself. He's beauty, wonder, and glory. But He's Spirit. We are created as spirits; we're not just outer forms. We are ourselves in outer forms. Now through the Fall we lost sight of this. We don't realize we're inner people. When we came to Jesus, a change took place. You can't find Jesus down here in the flesh because He has been crucified and risen. He had come here to be our Savior and then having taken away our sins by His precious blood He arose from the dead. Now you can't find Jesus on an outer level because as spirit we never really know anything on the outside. You only know a thing when it's become inner knowledge to you...in an inner consciousness. Now we know God like that. When we find our *need* in our lost condition, our sins, the judgment on us, and the wrath, we want to get right with God. We want peace and the gift of eternal life, and we put our faith in Jesus Christ. But the faith isn't in a Jesus Christ down here. We put our faith into the *risen* Jesus Christ! Now that's putting our faith in a Person who doesn't belong in this dimension at all. He's not visible, not tangible. He's a living Person, a real living Person, but not in outer form. *The real living Person is the Father through the Son and Spirit.*

So when we are born again we take a step of faith by which within ourselves we receive Jesus Christ as Savior. So by receiving Jesus Christ as Savior we are receiving not a person we see down here, but a Person who arose from the dead. That's what we call "the leap of faith." A person only takes that when they are in so much outer need. We know our sins...our lost condition. We know the grace of God offered us in Christ. We want to have God...and we take a leap and we put our faith in a Person we've never seen. It's conveyed to us through the Word of God.

That's the value of the scriptures. Scripture conveys the facts to us, but we aren't saved by just believing the scriptures. We are saved through the scriptures *by receiving the Person* they tell us about, Jesus Christ. And so we receive Him. Now, the law of faith is that what you take by faith you receive, you experience. You take food, you experience it. You take coming here this evening, you experience it. You sit in a chair, you experience it. You take up a profession, you experience it. Life always is inner experience. Why study a profession? Not that we take a profession; it takes us. You study medicine, you become a doctor. You study teaching, you become a teacher. You study carpentry, you become a carpenter. You become that thing. Life is what we are inside, what takes us over inside. What you take takes you! That's faith. This is what life is. Then you are at home in the thing. If you become by experience a teacher, or a lawyer, or a doctor, or a carpenter...you practice it. You know how to do the thing. It's become a part of you, it's easy to you. So faith makes a thing real to you so it's easy to you.

Now if we're born again, Jesus is our inner Moses. We become conscious of Him inside; we become conscious He is my Savior. That doesn't belong to this world. That's not an outer thing because we have a new experience – we become conscious of Him. Why? Because by faith I took the living Person Who is in the spirit dimension. Not matter...Spirit. He comes to me as Spirit and in my spirit He witnesses and says, "I am here. I love you. I have forgiven you. I have accepted you. I'm your savior. God's your father." Now you come to a new *settled* something which is new to you. This is the new consciousness. These outer things fade because they are only passing. This is the real consciousness. I've now become part of the heavenly family – spirit family related to the risen living Jesus Christ, the Holy Spirit, and the Father. And as a consequence, also, I begin to express a new way of life, because my old fallen self way of life was *for* myself. When I was captured in the Fall by the spirit of Satan, the spirit of self-for-self, I lived *for* myself. Now when I come in my need to receive Jesus Christ...His Spirit is the spirit for others – God is the spirit of love...other love is born in me. And so when Jesus Christ comes into me and this consciousness comes to me, what happens? I begin to love. I'm a new person. I can't help myself! Where I was always loving myself I *now begin* to love Jesus, love God, and love other people *by His love* shed abroad *in my heart* by His Spirit. This is what it is to be a son of God. Because God is a lover God, He loves His universe and exists to fulfill His universe. Now His purpose in having a Son and sons is to have those by whom He can express His perfecting love in His universe. The reason why this world is in the condition it is is because it's been seized by the god of self-love. Everybody loves himself, so he fights wars, has jealousies. Basically each person wants to get for themselves so it's chaos, disharmony.

Now, where there's love, there's harmony. Where there are persons who live for each other, there's harmony. That's what God is. God is harmony because God has no interest except in us. That's why He gave Jesus Christ. He exists so that we may be completed. So His purpose is to have a vast family of harmonious sons who express His Spirit of Love. They're loved sons and they're lover sons. They exist to love and complete and fulfill that for which they're responsible. That's what God's purpose is – a vast family of saved sons that are safe to manage His universe, because they won't manage His universe for their own ends. They'll manage His universe as He manages it for the blessing of the universe. Now that took place when I received Jesus, because I began to be a lover. God's love shed abroad in *my* heart caused me to love Jesus and love others, and want to be the means by which all have God's love and God's peace as I have.

But the further lesson I have to learn to be the son I am in Christ is that I still have this mistaken idea of myself. The only understanding of ourselves we have is Satan's *lie* of independence. Now back in the Old Testament days, Israel in the wilderness didn't know that. Though redeemed and under the blood, they only knew God at a distance. Now Moses did know. Moses knew an inner God. He knew how to walk with God and talk with God and to work the works of God. He could function as God because he and God were one. He discovered that in the burning bush when he found the fire as God symbolically burning out of the common bush. That's what we are – common bushes aflame with God!

But the Israelites didn't know that. They only knew a distant God. What you know outside will *never* hold you. You'll never learn your profession by what you know outside of it. So when all we have is a relationship to an outside God, when needs arise we can't find Him and we can't be sure of Him. You can only be *sure* of what you've got *inside* yourself...that's all! When you've got God inside yourself, you're sure because you *know* Him. He is the real me when you know Him just like you know yourself...and you know the true self to be Christ *in* you *as* you!

The Israelites didn't know that. When we're young Christians we don't know that. So we have to start the Christian life as the Lord's and wanting to follow the Lord, but we can't conquer our battles and our temptations and our difficulties. We know He is our Lord and our Savior and we ought to be better kind of people, but we don't know that independent "ought to" self is really still Satan's self as us...and we have the problem of our temptations like these men in the wilderness. They had never handled a situation where they hadn't got food or water or whatever it was. As separate selves, where could they find it? Because you can only practice faith on something which is within you. When you've got it, you can practice faith in it. If you've got to try and get it, you can't do it because when you want it, where is it?

Now this is what happened to the children of Israel – the type of us in our new birth experience. But when Joshua took them into the land of rest...took them into the Promised Land...Joshua had learned Moses secret and how to trust God...and some of these with him when they entered the land of promise. That was the *next* outer picture for us in the days of Joshua. For us the Bible says, in chapter 4, the *real rest* is Jesus **in** *you*. So the real rest is when we in the inner consciousness know "I'm not I, but Christ in me." Christ, my rest. So we enter into His rest because rest is when *you*'ve got what it takes. He in you *as you* in place of false independent you, where you operate from strain, and you haven't got what it takes to operate...and it's only you. You operate from rest and you've got what it takes to operate. You go to a store to buy $20 worth of goods with $100; you operate from rest. You buy from rest. If you go to buy $20 worth of goods with $1, you operate from strain. You haven't got what it takes to operate. Until we know Who is our inner operator *in place of* the satanic lie of independent self, we're like that. We don't know how to operate life because we want to be right, but with *only* ourselves and an outer Jesus, we haven't got what it takes. We don't know how to find God and have His presence and His power when we need it – with this mistaken idea that I'm an independent person. This is the illusion that remains from the Fall. When we think we're independent, we've got to call on God and pray God and seek God...and we don't know *where* we can find Him.

The second stage then is when we find that to be a true son is to take the second step of faith. And the second step is when I see that this old independent self of Satan as me that I've known as "I am," *has been crucified* with Christ as far as being independent is concerned. The independence was the sin – Satan as us. Independence is Satan's self-loving self. When Jesus Christ was crucified *that* was crucified; the sin-spirit went out of Him and thus *out of me.* Now then, I, as an independent self, am crucified, but now I live, my God-made human self, freed from that false Satan-self, risen with Jesus Christ and now Christ lives **in** *me*! So I live – my human self is now Christ living *in me as me* in place of Satan. Now then, when I know that, I am free to be myself. And I have all the peace...and all the power...and all the guidance...all the wisdom in me when the living God is in me. I have the lot!

So to be a son of God is to be my *human* self – a real person, but *God expressed* in His son form. This is what Jesus said after the Spirit as a dove came down, and was in Him at His baptism, "I do nothing by Myself. I know nothing by Myself. I do what the Father does." Now that's *my* consciousness. You live by inner consciousness. And on that basis whenever I speak, I know it's the Father speaking through me. I'm doing deeds with the Father's resources. Now I've got what it takes! That's entering into His rest. That's what the Bible calls "ceasing from our own work." Your own work is trying to do it by yourself. If you're born again you're *not* by yourself. It's a lie. You're under illusion while you think you're *just yourself* with God helping you or something – or Jesus Christ *by* you. He isn't *by* you. He's you! He's taken your place. He's the real you in you! You as an independent person have been crucified. You live; He lives in you! That's why in chapter 4 it says, "Let us labor therefore to enter into that rest, lest any man fall after the same example of unbelief." What is unbelief? Unbelief is that I'm not relating myself to a fact given me. All life is relating myself to facts given me. When you come here this evening, "Shall I come? Shall I come? I'll come." That's faith. Labor means "study earnestly," "catch hold of what it means to believe." Realize this is what the Bible is saying to you. The Bible is saying to you – Christ is not only the Savior, but He's the indweller; He's the one Who's joined Himself to you. He's not only your Savior, He's your life! Study is to recognize this. Then you move in by faith and say, "That's what I'm taking!" So the Bible is to teach us what we can take. The Bible can't make us take it. To study is being interested in a thing. Study is not boredom. Study is "I'd like to know that." And, "What's that?" I'd like to know Jesus Christ living in me. It's by *faith*.

We enter into this rest by the same way as we entered into Jesus. To take Jesus you and I had to take a step – discovering we were sinners...wanting Him as a Savior...wanting to have eternal life...wanting forgiveness...wanting to have God as our Father. What do you do? As a free person, you said, "You told me that if I receive You into my heart, You come. Jesus Christ, I've herewith received You." Now by the *law* of faith, what you take takes you! So by the same way we enter into His rest and discover that it's no longer we living – it's Christ living in *my human* form. You haven't found Him; He's found you. *This* is the rest.

Now he was telling them that they should get hold of this. He was writing to these Hebrews who were in *this condition*. They didn't yet *know* Christ as their rest. They were saved...they followed Jesus...they suffered for Him...and loved Him and Paul said, "God is not unmindful to forget now your labor of love." But they hadn't got *this*! They still had the idea that they were *serving* Christ, but when they were in difficulty – *where* was Christ? They were still in the *delusion of being independent* selves. And he was urging them to possess their possessions. They're *not* people apart from Christ – *they* were containers of Christ. That is this rest!

Now he said (chapters 5 & 6) there's a third relationship we have to the Son. We're *co-sons* with Him as *perfect expressions*. The Bible says, "as He is *so are we* in this world." *As* He expressed the Father, we express Him. Thus there's a third way in which we're to understand our union with Him. The one who revealed Himself to us as the Savior now reveals Himself to us in us, first as our Moses, then as our Joshua. But *now* He expresses Himself also as Melchizedek, the high priest, and that is the purpose of Paul's letter. The meaning of a high priest is that he is for others. A Savior for is myself...a high priest is for others. In chapter 5 the meaning of the high priest in the old days was that he's the one who related the people to God. In those days their relationship was through the tabernacle, and the high priest represented them to God and made reconciliation by taking the blood into God's presence in the holy places the holiest of all. So a high priest is one among them who's been ordained for them to relate them to God.

The High Priest is Jesus Christ, and Paul is showing them that we also are royal priests...with the priesthood ministry. He began to explain to them how a high priest is identified with the people...enters into their lives... suffers with them. Then in vs. 11 chapter 5, he had to stop short. "I can't actually take you Hebrews further on because there is a blockage. I'm now going on into spiritual dimension, the heavenlies, where God is for others. I can't take you there because you've got blocked up by yourselves. You don't yet know that lie of thinking you are independent, separated selves. You're blocked up by your own apparent separate needs and self-pity and seeking for your own self-deliverances. You haven't found the secret of *freedom from* that false Satan self-relying form of self...and *being* a Christ-expressing self. He's your sufficiency and you're free to be your true self when you know Him as you in place of Satan as you. But you haven't got there." So he had to stop there in what he was saying to them. "You see, I'm not likening Jesus Christ to an earthly priest like Aaron. I'm likening Jesus Christ to the eternal heavenly priest. And that means moving into the eternal purposes of God out of the temporal to the eternal.

Before we go further into the revelation of our Lord Jesus Christ as the Great High Priest and ourselves as priest-intercessors along with Him, with the central emphasis all through of the keynote of faith as our life-basis, I will go over again something of our necessary *personal foundations* for the life in the Spirit. These Paul has given us through the types of Moses and Joshua, starting back by the reality of our lost and separated condition from the Fall in the Garden of Eden.

We have first to recognize our **separated** condition in the Garden of Eden and the Fall. I'm not going to introduce this at any length because it doesn't come into this letter, but it's the background of being purged from our sins. Sin is the term used by definition of being **purposely** the *opposite* to God, called "the transgression of the law", which was Satan in action. The law of the universe is the One Person who is love, and when the nature of the One Person who is the universe is self-giving love, when by Satan we purposely become self-loving love, we're the opposite. That is sin, Satan's nature. That's what we have to be purged from. That's what we fell into. Through the temptation and through response to temptation we came under the control of the spirit of self-centeredness, the spirit of error, the spirit of Satan. The taking of the fruit symbolized taking the person. That's our sin condition opposite to God. He's the person of self-giving love. We're the persons of self-loving love. And in the control of the spirit of error we go to the destiny of the spirit of error, which is spoken of in the Bible as the spirits in prison, and spoken of as hell. That's why Paul speaks in the second chapter of him who had the power of death...and we fear him. In between our human birth and our death, there are all the sorrows and sufferings which are the outcome of that distorted life. True life is harmony. True life is God, Who is love and with love there's always harmony. False life is disharmony, so this life is a life of suffering and distortion, fear, hate, and being driven by things of which we are guilty and condemned, yet necessary because by this means we find that we are persons.

Now the Son comes into this situation where we have lost even the desire for our true destiny as sons of God and prefer to be children of the devil...and to find our satisfaction in what we know to be a distorted form of life, a self-centered life. He comes into that with His consequent sufferings as His first step of identification, the Son with the sons. That's chapter 2 of this letter.

It doesn't refer to what He did for us, but what He suffered in doing for us because it is His identification with us. It is a remarkable statement – that God *meant* this. It's a great thing to understand that God means suffering! It says in verse 10, "it became God," it suited God "by Whom are all things," in bringing many sons to glory to make the Pioneer of their salvation "perfect through sufferings." It's God's *meaningful* purpose that the background of glory is sufferings, because you can't have one without the other – one pressurizes and conditions us for the other. You have to know the opposite. You have to know the negative before you can settle into the positive. The expression is, "he tasted death for every man." Tasting is what it meant to be a Savior, and that touches us when we move into the intercessory life. We taste their sufferings. It's fear. It says that Jesus came to destroy him that has the power over death, the devil, and deliver us from the fear of death, which all our lifetime subjects us to its bondage. It wasn't death; it's what is involved. It's the fear, and the fear of death is the destiny of remaining in the hellish condition of distorted self-centeredness. That's why, when Jesus went to Hell. It says in Peter he preached to the spirits in prison, because our prison is our self – our distorted self is prison. Hell consists of spirits in prison. It's the *spirits* in prison, not the bodies. And we start out life by being spirits imprisoned here by the spirit of error. And now we become liberated spirits!

So this chapter 2 presents Him in *His total identification with us*. He didn't take on Himself the nature of angels. He took on Himself the seed of

Abraham, and became one with those whom He was to perfect with Himself. "For both He that sanctified and they that are sanctified all are of one" – not there referring to our oneness in Christ, but to us all composed of the same material. Therefore "He's not ashamed to call us brethren." A permanent eternal bond. Forever, He's our brother. Therefore don't be ashamed of yourself when He's not ashamed of us. Put the other way around...He's *proud* of us. So be proud of yourself...and we do that when we know we are God-indwelt selves!

And so it presents Him here as permanently identified with the redeemed family. "I will declare thy name unto My brethren....in the midst of the church will I sing praise unto thee." So He remains with the sons...praising the Father. And then He fulfilled his Saviorhood by being identified with all that we go through as our Brother to its ultimate limit which is death. Death means hell. So The One whose body died on Calvary, "Thou will not leave my soul in Hell," His body was left on the cross and didn't see corruption because it was raised again. His soul, which is His outer self, went to hell and "Thou will not leave my soul in Hell."

So He went the ultimate distance we go, but because the devil, tempt Him as he may, *couldn't* get Him. He was never under the control of the devil, and because He was *our* author and *our* representative as representing the whole family, He came up from that hell. It couldn't hold Him. *He'd went down, representing us – "made sin" with the spirit of error. He came out as us – the Spirit of Truth – raised again with the glory of the Father, quickened by the Spirit!* And by that means He annulled the power of him that had the power of death. The word destroyed means annulled. There *is* no more death. There's only the death of the body and we get a better one! The *real* death is abolished in Christ. In Christ we have eternal life. We don't really die when we die physically. We've already died in Christ. We merely *move on* to a fuller being! That's why death is a praising...not a mourning! Then, he says, the purpose of this is a permanent relationship. His coming as the Savior was a *temporary* condition...pioneering our salvation. His resurrection is the *permanent* fact as the great High Priest, which is His eternal relationship with us. So it says, at the end of chapter 4, "Wherefore, it behooved him to be made like unto his brethren that he might be a merciful and faithful High Priest." Faithful means carry out what He came to do – to *relate us to* God and then to *establish us in* God. This is what the letter moves onto.

Now Paul moves on into the full meaning of *symbolism* – the types which had been the only way by which God could first reach us as a *separated* people. He had represented Himself in His external form by standards we couldn't reach by the law, and *because* we couldn't reach them it would convince us of our guilt and of the curse which was our hellish destiny. And coupled with the law He gave them the tabernacle as the demonstration of His continuing grace – of His presence among His people by the sacrificial process, and with the high priest. He must be a chosen one of the people...a member of the people and go through all they do...but would be God's chosen representative who would link them to Himself by reconciliation and thus ensure His continuing presence with them. But we can never live by outer forms; only those who know the *inner* know the liberated life. Moses knew the inner...and Joshua. They knew the inner relationship, and so it was always possible for people to move into the inner, as was said of Joshua...and Pharaoh said about Joseph, "In whom the Spirit of God is." Yet the Spirit relationship could only come on a full scale when the *true reconciliation* had been made by the *true* Reconciler. So that now we all can move in to the Spirit relationship – the heavenly – which is the purpose of this letter. Paul now very wonderfully puts in Spirit focus the symbols...the shadows...the patterns of "the heavenly things" (5:8) in the tabernacle, but which *now* become substance.

Now he says the first shadow I remind you of is Moses. He was like a Savior to them. So the Bible actually says, "You were baptized into Moses in the cloud and the sea" (1 Cor. 10:1-4). In that *outer* form he was their mediator for a relationship to God. He wasn't the Redeemer. He wasn't the Son. He was one of us...the servant...and he could only give us a relationship **to** God. He was the head of the people of God. That's the best he could do. So it remains an outward relationship and therefore a variable relationship.

So here's God and here's a people. Here's a tabernacle where He dwells, and I'm related to Him and I have to have sacrifices continually to keep me in the right relationship with the high priest to do it for me. But you can't live by that outer! When the storm is blowing you haven't got the inner reality, which can take you through things. Now he says, "You know better than that. Jesus has come as your Moses. He builds the house." Moses was faithful in all his house as a servant. "Christ is Son over His own house, and whose house are we if we hold fast the confidence and the rejoicing of the hope firm to the end." We're the household now! This means the new birth to us. It's an *inner* relationship to a Savior.

So you've begun the inner life. That's why at the beginning of Chapter 3 he says, "I write to you holy brethren, partakers of the heavenly calling." I'm presenting to you the High Priest and apostle – initiator of our profession. Our profession is the inner one, but he adds, "If we hold fast" (3:5), and he says it's a warning of why it isn't, but might be. You are...you have the confidence, but there's a warning...*keep* it. Not *get* the confidence. Hold fast what you've got. Don't center on the "If you lost it." Center on the fact you *have* it. It isn't, "You might lose it." It's, "Thank God you've got it.! Keep on with what you've got." But when we don't know Who we are, we give equal negative warnings to others. We're *more familiar* with being lost than being saved when we haven't got that for ourselves. But now, he says, it's still a house relationship – we are a separated people. He is the Son in His own house – Son, sons, separated people – still, "Here am I; here's He." Still this *gap* which came through the Fall - that took form for the children of Israel in the tabernacle.

They hadn't reached the Promised Land yet. They were in the wilderness. They had come with Moses, through the cloud and the sea – what's *symbolic* to us of a saved relationship with Jesus Christ. They were disgruntled wandering in this tough wilderness. No food, no water, enemies attacked them, snakes, and who knows what. So they *hadn't* come into something which had become a *possession* to them, in which they lived. You *live* in the Promised Land. You're a *part of* it. You're **in** it! But they were still in the *illusory consciousness* of being separate persons from God. We all go through it in our new birth. We have Him, but I lose Him so often – I lose His fellowship...I get dry...I'm weak...I fail...I've sinned...I haven't any power. There's something missing! I haven't settled into finding something which is *wholly me*. You can't settle in a wilderness. You don't want to be there. *There's something missing*. And they expressed their disturbed feelings by their murmurings. They were more conscious of their disturbed selves. They were God's people but their consciousness was on *themselves*.

The Children of Israel were equivalent to being saved people. They didn't die and go to hell. They'd come through the blood of the Passover and through the Red Sea and Mt. Sinai. They were God's people! They were equivalent to what in our day we call 'redeemed people'. But they were *half-way people* – as we *appear* to be when we hadn't yet got this matter settled of *what a self really is* and *how it functions* as a real self – which is a son of God, a deified self! They hadn't got that and they could only learn that through a painful process. We can learn nothing except through painful processes! No suffering, no glory. They're out of the sufferings of the sins, which were symbolized by being under Pharaoh and making bricks and slavery. They were out from that. But they weren't out from under the *inner* sufferings. *All suffering is really inner* – their fears and dissatisfactions in this wilderness condition – and God apparently far off. So they murmur. I don't mean lost, but never having found the *released* life. We pay the price of what we are because we always have what we are. When we're in the Promised Land we enjoy it! We will never enjoy wilderness in symbol, because the wilderness is a type to us of it being *impossible* to enjoy life – I haven't got my dissatisfactions met. But we don't stay in the wilderness. We pass into the *satisfied life* – the Promised Land life.

For us the wilderness is dissatisfaction with *myself* – I haven't got what I ought to have...I can't conquer my sins...I haven't got the peace...I haven't got the way to handle situations. So I'm dissatisfied...self-conscious. *Apparent* separation is the problem, but it's an illusion because the moment I'm in Christ I'm *really* unified. Yet, I don't *know* that. That's this second stage, the Joshua stage.

So my Christian life is a real Christian life, but it *centers around* my dissatisfied self...maybe my murmuring self. Now we can remain there and physically die. That doesn't mean go to hell. It means our human life only comes *that* distance. It did for most of the children of Israel. They were God's people, but didn't reach the Promised Land. Why? Only one reason – because they didn't *believe*. That's all that was said (1, 2), which is the **only** thing we ever have to do. That's why the *only sin* is not to believe. The *only righteous* thing is to believe. That's all there is in life! There's no other activity in life, basic activity, except which way we're believing. Believing is my *inner self* in action. That's why in this chapter (3:17) it says, "He was grieved with them and swore they wouldn't enter in." That doesn't mean God's a swearing kind of person that bangs you on the head. He merely says *you have* what you are that's all...I'm sorry. The grief wasn't for God...it's for us. God doesn't grieve for Himself. His grief was, "Oh, those foolish people. I wish they could understand. I wish they could be like Moses and enjoy Me. Ah, those foolish people, but I have to let you know, you're in a *condition* in which you just don't 'get' it." That was God "swearing in His wrath."

While we remain in the *delusion of independent self* we've got such a negative idea of God, as if He is this angry person waiting around the corner to beat us up. There's no angry God at all! The only anger of God is His distress that we're such fools. His anger is *for* us. He's only saying, "You get the consequences of your dissatisfied, disgruntled and murmuring, suffering life." That's all. That's what the wrath of God is. It's *in you*...not in Him. And only the grief is in Him. Jesus grieved on earth. He grieved because *they* couldn't believe! The reason Jesus wept over Lazarus was because He'd already got faith that Lazarus was going to be resurrected. He *didn't weep* because Lazarus was lying four days in the grave. He wept over Mary. Martha was a wonderful person but she was mainly an outer activist though she had some inner life, too. So we could understand that Martha couldn't get it – that the dead could rise. But who could get it? Could we? Anyhow, he thought Mary would, so when Martha said, "Mary awaits you", he thought, "Mary will understand." And when He came, Mary said the very same thing as Martha said. "If You had only come, he wouldn't have died." He wept – "I thought *you'd* know." He didn't weep for Lazarus. He wept because He was sorry that even Mary *had not moved in by faith*.

You see, it's always for us! We have to come to the *limit of our disillusionment* before we're ready for the truth. The children of Israel were His precious people. You remember where God said that. Never forget this when we tend to condemn other believers for not being 'there' or condemn ourselves for not being what we ought to be. Remember when the challenge was made that God should declare before the heathen by the voice of the prophet what He really thought about His people. Look at what He said. "It came through Balaam in the presence of those heathen Midianites who were waiting to destroy Israel, but Balaam had to declare God's word. In front of Balak and all those kings (Numbers 23) Balaam said, "Behold, I've received a commandment to bless." And he *had* to bless. *That's all there is in God!* There's only blessing! "And I can't reverse it." He had not beheld iniquity in Jacob, neither had He seen perverseness in Israel. These are His people! They wibbled and wobbled, but He wasn't going to let the heathen know that one. "They're My precious people. They're my special purpose. I'm not going to let you know I've got a few internal problems with them. That's My private matter." Isn't that wonderful! God doesn't behold these things in us? He sees us coming through as sons. So Balaam said, "The Lord their God is with them. The shout of a king is among them." What a statement!

So we have to go through it. Aaron did. Aaron was a man of God, but still in the delusion of his *self-relying* self. He gave way to those who made the golden calf. That's the way he learned! Being a precious man and having been with Moses, he learned quickly...and he came through. But you have to go through grief and humiliations to *condition* you. Somewhere along the line we find the *answer is not* in our helpless humanity...in that Satan lie of independent self. The answer is God *in* us *as* us. He's the sufficiency!

So where they failed was faith. In the same chapter (3:12) "Take heed, lest there be found in you an *evil heart of unbelief* in departing from the living God." Now, there's the danger. Doubt is not sin – *unbelief*, refusal to believe, is sin. Unbelief is an evil heart. Why? Doubt is a human reaction. You're unhealthy if you don't doubt. If you're a good believer, you're a good doubter! "It couldn't be. It couldn't be!" But unbelief is, "I don't and won't believe it." Unbelief is the *purpose* of the heart. So unbelief is sin! That's why God could take Abraham's laugh when God told him that he was to have a son at 100 years old. But God couldn't take Sarah's laugh, and that's how Sarah learned. Abraham's laugh was an honest laugh...doubt. Who on earth could take that? "I'm 100 years old and Sarah ninety years old and we're going to have a child!" He laughed... but he *believed* God. He said, "God, this is rather absurd." God enjoys a good laugh – that's partnership to faith! But Sarah, her self-relying self, didn't yet. This was how she learned. She was in the wilderness condition. She only had her own independent self and her own attitudes. She was behind that tent door when the visitor, God, said to Abraham, "In the right time of year, Sarah will have a son." She said, in her head, "Don't tell that to me!" But when God said she did laugh, she said she didn't. She was relying on a false Satan-self...a self-righteous self. So she denied she laughed when she did laugh. She *meant* to laugh in straight unbelief. That was how God exposed her...but she came through. Because of *faith* she conceived. It wasn't by birth (11:11). Sarah had the faith by the time she conceived.

What does believe *mean*? That when I am sufficiently disillusioned with myself...though not as an unsaved person now...there's a transference of my believing to what is *already given me* in God. We are all believing – when I'm murmuring my independent-self is *believing in evil*. My trouble isn't the evil. My trouble is my deluded-self believing it. There's no manna...there's no water...there's snakes. I'm believing *that* in my deluded self-relying self. This is this lesson *between* appearance and reality! Appearance...while I am seeing through my separated Satan-controlled self...is snakes and no food and no water and no nice leeks and onions (and all those horrible things!) and that's *appearance.* Reality is, "Israel, you're My people. You're My special people. I brought you with eagle's wings out of Egypt. I'm yours, you're Mine. I've got you in hand. Look what I've done for you...getting you out of Egypt. And I'm here...even when you couldn't seem to see it...I'm here. My presence is in the tabernacle among you." Now *that* is the crisis, but recognition can only come by revelation. First, the recognition that their faith was in the wrong direction – deluded independent-self is only geared to believing in outward appearances.

So instead of spending ten days in the wilderness, they spent forty years. But they *had* to learn! Even Joshua himself, among those twelve spies who were leaders...except for Caleb...couldn't take the appearance of the giants. When they got to the edge of the land Moses sent those spies in and they returned with the evidence of these luscious grapes, but there were these giants! Exaggerated by doubt...unbelief always exaggerates. But they moved *from* doubt *to* unbelief. They disturbed the whole people. That was where Joshua learned the lie of the *independent* outlook. He was one of the men that brought back the bad report. Caleb alone knew the truth for he was the one who said, "Let us go up and possess it for we're well able." Those giants are bread for us. He knew this union! He didn't know *separated* God. You don't say that with a God up there, or in a tabernacle, or on a mountain! You only say that when God and you are one person! "We'll do it." *That's inner union!* Caleb knew inner union as Moses did...and Joshua did from that night onward, because that's where he saw his final snare of his own deluded self-reliance in his confidence as a general...but his military competence had failed him then. That's when the whole multitude rose up the next day and were stoning Moses and Aaron. That's when Joshua moved over. Joshua stood with Caleb. That night he *moved over* from self-reliance (that Satan nature) in his own military ability, that "We can't conquer those giants" to that *inner replacement* in Joshua – of the spirit of Satan-self ability **to** the Spirit of God and His ability. He sided with Caleb and was prepared to take a stoning with Moses, Caleb and Aaron. That's where he got the *anointing* and Moses later spoke of the Spirit of God in Joshua.

And for us...now he moves in chapter 4 – Jesus is our Joshua. Joshua is the one who had given them rest. Joshua got them in and they did get into the land...and got in *by faith*! From being a multitude of slaves they became an army of believing soldiers! By the time they'd crossed into the Promised Land and shouted over the walls of Jericho, they had become soldiers of faith! Now, Paul says to the Hebrews, Jesus is *your* Joshua. Now, we're not talking about an outer Promised Land. We're talking about an *inner rest*. The Promised Land was an outer symbol.

So the Psalmist says...hundreds of years later...that God rests from His works on the seventh day, and "If you enter into my rest." So David said, in

Psalm 11, "Today, if you hear My voice, hearken unto it." And by inspiration of the Spirit Paul picked that up and says, "Today means that the real rest is *now.*" They didn't get the *real* rest...they could only get the external type which didn't work, of course, because outside things can *never* be the answer. But, says Paul, "You've come into this new dimension we're talking about" – this union with the *risen* Jesus...*not* an earthly Jesus! The 'earthly Jesus' is on the level of the tabernacle. He *had* to come that way otherwise we wouldn't know it. He had to come as a human...but He has ceased to be that now. He's the risen Jesus, in the *eternal* kingdom, in the heavenlies...and you're joined to Him. You became related to Him first of all as your Moses – in you are justified by faith and have peace at heart. You've got that far. You've entered into a spirit relationship, but there's been this *area* in which you remained under the *delusion of being an independent person in separation.* But, now, he says, through Jesus your human self is *out* from union with "the spirit of error" and is indwelt by the Spirit of God – *spirit joined to His Spirit.*

So, now, entering into His rest means you've entered into something more than the outer relationship to a Christ Who died for you. You've moved into an inner relationship in which *you* have died with Him. That's something different! You haven't died outwardly, obviously. When it says you've been crucified with Him...you've died with Him...you've risen with Him – this means that *within you* you've entered into spirit union with Him. *You're* in Him...in His death...in His resurrection. Baptism symbolizes this burial and rising. This is a new relationship – you in Him and He in you – presented by Paul's particular word, "I've been crucified...as far as being an independent Satan-sin indwelt person is concerned...but now I live, yet not in independence...Christ lives in me."

This is the second area...the second phase...the Joshua phase...the Promised Land. I've moved into the fact that what's really happened in His Son being the Pioneer of my salvation – is that He removed from my inner self its false Satan-sin indweller in his nature of self-centeredness, which was always by trouble. Self-seeking...self-getting...self-gratifying...self-magnifying! It isn't *only* that Jesus Christ took away the fact that we've broken the law and were under the curse. He also *took away* from us the spirit of self-centeredness...who *owned and operated us* in the fallen condition...and deceived us into thinking we are separated persons living an *independent* life. That's been crucified with Christ!

You *are* crucified with Christ – which means you *cease* to be that self you used to be, in that false relationship. You don't cease to be yourself because you rise again. You cease to be that *kind of self* you were. We are "dead to sin." Sin is the Satan-operator of self-centeredness. You're not cut off from yourself. You are cut off by faith from your false indweller. That's what's gone *out* of you. It's the Satan self-centeredness gone out of you – *that independence* has gone out of you. Now you rise in Christ! Self is always related *as* branch to vine to the god in us. You've *been* united to a false god. *Now* you *are* united to the true God! So in the resurrection you are *joined inwardly* to Jesus Christ...SO joined that really the person living is not you at all! "I live, no, I don't live, Christ lives in me." You're Christ in *your human form*! *This* is the new life. That is the Promised Land – when that's become *my* experience. Now you live by *consciousness*. When you know He's the real you, joined to you, you *live* there. We are temporarily pulled off by appearances into fears, questions, doubts, but we now know Who we really are because *this* has become settled in us.

This is what faith *is*. It produces *fact*. Faith is only faith when it produces substance, and substance means it's become real to us. Indeed we have to have a *maturer* understanding of what the word "faith" means. We tend to think, "I've put faith into something. I have faith in something." That's true only in its first stage. What it really means is something has *become real* to me. When I put faith in you, it means that you're real to me. I'm saying "put faith in *you*." What I really mean is I trust you. So faith is something becoming real to me. I always say all habits are like that. You eat food because you put faith in it. The food becomes you. Putting faith in food means I take that food...and it takes me. So faith is only faith where it's *accepted as fact*, and then it becomes *substance*. Like any kind of earthly fact. I say, I'll come here this morning. All right...I put faith in "I'll come here." Now faith becomes *action* in my coming and *substance* in my being here. The word is the fact presented you. It has to be a *heard* word. That's why in Romans 10:17 it says, "Faith comes by hearing and hearing by the word of God." It means the word of God alone isn't enough. It has to become a heard word. Faith comes by hearing and hearing by the word. The word's the *outer* fact – it was the historic Jesus. Now it's the risen Jesus given...as in the Word of the Bible. But they don't begin to be facts unless *I* hear them.

Now, that's where we have the change. While I hear myself, I don't hear God. When I'm more self-fussed, self-reliant, and in self-effort, I can't hear

God. I can't hear the word. Then somewhere a shock comes – opens up to me that the answer is not in this *independent*-self that is a lie and a delusion. Now *I* hear! Now faith comes by hearing and hearing by the Word of God. There's the word – speaking about Christ indwelling me in place of sin indwelling me. I *hear* it now. I move in by my word of faith, and act by confession with my mouth. Now moving in becomes fact. You enter into His rest. That means I've done it. That's a fact – the spoken word of faith is when I speak it. That's my ability as a free person – to attach myself to something...to do something...to say something. That's the word of faith! That's why a word settles it. A thought becomes *settled* in a word.

Now this is the word of faith and it therefore says that this is the rest – and the rest is "he that enters into His rest, he also has ceased from his *own* works as God does from His." Not ceased from work. All life is activity. It's flinging myself into something...and now it is God. God's my sufficiency! So it's rest because we've ceased from our *own* works. When I operate from myself, I'm inadequate...I'm troubled...I haven't got what it takes to do it or say it. That's strain. The *same work* operating from rest means "God's handling this." Now, I have my adequacy...that's rest! Rest isn't rest *from* works. It's rest *in* works – works operated from a rest level instead of a strain level. And that's the Sabbath rest. Sabbath doesn't mean going to church on a Sunday morning! We *are* the church! Church is very good for fellowships, but I don't go there to find Jesus. He's already found *me*! I go for worship and fellowship. But *this* is the Sabbath rest. The Sabbath is to cease from your own works. It says, "On the seventh day God did rest." That means that I'm in *a condition* of *total sufficiency, which is God*. That sufficiency is permanent rest.

Then he adds one advisory note...not a warning...a contributory, helpful note which *stabilizes us* in this rest. It is the keenest spot to which the word of God will lead you – sharp like a two-edged sword to divide between soul and spirit (4:12). This is what will help you in the poise and establishment of this rest life. To divide asunder the soul and spirit – to divide asunder! Therefore there is a *radical* difference between soul and spirit. That's clear. And an illustration of that difference is the joints and marrow. I'm not a doctor, but roughly speaking we can say that the *marrow is the life* of the bones and the *joints express that life*. The marrow is the spirit. The soul is the joints. In other words, the marrow is the life. That's what you are in yourself – Christ in you. The soul is the joints which express the Life. The Bible doesn't go into great length on this. It is for special people –

specialized for those who pursue. So it says the word of God pierces even that distance. The Bible says we are a tripartite as in I Thess. 5:23, "I pray God your whole *spirit* and *soul* and *body* be preserved blameless." We're not just spirit and soul mixing the two up as if it doesn't matter, and then body. We're spirit, soul and body. Then this scripture comes along and says...yes, there's a *distinct difference* between spirit and soul.

In simplest terms, we're told quite plainly we're spirit. "God fathered our spirits." (12:9) "He that is joined to the Lord is one spirit." "What man knows the things of a man save the spirit in him?" "God is spirit," said Jesus. That's what God **is**. That's why you're in God. That's how you can be one with God – because He's Spirit. He's *the* I Am. I'm *an* I Am. He's the *deity* I Am. I'm the *created* I Am. That's my real self! That's where I know and will and desire – knowledge, love, will.

Now that inner self, like God's, is invisible *unless* it has a means of manifestation. My soul with my body is my means of manifestation – of expression. It isn't the person. It's the invisible means of manifestation and will continue as such – where the body is 'left behind' and the body will get changed. The soul is where we are *different* from each other. The spirit is where we're *undifferentiated* – one Spirit. We're all one in Christ Jesus. There isn't one greater than another. We have *varieties*...and if there wasn't there wouldn't be an expression of the variety in the *personality* – we should all be just like unidentifiable spirits.

So the soul is the *means of the expression* of the spirit. And the two main ways in which we express ourselves are by our *emotion* and our *reason*. Our reason is our necessary guide...it's not the final arbiter. The *final* word is the spirit...but reason *guides*. So our reason and our emotion express our *selves*. Your spirit is your *fixed self* in Christ – *unchangeably fixed* when you're born again. Your soul is open to all the winds of the world...as well as what comes from God. My emotion can be disturbed, shaken. But my **soul** is God's agent...and the more *I'm as He*, the more He's expressed by my soul – emotional life – in the right sense. We use our love life...our emotional life...our desire life – that's our *emotions*. And then our reason, of course, is that by which we sort things out, by which we operate...and is God's agency. We sort out God's Word by our reason. It doesn't confirm – the Spirit confirms. Reason is just material for confirmation by the Spirit.

When I'm fearful, or hurt, or feel cold, or feel worried, I'm *mistaking* soul-feeling for fact. Soul is feelings. Spirit is fact. So, do not follow your feelings if they're the wrong type. Of course, lots of our feelings are the right type, but when they come the wrong way, that is Satan getting me mistaking soul-reaction for spirit. That's the false thing – then we're back again in the illusion. That's the effect of *outer* circumstances on your emotional life.

So Jesus said, "Take no thought." You don't run life by thought. You run life by *faith*. Thought is geared to this world and we say, "Oh, that's impossible, it can't be." That's when our reason is expressing the traditions of the fallen man...and the *appearance* of things. But when the reason is in the right gear it says, "No, I'm taking what God says!" *Now* you go back to spirit. Then, I've related my reason back to God – "I'll say what You say." Now your reason has helped you to clarify some action or attitude of *faith*.

So this is what gives us a steadiness in our *rest life* – where I can discern between spirit and soul. Use my soul for what it's meant to be, as God's precious agent, but recognizing other things do come in from the world's point of view. At that point, I stand and say, "I'm not governed by what my soul is saying. I'm governed by what I am in Christ." Then, having said that, Paul has given us the foundations of our sonhood – my sonship with the Son, which has settled me in this *unified* relationship. This is the second grade. I now know, forever, that it's *not I functioning*. It's He functioning. But that is still around my own needs. It's more Christ in me *than* I in Christ. But I'm for a bigger purpose than *me*.

Now we move into His royal priesthood. In the old days the high priest was the unique leader of the nation, and the agency for their relationship to God. He only could enter the holiest once a year on their behalf...but that was these outer days of our outer covenant nation. Now, Paul says, the real High Priest has come, and we are going to see our relationship to Him and with Him as priests with the High Priest – now that we know *our settled union with Him*. So we move with Paul to the end of Chapter 4. We are with this great High Priest who has passed into the heavenlies. We've *been* talking earth talk. We've been talking about self down here – Christ in us. But it's still self down here – *my* redemption, *my* reunion. We haven't yet talked heaven talk which is "in Him." We've talked earth talk – "*He in us*."

But this is where Paul has to hold things up. He says, "I have to stop here because I'm no longer giving you an earthly type. I'm in a difficulty here. I gave you earthly types – Moses, Joshua. Now I've got to move on to a reality which isn't earthly...but I'm in difficulty because you haven't yet been those who have had this *human self* put into its focus in this rest relationship. So you haven't entered into the *consciousness* of the heavenly self-for-others as a *permanency* – the spirit realm. You've lived geared to the outer human – self-interests and self-reactions realm. But our High Priest has "passed into the heavens." This is where He's given the name Jesus, the Son of God. It's Jesus, the man, yet it's the Son of God. And we're to be co-Jesus' – co-sons in the heavenlies! But it *is in* the heavenlies. But they had been obsessed with the problems centered around themselves. They hadn't yet passed into the Joshua *rest level*. So he couldn't take up with them the released-from-self reality – where it is the realm of suffering for others, while they were occupied with their *own*.

So he just touches on what a high priest is with his *total identification* with the needs of others (5:1-10). A high priest, he says, is one taken from among *men*. He's one of us...but he's appointed of God. So, if we are priests, therefore, we're called of God too! God had originally said to the children of Israel they were all to be "a kingdom of priests." Not a kingdom *with* a high priest – a kingdom of *all* priests. But you are only a priest with the call of God. No man takes this up on himself. He that is called of God...as in Aaron. But now watch this – *we* are the called of God. Each of us is called of God. Every redeemed person is a called person when we see it! But, then again, the word of God comes when we are in 'hearing distance' of it...if we're to receive it. So a high priest is called of God. He's called of God...yet he is the normal human with all the temptations, and weaknesses, and infirmities that go right along with our *normal right humanity*. So we don't judge our fellow humans. We are "all of one." But the priest-calling is calling fellow humans to who they are...when they know and receive it...sons with the Son.

So a high priest is taken from among men, called of God, but ordained for men...not for self. You're not for yourself, but shut up into God's people-purpose – not willing that any should perish, but all come to repentance and to "offer gifts and sacrifices." In Jesus, as now our case of course, He offered the gift of Himself – and that means many pressures on *me* "filling up the afflictions of Christ for His body's sake." "Travailing in birth til Christ is formed in them." "The prisoner of the Lord for your sakes." So, Jesus, the Man of Sorrows, Who "in the days of His flesh with strong crying and tears, offered up prayers and supplications to Him who was able to save Him from death." "He was heard in that He feared"...as in Gethsemane with strong crying and tears and bloody sweat. He was saved from death by going through death, and getting the resurrection for us all. He did not spare

241

Himself. He wasn't saved from death, from which He could have been. He said "Legions of angels could save" Him. But, He said, in effect, "In my Father's will being saved doesn't mean I won't have the *outer* death." In His outer death for everybody...but millions along with Him in resurrection. There is agony in it. There is travail and there is agony. But that is where it says, "Though He was a son, yet He learned obedience by the things He suffered, and being made perfect became the Author of eternal salvation to all who obey Him." Made perfect as a High Priest – not perfect in sanctification, which He already was. Now to be perfect as a High Priest...to be able to lead other people in.

Then "being made perfect" means made *mature*. When we've settled in this way of faith, then are we to bring eternal salvation to people. Not a hit or miss little bit of salvation! Eternal salvation means a *continuing* new grade of life. *We* can be the author of eternal salvation to others when we know the way ourselves. We can show the way of faith *having gone* the way of faith. We can be the author of eternal salvation when we *know the way*. We present Jesus, not ourselves...but we know the way. So in that sense we are priests as He was High Priest...to those who obey. The obedience of faith, not works. The way of obedience isn't the way of hard works and prayers. The way of obedience is to be willing to accept the position you're in *as from God*, and then move into the *faith* that God is perfecting something thru it.

But, Paul says, at that point, I have to stop because there's a remarkable high priest introduced into the Old Testament. *Just introduced*, then dropped and nothing more said about him. Yet it was a *radical* revelation! Never seen before...never seen again, and wasn't among the usual lists of high priests...and for this reason. The human high priests were geared to the old covenant of law. But, in order to prepare the way, even in symbol in the old days, there was an *eternal* high priest who didn't follow Aaron. Jesus has been our Moses...Jesus has been our Joshua. But Jesus is *not* our Aaron, because Aaron represented another covenant – a covenant of *law* and *works*.

Now, Paul says (5:10-16) that there is *another type* of high priest, and *this* is where he can't yet take those Hebrews. I can explain it to you, but I can't say you're there yet *because* you're still geared into this self-pity – of this deluded independent self – and questioning about your *separate* selves. So I can't bring you in, but I can present it out to you. This is heavenly. It doesn't belong to yourself as an earth person. It belongs to yourself as a heaven person – in spirit union! *This* was Melchizedek...and all that's known about Melchizedek is when he suddenly visited Abraham as the priest of the Most High God.

Now Abraham was the father of faith, but he was linked in the human fashion to earth relationships. So a high priest on Abraham's level wouldn't be just another Abraham. So there came into Abraham's life a priest that wasn't on the Abrahamic level. He was king of Jerusalem and the priest of the Most High God, but nothing else is known of him. He *knew* the Most High God. A priest knows the highest. He's in the holiest. He's at the throne. And that was the term Melchizedek used - the Most High God.

Now that saved Abraham at that moment. It was when Abraham was being tempted to take the spoils he had gained by his rescue of Lot from the kings with all the spoils of Sodom. He could have taken it and we can easily have the earthly idea that God can use this human wealth. That would not do for God's *eternal purpose*. He must have a person who *walked alone* with God – the absolute with the Absolute – who wasn't profiting by earthly gains...by which of course, he would have engendered all the hatreds and jealousies of the world's peoples around him. He was to be a *separated* person. He was to live in tents. He was to look for a city which had foundations – that heavenly city! And here was this moment of *vital preservation* under temptation. This man 'turned up' and Abraham immediately knew he was higher than himself. This was a priest of the Most High God! They communed together by bread and wine provided by this strange man. They broke bread together – which symbolized *union*. By this he conveyed to Abraham his union with the Most High God. He possesses heaven and earth, and *you in Him* are the possessor of *everything*...not a few wretched spoils from Sodom and Gomorrah. So Abraham lifted his hand in public...and renewed his vow to God. "I won't touch your things, not a thread of them. I am in union with the Possessor of heaven and earth. I'll give the rightful share of the spoils to the men who came with me, but I won't take a thing myself." Then Melchizedek blessed Abraham. The blessing was to confirm to him who he was. "You're the chosen of the Most High God. You're the progenitor of his whole purpose of blessing in this world." And Abraham gave him tithes, which indicates the lesser blessed by the better. It was plain that Abraham was greatly refreshed in his *own* vision of God!

Melchizedek was never heard of again. Just one mention in the Psalms, but that put the *whole* thing into *focus*. David there speaks of the coming

Messiah and says, "Thou art a priest forever – a priest forever – after the order of Melchizedek." You're not after Aaron because Aaron died. You're the *eternal* priest to introduce us to the eternal dimension – where we live as eternal sons...operate with eternal resources in *union* with the eternal God. So Jesus couldn't have Aaron as his type. For the ultimate position, the *eternal reality*, as High Priest, He must have the *eternal type*. So, "Thou art a priest *forever*." And then this is interpreted here in the next chapter. Melchizedek was like a person who had no father, no mother, no descendants, "made *like unto* the Son of God." It doesn't say he *was* the son of God. "King of Salem, King of Peace, without father, without mother, or descent, neither beginning of days or end of life, made like unto a son of God, abiding as a priest continuously."

Now Paul says he has to stop there. He has to challenge them again. He doesn't challenge them with doubt. These aren't negatives. He has to lift them up. "Come on up." "Let us have boldness to *enter in now*." He goes on to say, a little later on, "You *have* entered in." This is up, not down! But he has to be honest with them. He says, "You are not there *now*. I can't speak to you as those who recognize your *union* with Him as the eternal High Priest – therefore functioning *as* priests. So he had to rebuke them. "You need to watch out." That's why Paul says to the Philippians, "It is *God* that works *in you* to will and to do His good pleasure." Then you "work it out with fear and trembling." Fear is not of some negative judgement coming on us. Fear is a *rightful caution*. Everybody who drives a car has a rightful caution. You don't fear driving. You enjoy it, but you keep the rules. Fear is respect. We all have it for each other. We love each other, yet we don't go beyond bounds. Life has this basis of respect...for God...for each other...for ourselves.

But he says to them, "You've not been going on because you're still fussing around the elementaries." (chapter 6). That hits home to us because so much preaching is on the elementaries. I go to a good gospel fundamental church, but they so often *never give me anything but* the gospel. I'm hungry to be taught the deeper things of the Spirit! They're fussing around the elementaries. Paul describes what the elementaries are (6:12). They're the external relationships...the foundation of repentance from dead works...and faith toward God. The *first* steps! Then you go to outer forms to confirm it – the baptism and laying on of hands...*even including* the gifts of the Spirit...(You can have the Holy Spirit in the Pentecost experience of the gifts, and *yet not know the total* relationship.) and in the bodily resurrection and judgment to come. They are the *outward* forms. That's the future...a look into the past...a look into the future. *That's the elementaries!* Now let's *move on* to perfection...maturity.

"So, you see, the evidence is that you need to be taught when you should teach!" That's a valid point for us. We shouldn't need to be taught. We should know...and *live* by our *knowing*. John speaks about that (I John 2:20, 27). *Teaching* is only to *confirm* what *is*. But I shouldn't *need* confirmation! I may enjoy listening and hearing it again, but I shouldn't *need* it. This is what I am! We all give what we've got. You share what you've got. Now, he says, you should be teachers. You should have so much of a *confirmed inner consciousness* of this life of *Christ in us* and *we in Him*...that you're able to share it with others. That tests us out. A teacher means you're sharing what you've got. So he says, "You're not ready for strong meat yet. You can only drink milk." Milk is the outer thing. Solid meat is that which gets into bones and marrow and needs chewing. You're still related to outer things – you interpret things according to their *outer* appearance of good and evil. We say, "Well, that's good; that's evil."

But, he says, when *your senses are exercised to discern* both good and evil, you come to a new sensibility. And the new sensibility is this – it runs right through this letter, which is a letter of faith. *The only real evil is to be believing by outer appearances.* The good is to *discern the motive*, and to see how God is operating through *everything* (see Rahab!)...whether it's good or evil...whether it's the devil himself as Jesus in John 14:30. The *real* evil is *my* unbelief – seeing on an outer level, an appearance level. The *real* good is when I can say, "*God's* in this thing!" And when I'm in an evil situation I can say that's *God* working in it just as Paul in Nero's prison called himself "the prisoner *of* the Lord." That is discerning with right discernment! The elementary says, "That's bad; that's good." When my senses are exercised in a *right* discernment, I say, "Wait a minute, even if it is bad, God's *in* that situation." God means freedom – so He means a bad thing to *be* a bad thing, as with Pharaoh in Romans 9:17. But we say, "God, that's it! I know that's bad...as we call it bad...but *You're* going to turn it into good. I'm going to see *You* bringing good out of the evil." The good is seeing a good God in operation in evil situations. Evil is real...but the *only real evil* to me is my unbelief! When you see things as evil *you're* bound by it...and you make no contribution to it *except* as a negative. See Paul in 2 Cor. 1:8-10. That's the level of the servant...because you can't see it until you see **God** in everything. You can't see God in everything until you've come up into this heavenly realm. Until then you've got the divided outlook that we got through the Fall – God's here and the devil's there. Two powers. You can't see it until you see it in the wholeness of God. See what Jesus said to Pilate in John 19:10-11. Then you see good and evil from a different angle and you speak of it differently. You don't just say that's good or that's evil. You *watch for God* in it. That's against the way the world sees things. The whole concept changes. That's not a concept acceptable to the average believer who's in stage 1 or even stage 2. You haven't moved into the 3rd realm where you *only* see things from the spirit level, and you think you should condemn evil as evil and good as good as we commonly speak of it.

Now he continues with his word of exhortation...chapter 6 all through. It was to lift them up because he was always saying, "You're God's people. I want to lift you to the highest." So he continues with a word of exhortation to persistent faith. Anyhow, he says have *persistent* faith. Go on to perfection. He says, you're not among those who turn back. "I'm persuaded better things of you, things that accompany salvation." He lifts them up. The Spirit always lifts up, not down. "God is not unrighteous to forget your work and labor of love. Your ministries to the saints," and so on. But, he says, "At this spot I do warn you, you're not among those who are slipping back." Yet there's that basis of rightful fear there. "You won't do it, but there is a place where it's impossible to restore yourself again (6:4-8). I just warn you. You aren't there. But just watch that you are preserving and continuing in your way of faith." (6:4-6) That's all he says there. We make great argument of this, bringing in terms like eternal security. Oh we love to bring in non-Biblical terms and then fight about them. It isn't negatively that you *will* fall away. It's positive that you *won't*. "But I just say it to you. You've got salvation. Keep on with what you've got, and the one way of doing it is the persistence of faith." So he puts it in a few words on the endurance of faith...through faith and patience. "Be not sluggish but followers of those who through faith and patience inherit the promises."

Patience is best interpreted as endurance. It means going on. Then he used Abraham who patiently endured until he got the promised son. He says, "Stick to it." Faith is just stickability. Keep believing anyhow, because we are based on a God who can't lie. This is where he brings in that statement that it's impossible for God to lie – God even acting *as* a human *to* a human by confirming Himself by an oath. He swore by Himself! What He said would happen surely happens. We can surely see that – who are now members, part of the vast family of Abraham. To that he adds, "You have this Jesus now as a forerunner to heaven for you." He cannot speak to them of Jesus as the High Priest, but Jesus the forerunner taking *us* into the very presence of God – you're not outside. That's where you got the false concept. *You're* in the very presence eternally. He has gone within the veil which was split in half at the Cross. He's there as your forerunner, which gives you a sure faith like an anchor of the soul. So he puts that in as a confirming word. It is Jesus who has moved into the heavenlies on your behalf. He's your surety there, your anchor there. It was a temporary gap-filling word because faith is more gap-filling. Faith is more than sticking to it. Faith is glorying in the fact though you haven't seen it and you operate on that basis. So there's room for the patient enduring of faith...and he now moves in to the revelation of what the completion of the eternal high priesthood means to us, and how on that basis we can move in *side-by-side with Him* – the priests with the High Priest.

So we are now moving in to what the eternal high priesthood means to us, and how we are in side-by-side with Him as priests with the High Priest and *function with Him*. The point of what he's saying now is its eternal basis. The word *eternal* covers a great deal. We've already read where it says that He's the author of eternal salvation to them that obey Him. And it says that "Thou art a priest forever after the order of Melchizedek." We're now moving into the permanent fact of an eternal reality which we interpret in time situations...and the eternal is the spiritual. He calls it the "heavenly" – the "heavenly priesthood." The difficulty of it being named heavenly is that we're so *matter-minded* we tend to say, "Earth is *here*, heaven is *there*, hell is *there*." "We'll get to these places." "I've got to go to heaven." So in some ways heaven isn't the best term for us because it still so often gives us a *separated* concept. Of course, that's dissolved by the word of God and the Spirit. Paul says we're *in* the heavenlies...so the heavenlies must be *not* a location, but a *condition* – an inner consciousness, because we live by our inner consciousness. It's easier for us to use the spirit terms because we recognize ourselves as who we are as a spirit – an "I am" – that "I am" of the inner fourth dimension. You can't locate yourself. You can't because you're universal! We're forms of the universal – spirit joined to His Spirit. You can't know yourself in the outer sense. Senses can't *know* you!

This is where we move into the new dimension, which is knowledge. Knowledge is my knowing *consciousness.* Now you don't *know* a sense thing. You *sense* a sense thing. I don't know that chair. I sense it. Sense things come through our ears. Sense things come through our eyes, because the whole world consists really of these waves of light – electrical waves which take forms, and we call the forms *things*. I'm merely sensing the impact of certain light waves. Einstein found that out for us. Mass multiplied by the square root of the speed of light is energy. E=MC2. *Everything* is light slowed down in certain forms...and *God* is light! Now the senses can relate to the outer. We can *relate to* sounds; we can *relate to* sight. We can't *know* them. The main basis of our fallen life is our sense life, a living soul. But *knowing* is a quickening Spirit – the inner knowledge which is indescribable, which *knows* God. What happens to you at new birth? An *inner* light. "Oh, this is it!" A light has come. "That's it!" That's not this life, is it? Light is inspiration and ecstasy! That's how you *know* light. You know that, if you're born again. "Yes, Jesus loves me!" You don't even know that by the Bible. You *know* it *inside*. That's it. That's light.

Now we're *part of* the light...not its forms. We are *part of* the Eternal One. We've moved into eternal light – God is light. We're light! (Matt 5:14) That's how you *know*. I don't know you outwardly...I just see a body. *Knowing* is different. It's something *inside* in which we participate in something or somebody. That's the eternal! And it's imparted to us by a sense of inspiration. "Yes! Yes!" And all life continues to be *more* inspiration. "Oh, yes, I understand. I hadn't seen that before. That's good." And it's ecstasy because it's thrill. *Life* is always thrill...and in the union is *eternal ecstasy*! So when we're conscious of coming into union that's eternally an ecstatic *inner* level in us. It's the inner confirmation. This is the goods! And even in the midst of the things that are tearing at us outwardly, *this* is the goods. That's what Jesus had – the ecstasy...the glory!

How about those times when we don't know communion with born-again friends? We affirm it as fact. Get off the *appearance*. In that light is the ecstasy. You know it at once – the moment you see God in a thing. In the permanent union you get the permanent underflow of ecstasy which can reach great heights. It reached great heights in Jesus at the time of Transfiguration. It reached great heights in Paul when he didn't know whether he was in the body or out of the body. It reached Moses at the burning bush, and again when he saw the glory of God on the mount. And so, in all these men you will find they had their places where they had their super ecstasies. But the continual is the most important because we don't live much in the super; we live in the *continual*. Now this is this eternal One, presented in the 7th chapter in His eternal being. This is the Priest forever.

We're moving into a *being and knowing* in Him that is permanent. We're moving into the 'Moses word' in Psalm 90, "from everlasting to everlasting, Thou art God." He's eternal ecstasy and he sees the reality all the time. The perfection is always there. We're moving in a sea of perfection. *Everything's perfect!* Everything's not imperfect. *See* it as perfect. The disasters are only *temporary* outer phases. They're part of the perfection – *this* is eternity. So it's a very good word being eternal. It involves the changelessness – the perfection of God's operating everything...everywhere...all the time as Paul said in Ephesians 1:11. You only *know* yourselves in this relationship. You *are*. You just *are*. It's a difficulty of understanding. In that sense we can't know ourselves. It's a knowledge which is *beyond* what we call knowledge. We are into this new concept of union with God. It isn't, "There's a God sitting in a chair or a God up there." It's a knowing. Who is He? Where is He? Who are you? I don't know...you just are. So what you do know is – you are. "Well, I am anyhow. That's God in me anyhow." That's why symbols have to go. So He and we are one. And we're in the eternal One operating on this *being level*.

Yet this is the paradox – we do remain *particular* and we don't lose our *personhood*. That's why the Bible is balanced in saying, "I in you, you in Me." It never dissolves the two. "I live, yet not I, but Christ." It keeps the two "I's" because they remain permanently. And so it's always the dialectic – the problem of the duality which is a unity. This is the main part of Chapter 7. The simple scripture says, "This High Priest is not made after carnal commandment, appointed and then dies, but after the power of an endless life." It's a wonderful expression. Verse 16. See? You are yourself...in the power of an endless life. We're sons with the Son from eternity to eternity. This is just scratch pad en route. It's an interlude...except that it's an adventurous interlude! As we move into Hebrews 11 we find that it has the *adventures* of faith in it, and the *commissions* of faith which are thrilling, with a cost – with a 'price' in it. But it's part of this endless life!

Having passed through this era where we bear the marks of the Lord Jesus, we move into the eternal being and *operating* as such. As a consequence of what He has completed, in an unchangeable priesthood, "He is able to save them to the uttermost, them that come into God by Him, seeing He ever liveth to make intercession for them." Intercession is something that is completed and now applied. Intercession is, "I've gone through something for somebody. I've completed the going through of it. I've gained the

249

intercession." And the Bible says He made intercession at the Cross (Isaiah 53:12), when "He poured out His soul unto death and is numbered with the transgressors, bare the sins of many and made intercession for their transgressions." So intercession is a completed act through a plain, clear calling, and then, to use an expression my friend Rees Howells used, "the gaining of the intercession." You've gained something, and the fruits follow from it. An intercessor is one who has a specific commission to fulfill, a specific gap to stand in, and gives himself to the limit to do so. He gives himself over to pay the price for those for whom he is interceding, and pays the price to the uttermost farthing. In doing so, he, with the inner confirmation of the Spirit, gains his intercession.

"God looked for an intercessor." (Isaiah 59:16) He couldn't find one, so He sent His own Son to be the intercessor. And now, in the resurrection and ascension, He "ever lives to make intercession." That "ever living to make intercession" does not mean He's in a continual position of beseeching and praying. No. He has sat down at the right hand of the majesty on high, and His total fulfillment by the Spirit is He in us now, both in the saving and the keeping and the using. And we get to be intercessors. God is looking for those who can stand in the gaps (Ezek. 22:30). This is the high calling into which He takes us – where we're being used for others. This is the law of the harvest – the much fruit, which is born by the corn of wheat which has been sown in the ground and died. It's in all of our lives where we are intercessors. Jesus used that illustration of the corn of wheat (John 12:24). Leave it in a corn-bin and the nice little corn sits there. Sow it in the ground and it goes through the process of disintegration, and out of its death comes the blade, the ear, the full corn in the ear.

In the next chapters, Paul goes into revealing detail of the completed intercession and uttermost salvation of our Great High Priest. In the 8th chapter it is the new covenant that abrogates the old. The old was based on self efforts and the helpless condition of fulfilling it. It was an "if" covenant. In the new covenant it's a relationship which has no conditions. The covenant of law was based on "You do it," to show us that we couldn't do it. The new covenant, without conditions, is the uniting of us to Him by which He "puts His laws in our minds and writes them in our hearts," and we are spontaneous law-keepers. This isn't He giving us certain standards and telling us to live by them. He's our God...we're His people. By a spirit relationship of inner knowing, it will no longer be a matter of teaching your neighbor to know the Lord for "all shall know him from the least to the greatest." Teaching a person to know the Lord means they don't know Him, but every man knowing Him **is** an inner consciousness. Now we've moved from the outer to the inner for the *redeemed* relationship is an inner consciousness. All shall know him, from least to greatest. All. And the prophet Jeremiah said it hundreds of years before Jesus!

The High Priest, by His intercession, has brought us into this new covenant relationship of union...*and* He also brings us into a permanent *no-guilt* relationship. That's the ninth chapter – where the shedding of the blood for the remission of sins has become a *completed* fact in the intercessory work of the Savior. *Sins are no more an issue.* "Their sins and iniquities I will remember no more." The shedding of the blood is the life laid down – because the life is in the blood – the life poured out on our behalf. The resurrection means the whole sin issue is out of sight, "Raised again for our justification." (Rom. 4:25) And he takes some length of time in this chapter explaining how this one act of the great High Priest in one *completed* sacrifice of Himself has removed forever all the sins of the whole world! So that Paul could say, "He reconciled the world unto Himself." (2 Cor. 5:19) The one problem then that remains is *our guilty conscience* concerning sin. It isn't the sins that are the problem...because the sins are out. The only problem that can remain is *in the believer* himself...not in the Father or the Son. So the key verse of Chapter 9 is verse 14: "How much shall the blood of Christ purge your *conscience* from dead works to serve the living God." Dead works are somewhere where we slipped into something which is a *self-work* – which is a dead work of sin that gives us a *troubled* conscience. The blood doesn't purge the dead works because that's done! The shedding of the blood finished that...but what *has remained* is the effect it had on me because temporarily *I slipped* in my believing. I'm believing more on the *reality of my sin* than in *the reality of the blood*. And, as a consequence of that, I have the *consciousness* of condemnation and guilt. And he says the blood of Christ gives you the basis – cleansing your conscience.

Cleanse means *to remove* the consciousness of a thing. And you're free to serve...from dead works to serving the Living God. We're not free to serve while we're in bondage to our guilt or condemnation. The completion of our liberation and setting of us in the eternal union relationship is first of all the recognition that there is this union provided in the covenant which has been sealed to us in our great High Priest. Then we're to be undisturbed in that covenant. There's no further guilt or condemnation...and even when we slip into something which might produce guilt or condemnation, we move in and say it's not there. We move back into where we're free to serve, because we're free!

There is a great deal of false condemnation. We *mistake* the temptations we all have for actual sin...and thus feel condemned. James clears that in 1:14-15. In Christ, as new creations, we accept ourselves delivered from that old sin-Satan indweller, and he *replaced by* our Christ-indweller. We are actually "made the righteousness of God in Him." (2 Cor. 5:21) But as *only* tempted and pressured selves, we do not mistake such soul-body assaults on us as sins committed producing condemnation. No, they are spurs to faith in our Christ-indweller and keeper! Sins are only (as in that James 1:15) when, from our *spirit-center* – our heart – we *purposely follow a temptation* into a committed sin, which is really rather rare. But, even then we are in *temporary* guilt, but *not* in condemnation. We are honest. We walk in the light...confess...agree with God about the sin committed. But *when* we have done that, John says, "He is faithful and just to forgive us our sins and to cleanse us from all unrighteousness" – consciousness of sin, and that is what it is here saying in 9:14, our *consciences* are cleansed from those "dead works". The precious blood has already blotted out the sins, but also now it *cleanses from continued sense of condemnation*. We do not live in condemnation! "There is therefore now no condemnation to them who are in Christ Jesus." (Rom. 8:1) We walk free and continue to walk free!

The final of these four chapters (chapters 7-10) of our heavenly dimension in Christ is by the Intercessor – the restoration of the *whole* man in God. His shed blood removed the sins *and* their guilt consequences – "dead to sin" (1 Pet. 2:24). The offering of the body of Christ, His body representing us, was "made sin" (2 Cor. 5:2), just as ours contained the sin-indweller from the Fall; and in His body-death, as us, out went that sin-spirit of error and thus out of us, and in His resurrection in came His own "Spirit of Truth," and thus into us. So it now says, "We are sanctified (made holy, made whole) through the offering of the body of Jesus Christ once for all." "By one offering he has perfected forever them that are sanctified." Now that's the *whole* man – the *whole spirit, soul and body* – perfectly God's perfect agent. So we're to see ourselves as perfect! The whole of us is caught up and transformed in the offering of the blood *and* the offering of the body. The whole man is back into its relationship in which we were created – to be sons with the Son.

So this is *fully* saved, *fully* sanctified, *fully* unified. Eternal...in the heavenlies...in the Spirit...in with the Son...in God...in the union, which can never change because it has *no conditions*. That's the New Covenant! In the blood, which means nothing can ever be brought against us. And we learn not to bring anything against ourselves never brought against us by God. It has disappeared! Not only past sins, but any present needs for cleansing or future. The whole sin system is *out of sight forever* by the one offering of the blood of Christ. And by His body death and resurrection the *whole man is raised*. Not just our inner spirit condition, but the whole man! *Our* soul and body is the way *He expresses Himself*. As sons in the Son-family, *we* boldly accept ourselves. We should not see lack in ourselves. We do not keep looking at "Am I short here, am I short there?" Instead, *"I'm whole here; I'm just what God means me to be. If God wants to develop something further in me, He will develop it. As a growing person, a developing person, He can do what He likes, but I'm not looking at the holes in myself. I'm perfected forever – a whole man by which He can wholly express Himself!"* We so often look for holes in each other or ourselves and think we need further repairs. But God doesn't say we need further repairs. The Bible says we're perfected forever! The whole *human* entity in its faculties of spirit, soul, and body *are unified* in Him...perfected forever...by which now in this world condition He can live His life as He purposes to *by us*. So He calls them and us to a faith, which recognizes ourselves in Christ...and in this relationship with the Living God Himself.

So where he *had* said, "Let us have boldness," he says now, "Having therefore boldness to enter into the holiest by the blood of Jesus." So there's this element of boldness! We boldly *affirm* what is a fact. Don't listen to what man or the devil himself says. Affirm we *are* what God says we are! Because we are those who have entered into the holiest...right into the center of being. Now we're in the holiest. The holiest is the total...the final...the center of the universe – Him. We've been brought now into this *permanent relationship* with the Father and the Son. Union with the Son in the Father – we are one!

So as we move in by faith, we have the full *assurance*. "By this new and living way we draw near in full assurance of faith." And we help each other by getting together in fellowship. Some take that to mean by normal church services. But no, he says it's for *mutual participation*, not for preachments, "not forsaking the assembling of ourselves together, but exhorting one another as ye see the day approaching." Exhorting is for encouragement or challenge. The best way is to recognize persons as who they are and encourage them to recognize who they are. Not to say "you ought to be" or "might be" or "should be", but "you *are*." Now as you are in this *permanent union* with the Living God...recognize it and stand in it!

This Hebrews letter is to encourage them to *recognize* who they are and *stand* in full assurance of faith. And faith is its own witness when it's affirmed. "He that believeth hath the witness himself." And there are warnings, but he affirms the positive. "Call to remembrance the former days, in which, ye were illuminated, ye endured a great fight of afflictions...and suffered compassion in my bonds." That's what you are. Don't let anything touch that. There is the possibility that a person might fall away, but don't regard that. This is a simple warning because in all life there is an element of caution. It's good to have a background warning: Be awake when you drive; don't sleep. Don't go driving on that left side of the road. But I'm not to say it isn't there. But the whole basis is, "You're there. You're caught up. You're in the consciousness. You're fixed. You're grabbed. The Holy Spirit's got you! You're joined to the One who keeps you to the uttermost and will save and eternally keep you. But there is another side, too. You are a free person. And there are warnings. All life must have it. If you walk on these icy roads today, look out for ice. All life's like that, but we don't live afraid of the ice. We just live! So life has its background of caution which makes it healthy. It's the positive-negative relationship.

And now, the completion of what he's saying to them is what the whole letter's built on. *The only activity of life is faith.* And my only activity is to what I'm relating...and what I'm inwardly relating myself to holds me. If you're relating yourself to your doubts and fears, the hurts, these are what are causing you to have spiritual recession so that you're not going on to perfection. Now, restore your believing to what you really *are*. I've made plain to you who you really are now in our great High Priest. Now restore your believing to who you are, in place of this diverted believing in these things that appear to be hurting you. You have slipped back into the Satan-*delusion* of being an independent self-reacting self. But you are a son of God with the Son in the Father in the union, *co*-sons, *co*-heirs...and when you can take it, *co*-intercessors with Him!

Now, to give you a glimpse of the *real purpose* of this restored union, this recognized union, which has been the open door to this full assurance – not something you're getting but something that's *got you* in this eternal relationship, in the heavenly dimension, I'll give you some illustrations from past history. We'll take some famous or sometimes less famous people in the Bible record and see what was the basis and outcome of their living.

Now we find one significant fact about these men and women and what were the products of their lives of faith – it was always *for others*. They'd left behind what they needed for themselves. They were on a settled foundation, and so free for the *true purposes* of their lives. All the exploits and experiences of faith which we read about in this famous 11th chapter are God *by them for others*. This is how He comes through in ever fresh revelations of His living Self...His living grace...His living power in this darkened world...taking *their* share in the world's salvation, which is the *ultimate purpose* for which Jesus came.

This is the hidden secret in the background of this letter, which could only come out in this "faith" chapter because they were still needing to get their own position right...and it is clear they weren't even in the resting position yet. They were in the Moses position – redeemed, but not yet in the Joshua position – the *rest of Christ in them*. Still *less* therefore were they on the high priest level in the heavenlies – where the whole purpose of being there is related to the fact and privilege of being self-giving selves – that the whole family may be completed, the millions brought in – for God is the other-lover *completing* His purposes from the beginning through his Son and sons. Now that has not come out so far, because of this necessity of affirming who they really are in *full assurance*, which is only the background. The functioning in the third high priestly intercessory level – not what He has done for us, but how this is transmitted to others. He had never said that because He knew how far He could go. Only when you're free from *yourself* can you be free to take the freedom to others!

So that has been the preoccupation of this letter – to free them from the independent self-*delusion* in Satan *into* the Christ-self, and then to show how *you* are now a commissioned person by which other people can find the freedom you have! The whole meaning of being a person is to be a person for others...for the only Person in the universe is God, Who is for others. He's love. He's nothing else! His whole life, and ours, is ecstasy, involvement, perfection, completion of His plans from eternity to eternity. It's the perfection of His universe. God all in all in the vast dimension of love.

So finally when he gives illustrations of these unified sons of God, who are operating by faith – no longer an operation of faith to *gain, retain*, or *be in* their own God-relationship, but outside their own relationship for some purpose He's fulfilled by them in their generation. This is the *complete* – the perfect person. This is the person who is the priest. It's the High Priest expressing His priesthood by us *called out from among people* to bring them to God, and pay the underlying prices in doing so. These, he says, are the illustrations of faith I give you – *God in action* through these men and women in the Bible. Look back and see these older generations. By this they obtained a good report. In each case under a whole variety of guidances, they expressed their faith in some outward way, which would give a revelation of God, the Living God of peace and fulfillment, to those who have lost their way.

He starts by a very primitive illustration. Abel, as the first one who launched out from Adam and declared by his faith that "all I deserve is death," and "I offer to God a symbol of the death I deserve. I have faith that You've made a provision for Adam, my father. You gave them skins to cover themselves. Here is the firstling of my flock to cover me in my death condition, and by which you accept me by grace." He was the first one to make this symbol of worship by sacrifice by the slain animal, which ran clean contrary to the lie of self-sufficient selfhood which had captured true world as in Cain. "I'm for myself. Here are some of the fruits I've grown, to show how good I am and what I can do. Hiding, of course, the basic sin of self-centeredness and the sins it produced..."Sin lieth at the door." Cain was antagonized because he saw in Abel the assurance that God had accepted him. There was a 'new birth' quality of life in Abel, with a peace and joy and a recognition of union and communion with God – "God testifying of his gifts." And darkness fought light, as it still does, and Cain slew Abel. So all through history Abel presented to the world how God accepts and welcomes and loves and makes His own anybody who comes that same *way of faith* – and Abel participated in the atoning sacrifice of "the Lamb slain from the foundation of the world." He being dead yet speaks! That was the first historic operation of *faith*.

This Chapter 11, at its beginning, lays the foundation that *by faith* we are able to discern that the *visible comes out of the invisible*...and that's how we live. "Worlds are framed by the word of God and so by our words of faith." So *I'm* going to operate with the invisible now, as he goes on to say about Moses who "endured as seeing Him Who is invisible." They all did, but it spoke of Moses here. Then the whole great chapter lists the instances of faith expressed in God, and costly actions with the *certainty* they would happen...and by them in some new way God would unveil Himself as the God of grace, truth and fulfillment in this last world.

With Enoch, just a plain daily walk of faith, yet such a walk that his body was raptured. But the real point was that "he pleased God," and the comment then from those earlier days was that he set the standard for us all – simple, persistent, plain faith in any walk of life is pleasing God, and higher than that no man can reach...for that is in fact Christ walking *in us as us*. So Enoch sets the standard for the multimillion body of Christ of today.

With Noah in a world so Satan-possessed that God had to drown it and start over again, that faithful man made no secret of their condition. He did not cease "preaching righteousness" for a hundred and twenty years, and amidst what kind of mockery? A total fanatic was given foresight of the coming flood, and built this ark as large as the Titanic for his whole family though there was not one other who joined them in faith.

And so to Abraham, a product of the godly family of Shem, and with the listening ear though surrounded by idolatry, *conditioned* in the Spirit to see beyond himself, and be the father of God's multi-million faith family. "Come out, follow me, Abraham." And there was glory in it...as there *always* is when God speaks to us. The God of Glory appeared to Abraham and said, "Come, Abraham, out from your father's house, and I'll bless you and make you a blessing, and in you all the families of the earth shall be blessed." What a commission! By this God was proclaiming to the world that He is the God of love – the opposite to the blinded interpretations men in the flesh have on the Old Testament, as if God is a God of wrath and judgement as which He has to *appear* in these *distortions* that sin brings. His first revelation of Himself was – "I'm here to bless. I'm going to bless the whole world." The whole world will come to its *perfection* – everybody perfectly happy, perfectly beautiful, perfectly fulfilled and perfectly loving one another. So, He says to Abraham, "This is the God I am. Move out as I tell you, and as you live this life of faith, now, your whole life will demonstrate that you're connected with the Person Who has a world blessing. Your blessing isn't these earthly possessions, which can only bring you destruction, hate and war. Yours will bring the peace and love and prosperity of the life when *lived for others* and God. You're going to be the demonstration to the world that this is what I am and you all are going to be."

So Abraham moves out, not knowing whither he went...not the great adventures of the *way* of faith. This is true of every believing life. All of us, in all kinds of conditions, are picked up by God when we have *hearing ears* and *seeing eyes*. Watch this! What he's really saying is, "In Christ you *have* hearing ears and seeing eyes." Pick up that God has something for *you*! The God of Glory appears to *you*! *Be free* in Christ from the Satan *lies* that you are an independent self-for-self.....settled by faith in your union relationship and you've got open, hearing ears.

So the list of the men of faith continues, some mentioned, but so many others of whom Paul said, "Time would fail me to tell you of them all. Here are just a few." Gideon, for instance, was just a farmer threshing his wheat in the winepress to hide from the marauding Midianites who were dominating Israel in their disobedience. But Gideon had a heart for God. He questioned this defeated condition of God's people and back came the answer, "Come, Gideon, you'll go in *your* might and save Israel." Of course, he had to learn this same secret we all are learning of that might being God expressed *by* him! But he moved out in faith... and to an almost comical conquest of the thousands by three hundred men with torches and trumpets and shouts of faith-victory! How God makes a mockery of the appearances of earth-power where there is faith!

David is another famous one. A shepherd lad, but with that heart for God...as in those great psalms of his. But just as a shepherd, he said, "If I am God's shepherd, no wild animal will seize any of my flock." And he seized a lion by its beard and rescued the sheep. And then it was mighty Goliath! And then it was the greatest expansion of Israel by conquest after conquest in the land God gave them. But above all...*above all*...the one with that highest word said of him, "A man after God's own heart."

Then others, some mentioned in this chapter, some from other Bible records. Jeremiah...young with a heart burning for God, but plenty of negative self-image. But God said to him, "Say not I am a child. You'll go to all to whom I send you and speak out all I command you to." And he did! Mary, a young girl, but with that same obedience of faith. "Be it unto me according to Thy word." She paid the price of an apparent illegitimate birth, but was picked out as the mother of the Savior.

As we trace all the way through we find *ordinary* people in ordinary conditions, and the Holy Spirit saying to their hearing ears, "I'm going to do this through you." This is priesthood faith. This is intercession – out from yourself in your *conscious Christ as you* in place of Satan's delusion of independent self. And this chapter demonstrates this. "I'm *free* from myself now. I'm concerned that other people find their sonship...and in my commission I'll do it." As matured selves we're now able to help others. *I* know how to do it. *I* can explain to you what this union life is in you and as you. See yourself by faith as a perfect agent of God. *I* can show you the Intercessor Jesus and *you* as co-intercessors. Somewhere with the hearing ear, the seeing eye, something comes to us in which God is involving us. There are a thousand different ways. "That's it! *I'm* involved in this." There's the start.

Certainly it includes a dropping off from many of the things that claim us in life. That is the difference between childhood and discipleship. It's to the disciples Jesus said, "If you're going to follow Me and be as I am and be 'another Jesus', then there's what looks like a hate for father, mother, wife, children, houses, lands. Yea, and your own life also, for taking up the Cross means, as Paul said, "God forbid that I should glory save in the Cross of our Lord, Jesus Christ." It cuts me off from the world and the world from me. The world's crucified to me and I'm free to bypass it, and the world regards me as way out and they bypass me. That's discipleship...remembering always that we're now in the voluntary level. There are *no* laws in this life. There isn't a threatening demand on you, "If you don't do this there's trouble." The fact is you can't help it! The law you didn't want...and didn't do it. The commandments you want to do. Maybe in your soul life you are sometimes *temporarily tempted* to not want them. But underneath, in your spirit, you *want* to. Jesus didn't die because He had to. He died because He *couldn't help it*! It *had* to be.

So this is this priesthood life. Sometimes in your own home you have the opposition...or in your church...or there are things that others can do, but you *cannot*. This life of intercession has a *death* in it. There is *suffering* in it. Somewhere. It will cost you your time, your money, your reputation, your health, but it's glory! "Our light affliction works for us a far more exceeding weight of glory." (2 Cor. 4:17)

Look at Rahab in Jericho, for instance. What an *unlikely* heroine of faith to be mentioned in that chapter. She was a harlot, evidently practicing her trade. Two men of Israel were sent by Joshua from the other side of the Jordan to spy out the conditions in the first city, which would confront them in their Promised Land. They slipped into the city, but the king was informed about them. They were in the harlot's house. Who would have guessed that this harlot was the *only one* in the city in whom the Spirit of God had *implanted* faith? She spoke to the spies of her *knowing* that they represented the Living God and were going to take the city...and she knew the history and reputation of them as *God's people* since they had come out of Egypt. Suddenly the king sent to Rahab's house to arrest these men. Faith is no sudden soul-emotion, but a *rooted conviction* and stands the test in the crisis. She knew if she concealed these men and was found out, she would be the one to have her head off. But she told a lie and said they had just left the city. *Sometimes* a lie is the act of God! She had hidden the men under the flax harvest on her roof. The police left and then she made that *bargain of faith* with the spies – that when they came to capture the city they would preserve her and her family as she hung a scarlet cord from her house on the walls. And Rahab is listed among the progenitors of Jesus! Had not Paul said in this letter that *only the mature can discern good from evil,* and God, who knows the "thoughts and intents of the heart," was doing His saving work by a harlot's lie, we'd have missed this glory!

This is the faith which always takes some substantial form (11:1) "The substance of things hoped for." It has its *temporary* and then *final* answer. The final answer is like the whole cake. A slice of the cake is what God gives now. This chapter gives illustration after illustration. To Abraham, a son in the impossible...by Moses he delivers the people from Egypt, opens the Red Sea, gives the manna...by Joshua the people cross the Jordan, the walls of Jericho fall down. These all, he writes, "died in faith, not having received the promises, but had seen them afar off, were persuaded of them, embraced them," and confessed their faith by their way of life and the risks they appeared to take. Abraham with all his prosperity in sheep and cattle, "dwelt in tents with Isaac and Jacob," as "strangers and pilgrims on the earth," for "they looked for a city which has foundations whose builder and maker is God."

In all these we see the *varieties* of the faith life. *Tremendous* risks taken in the obediences of faith. *Tremendous* achievements. *Tremendous* sufferings in Abraham – the faith achievements on the family level...right up to faith acted out in the resurrection of the body...by *this man* called "the father of the faith family." In Moses, the basic renunciations which made room for the mighty *operations of the Spirit* through that trained mind and disciplined body, "mighty in word and deed." A palace life and membership in the royal family renounced by choice. Greater riches found in the "shame" of identification with God's purposed plans through a slave nation than in Egypt's treasures! A life time of desert conditions with God's people more satisfying than all the temporary pleasures of sin. And *what an outcome* in the building of the earthly nation by whom the world's Savior would come to build from it his eternal family! In Joshua...first a *radical inner replacement* of reliance on his military ability by reliance on the leadership of God. Then a series of successful military campaigns unequalled in history and establishing the nation in its Promised Land! There is prosperity and success in the walk and warfare of faith, which we can expect to experience while we obey and listen to God's word. "Then thou shalt make thy way prosperous and then thou shalt have good success."

Many souls we haven't seen yet saved. Many areas not won over. But we've seen some success. That's a good word in Joshua 1:8, 9. It's a good verse to underline and live by. "Then thou shalt make thy way prosperous; then thou shalt have good success." To get that to our spiritual bones. God's saying, "That's what *you're* to be in the present. Then the perfection later on." And we say, "OK, God. That's it. It's going to cost and I'm going to suffer, but this is my glory. I'm involved. This is the death *I'm* participating in and there's the resurrection! I'm going to see things happen *now*, besides what's going to happen one day."

Then in 11:32-34..."They subdued kingdoms, wrought righteousness, obtained promises, shut the mouths of lions, quenched the violence of fire. Out of weakness they were made strong." I've often used that! "Out of weakness made strong." We're always weak...faith makes us strong! Faith is "God's doing it!" There is the shock of the opposite. In most of this chapter it is *achieving* faith. A few are *enduring* faith. In achieving faith it happens! There's also the enduring faith where the happening is the glory in *your* soul. You die glorying – the achievement *is* you die gloriously! *You* are the achievement. In a sense we all start there, we all start by being the achievement...and sometimes it ends like that. You die like that. And that's your witness! You have received the promise because the *promise is Christ as* you, *in* you. This is God's purpose that you should die...and so it says here they didn't accept deliverance. There were some whose children were raised again. But don't point fingers when some are not healed. It says here, "Others were tortured not accepting deliverance." *Not accepting.* They wouldn't take it! "I'm standing for God, and if I die, I die. I'm not going to try and run away from this by telling a lie or something. I'm awaiting a better resurrection." The whole series then – trials, mockings, scourgings, bonds, imprisonment, stoned, sawn asunder, tempted to renounce, slain with a sword. They wandered about in sheepskins, goatskins, destitute, afflicted, tormented. They wandered in deserts, mountains, dens, and caves of the earth. Too valuable for this world – here are God's crown jewels. There's the glory – the glory that magnified Christ! It is good that this greatest chapter in the Bible on faith ends with *this* quality of faith.

I am in Him, but now it is He moving *me* out by which *my* Christ is manifest to others. I am a co-intercessor, a co-priest with the High Priest...but for the reasons given earlier in their present self-disturbed condition still caught out in the lie of being independent selves...he has just to illustrate this to them by this heavenly "Hall of Fame" mention of some of these greatest men and women in human history.

Now, surrounded and spurred on by this great cloud of witnesses, he says in Chapter 12, "Come on." "Lay aside every weight and the sin, which does so easily beset us." Obviously the sin which besets us is *unbelief*. The whole letter is on the lie of unbelief. What beset them was *seeing* life from a self, which is really a Satan-self point of view. "I'm in a terrible position." Lay aside this negative outlook on your situation. "Run with endurance the race set before you, looking unto Jesus." He doesn't speak about being "**in** Jesus" – the replaced inner Spirit-union with the Spirit of truth taking the place of the spirit of error in us through the Calvary body-death of Jesus. So he's speaking to them about "looking *unto* Jesus." It's a glorious truth when combined to the union reality – the Beyond in the midst. But left to itself, it is an inaccurate translation. "Looking off unto Jesus" implies separation from Him...and to the Hebrews, whom he had regretfully warned that he could only talk to as babes...and merely outline to them the total union "heavenly" truths of chapters 7-10. But in our *inner union* with Him, we just see Him! I don't know how else to put it.

To the glory of our "Christ in you" reality, we *also have* our "we in Christ" reality...and with Him in His world purposes. We are now with Him in "the joy set before Him in enduring the Cross and despising the shame." That joy with its Cross and shame and then glorious fruition in its "corn of wheat" harvest...*already* His in this present day countless millions of Spirit-born lovers and knowers. And so with us!

Now a few final words. You are having your share of suffering, but don't *mistake* chastisement for punishment. Never say of our loving Father that He punishes us, as believers under pressure are often tempted to do. Don't children always have *correction*? That may be a better word than chastisement...teaching us lessons which we are afterwards glad to have learned. They may *seem* painful to our soul-reactions, but we know inwardly their *true* value. So lift up in praise hands that hang down! Don't say you are too weak to walk. Go straight forward in the walk of *faith* and you will find your feet and knees are in walking trim. Keep to the highway of holiness, "without which no one shall see the Lord," both from outward sins...and *even more subtly* from inner bitterness or resentments, which if they have root in us spring up and out into a defilement of many. Esau had that cynical defiant spirit, which was so rooted down in him that there was a point of no escape when he, at least for his own convenience, even wept for one. We know we have the answer to such *inner* disturbances in our great High Priest who has saved us to the uttermost by inwardly replacing that spirit of error in us by His indwelling Self.

And what a difference for us compared to our forefathers! They could only approach at a trembling distance to a God on a fiery mountain, which even put fear into Moses himself. But we are now actually on that Mount Zion – not shall be, but *are*! We are actually members of that vast company of brethren in the city of the Living God...surrounded by an uncounted number of angels...members of the church of the first-born...perfected in our spirit-centers...sealed in the new covenant of His blood by Jesus our mediator...and justified by the Judge to whom all have to answer. What a declaration of our eternal independence from *all* that could divert or assault us!

So he sums up his love letter to his Hebrew brethren, and indeed to all us readers, with a few last words of exhortation. Always be welcoming to strangers; you may find a very special blessing in the ones you welcome. Retain the sanctity of marriage in this sexually permissive world. Be loyal and have respect for those over you in the Lord and supremely *centered* in our changeless Jesus Christ "the same yesterday, today, and forever." Glory in your badge of identification with Him in being fellow outcasts in the scorn of this unbelieving world, "without the camp bearing His reproach."

And finally with one *word of faith* for them, as it were laying his hands on them, and let all who read this, read it for yourselves in 13:20, 21 "The God of peace, the great shepherd of the sheep, the blood of the everlasting covenant, all combine in the certainty of perfecting them." So farewell...and that they will pray for him also and graciously *accept* his word of exhortation to them. What a word!

JAMES

James is the psychologist of the Bible. He puts it very plainly. He says, "Every man's tempted when he's drawn away of his own lust." But the word lust isn't just sex...we've become so sex minded. It's just desire of any kind. The word in the Greek is just desire. Any man is tempted when he's drawn away of his own desire and enticed. Now enticed means you'd like to do it. So temptation is...you'd like to. That's not sin! That's first normal reaction to something.

The Meaning of Life

Now then, when all the "doubles" of James turn up (double mind when needing wisdom; double attitude to folks as rich or poor; double tongue - 3:9-12; double motive in our prayer life – 4 etc.) we do not struggle as if we are double and take condemnation, No, we boldly say, "I am NOT DOUBLE, I am single – Christ in my form, with single faith for His wisdom; single seeing of all God's children equal; single tongue (which can be tempted by a muddy trickle getting in, but the fountain – Christ as me – is pure"; single motive in my desires and prayer (4:1-4), not an adulterer having an 'affair with Satan', though we may be tempted (4:4).

And finally, we come to the bold declaration of 4:7-9. Get clear in faith that I have cleansed hands, pure heart, and the devil has nothing to say to me.

So I think that to me is the secret of James, which I believe, is missed. It is not a struggling to do good works, condemnation for failure book. No, it is the glorious life of practical outworking of our faith – declaring who I am – single, sole, not double and I AM the right ways of Christ expressed as me. I am that wisdom from above of 3:17, 18.

And then from then onward I meet all the doubles of that Letter of Temptations with the laugh of faith, which says Satan may make me feel like that, but that is his lie. I am Christ as me; I am love; I am purity; I am single-tongued; I am singly motivated, and as I boldly assert this by my word of faith, the Spirit bears His witness to me (4:7-10.)

Knight of Faith Volume I

JAMES

James is different from any of the other letters...somewhat the same way the book of Esther is different from any other book in the Old Testament. There is a profound work of Spirit; yet, the Spirit and God are hardly mentioned. James is a little like that. He almost by-passes all the depth of interest in all of Paul's, John's and Peter's letters. His letter is a class by itself. He is entirely concerned by the practical outworking of Christian living.

In a sense he takes the background for granted...yet, in a very subtle way doesn't take it for granted. All he really says points back to what the background really is. So there is a subtlety tucked away in his presentation. The background, of course, is what we have continually learned through Paul and John.

We have learned that a true person is in conscious union of conscious unity. We are created for that and we are created for that in Christ. The whole purpose of God through the ages is the Spirit unity with His redeemed family — His Son and sons. He expresses Himself and operates by a redeemed family. So it is God operating Himself by His redeemed human people — human forms! The basis is a conscious Oneness. You are operating from conscious Oneness. So it is always God operating Himself by us, God speaking by us, God working by us. God — meaning the whole Trinity — Father, Son and Spirit. This, we understand, is the ultimate of the Gospel. This is the purpose of God through Eternity, chosen by Him before the foundation of the world.

James makes a plain statement of where he starts. Then he makes a very pregnant comment to follow, which is really the secret of his letter. His plain statement starts by saying, "I'm a servant of God of the Lord Jesus Christ. I'm speaking to you, the brethren scattered abroad." A servant is the highest form of son. So we are delighted to be servants! Jesus' highest level was to be a servant. God highly exalted Him because He had gone to the bottom roots of taking our place. So to be a servant is the highest glory. We are a son to be a servant and delight to be a servant! This means that your interest is to fulfill other peoples' needs. So James just says that, "I'm a servant of God of The Lord Jesus Christ." So his basis is there for himself.

The hidden secret of the letter and its real point is that his hearers have to find out what the secret is of which he speaks – as "the perfect law of liberty." An unusual phrase, nowhere else to be found in the scriptures! In 1:25 he says, "Who looketh into the perfect law of liberty." Perfect! His letter of perfection, which he has left for the moment, but he continues to go back to the perfection.

So he is presenting us with perfect Christian living. He speaks once again of being judged by "the perfect law of liberty". He speaks about that in terms as being the royal law according to scripture, "Thou shalt love thy neighbor as thyself." This is the top of all scriptural laws. He means that this law is the normal form of operation. All life is law. We are in the liberty of that law when we are functioning normally. There are certain ways laws operate, and we are part of those laws. As we happily function in them we are in the law of liberty. The whole universe is law because God is law.

There are these hidden 'background secrets' to law that do not come out in James when we say that all is law. We say the law is the way things work. The law of our bodies is the way our bodies work, while, we are reasonably fit, we are in harmony, and we are in liberty because we are expressing the law of our body. As our body functions on the ordinary level that is the law of liberty in our body.

The law of liberty of the universe is The Person, Who is love. The whole universe is One Person, Who is love. That is the law of the Universe! The whole Universe is a Person operating everything in love, everything in perfection. If the universe is imperfect... operating to restore it. So the Ultimate is a vast universe of acting love – loving one another. That is the ultimate universe in which we participate.

So we are in the law, when we are expressions of God Who is love. When our human spirit has become united with His Spirit, it is really He by us or He as us! We are in the law of liberty, because we are then expressions of Him Who is love, and we are love and that is liberty. That's the hidden secret of the law of liberty. He speaks of it as a law because he wanted to get it practiced...he talks about practice.

He was a man who discussed the outer forms...the 'outer' shell of life – Christian behavior. So he used the law because that is how the law operated producing Christian behavior. When we, as person (human), are expressing God, we show it by outer forms of love, which is the law of liberty. So he

267

calls it law. He did it in the forms of love other than the principle of love. That is the difference. Behind the functioning of love is the principle of love. Unless you are in the principle of love you cannot express the functioning of love. The principle of love is this hidden union. This is the secret which he doesn't mention, which is the whole basis!

His whole problem is how to face the double in life? We are not double, we are one. The whole of his letter consists of being confronted with apparent doubles. How do you handle your doubles, your inconsistencies, and your opposites? He is talking to believers. The truth is we are not double, we are one. That is the secret. We have to know that we understand what it is to be one, function as one and that absorbs the double. The double is only something that sparks up the one, like the negative sparks the positive. So the invasion of the double sparks up the affirmation and operation as a single, God expressed by me in the right form, single, the true form, the love form. That is what the basis of this letter is.

Really, James speaking here of perfect...speaking of perfection...is God expressed by me, so I am an expression of God! That is perfection which is love. All his letter is perfection.

He is evidently writing, as we say, to all God's people – to people who don't know or don't show much sign of knowing that union. That is what we are talking about that union-life. It is rarely known. Most people are living in this dual – there's God; here am I. How can God help me to live, to resist what I can't resist? Here we are back in Romans 7 – a separate outlook instead of a unified outlook. We all know that this is the second stage.

Then he brings out all the negative all the way through – the imperfections. "What am I going to do about this? What about that?" He is implying for us to find out. Here and there out pops the secret, which we see all along here, which is the union. This is it; he doesn't tell you how to get there except by implication. He lets other people do that. He just presents the problems – the opposites, and says "Go to it" because it is a letter of faith. It is 'how to operate by faith'...but a faith which works! He is the one who brings this out.

Faith is something which produces goods! It works! Like our being here. We are here by faith, which means we are living here. Our faith operates by being part of the family here. Faith isn't only that I'll come here, I'll accept, and I'll go. It is our being here. We are living 'the Life' in relation to this weekend. Consider our being here and functioning as two different ways of functioning. Functioning is faith and faith is functioning. Faith is works. This is the coping stone of James on the outer line – the operating of life. This is faith that works in the real operations of life. Faith is works; if it isn't works it isn't faith! This is one of his great statements, so it is a faith letter.

In the very beginning he says now what we are talking about is the trying of your faith that works patience – that you may be perfect. He jumps all the background. You are to have plenty of joy and plenty of trials! The very first step my brethren is that you will find total joy and total trials. Some statement! Why? Because the trial being the point of the negative strengthening you in affirming the positive. You cannot affirm a positive without a negative. You cannot see the dawn unless it swallows up darkness. You can't cook a sweet plateful of something unless it has swallowed up the non-sweet element. It always has to be that way; it is the law of opposites. One works the other! Now notice the word work. It says here "Count it all joy when you fall into diverse trials, knowing that this trial of your faith worketh patience."

Patience is the constant recognition, "It is God." Patience is endure as seeing the perfect will – patience. Moses had patience; he endured. Endure is rather a tough word. I like the word endure and joy better; it is a mixture of the two. You enjoy enduring. Endure is seeing through to His blessed patience – I am seeing Him! It is not so hard to endure when you can see Him. You know that He is pretty good! I endure – "Ok...I'm enduring as seeing Him Who is invisible." That is a contradiction in terms; that's Moses! That is probably the perfect statement on patience given in the Bible. It says here "that trials worketh it."   Work means produces it. You can't have one without the other. Patience isn't a sort of something to help me. It is necessary, it works, and it produces. We cannot have the steady walk in the visible unless it works in us...the unsteady pulls of the other kind of life – the trial life. One works the other. Like Paul says – the life of frictions works exceeding for us with the Eternal way to glory. "Tribulation worketh patience." So it is very significant; we need to relate the two. You cannot have one without the other. You can't have the positive unless it has the background of the negative, which has swallowed up. The two make the one. You can't have the one without the two.

It says here that God cannot be tempted with evil. He can't be tempted by evil because evil is the opposite. Evil, of course, is self-centered self instead of the expression of God which is self-giving-self. So there is a place where the Eternal Person must have swallowed up the opposite. The opposite must be so much the hidden basis of the positive that it is non-existent. I take it that is the life that we go into.

That is why it says "God cannot lie" He isn't bothered with lying. He isn't tempted to lie...doesn't count it. It isn't there. We know a little of this, in our experience of being "saved." Our sins don't bother us. They have been swallowed up. They were there and they condemned us. They have disappeared as we see ourselves in the Blood of Christ. We just aren't bothered by 'once a sinner'...except to praise God that I am not now! So we have a little taste of where the positive swallowed up the negative.

Generally speaking, when you sit in a comfortable seat you are not conscious of the hard frame work...or very faintly conscious. It just gives a little firmness to the seat. So it is swallowed up. When we eat food, we aren't thinking, "Well this is a horribly bitter sour thing that you have made nice and sweet." We don't think of that. We just enjoy the sweetness.

So you see there is the law of opposites. One works the other until it settles in. This is a great lessen I had to learn. I have to relearn and relearn it every time. "Oh, what? Wait a minute. That is meant to be." That is precisely how God can get something up, and up through me because I have a down and down here. One works the other.

So he started with a profound truth here. He says that this is what we hear faith is...the living...in the sense that it is God living it. That it's God coming out, because faith is works. You are living a life. It really is that underneath you know it's God coming out. You are not being fussed about by diversions, sins, and the little things that happen. We have come out of being flesh minded, sin minded, and temptation minded. We have come into being God minded and asset minded! Being God's temple, being a form of God, we are on the up and up. This is what faith is. Faith is to mature us ever more quickly – transferring from the impact of the trial to its effect. Thank God, that I know God is in the situation. It's patience. It's perfect work that we may be perfect entirely. That's the stuff! The perfection! He says this several times over. He is the only one in the Bible who speaks about perfect faith.

He speaks about Abraham's faith. "By works his faith was made perfect." Chapter 2:22. He speaks about when we have properly managed the tongue, which takes some management. He says in Chapter 3:2, "the same is perfect man." We like to get out of the word "perfect" and say "mature"...which isn't the way out. This is the King James Version's words.

He says if you are not showing perfect love and respect to all of God's people; if you are preferring one over another because of any reason – money, social prestige, or what that person can do for you, it's sin. That sin comes out of the same law. We might call it a little sin, and is just as big as murder or adultery! So he stands for perfection. We can speak about being perfected – by the perfect Christ expressing Himself through us. So we are to take it that our common lives are perfection. It is Christ coming through common ways! If Jesus Christ was God, not just some image of God, but was God, then He sleeps, talks, walks and eats. God is a very common person. Jesus Christ was a very common person. He walked about Palestine and did common things. So common things are God! It is all God and therefore it is God's perfection. I'm an expression of God's perfection!

Now, he starts right away handling our problem, which is the invasion of His opposite. He says in the course of this walk, when you are in any kind of trial, you may lack wisdom. You may want to understand which way you should go? How shall I handle this situation? You lack wisdom. Then he says you've come to God who likes to give. He does not upbraid you for asking. He is glad that you have come, and that you are operating on the level that this is a situation where there is a need of you functioning as God. Therefore, how does God cause you to function in this situation? Then comes the invasion of "Oh, I don't know. I don't see any answer to this; maybe God doesn't have an answer for me." So you begin to waver that is the double coming in. It is the first thing that he mentions. He speaks about the double mind. "Let him ask in faith not wavering. For he that wavers is like a wave of the sea drawn with a hard wind and tossed." He doesn't receive anything because 'double' can't see. Only a 'single' can see. The simple illustration is that you can't see a reflection in a disturbed pool. Only in a still pool can you see a reflection. So we must have still minds or still spirits, if God's word is going to come through to us. He doesn't tell us how to get out; he just tells us a double mind is no good. This doubt in faith – "Will God show me what I need to know? Will it be so?" – is a double mind. Therefore he is always pointing back to the "law of liberty", which is perfection.

We only have one mind – the mind of Christ. You don't 'take' the other. The opposite is that we are not these – worries etc. You don't fight it as if you are the two. You don't fight it as though you have faith, and then as if you don't have faith. Now, you are faith. The other is just an invasion. You do not take it. Advice, reason, appearances may cause me to hesitate, but I don't take them. I'm taking – "I've got God's mind...I've got God's wisdom... and I'm going to wait for God's way. Somewhere God will show me, and until He does, I won't do it." That's the unified mind operating which overcomes the other by affirmation of faith – "I'm not taking that!" Not that I struggle against it – I'm not that. That has gone out in that old 'doubts line'. It has gone out in Christ, the Cross, and the crucifixion of Christ. I died to being that kind of person – I have to find my own way, and scheme my own. I died to that one! So I'm not answering the double by fighting. I am answering the double by saying, "It isn't there." Now we come back. We do not see the other...don't see evil...don't see questions...don't see them. That's why when I saw that statement in Zephaniah, "Neither sees evil anymore"...one or two like that...I took that line.

This is first touch on the being of a whole person...on this level of guidance. You don't take the disturbances. You just say, "They aren't there." They are not there because you are in the Person Who is perfect. The perfect soon will come. If you wait until it does come the light that you need for the situation will be there.

All the way through James, his mind is settled on practical things. As far as we can see, he jumps about quite a bit. He jumps to different points which he thinks need dealing with and brings them in. He brings in self-image here. He says, "Now find your new self-image in Christ. You are Christ's person! Don't have a too humble or too exalted self-image."

I don't know that I should say, but perhaps wealth and poverty was more of a problem there than it is here. It comes in quite a bit in this letter – the dangers of wealth as against poverty. He also talks about background. You can't say you have a family background or financial background or high lots. In other words you are a brother of low degree. Rejoice you are God's son! You have all that is necessary. You can speak with God. Stand up! Accept your God image – you need to be exalted! You need to come out of the idea, "Well I'm just an old nobody, I'm not like somebody and I haven't any background and all that. I'm ignorant." Cut that out! "You are God's anointed son; you are God's anointed expression." A little further on he speaks "you are real rich in faith." That is a lovely expression. I think that he is the only one who says that. That comes in the next chapter.

He says, "You despise the poor. Has not God chosen the poor of this world 'rich in faith'"? Isn't that great? "Rich in faith" of course means rich in what we have, because we are in faith in which we are inheritors of the universe. "Rich in faith" is that which makes it real to us. Faith always makes things real. Faith isn't a theory. This has now become a reality to me. I function as such. Come out of the false inferiority complexes. In actual fact everybody whether you are rich or poor have an inferiority complex. Because bottom self hasn't got it. It is busy hiding and trying to build up something that makes him superior. In fact it is only when I recognize that I am inferior that I recognize that I am superior...because my superiority is not I, but He! Again my inferiority is permanently swallowed up in His superiority!

So there is an attitude in which we are apparently boastful people. We speak out as to Who we are to the world. It takes a dim view of that...as we know. At the same time watch if you are rich. We all have to watch this. We have perhaps a background etc. No! No! You have nothing in you, except what is God-expressed through you. James says, "Watch out, if you are rich, watch out. That is only grass which will fade and burn in the sun. So also will the rich man fade away in his ways." Just be sure that our advantages in this life are for the use of God. What we call an advantage is not an advantage to God. We are God's advantage – human beings made in the image of God. That is God's advantage! It isn't some special gift. We all have gifts that come out.

Then James moves again to the temptation/trial bit. He wants to get that a little plainer for us. He has already said that the background to perfected living is the negative working into us, and becoming the establishment in the positive. Then he says that is the crown of life. "Blessed is the man who endures temptation, for when he is tried he shall receive the crown of life." So the top of the crown, the reigning in life comes through having lived this life where the temptations are replaced operations of God in and through them. That is what life is – trials and temptations pressing us into the replaced recognition. This is God operating in all of these situations.

He defines temptation – the great definition that we so often use. Again there is nothing quite like it in the Bible. It comes out of our self-reactions. A person is tempted when he is drawn away by his own desires, lusts. Lusts may be in any form. We are all lusts and strong desires...that is all. Everything is strong desire. All life is strong desire. We should be strong people...for God must have strong desires to expect that His own strong desires are done through us! Our precious Jesus felt strong desires. He

273

knows what lust is. I know what James is talking about, it is more our desire being directed toward a definite way...a definite thing that I would like to have. So temptation comes...and I'll always be having temptation being a human. These are the sudden pulls to reacting this way or reacting that way...through my flesh...through my spirit...through my words...through my mind...or through my body reacting. Temptation is to go some way that is pleasing...self-pleasing. James is saying that it is the very background that establishes us in Christ having His way by our lives. Establishing the transference into recognition! That is why we must have union before we can handle duality. The duality is always going to be there. Jesus had it. That is why Jesus is so valuable to us in that sense. He, as God-man, was precisely what we are. He handled all life as we handle it..."tempted on all points". Temptation means that you want to do a thing. James goes the full way in his explanation here. "Every man is tempted when he is drawn away of his own lusts and enticed." I'd like to do it! Therefore Jesus wanted to do everything that we want to do. That is very interesting! If He was tempted on all points temptation is not only drawn, but enticed. "I'd like to do that." That is not wrong.

One of the great lessons that we have to learn is to get settled into this life. This is what condemns those who haven't seen union more than anything else. They are not settled in to the fact that they are not themselves, but Christ! They act as if they are a separated person, a wrong person. "Oh, look at me! I want to be angry. I have a lust of the flesh that I want to fulfill...like this, or I don't like that." They are a tempted person. That is duality, when I'm seeing myself here and Christ there. I have to try and find Christ to help me through, which He will of course.

I am a unified person when the fact is settled into me that I am a unified person, and that it is not I, but Christ. Now I'm tempted. Yes, I'm tempted and I want to do it, but I know that Christ is taking care of it as me. Actually, we are not tempted so much when we are dwelling in the positive. A lot of our temptation comes from thinking toward temptation - sensitive to it within. That very sensitiveness activates the temptation. So when we are "in Christ" in many ways we are less tempted, because we are freer. But temptation does come and then we learn "Now wait a minute...that is not it. That is an illusion." I'm being pulled out to act as if I'm an independent self – to follow out my physical, spiritual, soulish desires. So I don't condemn myself with temptation. I shall always be tempted. That is what makes me part of the real world and confirms me in my own Christ walk, and levels me up with my brothers. I can talk with him because I'm on the same level co-tempted with him.

Then he adds what sin is. Sin is when you accept the temptation. James says, "Every man is tempted, when he is drawn by his own lust and enticed. When lust has conceived, it bringeth forth sin." When we do the temptation...that is sin. Sin has come out of the acceptance of the temptation, which is produced by faith that has worked its own way. Instead of the works of God it is doing the works of flesh. Sin is moving into something that you know you shouldn't do...and you have done it. James warns that this is the way to death.

So he has defined for us the operations of temptation, which is this process by which we are established in our perfection. This is the law of liberty which is Christ operating by us. Don't say that you are tempted by God. God can't be tempted by evil. Temptation isn't from God. It is to do with our flesh reactions. I know, therefore, that it God in the sense that we are forms of God in the origins. That is all.

Then he moves into the understanding of God in all His outpoured goodness. How you function and continue is in the law of liberty. The rest of this chapter is on that. He starts out by saying that God is nothing but goodness. "It is one stream of every good and perfect gift comes down from above no shadow of variance turning". God is just one great stream of Self-giving love!

James says," The remarkable thing is that the special form of that Self-giving-love has been bringing you into 'new birth'. You began to find yourself to be a new creature. You began to find that you have His nature. You began to find that is Christ expressing Himself through you! This has been the outstanding operation of these "every good gifts and perfect gifts" in verse 17..."Of His own will He begot us with the word of truth that we should be the first fruits of His creatures." This is His abounding love! He has picked us up...the whole creation. This is going to be something unspeakably glorious. All creatures are involved. The first fruits are that we ourselves become expressions of God. The whole universe is to be an expression of God – God in full manifestation on their levels. Humans, of course, are in the conscious wave of His manifestation. Animals are a form of His manifestation on their level. We are gods. We function as God. We are His first fruits of the whole universe...everyone on his own level going to 'be' perfect manifestation – perfect God of outgoing-love. This is what James has been saying to them here.

He says, "Listen, you have forgotten now." This is the trouble – they have forgotten, and don't know how to handle it. This is the 'double' come in. You've forgotten that you are a child of God. You know Jesus Christ as your Savior. You belong to Him. You've begun to be a new creature in Christ, but you are being torn by these doubles that are assaulting you. You do not know how to handle them. Listen. Now you must have the spirit of listening. Don't think that you have it all. You need something more. He says "be swift to hear be slow to speak, slow to wrath"...and slow to arguments. Try not to talk it out or argue it out; have the spirit of listening. And all these other forms of self-activity – laying aside all other disturbing elements...may be theological thinking that you have it - anything which can divert you.

I was talking in a meeting in Bermuda. We were talking about this life – how Christ operates through us. And a lady said, "How do you put that to the Africans?" She didn't want to be talking about herself. I said, "Oh I'm not interested in Africa, I'm interested in you." She wanted to escape something. We don't want it to get too close, so we turn it to "Tell us how to interpret this life to the Africans." That wasn't the point at all! We want to know how to interpret it to ourselves. So you see these things can flow in, overflow superfluity, so that we can't get the listening word that will put us into focus.

So he says don't over talk it. There are some things which you need to be catching on to rather than talking about until you are more sure of what you are talking about...until you can become the "doer of the word". He says in verse 22..."the doer of the word, not the hearer only." He puts this curious illustration in "Don't be like the person, who sees himself in the glass (the mirror)...sees his reflection...forgets all about it just goes back as if he had never seen it." James says don't be like that, because what you see in the mirror is what you are. What you are is Christ in you...oh! What you see in the mirror is Christ in you in your Elizabeth form, or whatever. Christ has come to express Himself by His redeemed sons. Now, you are a reflection of that! You are a reflection of what you are.

Now that is "the perfect law of liberty." This is where he says, "You look in to the "perfect law of liberty." verse 25 Don't be like those who look and forget you look into the "perfect law of liberty". What is the "law of liberty"? God is perfection of love and you are a form of that law. You were created to be that law! You are the law because the law is Christ in you expressed by you. You are that law – that "law of liberty" – when you are you are self-giving love. You are living on the liberty level, because that is what God's nature is. You look at that perfect law. Now James says, "Continue in it." That is all he says about union-life.   You look at that law and continue in it. Don't be a forgetful hearer, but a doer of the word. Doing the word, you express in your life this being of God – this love being of God.

Then James begins to say certain details that will affect your tongue. He speaks quite a bit about tongues. It effect – the way we talk about things, the way we talk about people expresses our habits. He says you are unspotted from the world. In this new life you won't be interested in the worldly things. The world won't be able to pull you. You won't be interested or mixed up in things which do not express Christ...unless you go into something by which you can witness to other people. It isn't that you go into them because you are interested in the things that are happening, but because of your witness. You are an attached person inside. You're unspotted from the world's affections and world interest, which would smear us, and we naturally serve others. So it comes out, this pure religion before God and the Father to want to help other people...the fatherless and widows. You are a lover of people in their situations!

So here is where he presented to them, what is really in the inner sense the key to union life, the meaning of union life. Yet, you have moved on from the Begotten, and you have listened because you discovered that you didn't have what you ought to have. You have these disturbances, these superfluities, these naughtinesses, these 'self and flesh' coming different ways. You then look in and you have seen what Paul taught. This is the law of liberty – Gal 2:20. The law of liberty is what you are in Christ – crucified, risen, ascended, joined!

"Look into" means you reflect it. A mirror reflects. This is what you are. This is your new self. When you find this new self you walk in it. In walking in it, it changes your conversation. New interests develop that occupy your time and interests. It changes your habits of your life in the world. It changes your actions of service. There is something in you that wants to help and bless those who are in need. This is practical Christianity!

James, I take it has to write these things because somebody has to say them in practical outworking. Paul does it incidentally, of course. He talks about husbands, wives, servants and so on. Peter to some extent does. But James hammers on this! This is his message. It has a totally practical outworking. It is a real living faith that has a practical working letter. Now of course, that could run us into bondage if we didn't know better.

It doesn't dump us into bondage, if we know "the law of liberty". However, it does dump us into bondage, when we see two, "Oh! I ought to be that, but I'm not". We have already seen that. That wisdom I ought to have...what shall I do...and I'm all fussed up. Therefore it doesn't put you in bondage when you know to say...this is what I am. Don't say...what I ought to be. Say...this is what I am; this is what is happening. And when it doesn't happen, catch yourself up again. That's all! It is all right – I slipped a moment. Don't say that I am that. No, I was tempted to have a double mind about that; I don't take that! God can give me wisdom. You keep on the 'I Am level'. That's this life! We are level...the Christ, we are One. This is the secret. James's job is not to say too much about that (others have said that) except to present it in its perfection – to say...now this is how it will work out.

In the first part of the next chapter he talks about the class distinction among the brethren. That doesn't mean that we don't respect people in their titles. You respect the President, not because he is Mr. So and So, but because he is Mr. President. It helps very much if you can respect the person, but we respect Mr. President. That is right, that is not a wrong title or respect to give honor to the Jews. The Bible says that. It is all right not to honor the person, but to honor the office.

In God's Kingdom we don't see offices. In churches too much respect is given to elders and so on. We are getting out of that a good deal. I don't know where this comes in too much – this beware of honoring too much wealth, position and family influence. In the slave days in Bermuda, in the Church of England the slaves had to sit one place and their masters in another. Those days have gone, I believe, in this country. The question is watch again giving prestige to those who have money, influence, social prestige etc. We are all brothers in Christ! Here again we come back to that self-image. If high, too high, we need to lower it. If too low, we need to have a higher-better—image. James talks about the danger of riches frequently in this letter. It is quite a social touch in this letter. He brings up how the rich misuse the poor. Of course we have had slave days, sweated labor days, we have had race slavery days and so on. We are coming out a bit. We always want to point that these things aren't there.

Then he says the law of scripture says, "Love your neighbor as yourself." That is the law! That means you love your neighbor you are...when you really see it...really only one person. I am you! When I really 'see through', the whole universe is one...and I am everything and everything is me! That is a great mystery that we haven't penetrated very far. As we understand Psalms it says, "Every thought that we have touches a star." We can't understand that. The speed of things has begun to touch us. We have some idea of the speed of light and so on. Even that knowledge is only in the third dimension. Speed of light is only 186,000   miles per second. That is peanuts in eternity! That is only in the third dimension. The fourth dimension...the nearest that we get to that is the mind...it is a place of the moment – the fourth dimension of being. You can be here...be there...in a second. When that happens to us in the whole new dimension, we are there like that – like Jesus walking on the water, and His appearances and disappearances.

I am trying to say there is a secret that we have hardly begun to learn – that we are actually each other, because all are one. That is a great help when you understand because that is what Jesus said. "Love your neighbor as being yourself". Jesus put in terms, "If you don't visit prisoners you don't visit Me. If you don't feed the hungry you don't feed Me. If you don't clothe the naked, you don't clothe Me." Several other incidents in scripture, on the Road to Damascus, "Why persecutest Me?" Paul persecuted the Christians and imprisoned them and insulted them, not Christ. However the Christians and Christ are one. So if he did that to Christians, he did it to Christ!

So if I can begin to catch that...and I'm dimly catching it...I'm you! Now that is not judgmental. I never judge myself. I am always nice to myself. I am only nasty to you. See what I mean? So if I am as nice to you as I am to myself, I'm pretty nice. When I see that, it really stops me. I do catch it every now and then. Wait a minute – I'm that person.

See him from that point of view. Don't judge him. Take them as they are. That is what they are meant to be at the moment. They may have those affects to them, but they are God's same as I'm God's. And I'm with God...now moving in until we get sons and get them to know they are sons, as I know I'm His son. Now that is the royal law!

The moment that you say, "Oh, that is an important person; give him the important place in the fellowship" you are not loving him as you "are loving your neighbors." You are loving him not just as a common servant, but as a special person. That is where James says, "Don't kid yourself all sins are alike." He says, "If you have respect to persons, ye commit sin and are convinced of the law as transgression." Then He adds, (He's sharp...any lawyer will tell you) "If you keep the whole law, yet offend in one point, you are guilty of all." You are simply guilty of a broken law. Therefore he said, "Do not commit adultery; also do not kill. Now if you do not commit adultery, but you do kill, you are a transgressor of the law. So speak ye, and so do, as they that shall be judged by the law of liberty." That is something that we are to learn. A physical adulterer isn't worse than me when I'm saying unpleasant things about people. That's something isn't it! Our attitudes, amazing things of mind and matter, in God's sight are just as heinous as a murderer or an adulterer! That may help us to take some of the judgmentalism off.

So your standards and your judgments are to be in the perfect law of liberty. Judgment doesn't mean that God is saying things from outside. It means to show you things that help you. He is showing you what you are. "Come back, come back." Judgment isn't some awful thing that God is up to. "I'm going to show you what you are." It is God's mercy saying come up...you've slipped a moment. Okay? This is the law. This perfect love which is God in everybody and for everybody is this Oneness. This is the law and operating on the level of it. So if you slip, come up and take the judgment...take as your standard...the law of liberty.

This is where he brings in that famous passage that faith is works. Paul couldn't say that because Paul had to combat false works. We build life on works...self-works. We carry those self-works right into our early Christian life. We try to fight them, but we are conscious of self-works. Paul had to help them to see that this thing had gone out. And the law — that kind of law, which was there to oppose me...to make me know I wasn't that — that has gone out. Why has it gone out? Because He has come in! The law being crucified in the Cross of Christ and resurrected as me. I'm that law now! So I'm free of its dominion, which came to me as an enemy when I was told what I couldn't do, didn't want to do and made me guilty. Now Jesus Christ wiped out the guilt and the law. The whole thing went out! Not that the law might come from the outside into the inside; I'm the law and function as such. Therefore James can say, "Now then you are the law."

Faith is operated on a given level; you are functioning on a given level. Faith is being. You move inside your being. This is the place where he differentiates between believing and faith. Here he distinctly says, "You can

280

believe but not have it…" This is where he says, "You believe there is one God you do well: the devils also believe and tremble." So he makes a differentiation between believing and knowing. Really, I'm saying that I'm believing something…it is just as well to say that I believe it.

Faith is a whole being involved in something. Faith is involvement! All life is faith…and faith is works. As illustrated in the first part of this tape – by our coming here etc. Faith is always works – works from the level of faith. So James isn't putting away Paul. He is putting something around Paul. Paul isn't there to say anything. Paul had to get the tremendous basis right. James comes in to operate that basis. You are operating; see what you are? It is interesting he went to the two extreme involvements. There are times when we get into the depths of things governed by love. The two instances mentioned by James of perfect faith – the offering of Abraham of his son Isaac, and Rahab showing the spies the way out of her house. In both cases God guiding them! Both listening to God and doing what He wanted them to do. Abraham having to see and prove his faith…knowing that it was all God and that God would take care of seeing that God's promise to him would be fulfilled. Rahab knowing that these spies were God's men, and showing them another way out. She was a believer! These men went back, and from this Joshua was able to take Jericho. The land was opened to the Israelites!

They gave us a magnificent headquarters in England for our mission – quiet center for fellowship and so on. I was there when it was opened, and I said, "Does the Holy Spirit come out of it?" That is a good question to ask of any edifice that contains God's people. Does the Holy Spirit come out of it? If not, the place is not of God!

We have to watch that. What's Union Life? Nothing!!!! What's a magazine? Nothing!!!! Unless it is Christ coming through. You have got to watch against "Union Lifers" and stuff like that – sects or something. That moment they become death! The point is – does Life come out?

Don't judge – leave the person to God. If we think they have made a mistake, let God take them the 'mistaken way'. Certainly people would have thought Abraham was a fool. He probably didn't tell Sarah until it was all over. Jesus was in the eyes of the world a fool. He died a criminal according to world standards. Jesus died a failure. He didn't leave one success behind Him on earth. His success was only in another dimension…in the resurrection. So the lesson to us is, "Don't judge!"

So James is saying (his whole letter does) faith is something which produces. We know that now we do not take condemnation. We are producers. If we are not, the Holy Spirit better get showing us! So faith is production. Faith is a new life lived, which is the inner background. This is not the same "as trembling as the devils", but is not followed through by the devoured life.

Then he moves into something altogether different...the tongue. This is, again, the 'outer' aspect. A tongue is a physical member. It expresses a mind, a spirit, a voice and a word. When it come to the tongue, he always deals on the 'outer' level – tongue speaking, what the tongue produces. The tongue is an agent, like we are an agent, of God. The tongue is an agent of the spirit that goes on inside of me – the thoughts that I have, and the expressions that come up to my tongue. (He gets that old word "teachers" there). If you are a teacher be sure that you know what you are teaching. James says, "My brethren, be not many masters (meaning teachers) knowing that you shall receive the greater condemnation" – judgment. The negative words mean the greater judgment than what you teach. "For in many things we make mistakes." In others words, if you are teaching know what you are teaching...that's all. Be a teacher if you are given that...be a teacher. I'm a teacher! I need to know what I'm saying. If I'm mistaken I need to know I'm mistaken. It must be to me the truth. I must give what I think to be the truth. I mustn't try to pretend something...for I'm responsible for what I give out. The Christian message couldn't be expressed in books in those days, because they didn't have any printing. So we can say the tongue includes the printed word today!

If you are a teacher, know what you are teaching. Know the facts that you believe so that you can have interchange with others. Your brothers will pick you up. "Are you right? Why did you say that? What proof have you got of it?" And you should know! Any of us who do know the facts are becoming Who we really are. Thank God! Don't be afraid. Don't hold back! If you have it, give it! This 'little warning' – be sure that what you are giving is what you understand to be truth...not just something that you've just picked up and theorized. Kierkegaard said a word which is great to me, "The truth that edifies is truth to me." The truth is that which feeds me. Of course we try to relate our truth to the word of God. That is why we keep the word of God as our safeguard. It must edify. Oh, that is real to me! Then I can give to other people. We can only give what we really know – experience. If we speak from the heart...heart speaks to heart. Heart is edifying!

I'm only giving what's real to me...and something echoes in you – heart to heart! A mind bores so often because you know it is only mind. That comes down to the edifying...truth. I like that phrase, "Truth that edifies is truth for me." That's what I pass on.

Then he again speaks about the power of the tongue. We are ruled by tongues – we come here by invitation. Most life is geared to what we hear in detail (advice) and what we see. We come here through the phone. The tongue can be devilish or heavenly. It can be stirring up hates and fears...pornography and all that stuff...or it can be pointing and uplifting people in truth! So it is well that you look at it. Most everything comes through the tongue. He compares the tongue to the rudder in a ship or the bit in the horse's mouth. So the tongue is a real power for good or evil.

There is a devastation tongue. It is set on the fire of hell. This is the negative aspect – tongues of fire. We get a little touch of the spirit within, because spirit is fire – God's fire. Fire isn't this thing that burns. This is its outer form. The sun is the outer form. God is fire...life is fire...everything is fire, really! That's why you scratch a thing and it sparks. It is only half fire...hidden. Atomic fire!! Spirit is fire.

Then James says, "The tongue is a world of iniquities. It defiles the whole body, sets on fire the course of nature and it is set on fire of hell." So James puts hell where it belongs. Hell isn't a place out there, a lake which you go to one day. It's here! Hell is a condition – a spirit condition – a condition of self-centeredness. Hell is – I'm for myself! Therefore I hate this and love that and grab this, and all of this that comes out as self-centered-self. Behind that is the spirit of hell...set on fire of hell! That is all hell is. Hell is merely what heaven isn't. It is not truth. The only truth in the universe is heaven and God is love! Heaven, of course, is the whole thing. This is the kingdom of heaven. Heaven is God's expression of love. The other is hell because it is geared in selfishness, hates, jealousies and fears, lust, and things that stream out of our tongues. Now he adds a little touch here "No man can tame it."

He says, in Chapter 3 verse 7, "For every kind of beasts, and of birds, and or serpents, and or things in the sea, is tamed, and hath been tamed of mankind. But the tongue no man can tame, it is unruly evil full of deadly poison"

Then he suddenly says, "You've got a problem; you have a tongue like that! You are a redeemed person. You are born of the Spirit – begotten." (Actually I missed one little thing proceeding from the begat – into the law of liberty.) He says, "Watch for the engrafted word". It is very subtly put here. I go back to that "Listen, to the engrafted word". Now that is the inner word. So he slipped it in again. You move from the outer word to the word of truth. We are begotten as the first fruits. That is wonderful! In His own will He begot us! Now he says, "Listen and don't get your noisy tongue in the way. Don't get into arguments." Don't get rushing into forms of self and self-expressions, which get in the way. Listen...listen for the engrafted word. Chapter one verse 21, engrafted – produces, put into. It is part of you – word has come to you! That's the inner word; that's the inner Christ! That's the law of liberty! Listen to that one. Move into that one. That's where he is moving into the union life.

Then he brings up this problem, "Now what?" You aren't the way you used to be – at the time just a hellish thing. But he says that we have an ambivalent tongue...never a double tongue. You are Christian now. As such, we are pretty good at blessing God. We are also pretty good at saying unpleasant things about man. But, of course, God doesn't say unpleasant things. God only sees blessing and cursing. The Bible doesn't see gray it only sees black and white. So to say an unpleasant thing is to curse a thing in God's sight. It says here, "Thereby bless we God the Father and we curse men." We don't intend to curse but we are cursing. We dam with faint praise – that's cursing. That's Shakespeare! He said a good thing every now and then. We do that. Now what? We are new people and we praise God, and of course that is part of union.

It took me a long time to see that. It is like that speck in 1st John where John says, "If a man says he loves God and hates his brother. He is a liar. He that loveth not his brother whom he hath seen, how can he love God who He has not seen?" I said, "That's not fair, because God is very nice and you are very nasty!" It is quite easy for me to love God, but I can't stand you...until I find that you are God. See?

Then if I say that you are God...if I don't love you, I don't love God...because that is where God is! That is an odd one! That is the union coming out. James is saying the same thing here. We bless God the Father. I can't stand that person. I'm cursing him. (Double tongue). Again and again the subtlety comes in almost unspoken... catching the logical out – those who see it!

Really, you have to go back for your answer to Paul. James goes on and says, "You can't have a fountain sending out two waters. It can't send out sweet water and bitter." You can't do it. "You can't have a fig tree bearing olives or a vine bearing figs." See the logic? You have something wrong. You can't. We are not both. We can't be both! You are one fountain. You are the new fountain. You are the fountain of the Spirit!!! So the pure fountain of the Spirit produces positive word about brother and sister...as He produces the positive word about God. Therefore: not from the fountain is a little mud coming en route as the water flows out of the fountain. It is mudded enroute that is all. Don't mistake the mud for the fountain. Do you see?

Find out what you are!!! You are not a double person. You have not got double partialities or double estimates about who people are or double questionings about God's guidance and so on. You are not a double person! You are a single person. You are in the law of liberty! Don't say double. Affirm that you have a pure fountain – a fountain of love, a fountain of appreciation. We go with it and I think we speak more and more positively. I find that I check myself very much quicker. I see that I have said something that is quite unnecessary and have the wrong 'side of' to it, because I see that I should see God's side about that person. We check up and see that. That is another false thing coming in...the double coming in through the flesh, tempting me. This is something that my outer mind sees. Out comes my response, "That is not I. I say that is not I. I don't take that."

If it is said, it is forgiven, "Don't take it! Stay on the positive! You are a fountain. A fountain can only produce one kind of water. So you see how he catches them each time and brings them back out of the double – double mind, double involvement – into the single. Then he said...There is a heavenly wisdom and a hellish wisdom, which comes out through the tongue. Have your conversation in meekness of wisdom, heavenly wisdom, so that the out stream is mainly pure because it is genuine, peaceable and easily to be entreated. It produces peace; it is sincere, honest and impartial. That is the sweetness of heaven coming through us!

That is what is called "wisdom from above." That is the character –the gentle, easy one – who can accept what others are saying. This is Christ. Sometimes you have to challenge, but you don't live there. Even then the point isn't the challenge so much as the love. This is the Heavenly wisdom...and we know it ourselves.

James also speaks of another kind of wisdom. He doesn't say too much about it. He says that that is where bitterness and strife come in. We know it when we watch these arguments. Envy is a bad word. Perhaps we have it more than we think. I'm not so conscious of that one. Envy – because we basically feel someone else has more than we have...or something. It produces the discord. So the real is a concord and a discord, isn't it? Generally speaking ours is a word of concord, peace, love. The other word - discord. "Watch it! Watch it!" By operating on the peace level we produce a flow of life. The fruit of righteousness is shown by that – meaning that is harmony. That is what he says about tongue.

In covering the last two chapters we see that apparently there is a great deal of worldly greed and competition going on. He was speaking to believers! He said, "You get fighting among yourselves. You have desires that you want certain things and you can't get them, so you even kill to get them. You might kill a person's reputation, as well as their body, to get them. You still can't get them. One reason you don't get them is because you ask not. You don't get them when you do ask, because you ask for the wrong motive. That is a pretty gooey picture! That is the first four verses of Chapter 3. So we have desires...earthly desires, ambitions and covetousness for this and that. Even fighting your neighbors about whether it was in church affairs or not! (It doesn't say here.)

You even use prayer as a means of getting what you want. This isn't a passage on the technique of prayer. It is on the misuse of prayer. Then he comes right out and says, "If you have any other love but Jesus – God the Father, Son and Sprit – any rival love is adultery...if you give way to it. Of course you will be tempted. He doesn't imply that it goes much further than temptation here. He was going into things which are divided objectives in life. Get it clear you can't have two loves. You can't love Jesus and then be grabbed by some love of this world. It may have to do with finances, position, persons or family. You can't have them. That's drastic! If you have any other loves greater than Jesus, you are an adulterer. If you are having an affair with another woman, you can't have that. That is strong measure isn't it! It can rise in subtle forms such as more money in business, better salary, by-passing this person, or down-grading that person so as to be able to step into his position. So other loves other than Jesus can rise in subtle forms.

Sometimes the wife, husband or children take the place that belongs exclusively to Jesus. Because, if you are in union you must have that –

because union is that! Union is you. So poor you! You are not you; you are Christ in you. You're finished; you are that life. It isn't really love with a person. It is like you are that person. I'll admit there is a duality in the unity. When you have unity, it isn't like "you love him, too." People who do not know unity get mistaken about that. They say, "Well, I have God, and I'm going to meet Him face to face. How can I say that I'm One?" You can't say it, you only know it.

Course it is the same principle as the Trinity. How is the Trinity one? Yet three? They are One, yet Three, yet, They are One! So you can't argue. They only pick something up from you, that you know. This is your center, your peace, your sufficiency and your all. I am not I; I'm this person lived through me. Therefore of course, I only have one love, because I am that love. I can't have a rival love. I'm never tempted. I can't have it! If I don't know that, I can have rival love. That is what we are getting at here, getting at those who have a divided outlook; they haven't recognized that...that is a false thing and has been crucified with Christ. It is not real. They, with Christ, have been crucified with Christ – those affections of love.

God forbid that I should glory in anything except in the Cross or our Lord Jesus Christ! I am crucified to the world and the world to me. Galatians three times over says, "I'm crucified", "the world's crucified" and "I'm crucified in the flesh."

So they are not stopped really. What's crucified isn't real to me. It's way up there...so it's a falsely rival love. It doesn't appear rival until you know this union. Then I say, "I'm not that." Then you come back. The only answer is to know the union. Because they didn't know the union they were being caught up in some of these things. To some extent they were involved in rival loyalties and even twisty ways of doing things and gaining things – by which they can be called an adulterer. You are in love. You are in love with another 'woman'. That woman is the world!

So it is good for us to be searched. I trust that we have been searched but say, "I don't accept that. I may have temptations that way; I don't accept that." Or we can appear to be caught out. It is an appearance really. It may be real to us. We may really have a rival love and do battle with it. Our trouble is doing battle with it, of course...because we have mistaken an illusion for reality. So it is possible, if you do not know the union to be grabbed by rival affections...rival anything. We know that. I've known that but I don't take it. If you fight it, you take it. There it is. You say, "No that's not real. I only have one love – that's God. My love is to love people for their sakes, not for my sake. Love things for other's advantage, not mine. Then you are free. In other words, we are free! So it may be that they were caught up by rival love...those to whom James is speaking. They didn't know how to fight it. So they had to falsely admit that they were slaves and adulterers...slaves to rival love.

In this case James deals rather drastically He says, "There has to be exposure, cleansing, humbling and crying out to God. He says, "Don't you know that the spirit that dwells in you lusteth to envy?" It is a queer phrase and there are two interpretations. One is that our spirits lusteth for what they shouldn't. I don't think that is right. Don't you have the Spirit of God in you lusting to get you right? He is jealous for your being wrong! He is there working on you. I like that interpretation much more! Don't you know that the Spirit of God is working on you to deliver you from these false things? It is there because God did bring abundance of grace! God will give you more grace...abundance of grace! Again this is the second area of grace...plenty of grace! Of course, it is not explained. The grace that we know – the born again – the recognition, the affirmation and the union, and the realization of the union...and the illusion of the other. It is in the Cross. You have to explain that. God does give grace, but you have to humble yourself.

We have hope that the believers were humble. We hope that we will find that they were. They knew that they had no business to have these rival loves. You can't resist the power if you come out and say I shouldn't have them. Now you are stopped. Then you should submit yourself to God. Then he says "resist the devil" because there is submission to this – when you can't see two ways. You submit yourself to God; you can't see the devil...he's out! We resist him by saying who we are, not by fighting him. The more you fight a thing the more it is. The more you resist a thing the more you have it! That is why you don't answer temptation by resisting. You claim it is not there. That's why I use that phrase that Jesus used on the Sermon on the Mount "Agree with thy adversary quickly". You say "Away with you!" because you do not agree with him. He'll grab you and put you in prison until you pay the utmost farthing. The idea is, if you fight your adversary – your temptations – something grabs you and you fight them...he gets you. You say, "Okay you are there but you are not really there. Okay, I'm tempted but that's not what I really am at all." You have agreed with him so that he can't fight you. "You are there, but I don't take you, for I'm in the Other – in Christ! So you resist the devil by submitting to God, and drawing neigh to God.

James does say, "Cleanse your hand, purify your hearts ye double minded." Double mind comes in again there. Afflicted...more than a 'wink'! Again, he doesn't say how our hearts are purified. They have to find out. They may have to go this way. They have to clean things up and cry to God. This is where he says, "Stop being happy". "Be strong, be afflicted, morn and weep. Stop your laughter; turn your laughter into mourning and your joy into heaviness. Humble yourselves in the sight of God and He will lift you up." So there are areas sometimes that people have to be broken, aren't there? They have to admit, "I've been wrong there. I'm on the wrong path. God have mercy on me. I have to (even though I'm a Christian) find the way." 'Course the actual fact is that when you get there you don't purify you heart – it is purified by faith! The great scripture of purity of heart is Act 15.

Those who don't know the union still bring up that Jeremiah statement. I get it all the time. "Oh the heart is deceitfully wicked, above all you can know." But that's unsaved of course! Your heart is like that...not saved. When you are saved of course your heart is not deceitfully wicked above all things! Peter speaking after he had been to Cornelius's "And God which knoweth the hearts, bare them witness, giving them the Holy Ghost, even as He did unto us; and put no difference between us and them, purifying their hearts by faith." Act 15:9 Purified done and finished! Why? Because a pure thing is seeing single! So a pure heart is a single heart. When we have moved into union with Christ we have a single heart, because His love has been shed abroad in our heart. The love of God has taken us over! We have the single heart because God is love. The actual fact is that everybody has a pure heart...depending on which way it is pure – evil or Christ!

Purity of heart is to will one thing. Heart is where you choose. You will one thing – that is purity of heart. Now, we used to will self. We were purity of heart for the devil. To be pure of heart for God was taken care of by Jesus Christ when He died in our behalf! He died and took out this false love. That's sin – the false love. And there came in the new love! Now the change of purities – our hearts are now single for God. (I suppose James means more in the set of the affections.) The actual purifying is that you are made pure in Christ! So he speaks strong words to them there. That may be the times of heart searching, the braking down, confession and restoration. Actually we all do it, if we come into union...where we searched and thought and mixed up with self-condemnation until finally the truth was revealed to us. That is the last of the doubles that he mentions.

Then he comes back again to the tongue. He is very sensitive about the tongue...about speaking evil about one another. He puts it in an unusual way. It makes you think. "If you speak evil about your brother you speak evil of the law." That is a curious statement. "Don't speak evil one of another brethren. If you speak evil of your brother and judge your brother, you speak evil of the law and judge the law. If you judge the law, you are not a doer but a judge." 'Course our old idea of the law is something 'out here'. That doesn't make sense you judge the law 'out here'. But of course, you see, we are the law. What he means is the perfect law of liberty. If I judge a brother...that brother is an expression of this law of liberty...I 'm judging which he is expressing. I'm not judging him; I'm judging that which he expresses. So don't judge your brother. That is God's business. If he is one who claims to be Christ's person and son. Don't judge him! He has claimed all that. That is Christ taking him that way! Let Christ take him that way. If you judge him, you are judging the law. He is being controlled by the law of love. The law of my understanding is God in him! That is the law – the law of liberty – the living God Who is the law of the universe expressed in him. Don't judge that! So it is a subtle way around of saying you are judging Christ – because it is Christ in that person! The Spirit of Christ is within him! Beware of doing it. Do leave that alone. Just leave Christ to do His own merciful, positive, edifying operation in a life. He never is destructive.

Then James jumps again. He says, "Don't you people say, 'Now tomorrow I'll go to such and such a city and stay a year and make money'". The idea is – I'll get my own gain there. But you don't know that there is a tomorrow. Your life is only a vapor that appears for a little time and then vanishes away. You ought to say, "If the Lord will, we will do this or that." Rejoicing in your own choices – that is boasting...and that's evil!

I would think that we who have moved into union life would have that normal. We don't always say, "If the Lord will"...but we mean it. At bottom we are always meaning to do what we understand to be the Lord's will. We aren't cogitating...I'm going off here and make gain and don't give a hoot about God. So again, there is a division here of double mindedness. If you are the One, you aren't always saying, "If the Lord wills." You are just taking that to be saying something, because underneath is your inner conscious life...as far as you understand it. It is all being God acting through you in whatever His ways are!

While in the double-life again, you get it: that comes in this false one – I'm myself. I'll go there, for I can make some money there. I'll go and get on with that for a year's time. Haven't even consulted God. That is what he is getting at. You are enjoying that you may be able to make some cash on the side or something. He says that is evil.

He has a final passage again on the rich. Again he doesn't seem close to us, because he speaks of the rich men in their worst form...as those who are accumulating masses of money. It says "rust on them and burn them." And those who get their money by cheap labor...so there is a certain social touch here. "The cry of the laborers who reaped down your fields cry out against you, into the ears of the Lord Sabbath, Holy of Hosts. You haven't paid them their wages or again you use their wages for your own sensualities. You live in pleasure, you have nourished your hearts as in the day of slaughter. And, you have condemned and killed the just to make your way." This is a picture of course of all the rich in the world. There have been plenty through history, hasn't there? Obviously riches are hard and dangerous. Jesus said so. It may not directly apply to us here. It helps us to watch to see that we are good stewards of what we have. What is the point of storing up this wealth? It will burn you one day...turn to curse you...storing up your wealth, instead of using your wealth. As far as we have any prosperity our privilege is to see where it can be of any use to God and His purposes in the world.

Then he moves on to the final word on patience. There was a persecution there. It doesn't touch us so very much these days. We must have patience of the coming of the Lord. We find that when we read Paul, Paul did that. He was under great pressures. He likens our waiting for the coming of the Lord to Job. This is where Job is mentioned and the prophets of old suffered all afflictions...and had patience. Again he says that you are happy in enduring. That is a good phrase in verse 11. You are happy when you endure. You have heard of the patience of Job. Remember patience included joy. Job came back to a joyful life. We should praise what we are doing. So I would say...let's be more occupied in praising the Lord now. Be more occupied in His present coming than in the future. We must each go the way we are led.

Many of God's people are normally intrigued by the Second Coming. They say that book by Lynn something has gone into 2,000,000 copies hasn't it? To my mind a lot of it is just 'Christian movies'. You see a nice picture. I do not live a detached life – I don't live what is going to happen one day. I'm living very much 'what's happening now'!

291

So I don't personally want to be too interested in that. It will be wonderful when He comes...it will be perfection. That is not my basis. Yet, I find on the whole that it is the main basis of most Evangelicals. They are interested in what they can say about the tribulation and the judgment coming. It also makes you very negative. It makes you think that God is judging this world. Well, if He is, there is a pretty good blessing packed up in the judgment! So I can say, because this is a day of blessing – day in which we are able to move out with the Gospel! A day of freedom! A day of response! Tremendous days worldwide! I'm not going into missionary affairs now. I'm a missionary, so I'm able to know missionary affairs.

Anyone who knows missionary affairs knows that tremendous blessings are happening. Tremendous days in Brazil, Africa, Indonesia, and even countries like Japan, Thailand is moving. All over the world, the Spirit of God is moving through the people! So these are streams of blessings today. I think it is more, to my mind, in the foreground than the judgment! That is why personally, I somewhat doubt their interpretations. It isn't the present working out. For 50 years they have been saying this kind of thing. When I was a boy I heard these kinds of things, as if it was just happening or about to happen. Well they haven't happened and instead of that, there is this coming greater and larger working of the Spirit of God. So I'm more occupied with that. Nor do I think that we should be saying that we will escape the tribulation.

I have known a great soldier, C.T. Studd, who believed in soldiering for Jesus...suffered for Jesus and gave his life for Him. He was so contemptuous of those who wanted to escape the tribulation! He had a sign built, "FOR THOSE WHO WANT TO ESCAPE THE TRIBULATION". But no one joined it! If we go through tribulation...glorying God by glorying in your suffering...you let people see Christ coming through you in your sufferings! That's more the tone of the Bible, I think, than going out and saying, "Oh Good, I don't mind what happens to the people left behind. I shall go!" That's not the gospel. Escape! It's being with them! So I doubt the whole presentation myself. I think it is more speculation than interpretation, or so called interpretation than necessary truth. But others don't see that, so God bless them. Follow what you have got. If you are one who gets a great deal out Of this, well give what you've got. God has used it. Many people have been brought up to face their need of Christ through the Second Coming. So there's room for it.

He moves on to a final word or two...a little touch on language. "Don't swear." Now he isn't talking about vile language. When Jesus said, "Don't swear by Heaven etc.", what He was referring to is the weakness in saying a thing and having to have something to confirm it. That is really what it is. It is an admission that you are not confident of what you are saying. You don't have to put something in as a confirmation, "By God, I say this." Of course we wouldn't say that...the world says that. We may use different phrases, which we really use to confirm our word. James says, "Yea" they are good enough. If you are sure just say what's true. Say the truth. "Yes" or "No". You don't have to add something because you are a little weak. That is all he means there.

Then he has that well known statement on sickness, which I think has considerable subtlety in it. He is saying...if you are sick to pray practical. If you are very sick, sing Psalms. If you are sick what does it say? It says, "If you are sick and you want to have 'outer' symbolic help – symbolism – call the elders." Not they call you. You call them! Get them to pray over you and to anoint you with oil in the name of the Lord. "The prayer of faith shall save"...not heal. Isn't that a little twist? He didn't say that the prayer of faith should heal the sick. He said, "The prayer of faith should save the sick and the Lord will raise him up." Rising up is not necessarily physical. If he committed sins they shall be forgiven him. The center was getting the 'inner' healing. The center wasn't the physical healing. It was in order to save you, and put you into a saved relationship – a liberated relationship! If you have sins swept away they actually disappeared in Christ! That's what really matters. Our true health is being in Christ. When we are in Christ it may 'come down' to the body. James uses different words than we use.

He says, "Confess your faults one to another and pray for one another." That is going beyond the question of the elders and a sick person. He moves into a new section there, I think, although we use those two phrases a good deal together. "Pray for one another that you may be healed". Then he speaks about "the effectual fervent prayer." The body...what does the body matter? The healing is to the whole person. The whole person is the person in whom Christ is manifested. It may be through a sick body or not through a sick body! Physical is a minor matter.

You'll find that Paul made very little of it. After all, can you get a better teacher than he? He said, "My outer man perishes; my inner man is renewed day by day." He says, "Christ will magnify whether by life or by death." So he didn't say...I shan't die. If I die then I glorify Christ – magnify

Christ! So it is all in the flesh, which comes up in II Corinthians. I only mention that here because I don't believe the major point is that a person will be healed in their body. 'Course we are human and we hurt and we want healing. If you look at the dangers of the first "I want healing" you are back on selfishness again. It isn't the first thing. That should be "I want the will of God. God is now living in me. I want the will of God." Paul very plainly says that!

We have to only read Romans 8 to see that the first thing is not healing of the body. Romans 8 is the victory chapter! We are more than conquerors...and so on. That is where he brings that right in the middle..."For the world travaileth until they get the glorious release through the sons of God." We are heirs and co-heirs and are more than conquerors in this chapter...more than conquerors through Him who loved us! He says, "The world groans and travails in pain until the final release comes. Not only they, but also ourselves."

In Romans 8:23..."which have the first fruits of the Spirit, even ourselves groan within ourselves, waiting for the adoption, to wit, the redemption of the body. For we are saved by hope, but hope that is seen is not hope; for what a man seeth, why doth he yet hope for? But if we hope for that we see not, then we do with patience wait for it." So, the salvation by faith of the spirit. Salvation for the body? He doesn't say too much about faith for the body. So, we are not given total redemption of the body. So why bother about the body? Why don't I just be occupied to see whatever I am, Christ is coming through my body. The actual fact is that when we are healed spirits it does affect us – in there is a quickening. The word that Paul does give us is "quickening". Quickening isn't healing. It is life in spite of the condition. A quickened body! A quickened body...sort of quickened your mortal body. Probably the real meaning of that word is resurrection. Spontaneously things happen which quicken our bodies. Some get healing. So I don't see that the New Testament is putting the emphasis on physical healing as we so often hear.

Finally, he says prayer does get answered. He makes the final reference to Elijah. Prayers get answered! The highest thing of all you may be the means of bringing other people back to Christ – can convert a sinner from the errors of his ways! So he keeps adding these little words. There he finishes! That is what we have to say on James.

I JOHN

My sorrow is that so many of our evangelical Bible-believing brethren seem far more anxious of preserving the false garments of independent self-relying selves seeking to maintain our relationship with God, even when born again, than boldly moving in with Paul and John (and Jesus in John 15) into a fixed union where HE does the maintaining and preserving and fruit-bearing, and we are the spontaneous enjoyers and expressors of that glorious grace-relationship, as John says, easily and normally "walking as He walks", "knowing as He knows", "loving as He loves" as in I John 4:17. Great abounding life! As that naughty C.T. Studd said, "Evangelical believers are more concerned with preserving their sinful imperfection than enjoying at least the outreach into sinless perfection"!!

Knight of Faith Volume I

The new man drive is a basic drive...you are a safe son. We are safe when what we are doing really is for the benefit of others. That is why I John is one of the great discourses. I John is a great...the main...letter which interprets love to us.

I don't believe really in teaching, because I believe there is only one Teacher and He's inside us, because the Bible says so. Biblically I John 2 says if you have the Holy Spirit, no man need teach you because you know all things.

The Meaning of Life

I will send you some talks which were taken down unknown to me when I was recently speaking, called "The Key to Everything." It touches on this. **I John 4.7** onward is unmatched on this. The proof of our new birth and God's indwelling is not that He loves us, but that He loves thru us.

Knight of Faith Volume II

I JOHN

We are following through with his first letter. John was the man deeply established in his union relationship with God. Of all the New Testament writers John was the one...they all were in their different ways, of course...who was deeply established in his *union* relationship with God. He had that union relationship externally with Jesus on earth in a very special way. Communication of the Spirit through one of His great servants, John, in his first letter and centering our thoughts around what he said to us in that letter, and what we can catch onto from it. And we are saying that it's the *basis* of all those who wrote the letters by the Spirit of the New Testament, but perhaps it may be said in a special sense...John's *consciousness* of his *living union* with God. He'd been the one who'd been especially in union with Jesus on earth.

Well, *thank God* Jesus had gone out from the body – because outward union is never union. *Inner* union is union because we are spirits and He is spirit. And true union is true *unity* – is where the human is in *conscious unity* with the living God. It's just a fact! And we're as much a conscious 'we are not we', but He expressed through us...*as* we are conscious of ourselves. You see, we live by the inner consciousness because that's *all* we are. We are spirits. Spirit is that in you which is the "I am," "I know," "I will," "I desire" – that's you! God is Spirit. God is the I AM of the universe *manifesting Himself* through the universe. Because the Spirit is meaningless unless He is manifested...like we are meaningless unless we have our *souls* and *bodies* by which we *express* our inner selves. But our true self is spirit because the true Self of the universe is Spirit. The whole universe is spirit. It's the Fall that made us think the universe is *external* forms. They are passing phases. They are only electrical waves, that's all. Impacts come and find impacts on our 'ears' inside. That's all they are – because electrical wave is light. God is light...and they are forms of God in light come out, in matter ways – that's all it is. And so, this outer world is not real at all. It's just a *passing* phase. That's why Paul said it's temporal "Things that are seen are temporal, things that are not seen are eternal" *by* the eternal Spirit.

So the *real* I is an inner self...your inner self, which says, "I am," "I have desire," "I desire," "I know," "I will" – that's you! The rest is just outer form. That's the real person.

Now the real Person of the universe is Spirit. Jesus said that "God is spirit." So the real Person of the universe is an "I AM" – invisible, immortal, eternal. Just as I am; just as you are. He is the I AM. And He is the One – He's the thinker, the desirer, and the willer. And the whole universe is this Person Who's come out in different forms...so that when we've really got *ourselves* into focus, we are inwardly persons *conscious of God in a union*. We live by inner consciousness. And you're conscious..."I'm in union with this Person. It isn't really I living. It's the living Christ living by *me.* I'm in a permanent unity." That's the *basis* of our union consciousness.

Of course, the consequence of that union consciousness is – because it's this Living One joined to me, He's expressing Himself by me. *I* am the means by which He expresses Himself. Precisely as Jesus said that! Jesus walked on earth as a common man. But, the real Jesus wasn't the outer form at all. Of course, we know that! The real Jesus was *inner*, while expressed through His outer form. And that inner Jesus was always saying, "I do nothing by Myself. I do what I see the Father do." Now, we've become fallen people and fallen into this *consciousness of separation*, which is illusion. The whole world is a unity if you see it. The separation is only illusive appearance. Because we fall into that *illusion*, we even think God's away up here somewhere. And so when Jesus said on earth, "What I do as a Son I don't do by Myself; I do what I see the Father do." They thought He had some distant sight – He could see God up there then doing things. And when they asked Him about His judgments, He said, "Oh," He said, "I judge nothing by Myself. As I hear I judge." Well, they thought He must have some long hearing – He could hear up here somewhere.

Because in this fallen, mistaken concept, we think God is something far away...up there. And so, around the supper table they asked Jesus. He said He is going to the Father – because we have these third-dimensional geographical outlooks. There is no geography in *eternity*. It's just...there is **no** space/time. It's all one...just one permanent presence. God is a permanent presence everywhere. But we don't see things like that. We think in space/time terms – third dimension. So when he said, "I'm going to the Father" they thought up there. And so one of them said, "Show us the Father, will You? You've talked a great deal about the Father. Show us where You are going to." "Oh, yes," He said, "You see, if you see Me, you see the Father." That's a shock! Because this is the Son walking about on earth as apparent outer form – the inner Jesus through His outer form. How could you say, "If you see Me, you see the Father?" You see, you've got to learn a new secret – Spirit is unity, Spirit is unity. He says, "The truth is this. When you see Me you see the Father. Why? I'll tell you. You've got to have a new concept of truth, which is – the real "I" is in the Father, and the real Father – Spirit Father – is in Me. You've got to believe that I am in the Father and the Father is in Me. That's not *external* truth. External truth is we are outside each other...outside God. Real truth is, I'm in Him; He's in Me. He says, "You've got to believe that."

Now He says, "Just to make it a little clearer what I'm meaning," (of course, John was there listening to all this because he was the special disciple) he said, "It's like this"...I'm quoting what he said. He said, "I speak words to you. You hear My words. You think I speak them? Oh, no." He said, "I speak words, I don't speak them of Myself." What, then? "The Father." Where? Is there some long voice coming down here? No, no, no! "The Father dwells in Me. He does the works." So you see I'm a Person in permanent conscious union because there is no space/time in spirit. In the spirit dimension there's no space/time, no here, there or everywhere. It's just one everywhere. And so he says, "This Father isn't someone up here. He and I are one Person." And he said, "I and my Father are one. And the words I speak unto you I speak with My outer voice. You hear an outer voice. You may think they come from my inner self. Oh, no! They come from my inner self in a union. And the *actual one speaking* through *My* inner self is My Father's inner Self. The Father that dwells in Me...He turns My words into works." So Jesus gave the inner truth there. And that's the *inner* truth into which the gospel has taken *us*!

Now we can't go into that much tonight because the object of John's letter was how *we* operate from the basis of that inner truth. But, of course, the fact of the truth is that in God's purposes – which is to have a vast family of millions of sons who run His universe – they are to be brothers with Christ, co-heirs with Christ. *They* are to run God's universe. So His purpose was a vast family of sons who were created spirits. "He fathered our spirits"...in souls and bodies. They were created in His likeness – Spirit can commune with spirit – to be in the same union with Him as the Son is, and to operate as human sons...and yet really the inner motivation in us in operation is the *Father* through the son. This is His purpose.

Now, the character of the Father is nothing but love. We've been reading about that today. He *is* love. That's the great revelation from John. God *is* love. *Is* love, isn't *has* love. So the universe is a Person Who is love. Love isn't a thing. It's a Person! It's a living Person who is love. Love means He's *for others*. Love means *you exist* that others might be perfected and fulfilled and completed and have everything they need. You live that *they* may have their needs met, no matter what happens to you. That's love! Now, that's the character of God, the being of God. He exists to bless His universe to create His universe, bless it, fulfill it, and perfect it. And *He's* perfectly delighted and perfectly filled when the whole universe and the people in it are what they are meant to be — which is what we are going to come to. Now, His purpose all the way through is to have sons by whom He'd do it. Now, He first of all had to have His own Son because the Spirit is invisible. Your spirit is invisible.

So the living God is an invisible, unknowable Person unless He comes out in a form by which He could manifest *Himself*. So from eternity, in His own Trinity in Himself...He's had a second form which is His Son...which is His *manifestation*. That's the Son who becomes the Lord Jesus Christ...among us, of course. This is the Son. Now, it is through His Son — by means of His Son, the manifested Son — He's going to bring into being a manifested universe...and His Son will be the head and developer and manager of that universe. And His Son, of course, because He is in a union with the Father, has the same *character* as the Father. He is the lover-Son. You see, God is *ever* love — a lover-God. And He's the lover-Son Who lives to love and complete other people.

He has sons. Through the creation there comes into being a family so that He may have a vast family of sons who will be co-sons, co-brothers, co-lovers, co-managers of His universe. This is our destiny! So you have the human family in existence. Now the problem with the human family is this — we must find ourselves as *persons* because we are to be persons forever. We are to be real persons — thinking, willing, acting persons. Our personhood doesn't disappear. It gets *affirmed*, it gets *developed*, it gets *emphasized*. So we are to be real persons. But, of course, we are to be persons in this inner union so that *our humanity* is expressing His love. We are expressions of the God Who is love. But first of all, we have to *find* ourselves.

Now the only way you *find* yourself is to be *for* yourself. You find yourself to be for yourself – that was the Garden of Eden, of Creation, where Adam and Eve were tempted to be for themselves, and went that way under Satan – take things for themselves. By that means, they found themselves necessary. They found *they* had appetites, faculties, and abilities through which God could come. But they were used in the wrong way. They'd become distorted. That's sin! They'd become selves for themselves because they gave in to Satan and they came under – became captives of the spirit of self-centeredness. By taking the fruit they got the wrong person in. Taking fruit isn't a sin, but what you get inside you, of course. Like this taking the Holy Communion isn't a sin if you've got Jesus inside you. So taking the wrong fruit is taking the wrong person inside you. And so the human race got the spirit of error, the spirit of self-centeredness into it instead of the spirit of God!

So they became lost people *separated* from God. That's why we *see* things as separation. We've lost the sense of unity by which *all* these things are only forms of a God of love expressing Himself through every form of wonder. We've lost sight of that. When you are in union with God you are a see-througher, not a see-atter. Because, you see, everything is a *form* of this wonderful Person. Even evil is turned into good! Every person, every thing – some form. He's there working that thing for a perfect end, whether it's evil or good. You only see through everything to Him! Just the same as Jesus, I would say en route – when Jesus was attacked by Satan at Calvary. It was Satan came through Judas, wasn't it? It was Satan came through Pilot. It was Satan came through Caiaphas and the Pharisees. Who did Jesus say? "My Father's cup." He said, "That's My Father's cup." Satan was His Father's cup! He didn't see Satan except as a cup given Him by His Father. So Satan is *only* God's convenient cup, which He gives us. As we take it, it comes out in eternal life! He turned Satan's attack into eternal life for the world. So, you see, this is what it is to be a "see-througher."

Now we lost that in the fall. Instead of being people who see through one living God of love expressing Himself through everything, we see selves wanting things for themselves. So we've fallen into the concept of separation, when "*I* must have this; *I* must have that." And we see life in these *false illusory separated* forms.

They are not separated! Even atomic science begins to teach us that – the wave system which unites all, and so on. And so, you see, we've fallen into an illusory condition geared to self-centeredness. Now we had to do that because we had to find what it is to be persons. And in life you never know a right thing *until* we first know a wrong thing. You've got to know the wrong thing and discard it before you have the right thing. All you folks here who have a profession or you may be a housewife running a home, cooking in the kitchen, or you may have a business, or you may be a secretary, a teacher, a lawyer, or something. You only function competently because you knew the wrong way and discarded it! You ladies who cook, the only safe cook is you discover how not to cook before you cook, or your poor husbands! You professional men, you're in your profession and you say, "I don't run my business that way; I run it this way." "I don't run my engines that way," "I don't teach my mathematics that way; I do it this way," "I don't operate my medicine this way; I operate that way." You've always had to know the wrong way and *discard* it before accomplishing it in the right.

So if we're to be real functioning humans in the right activity, the right activity as the expression of God Who is love, we first of all have to be wrong kind of humans expressing self-loving self. Instead of being an expression of God in self-giving self – love – we had to be by ourselves, self-loving self – that's the Fall. Now, that's why the Son came, His own Son came – to identify Himself with us in our fall to remove the fallen spirit from us, and restore us to a right Spirit. So He became the head of the human race. He becomes our Elder Brother. We are sons with the Son and He is the Elder Brother among us...so that we may all be a vast family of co-brothers by whom we manage the universe. But the *central* thing to managing the universe is – He *must* have persons who manage it with a self-giving, not a self-getting, spirit.

See, this world is in chaos because everybody who has got power uses it for themselves – like kings and powers, rulers. The whole world is torn up because everybody gets what they can for themselves...so there's hatred, and jealousy and fights and war because *self-loving self has discord.* Self-giving self *blesses*. When I'm for the other person and the other person's for me – when my object is to bless you and your object is to bless me, we're in harmony! Now, that's the ultimate that God should have a universe run by sons who are lover-sons...so that they exist to bless and complete the universe...not what they've got to bless and complete *them.* They've been changed *from* the self-loving, self-grabbing, self-getting kind of self *to* the self-giving kind of self. That's what a true son is!

Now, in order that we might be that, we had first of all to be wrong sons...self-loving, self-getting...get disillusioned! The Son came as a man –

that's the incarnation. And in His death, going through with Satan, He took upon Him all that would come to us. He, as it were, was grabbed by Satan in death and went to hell. He said He went to hell where we self-centered spirits go – the place of Satan. Went there on our behalf! It couldn't hold Him, because He is the Son of God whom Satan never had a hold on. And although He represented us, He rose again. And in rising again He brought out the human race to be possessed by the Spirit of God who is love instead of the spirit of Satan, if we freely receive Him. Now we never lose *our* freedom. That's why we're real persons. Therefore when we freely receive Him, this change takes place. And all of us here are probably born again. If you're born again it *has* to take place in you. And that born again is a very important matter. Why? Because you've moved *from* matter to spirit.

Up until that moment your outlook on life has been related to the philosophies of life and maybe even your church forms and your activities on this human level. If you are born again, you took a tremendous step because you put your trust in a Person you can't see. You've put your trust in a Spirit Person. You didn't put your trust in a Christ Who'd been crucified. You put your trust in a Christ who had been crucified and is now risen! Now, crucifixion is history. Anyone can prove crucifixion through history. Resurrection belongs to a new dimension; it's a spirit dimension. And Jesus Christ rose in the Spirit by the Spirit. He had a new body, but that was just incidental. He became the new Person in the Spirit dimension – back with Father, Son and Spirit. Now, you see, when we in our need of a savior took this step of faith, because our need was so great, and because He'd been presented to us by the Bible – He loved us like that – we took not a Savior who just once died, but a Savior who now lives. But if He lives He's in another dimension. And you are a human spirit who is related to a Person who is in the Spirit – a Person who is Spirit and not matter. And so that's why if *you* are born again you have moved into the spirit-consciousness. The proof is this – the whole law of experience is what you take, you experience. That's the law of faith! What you take you experience.

Faith is the capacity in which we freely take something and experience it. You experience being here tonight, if you took it. You *were* back home. You said, "I'll come." All right, having said, "I'll come," which is you inwardly taking it. In this case you took your car and came here. And now you're experiencing being here. The whole of life is – we experience what we take and it becomes real to us. You take food and it's real enough inside you. You're sitting on a chair, some of you (some of you are not quite so comfortable), and you experience the chair under you. As I said, you people take a profession and the profession's taken you. You know what it is now to run your business and so on because it's taken you. So all life is the ability to, what we call faith, whereby we take something and experience.

Now we born again people did a tremendous thing. We took a living Jesus, not a dead one, who in His death had cut us off from the old spirit of self-centeredness — the old way in which we lived under the dominion of the spirit of self-centeredness — and restored us in His resurrection to His own spirit...His own spirit of love. As the new birth means — you've moved in your heart, your faith, away from history, away from matter, away from time, into what's given you in the Bible. You couldn't prove it — a Person who's risen from the dead. You've said, "Jesus Christ, I join You. I receive You." Now when you did that something happened to you which has changed your whole life, which is an inner consciousness. You see, Spirit is living by consciousness.

I told you that in the beginning — all you are is a consciousness. You are what you know, that's all. Not what you have outside you. They're merely passing. You never *have* a thing just because it's outside you; you merely use it. You use things outside you; you *know* what you've got *inside* you. That's why, again I say, you people with a profession, you don't have your profession because you learned it from outside...because having learned to be an engineer, or doctor, or teacher, it's got you inside...and you're at home inside. You practice your medicine, your teaching, or your law, or your secretarial work, or your home. You see, you've become inwardly a knower, and you live by inner knowledge — consciousness. Now the supreme consciousness, if you're born again, is that there's come into your consciousness that Jesus is your personal Savior — that you're joined to a living Person and He's your Savior, He's your Lord, God's your Father. You've become a part of a Spirit family and you know it! And your inner consciousness is that's where you belong – to Him.

This is the greatest thing in life. You'd throw the world away to keep that one, because the world is nothing and this is real! So you've moved into a Spirit consciousness. And in doing so you've, as we speak from John's point of view, you've moved on one further step. Now that's the first step you take, when as a human being in need as a lost soul having presented us the wonder of the love of God — that Jesus loved us like that — and we may not fully understand it, but in His death and His blood He took away your sins and took you away from the power of Satan to make you a new creature.

You understand that, and you moved in...in yourself and you took Him – you received Him, and He received you and there's come into you the consciousness that He's received you, accepted you, and that He's your living Savior and so on. Now, you have to go one further step and that is to find that this life is a unity.

That means a further disturbing revelation about ourselves. You see, we've got used to being *independent* selves. Independence is the Fall. Independence is my self-loving, self-relying self, doing my own bit...doing my own stuff. That's the only way we know how to live a life. I said we're independent. We're *not* independent! Actually the *whole world's* a part of His being. The Bible says every human person, not the saved (Acts 17), "they all live and move and have their being in the one Person." But you don't know it. As free persons in the Fall we refuse to know that. So we don't even know we're in His being! We think we're just independent selves...and so we've got this independence.

We've got to find that human independence can't work the works of God. As humans in our independence we're captured by the pulls of the world and the weaknesses. We haven't got what it takes to live the life of peace and power and assurance of victory. We can't do it! And so we have got to go through a further stage where we find, although we're redeemed people, we can't make it work because somehow we want to be better people and we don't become better people. We think God should change us. We think we should become better people...and be more holy...and more loving...and more patient...and have more victory over sin...and less anger...and less hates...and so on. And we're looking at ourselves as if God will change us.

He'll *never* do so, because we haven't yet regained the true secret that a human is the agency of a deity. The human is the negative end as it were...the agency of a deity. So the Bible says we *humans always are vessels*. Now a vessel is something which contains something. It isn't what it contains! The Bible says we're all vessels of wrath or vessels of mercy (Romans 9). Now a vessel of wrath is a human containing the spirit of error in the Fall – the spirit of self-loving self. That is a vessel of wrath. A vessel of mercy is the same vessel which has a new God inside it. So you see all the gospel is a change of gods – not a change of vessels!

We're mixed up when we think the vessel ought to change. A vessel never changes. Your *humanity* never changes. It's a beautiful thing! Your body is beautiful – made like God to express God through appetites, faculties. You're to be an expression of the Living God! You don't change. **You** remain the person with your normal expressions, your appetites, your faculties and you never change. You're a vessel. What *changes* is the god in you. What the gospel did for you is to remove the god of self-centeredness out of you and put in His own self, Jesus, the Holy Spirit, into you. Now, because you don't get that into focus when you're first saved, you think you're looking wrongly, "God will change me." He'll never change *you*!

So you've got to come to a fresh laying down of yourself. Shall I put it like that? The first was – you came as a sinner. "I'm a lost sinner. God have mercy on me. Take care of my sins. I'm going to hell. Forgive me." He accepts you. You remain yourself, as it were, accepted, loved, cleansed, like that. Now you've got to not only lay down your sins, you've got to lay down your*selves*. Now you've got to say in the sense that my self has got it wrong...that I'm a person who is going to do something and become something. I've got to lay that down! I've got to discover, "No, I'm not, Paul, because I am crucified with Christ." That means I am crucified so far as being a person running my own life.

You see, the Fall made me a person running my own life. "I'll run my own life my own way." Now, on the Cross with Christ I became crucified in Christ to being the kind of person under the spirit of self-centeredness, which runs his own life. Now I arise again, the same I, but now this new I is the container of Christ! Before, it was the container of Satan. Now Paul says, "I've risen. Oh, no, no. I'm alive. It isn't I now, it's Christ in me. Oh! I'm a container of a new Person. I'm not changed, I'm just a human. I still have my appetites, my faculties, my wonderful liabilities, all that God can use. I'm not changed." The vessel doesn't change, but the God in me has changed – and now it's *Christ* in me!

You see, it usually takes a certain period, what we speak about as the wilderness period, when we're trying to make the Christian life work...with God...with His blessing, but as if *we're* the people who ought to be better...and ought to do it...and ought to have the faculties...and the capacities...and the patience...and the peace...and we don't find *we've* got it. You never will! Because the vessel is just the agency *through which God's spirit expresses Himself*. He's the patience...He's the power...He's the life...He's all. Now you, it isn't a thing He give you, like patience, power. It's a Person – because the whole truth of the universe is One Person – a Person

Who's the peace, and the power, and the love, and the wisdom in you...and He'll express *His* love, patience and power through *you*.

Now, you'll do that, when you've learned the second lesson – which is, you transfer your attention first of all as a lost sinner to His blood, and His blood has removed your sins. Now you transfer it to Him...Himself in you, and you step into what is the real truth – a unity, eternal union, spirits united – that you hadn't realized before. You are now in eternal union! You're one person with the Lord Jesus Christ inwardly! You're one person with the Holy Spirit! You're one person with the Father! And as you're *conscious* of this...now in this unity He's the major...you're the minor. He's the all...you're the nothing. He's the vine...you're the branch. He's the head...you're the body.

Now then, when this becomes your consciousness, now, you've got a new center to your life, because as you're human, as you operate and you've got your problems and so on that will arise. "Oh, what shall I do about this? Wait a minute. I'm not myself. *You're* handling that." "Oh, I'm worried about that. Wait a minute. *You've* got that in hand." "Oh, I don't like that person. Now, I don't, but You do. All right, I'll love them with Your love. I can't think how You do it, but I'll do it anyhow." Because, you see, you've changed your center. Your center's changed from "'I" doing something...or God making me more loving, which He never will...or more patient, because it isn't you; you're a vessel. You're just an old tin pot, that's all you are. And you rattle too much, that's your trouble. A tin can! But it's not bad being a tin can *if* inside the can is God! It's not a bad exchange. And you're a tin can that contains God. All right, adjust to being a tin can like that. Now then, so you transfer your attention from the vessel and its human reactions. Of course, we're more than vessels; we're persons with human reactions...because when you've entered by faith into this union relationship – now I'll tell you when faith becomes consciousness. I'll tell you that in a moment.

Faith means you *experience* it. I say you've come here by faith. You experience it. Faith produces experience. When you enter by faith and experience – "Now. Oh, God. Yes. There's this pressure. You're handling that. I'm impatient. Forgive me Lord. I made a slip. You'll make me a bit quicker, but you're my patience." And don't bother about your sins. You sins teach you to have more sense next time. Don't get sin fussing...get Christ centered instead of being sin fussing! Don't bother about yourself. Forget it. *Be yourself.* If you slip, *He'll* teach you to be a little quicker next time! That's all. Say, "Sorry, Lord. I wasn't quick enough that time. But

You're in me. You'll handle it." And then you have a *free life* because you're on the **new** center. Now, you see, for most of us that's a second step of faith. The first step of faith is, "I'm a sinner...God, You've taken my sins away. I'm taking You as *my* center. That's a big step! I know I belong to You. I'm a *new* person in You." That's a big step! Yet a bigger step when I say, "Oh, it's no longer I...It's no longer how I do things *my* way. It's Christ and He's handling things and if you don't like the way He's handling them, tell Him you don't like the way He's handling them and "get to changing me, will You?" Don't bother.

I spoke to a business man just recently and he said, "Oh, I'm a Christian man," he says, "but I'm not at all sure I'm willing for God's will in my business." He owns a furniture store. He said, "I'm such a sinner." He kept saying, "I'm such a sinner." I said, "Haven't you found the Savior?" He said, "Oh, yes. I'm a Christian man. I'm born of God's spirit, but I'm not sure I'm willing for God to run my business." There's something going on which shouldn't go on, I suppose. I congratulated him. I said, "I congratulate you, brother. You've found yourself at last. You're not meant to be willing. You're not *meant* to be willing. You, as a human, have a human reaction, and that human reaction doesn't like a thing. Ok, tell God you don't like it and say, "God, get changing me, will You? Get changing me, will You?" "Oh," he said, "I don't mind doing that. That takes the heat off!"

You see, the heat is on when I try doing it myself. When I think I *ought* to change myself. When I say I *should* be willing when I'm not willing. When I say I like a person when I dislike them. The heat's on because you don't do it. Well, you say, "Of course, I dislike that person. Of course, I'm willing for that. Of course, I don't want Your ways, but get on with me all the same. You've got me. Poor me...I'm grand anyhow!" According to your faith, what you take will take you...and you'll find God grabs you. And he changes your will and makes you able to love a thing you couldn't love, and do a thing you couldn't do. This is this new *union* life! And that *union* life has become the fact by consciousness.

Remember, faith means you've moved into something which moves *back into* you. Faith isn't what we often think – just I myself putting myself into some trusting. No, it's – I'm putting myself into trusting something which I relate myself to...and it comes back to me. Like I put my trust into coming to this meeting this evening by the kindness of our friends. You put your trust in that. You come; here's the meeting. So *faith always is substance*. It comes back as a substance in the thing you put yourself into. So faith is not faith *until* it has come back as substance.

Spiritually substance is *consciousness*. Spiritually, substance is something inside me because the Spirit just knows inside. Already you know Jesus. Now this is, "Well, He's here forever. This is simply that — He is me. I'm really Christ in human form. He is me! This is the *living* Christ. No matter what I am, I'm just His humanity. He can do what He likes with it. If it's a messy humanity, it's His fault for making me a mess. It's His trouble, not mine." See, but oh, now when you get that consciousness — now you become free because you're under the consciousness underneath. "Oh, this One! He's love...He's power...peace. This One's running it." And you know when the consciousness is there you're able to operate by the consciousness. You haven't got to find Him again. He's got you! He isn't way up here. He's here. He's you! He's you! He's you. And so look around here. "Thank You, You're here, Lord. Get on with it, Lord." And He does get on with it. And if He doesn't, you slip, you say, "Sorry, Ok, Lord. I know what a silly person You are." Get up again and do better next time. That's all. It's quite easy.

This I John letter is John going through with us what kind of people we are — how we *function* on the basis of this union. That's why I've spent so long on this. The *background* of this is this union with God in Christ. That's a **settled** matter, and this letter is explaining how we operate on *that* basis. He's first of all begun by making it plain that we know Him by the Son. The Son's **all**. Everything in the universe is a product of the Son. It's all related through the Son, the Lord Jesus Christ. We ourselves have come back through Him as our Savior for Him to be our brother...so eternally we're related with the Son in the eternal purposes — the Son expressing the purposes of the Father.

So, he says, "This is how you know Him." He says in the beginning, we've touched, seen, and handled the Word of Life. Life is a Person. He starts by saying, "I'm going to talk to you about eternal Life. That Life's a Person and we've seen and touched, and handled Him." Now we can't do that now. It's good we can't because Life's *inside* you, not outside you. But thank God because we're outside people that were in the Fall. He had to come in outside form, to show Himself to us as the Life so we'd know that this is God's Life in human form! It's going to do certain things for us to deliver us from the false life and put us in the true Life — His death and resurrection. And then He disappeared as a person. So we don't know Him. We don't see, touch and handle Him like John said he did. It's a good thing we don't because we touch and handle the real person within. We're in living contact with the real Person when we have the inner seeing...and the inner touching...and the inner handling in our inner consciousness in this inner union. He says He has *come*! He's a valid Person. We've seen Him. He came as such on earth. And this was the Person.

He's gone now as far as that's concerned, but *this* is the eternal Life. Now He's gone. He's gone in order that *you* may enter into what He really is — Spirit, Father and Son! It says here, "You may fellowship with the Father and the Son." He's gone back to the Father because the Son to the Father — that we may be at home with the loving Father. And be more than that — be the ones through whom the Father can fulfill His greatest purposes in the world! And so we've become at home. Fellowship is being fellows in the same ship with Him. This is what it is. And that's why he says, "His joy is full." Because we've got to find one day — God is love. That's joy! Other-love is joy...not self-love. A God Who is other love...Who fulfills His love through eternal joy.

And when we've begun to come into a relationship with Him we've begun therefore to experience this joyfulness. Now, he says, the first way in which you know God is He's light. That's the first revelation given us here in verse 5. "This is the message that God is light...in Him there is no darkness." Now, we're in union with the Light. We walk in the Light. What's light mean? Now light isn't outer light. You see, the outer man knows outer things — you don't *know* Him, you just 'contact' Him. Light comes to us in sound form and sight form and sun form. We contact light. All these things are really forms of light. We just contact them. We don't *know* them. We just contact them.

Now knowing is *inside* you. Now knowing light is knowing *how* you know — by inspiration. That's light! Now that's what's happened to you if you're a born again person. Oh, something's happened to you in which you're conscious of light. Isn't that so? You're conscious somehow — Oh, I'm in light now. This is *light* that God loves me and Jesus saved consciousness that I'm in union with the Living Person. So real light is not a *visible* thing at all — me and I'm His child. Oh, I'm in light. That's light...so inner light is inspiration. It's the invisible consciousness. We *are* that light now. It's come down through us. So he says our first union with Him is light.

Now he says you can always know when you're not in light — because you're in light when you're walking in ordinary life...and you're in inner harmony with God and Christ...and you're just living your life. Underneath there is this sense of light shining. This is the consciousness. You *know* that. The moment self comes in there's darkness. The moment you turn in to self-reaction and you get caught up with prides and hates and fears, darkness has come in. And that's the sign to you. The light's always there. You're always a part of it now, but you've lost any consciousness of it because you've temporarily moved off from this relationship – when you're in the light to one in which you've *temporarily* followed some form of self reaction...hurt, pride, whatever it may be. And this is why it says here, "You can always know if you're walking in the light because there is this light – when there's this disturbance you're not in the light."

I lived with Africans; I was a missionary in Africa. They had a very wonderful way of putting it. They'd say, taking this verse – you see this union is fellowship with the Living God and the Living Christ. You walk about this life. Inside you have a consciousness of this union with Christ...of God, and we have this sense of peace and power and so on – we're in fellowship with Him. That's how our joy is full. Now, he says, they put it like this, they say, "That's like your cup running over. You're like a vessel and the water of life is running in you and running out to other people. You're like a cup running over." Now they say when self comes in, "My cup doesn't run over." And you're conscious of something which has disturbed your relationship. Now that's the warning to you that temporarily you've stepped out of the light into self. Self is dark – self-loving self is darkness. God and we in self-giving self is light. Now he says, "That's the way in which you know" and on those levels all you do when you know that if you're in the light...automatically you're forgiven. Don't bother about yourself. Don't fuss about trying to explain your sins. God will show you where the sins are. Don't fuss about them. Take yourself...walk in the green light, not in the red. Take it that you're free in God and get on with it! Don't live in the red light hoping one day you'll get in the green. You *are in* the green light. You're in it in Christ. Get on living it! The red light is only when this warning comes up.

When it does come up, normally God is just showing you you're accepted in His union. When the red light does come up, by the way, then he says, "It's quite simple. All you do is inwardly admit it." "Yes, I see that." The Africans would do that. They'd come and tell us in the evening. And they would say, "Brother, it's like this" they said, "I was walking in the light enjoying it." One man I remember told me this...I was visiting there. I was walking down the road to the hospital, myself and the doctor a missionary, and we passed two of the African brethren in the earlier days and he greeted one of them. He didn't greet the other one. He was busy; he was talking to one of them...he didn't' greet one of them. He just greeted the one of them...went on with his job. In the evening we had the open fellowship and the other brother, who hadn't been greeted, came up to him and said, "Brothers, I want to show how I've been brought back into the light, how I've been cleansed in the blood of Jesus." He said, "I was happy with Jesus and happy with my brother until the two white men came by. And they neglected me, as if I wasn't there. They didn't ever say, 'How do; How do," to me. And they talked with my other brother," he said. "I found the cup's not running over. I wasn't in this fellowship with Jesus Christ. Light shines; light will show you the truth," so he says, "I turned to the Light and said, 'What's wrong?' Oh," He says, "It's quite plain. You've got two sins. You've got the sin of pride and the sin of jealousy. You're proud because you think you ought to be spoken to, and you're jealous because the other fellow was spoken to." "Oh!" he says. So he said, "Thank God that's what the blood is for. They're not *there*. Praise the Lord! They're gone. So I've come to tell you I praised the Lord and told my brother. And so they're gone." Now, that's walking in the light!

Walk in the light, whatever a thing does. Don't make a big fuss about it. If the thing comes which has bothered you – "Wait a minute. What's bothering me? Ah, I see. I've got some unbelief there. Some fears. Admit it. OK, it's there. Thank God, it's *not* there. It's gone in the blood of Jesus. It's gone. I'm back again." And you walk on again. That's what this being in the light...now we *are* the Light. *We're* the Light of the world! So you see the positive is to be free, be yourself. Don't bother about it. Just be yourself. Run your life. That is the green light. Christ and you are one Person expressed through you. This is the new life! But where something which has come in to disturb – if it's disturbed like that, bring it to the center of your consciousness and recognize if we confess – the word confess only means "say with." It's not a word with a big noise. It's a Latin word "to say with." Say with Whom? With God, of course! So the moment I say, "OK, God. You're right. I did get a bit hurt where I shouldn't get hurt." OK. If you confess your sin, it's not there. The blood – it's forgiven in Christ and it's cleansed from my consciousness, and I go on again. So that's how we're taught here of the first relationship with God who is light.

Now the whole letter is a top line letter and has to be understood as such because the basis of it, as I say, is not we living it...but *Christ* living it. So the letter all the way through is saying *we* walk as He walked. *We're* righteous

311

as He is righteous. "As He is, so are *we* in this world." It says here, "If we walk in the light as He is in the light." So all the way through, it says in the next chapter – *you* walk *as* He walked! Then (verse 6), "you ought to walk as He walked." In verse 29, next chapter, "we're righteous as He is righteous." Verse 7 of Chapter 3, "He that doeth righteousness is righteous, even as He is righteous." Chapter 4, speaking of love, verse 17, "As He is, so are we in this world." Chapter 3 says, "We purify ourselves as He is pure." Early on in Chapter 3. So you see we're talking here about *top line standards*. *"As He is."* How can that be? The Bible says it is. How is it? Because He's in you, you see. You try this by *imitation*...you're in for trouble!

It's impartation, **not** imitation. You see, it isn't "I imitate Him." That's out! You're no longer an independent self. That's an illusion. You're no longer an independent self. You're a united self. *You're* joined to Christ. That *independence* is a lie! That went out in the redemption in Christ. That's crucified with Christ! It's out. So if you say...*I'm* to walk as He walked...you're in trouble. If you say, *I'm* to be *like* that... walk as He walked...righteous as He is righteous...love as He loves...as He is, so are we in this world. Whoa! Who's that? The moment you see yourself – phony!

But you're not 'yourself'. You're no longer an independent self. You are a united self. Your real self is Christ in you. Now then, when you say walk as He walked, "OK, God. You're doing the walking. I don't mind that. I'm walking as long as You're doing the walking. I believe You're doing the walking in me and by me. Ah, well." That's stated in 2 Corinthians 6. "You're the temple of the Living God. I will dwell in them and walk in them." That's a very good statement that in 2 Corinthians 6. We're the temple of the Living God. As sayeth the Lord, "I will dwell in them and walk in them." So you see He's the walker. Now you see, "Love as He loves." Ridiculous! With Your love...I love.

We'll get on a little more, if you've got time to what love is. Love isn't an emotion – it's self-giving identification; quite different! So you see the point? If you take these phrases and you're on the old idea of yourself...they sound ridiculous. If you're on the new fact – you're now never you again. Never. It's eternal union! You are He in you...forever. If you deviate, the deviation isn't on His side; it's on your side. He hasn't changed with you. He never leaves you. It's your foolish imagination...it's only imagination and the blood wipes that out anyhow. So there's never a change. Romans 8 says there's no separation! So you see, it's on *that* basis you can do it.

And so he's saying, now, in this next chapter "If you've got this momentary sin question settled – momentary sins may come about when your cups aren't running over and little darknesses come in. You recognize the darkness – that somewhere you've fallen through with sin or the flesh somewhere...and you come back and admit it. God says, "OK. It's not there." That's what the blood of Jesus Christ does. "OK, Lord, that's great. We'll go on again." So if you have quick sinning, be sure you have quick cleansing. Replace sins by cleansing. The biggest sin is not to be united to Jesus. That's what hurts God most. See what I mean? Your sin doesn't bother God. It's just a slip because He knows He's got you. You've just slipped. He knows that. It doesn't bother Him. It only bothers you. It doesn't bother Him also because He wiped it out with the blood of Jesus Christ.

What does bother him is when you stew on in guilt instead of saying "I'm cleansed." The stewing is the sin. Stewing is unbelief. Stewing is believing your sin is more (it's your pride, really) your sin is more real to you than the blood! Because you're so proud, you think you oughtn't to have done it. So guilt cries, "OK, I did it, Lord." So you see the bigger sin *isn't* that you did it – it's that you're *not believing* it isn't there. So if there's quick sinning, you be sure there's quick cleansing. Now that's just –these things, too. We don't live there all the time, thank God! We don't live there all the time, but these things do happen. Don't get sin-fussing...don't get self-fussing. Get Christ-fussing!

You get that again? If you're in the new consciousness – in the new consciousness you're more conscious of the amazing fact – this is Christ running your show! This takes you and you're less concerned about "my poor self." You aren't a poor self! You're God's precious self. Don't run yourself down. *You* are beautiful to Him. You're His agency. All your powers are for Him to use. You're a beautiful self...and so don't get self-fussing. "Oh, I'm so poor, I'm so weak. Oh, I do things." *Stop* that whole business! If you do things...all right, go on with God and say to Him, "Well, Lord, You ought to have kept me. It's Your fault, anyhow." Put a little blame on Him – be Christ-centered, not self-centered. You see what I mean? So you don't leave it in "Oh, dear, I've sinned." No! No! You live free. If you do slip, here it is – if you do slip, *Praise God!* That's settled for...get on with it!

Now in Chapter 3 you're walking. Now you're to walk as He walks. And you're to keep His commandments. Now you see, if you don't get this right you're headed for trouble! You see in the old life we're so used to being selves, "*You've* got to do this. *You ought* to keep the commandment." That's how God taught us. We hadn't kept them, of course. The law was their teacher. We hadn't kept it. But we did our best. We thought we did. We tried to keep it ...had our religion...had our good resolutions...**tried** to keep these things. So we used to be people who've tried to keep things, but haven't been very good at it. Now *that* law is out, because *we* are under no law, no condemnation...because we aren't selves running things by ourselves. We're "Christ in you". Christ is the law. So Christ writes His own law!

The law of God is the law of love, which is expressed in you. It isn't you expressing it. He *is* that law...so *you* are the law of God now. You're no longer under the law telling you to do things...because you couldn't do them. That self is an illusion − thing which is out. You're no longer an independent self. You're dead to the law talking to you as if you're an independent self. You're this new self, which is Christ in you...and He's the keeper...He's the doer...He's the law. So *now* you're not under the law, but here come the commandments.

A commandment isn't a threatening thing. A commandment is the way God says, "That's an absolute." This is what this life *is*. Now because we love to do it, it isn't, "Oh, I've got to do it." This is *how* we do it now. And so he is saying now, "You walk...keeping the commandments." Keeping the commandments means you recognize what the implications of this new life are, and fulfill them. That's in the first part of this second chapter, where he says, "If I say I know Him and don't keep His commandments, I'm a liar." "Who keepeth His word" ...see *is!* How do you keep His word? Ah, verse 6: "He that abideth in Him ought Himself also to walk...." See, it's you *in Him* and He *in you*. It isn't *you* keeping it. It's in this abiding relationship − it's a vine/branch relationship. You're part of that vine/branch. Now you're in Him...He's the one that's doing it! So the key to the commandments isn't a question of you doing it; it's a question of what you *recognize*. This is a *standard* of life. You accept that. That's the standard. I'm not running about telling lies and doing these things.

And then, far more, he says, that's all a bigger law. This whole book says there's only *one* law, the whole Bible says − the law of love...the principle of love. Now again, remember − law is the way a thing works. Law isn't a horrible word. You've got the laws of your body − that's how it works. It works spontaneously, and you just function by your body. That's why I use that illustration. If you suddenly break a leg or something − now you 'be' you and your body... you forget it. Your body's operating with beautiful laws. You see...think and hear...will and work...and so on, by those bodies. If you break a leg, suddenly you're at outs with your body. Your body says to "get that right, get that right." Now you've come under the law because you've got a breakage...come under the law, get it right. So the body says, "You get that right!" So law is being in harmony except when you're out of it.

Now, that went out with us in the Fall — that "get it right" went out in the Fall — went out in Jesus Christ. And now *we're* the law...keeping the law! Now he's saying here that the major law is love. The only law — and so he goes on here to the new commandment in the same chapter. Now the old commandment, verse 8, "I write a new commandment unto you, which is true *in* Him and *in* you. Notice!

The other great word you'll find all through the letter of John is "in," "in," "in," "in," "in." It isn't "with" or "for," or "by;" it's "in." Now "in" makes you a union, you see. Get it? This is a *union life*. It isn't, "I'm with Him...I'm for Him...I'm by Him...I call on Him." It's true <u>in</u> Him and <u>in</u> you! Twenty or thirty times over you find this verse — the truth is <u>in</u> you. He's <u>in</u> you. Because this is this new relationship — this inner union. Now he says, "You do this. You keep this commandment" because in you He's love and He causes you to love." Your purpose in life now is to love. If you're a born again person, a unified person, your desire is to bless people and complete their needs...and above all to bring Christ to them. You're under new motivation. So do you understand a commandment's easily fulfilled because it's He that's fulfilling it? It isn't — "You've got to do it." It's just — "This is the only way you can live the life." This is a life of love because God is love and you're love...and therefore you *know* at once when something comes into you, which isn't your inner self at all. And we all get it, "Oh, I don't like that person." That's not your inner self at all.

That's what the Bible teaches is the difference between soul and the spirit. Now your spirit is your inner self — your "I am" joined to Christ, which is love and you're an expression of love. And so your basis is His love's shed abroad in your heart...and you know you want to be a person who loves people...who loves God. You desire that — it's your purpose to be that. That's your inner *spirit*. Now your *soul* is your emotions and reasons by which you express your spirit. Your desires, you express through your emotions. Your knowledge you express through your reasons. So soul is your emotions and reasons. Now they can be influenced by all sorts of ways. So you may get influenced, "Oh, I don't like that person." Now learn —

that's not the real self. If it'd be your real self, you'd say, "I'm going to hate them." Now, that's another matter. But you don't say that. If you don't like a person, sometimes you can't help it. "I just don't like that person. They get on my nerves. That's about it. I can't stand them." That's not the real you. Learn to discern between soul and spirit. Say, "In my outer emotions I don't like them. But with God, they're God's precious people. They're as much God's people as I am. With God's love I love them."

And that's where love isn't emotion. Love is a *purpose* by which you want to give yourself to somebody. You want to do anything you can to appreciate them or bless them...although humanly you wouldn't like them. Now, that's love. So love isn't an emotion. Don't mistake the emotion which may vary. Sometimes you don't like people. All right...don't condemn yourself. Say, "In my soul I don't like them. But that's only my outer clothing. That's a temporary influence on me. In my real self with God's love, of course I love them. I love the world. And I'll set about now in any way God shows me in which I can show love and appreciate them, and I'll begin to do so." See that's it! That's where he says, "If you hate, you're out." He says in this verse, because if you hate a person, you stumble. This is the wisdom of God. Wisdom isn't cleverness – wisdom is love. Wisdom is *towards* people in what you think is the best way for them. That's wisdom!

If all nations knew *that* we should be different nations – it's what is the best for every nation. You see what I mean? That stumbles you. It says in verse 11 if you really are moving to hate a person and *accept* that hate, you walk in darkness – because that's self-loving self and you don't know where you're going...because you're looking at life from the wrong point of view... what *you* want out of it...how you react to it. That's always false. That's a lie! But if you walk in love, you *never* stumble, because love is – "What's the best thing I can do in this situation? I want to do the right thing." You won't stumble. That's wisdom. It isn't being clever and knowing. You are motivated by love as best you know how.

Sometimes that's not true he says...No! How can I best act in this situation, which is because I want that person to be blessed and so I want the situation to be right...and you find you do the right. So you don't stumble if you're operating by self-giving love in so far as you understand and can interpret it. So that's what he says is 'the walking'. You're walking, but don't make a fuss about it. You're walking. And your new purpose is...your command is, "Of course I'm not running about telling lies, though I might slip into something like that, and cheating. I don't go about like that; I've got a new way of life." But all that is fulfilled by love. If I love I won't cheat and lie, of course. And so my basis of the new life is – I'm walking in this love and I learn to walk...walk it step by step, and I learn, as I say...if things come up which cause me not to love, to say, "No, no, I'm not taking that. That's not the real thing at all. I'm going back to where I am loving." As I do that I shall find I'm walking in light and I'm not stumbling. I'm light to some other person. So this is what he puts out as the basis of the union life or the union walk.

He goes into a break-off then for a few minutes to admit that there are different levels of relationship – levels of understanding what relationship we were in, which is, in a sense, a relaxing way. He says, "I'm going to put out top line stuff. Now it could be you don't get to understand when I talk about union. Maybe you can't understand everything. You take what you can. I'll put out top flight stuff."

That's why I think preachers are wholly wrong who just keep giving the simple gospel. Give everything! Many pastors never give the full gospel to their people. They're afraid they might rebel against them. Best thing that could happen is to have a revolution rather than a revival! Best thing they can do! Don't say give me a simple gospel. Give all the works and let the chips fall where they may! Let light shine where it may and trust the Lord to suit the light given to the level you're on.

So here in verses 12-14 he breaks away to say, "I want to say there are three grades – little children, young men, and fathers. 'I write unto you little children" (verse 12); "I write unto you fathers" (verse 13); "I write unto you young men" (verse 13). And then he repeats it, little children, young men and fathers. And roughly they fall into 3 grades or 3 categories: infant, adolescent, adult. Now the point of infancy is an *infant* knows nothing except to depend on his outer parents – that's all it knows. He just knows his mother and father. His whole life is a dependent life. He doesn't know himself. He doesn't know what's happening inside. Now that's the first start. When my dependence has been on Jesus Christ who died on the Cross, took my sins away, that's all I know. I know Him outside as my Savior, my Lord, and my Father. I know Him outside.

Now you can't live on the outside and live on the inside. Now, an *adolescent* finds himself. That's why adolescence is ferment, because a young person's got to find themselves – get away from what their parents think and what other people think and be themselves. They've got to find themselves! And they've got to find that inside there's a battle between the good and evil. And so the Christian has to find, "Now I've got it inside. How shall I operate? Now I'm a growing Christian, how shall I operate? How shall I conquer the evil? How shall I conquer these temptations?" That's when I learn, it says here, "Oh, it isn't the question of the Bible...as Christ is the Living Word...the expressed Word of the Father...the Living Word coming to me...the Living Word is in me." So he says, "Now, young men, you have overcome the wicked one. You are strong, he says, verse 12. You have overcome the wicked one. I write unto you." And in verse 14, "You are strong and the Word of God abides in you." Not to you...in you. And you have overcome the wicked one. Now you've learned this union secret. "Oh, I say, evil," when I'm tempted in this way or that, "Christ manages that. I refer that back to Him. When I slip, He cleanses. He's the one who manages that. I'm not trying to manage that...He's the One." So you're an overcomer. You're strong because the strength is He in you now. This is the second one.

Not He for you as an infant; He in you as an adolescent. And that's what we call spiritual graduation – when you're conscious of this union. And you're living in the consciousness that you are crucified and it isn't you...Christ lives in you. Fact. Fixed. And you're living on that operation.

The third, *father* one is – a father's for others. Infancy and adolescence are for the development of the child. Fatherhood's for other people. A father goes out to contribute to the world. The world's his family. Fulfill his purposes in the world. So spoken in Christian language, a father is one who, having become free from my own problem...I can give myself for other people's problems. I've become free now to become a minister of Christ to others which we all are when *we're* right. Wherever you are, you know that. You want to be, don't you? You can't have Christ if you don't want other people to have Him. We're all ministers of Christ to find out how we can give ourselves, how by some means or other Christ can express Himself by word, by life, by witness, by me. And somewhere I can be a harvester for Christ. Isn't that right? That's fatherhood! And so the word given for fatherhood here is – a father "knows Him Who is from the beginning." Now that's a queer phrase. It says twice over, "I write unto you, Fathers, because ye know Him that is from the beginning." I tell you *knowing* is *always within*. It isn't sensing a thing outwardly. There's that sense – knowing is what you have inside you. The etymological or original meaning of the word "know" is "mixed with." I'm mixed with. I'm mixed with. Therefore, to know Him is to be mixed with Him. Mixed with whom? Him that is from the beginning.

What's that? The Person of the eternal purposes, of course. He isn't even given a name! The Living God who began and is in the process of completing. "Him from the beginning."

Now *I'm part* of this Person fulfilling His purposes of saving grace and love in the world, and I have the privilege of taking a share! That's fatherhood...to be united with Him in whatever situation I am...to have some calling which has some contribution to make to the needs of the people around me. I don't fuss about it. God will do it. Light isn't you shining, it's Christ shining. Let Him shine...that's all! He'll do it. If you have this concept...if you understand it you say, "OK, God. This is true. Somehow I'm saying You're making me a light for other people because You say so. I'm interested in other people getting something from me. I can be involved in something by which Christ can get other people." That's the fatherhood.

So you see he's saying here that, "I'm writing to you and you might be one of those three grades. A little child...you might not understand what we're talking about this evening. Even an adolescent who hasn't found the union. You may be interested about this union business... you may not understand much more. OK. Take what suits you. Take what fits your condition. And some of you can go on with what we're talking about...this top-line life. "As He is, so are we." But, he says, there's one certainty and that is every chance of love, because that's what you *are*. So he goes on to say, there's one certainty about all of us, whether you're little children, or whatever you are, your love no longer is geared to the world and what the world can give you to satisfy yourself. It's geared to the Father and His will. This is the change. This is the new love!

Previously you were self-loving self. You were geared to what the world could provide for your flesh, your ambitions, everything else – what's here called "the lust of the flesh, the lust of the eyes, the pride of life." The lust of the flesh is physical self-gratification. The lust of the eyes is accumulation, "Oh, there are all sorts of things I'd like to have; I'll grab what I can." The pride of life is self-magnification. So it's self-gratification...self-accumulation...self-magnification. "I'll be something for myself." Now if you're born again that's now gone out. If you're born again, that's not possessing you. You can't have two loves possessing you! You may be attacked by that. You may be attacked, but it doesn't possess you. So that's a test given here.

319

If you're born again the love of the Father is in you...because born again means the Spirit of God Who is Self, Who is love has brought into your heart the consciousness that Jesus died for you...and you can't help but love Him who died for you...saved you. The Father sent Him. You've got a new love – a love for God and love for man, and this is your new life. So you've changed loves. And you no longer love to gratify your flesh or to accumulate possessions in this life or to become the big noise. And that's the test of it. Now you may be tempted, but that's not controlling you as it did. That's the change. You see, that's the total change for any level – little children, young men, and fathers.

Now he proceeds on to the consequences, the effects of this union life in us in different aspects in relation to our inner knowing, whom and what we really inwardly know, by which our life is governed in relation to our outer conduct...that's Chapter 3. In relation to our *true* self which is our self-giving self...our love self...that's Chapter 4. And Chapter 5 is how you *operate* by faith, so that this remains a continuing experience in you...how you *overcome* by faith. Those are the 5 chapters.

So the remainder of Chapter 2 here concerns your inner knowing. Now, he says, there's only one safeguard – you *only* know this Father through the Son. He's revealed through His Son Who became a physical person, and Whom I know as a physical person to reveal the Father to me as the Father of love...and therefore fulfilled this commitment of death and resurrection to deliver us from this old life and put us into new. So all our knowing is geared to knowing Jesus Christ as Savior...as Lord...as brother...as all...and the One to Whom I'm united. Christ lives in me and I go along with Him. That's your inner knowledge.

You see knowledge isn't temporary understanding of outer things. That's not real knowledge. You may know how to handle a machine or something. You may know how to...external bits. That's not real knowledge. That's temporary application. Knowledge is what is really you inside – what's really new inside you is Jesus Christ the Son, Who introduces the Father, too. That's your inner knowledge. When you've got that you really don't need anything else because when you've got Him you've got all. You've just got to learn how He operates by you. So he goes on to say, you don't need any teacher. All you need is a flesh confirmation of the Person Who's living His life in you.

So here's as far as this inner knowledge is concerned. He says...rivals will come...antichrists will come. Verse 18. "They left us" and so, "but you (vs. 20) have an unction from the Holy One, and you know all things." Now, knowing is not having some temporary outside relationship with something by which you handle tools or something. We've done an immense amount by which we've applied science. That's not *knowing* it. That's taking what's been given us and applying it. We may have application ability, which has nothing to do with knowing at all in the sense of that's what we really are. It's not our real selves at all; it's how we are applying ourselves in certain external ways. That's how the world develops. So that kind of sense application is quite different from the inner knowing.

The inner knowing is Who I really am, which is Jesus Christ joined to me...and by Him I know the Son. And this is the key, the axis by which *everything* turns. So he says "You know all things when you have Him." You always know when you're out, when there's something which is attacking the Lord Jesus Christ. It says here, "he that denies that Jesus is the Christ." That's attacking the essential key of life. So he says, "Preserve the essential key, which is in you." It's in you...it's an inner knowledge. And so he says in verse 27, "Therefore, you have received an anointing and you need not that any man teach you. The same anointing teacheth you and is no lie, even as it hath taught you, you shall abide in Him." You see, we don't come to outer people for teaching; we come for confirmation – to affirm what we *already* know. This is where we are so weak. Unless you know *this is Christ* in you, you may want teachers.

When you've found "the thing" you've got all! Actually you *don't* remain hungry. Hunger is a dangerous facet...a dangerous faculty because it means you *haven't* got it. If you're hungry you want something, don't you? When you've got Jesus you're never hungry again, because He's your all. You're totally satisfied in the Living God Who is joined to you.

Now you may be glad to know more about how to experiment...how to know more...or how to apply more, but it isn't hunger. It's just the excitement of knowing a little more of how you operate in this relationship. So you get my point. So you see...we're not to go to outer teachers to be taught more. The real teaching is what is already our *inner* knowledge...and when we listen to people it may confirm us a little...it may refresh us a little...it may encourage us a little with what we've *got*. That's all. It may make it a little clearer what we've got. That's all.

321

So I never say, "I'm a teacher." I say, "I'm a sharer." I contribute to you, a contributor! I contribute to you, you contribute to me...like in the *Pilgrim's Progress*, an interpreter, that's all. We interpret to each other. We all contribute to each other. I don't believe in this "boss" teaching stuff. That's why I don't believe in all this standing up sermon stuff. They bore me. I prefer equal relation, because you know just as much as I do...and you have the same Person as I've got...and you can give *your* conviction as much as I can. That's a sharer. I'm not giving you a charge, am I?

Now we're going to move into Chapter 3 into the right walk...the right way of walking...the right walk...the standard walk. So it says at the end of Chapter 2, "You know that everyone that doeth righteous**ness** is born of Him." I'm not talking about doing righteous**ly**. He puts a little interlude in of the wonder that God's love has bestowed upon us...called sons and if we're sons the world doesn't know us, because they don't know Him. And we *are* sons. It doesn't yet appear what we shall be...because when He comes one day, and we see Him as He is we shall be like Him.

Because you always *see* what you *are*, you know. Life reflects what you are...that's *all*. When you see a thing outwardly it's *because* you see it inwardly! That's why when you see evil in a person it's because *you're* seeing evil. You're seeing wrongly. If you see a person as *God's* person despite their evil, you're seeing rightly. Things reflect back to you as you see them. And you're lining up as you see a thing. So as you see a thing bad it reflects bad things back to you. You say, "OK, it looks bad but God's handling it," then it's reflecting God back to you...and goodness back to you. Everything's got goodness at the heart of it because God's the heart of it. So you see we are *being* what we see. And so in this ultimate day we're seeing Him as He is and we're being what we're seeing!

In that sense as we see Him as He *is*...we ourselves in a more total sense *are being* what He is, as it says here. That's the day that's coming. Now, he says, rightness means you're *finished* with sin! That's the point of it. The right way of life – finished with sin. "You purify yourselves as He is pure." That's verse 3. He says, "Any man that commits sin transgresses the law" that's verse 4, "and sin is a transgression of the law. And you know that He was manifested to take away our sin, and in Him is no sin. Whosoever abideth in Him sinneth not, whosoever sinneth hath not seen Him, neither known Him. Little children, let no man deceive you: he that doeth righteousness is righteous even as He is righteous. He that committeth sin is of the devil, for the devil sinneth from the beginning. For this purpose the Son of God was manifested, that he might destroy the works of the devil. Whosoever is born of God doth not commit sin; for His seed remaineth in him, and He cannot sin, because he is born of God. In this the children of God are manifest." Children cannot sin – the Bible says so!

Now here he is saying you are *finished* with sin. How can that be? Find out what sin is. Sin is a transgression of the law, it says here. Sin is a transgression of the law. Now the law, as I kept saying is a word we use of how a thing works. We have all kinds of laws – of gravity, laws of science, laws of the road, laws by which we operate. We say, "That's how a thing works, and other earthly, temporary situations. The Law is how *God* works. How does God work? By love of course! So the law of the universe is a Person Who is love. That's the principle. The whole universe is an expression of the Person Who *is* love. That's *all* it is.

Now a transgression of the law is when free people...we're persons so we're free...as free people head it up by saying that's how it is up here. We said, "I'm not going to be a form of God expressing His Self-giving love. I'm going to be a form of myself expressing self-loving love." *That's* transgression – I'm *deliberate*. You see, I'm not going to be *with* God in Self-giving love. I'm going to be myself a self-lover – that's Satan. That's sin! All sins are products of **sin**. What you're removed from is the *principal of sin*, not the products, necessarily. The products are sins...only temporary details. The *principle* is a self-loving self which produces the hates and the lies and the greed and so on. They are all products of a self which is a self-loving self, which is Satan expressed in me. That's sin! So the principle of sin is this principle of self-loving love, just *the same as* the principle of rightness is God Who is Self-giving love. That's the difference. Therefore sin is a transgression of the law because it's self-loving love expressed in all the forms of sins. Now that's what we're cut *out* from! That is the character of Satan.

As he says here, He's here to "destroy the works of the devil." He said, "The devil sinned from the beginning." He was the *first* person to do that. Now Jesus Christ came to cut us out of any control of the devil. Now this person, who **is** sin...who produces the character of self-loving love...*has gone out of us*! We *were* that – we *were* dominated by the spirit of self-loving love. That's sin. The sin is where the hates and the lies and all the different things came out of it. That's sin. Now that went *out* in Jesus Christ. *We've* died to that. That's why it says we've died to sin...Romans 6. We've died to sin – because in Christ's Cross on our behalf He died for us, and then rose again. So He took upon Him the death, which is the consequence of sin...rose up from it...left all of that control of Satan behind...went out. He left any right of the control of Satan – who's the spirit of self-centeredness to motivate us by this spirit of self-centeredness.

If you're born again that's *all gone out*. If you're born again, you're no longer motivated by the spirit of self-centeredness. You're motivated by a new spirit – the Spirit of love. The Spirit of love for Jesus...love for people. You may think you deviate, but that's your basis and you cannot sin again because if you've been related to Christ in His Cross...Christ in his resurrection. You can't go back on the 'other side' again. You can't again be *dominated* by the spirit of self-loving love. You may *temporarily* express it, but don't let the devil lie to you. You see, the devil's a liar, a deceiver. He'll get you to have a self-loving attitude, "Oh, you're no good. You're full of yourself." Don't take that lie! Don't let man or devil tell you you're full of yourself. That's a lie! You may have a temporary touch, but if you're a born-again person, the basis of your being – love of God, love of Jesus, love His will, love people – that's your basis. Don't let that lie disturb you, because when you suddenly feel yourself self-centered, "Oh, you're a mess, you're just selfish." It's a lie. You're *no longer* a self-centered self. That's the devil. He'd like to get you to think so because he can bind you, if he does that. Don't do that. So, you **cannot** sin again! The Bible says so. Which means you can't again be under the motivation of the spirit of self-centeredness. You may slip and do a self-centered thing – that's sins. You may slip into self-centered acts, like a temper or something. You may slip into it. Come back. That's not you living that life. That's not sinning. You've slipped into the *products of sin* temporarily. Sin is no longer **in** you. That's what it says here.

So this is our liberty. We're delivered from being controlled by this old quality of self-centeredness. And we have in its place the Spirit of Self-giving love. And we operate from *that* basis! You only begin to get deliverance when you *affirm* those things. The boldness is easy you see...some of us are so confused. We don't, as it were, dare to affirm these things. We've *got* to affirm. What you affirm becomes you! If you affirm your union with Christ...if you affirm that you'll never sin again, because sin is the principle of self...you'll never do that again. You may *slip* into sin. You affirm that. You find that what you settle into is reality, and then you don't get bothered by the sins because when you slip you say, "OK, I slipped, but I'm not geared to that again. I just slipped." And come back. That's all. You learn something of this liberated life!

Now again he comes back to this and he says...the manifestation of the new life is that you don't do the old things, the unrighteousness, you want to do. In verse 10 he says, "The children of God are manifested and the children of the devil. Because whoever doesn't do righteousness is not of God – doesn't live this new quality of life – neither is he that loveth not his brother." Back he comes again. He says the true expression of this new life is loving your *brother*, not loving God! Loving your brother. This is the principle because, you see, God is operating in manifested humanity. He lives in manifest humanity. So it isn't a question of loving God as apart from humanity, but of loving God *in* humanity. Loving your brother. And so he says...that's the evidence! You love your brother. In this case, previously he said, when you don't love your brother you'll stumble. But walking in light and loving your brother gives you wisdom in handling a bad situation because you're handling by what's best *for* your brother – what's best in the situation. He says the evidence of loving your brother is you'll give your life for him. That comes out here [inside], he says. Sin will take somebody else's life. Love gives your life for the other person. Sin is the other person will take your life. Love – you give *your* life *for* them.

That's the evidence of love – that you lay down your life for your brother, and you'll do anything that will bring him to meet his need. That's love! So you see, you get the point...*love is not an emotion*. Love isn't a feeling. You may thoroughly dislike him in the feeling. But you say, "God, if there's any way you'll show me what I could do...something like laying down my life for that brother, I'll do it. He's precious to you. He's yours. You bought him with Your blood. Your purpose is to get him. He's yours to build your Self in him. Anything that I can do...here I am." So if you're born again you have the Spirit of self-giving love. The Spirit of laying down your life in any way He tells you. This is your new meaning of life. If by any means I can be the means which other people may have their life fulfilled – that's me. That's this love he speaks of here. And, he says, it does take practical form. That's the measure form. He says, "Whoso hateth his brother is a murderer." Self-loving love will kill your brother. "And you know that no murderer hath eternal life abiding in him." (verse 15) And verse 16, "Hereby we perceive the love of God, because He laid down His life for us, and we ought to lay down our lives for the brethren." So this is the motivation behind...and he says it's practical, too. It concerns the daily things of life. "If you have this world's goods, and your brother has need, and shutteth up your bowels of compassion from him, how dwelleth the love of God in you?" And so he says it takes detailed practical form as well as the general principal.

So he presented that as the practical way in which life is lived and walked. And he gives a warning against false condemnation – self-condemnation – don't judge your own heart. God's grace in your heart. He says, now you're a sensitive person. *Because* you're sensitive you might come under self-condemnation. You may feel you're no good. You may feel you've failed. Watch! Don't take those feelings. They come from your heart and your attitudes. They can tie you up. God is greater than your heart. He knows all things and you're precious to Him. He's accepted you in Christ. Accept your*self*. He says, learn this lesson...*Don't* sink ye into self-condemnation...a sense of self-failure...a sense of your sin...self saying you're no good. Those are part of your heart...really your *soul* life. They're a part of your soul life. You're not to respond to them. You're to respond to God. He's greater than your heart. He's accepted you. He knows all things. He means you to be what you like. You're precious to Him. All right, accept yourself and your preciousness as God in God's preciousness. In *that* confidence – that's where it is. Always, in any sense, in every way. Watch this arising of the self. I told you before, the moment you sense self...watch. There is something that has begun to come in you...something that is apart from Christ in you. And that's your trouble.

You're not any longer without Christ. You *are* Christ in you. But the moment you begin to react to things you know it. You know the shadow. Darkness. You know the shadow. You feel somewhere separate. That's out. That's a lie! You're responding to an illusion. You're not an independent self...a hurt self...or a wrong self. It's a lie. You're God's precious self – *Christ* living in you. And *He's* running you! If He is dissatisfied with you He has *nice* ways of telling you. If the devil's dissatisfied with you he has *nasty* ways of telling you. He condemns you. If Jesus is dissatisfied with you He'll tell you nicely. He says, "Oh, come along. It's OK. A little better next time." Jesus is always up and up. The devil's always down and down. Don't you listen to him!

So watch in any circumstance the moment that self reacts...watch. You slipped for a moment as if you're a human. It's an illusion that I'm *just* a human in a human situation...I'm a nasty human...or a weak human...or something else. Drop those lies! Stop it. Say, "No, no! I'm in union. All power's mine." It's tremendous! If Jesus Christ is in me...all power's mine, all ability is mine, all sufficiency is mine. Move in. Speak those words of affirmation and faith. I do not sin again! That doesn't mean I can't step into sin. But that's only temporary. I don't live under this old life I used to live of self-centeredness. I'm free. So you see he's calling us to freedom by having more confidence, by having more boldness. He says here, "If your heart condemns you, you have confidence towards God." And then you're bold in *receiving* things from Him, too – confidence. So it's to build up confidence, affirmation of Who we are.

We were looking into what the Holy Spirit might have to say to us through His very special servant John. Nobody is special to the Holy Spirit – only special in the sense that he had come into a special union and therefore an understanding of the things of God, and so we were looking into that, but didn't complete it last night. We were saying that he speaks on the top level. The letter doesn't deal with the background. The issue we dealt with last night of how real a person *is* – who's in conscious union with God. You and God are one Person and *you* know it. And the importance is that you *live by* what you know...you live by what you are. What you know is what you are! We all are what we know. My knowing is not outward knowing. That's the fallen knowing. Inner knowing is knowing in the spirit. Knowledge is part of you – that's what I know.

You can illustrate it a little bit on the human level when a person gets a profession, for instance. You don't operate your professions from what you've got outside, because you never live from outside. Outside is not real to you at all. It's just things you're contacting. You operate you profession by what gets inside you. So you study medicine, you become a doctor...study carpentry and become a carpenter...study teaching and become a teacher...or study cooking and become a cook. Now it's spontaneous because it it's inside you – it's you! You're a cook on that level. You're a teacher on that level. You're a doctor on that level – because knowing has been mixed with something, and you're mixed with this and it's you. This is how all life is lived. What we become mixed with – that is us. That's just on the natural level, to a certain extent. That's just on the level of the flesh. You can know things like a profession, and function spontaneously from the basis of that knowledge.

Now true knowing, because we are true spirits, is when God and I are one Person – when we know Him because we're spirits. We really only know *about* things, otherwise, but to a certain extent we've come into a fusion with them. But they're only on a thing level...a self-level. But the true knowing is when I find *my* real self is in Christ, which means I've had a death and resurrection – which means in Christ, I've died to being the person I once was, which is a self-centered person. And in Christ's resurrection, I've become the new Person which is not I, now, but the Holy Spirit, which is love. The person of Christ Who has become one with me because spirits unite. The truth of the whole universe is union. The whole universe is union! We've been reading a lot on that level, which I'm going to do this morning. And because the whole of life is One – it's when you see as one – when you see with the inner seeing you are seeing Him who is the All, and then you're seeing that all is Him expressed in all forms. He's God, All in all!

And so your seeing starts with seeing, first of all of course...*before* you've seen your lost self...now you see yourself as a saved self. You see that you've been accepted by Jesus and you're cleansed by Jesus. You've got eternal life and you've got a relationship. That's the first knowing – like a relationship with the Christ Who died for you – the Christ Who lives now, has come to live in you, has related you to the living Father. And then as the knowing goes on you come to find it isn't a 'relationship' at all – it's a unity, because spirits are One. The whole universe is One, because all the universe is spirit manifested in outer forms. So these are just outer forms. Basically everything is One unity. That's one of the flashes of insight – that's God All in all. God Who is the All in all His forms! This is what the whole universe is when you see it now. The Bible says that's what will finally be known in the whole universe when the last enemy has been destroyed, which is death (1 Cor. 15) and the Son rose up and is seated with the Father...and then God will be All in all. If God's all then there's nothing else, is there? If God is all there's nothing else.

The Bible says that God may be All in all means that the One *is* All in all His outer forms...but we who have moved into union with Him know that now. We now see that He *is* All in all. And though we live in this fragmented outer world we are living really in the inner knowledge, which He and I are one. I'm a form of Him – I'm He expressed in my human form. This is the union level. What it means to be a true person from which John is speaking. And we went into some detail which we can't go into this morning.

It was asked last night *how* we move into the consciousness of the union – how we find that the self that is the independent self has gone out, and the *positive* independent self we've become (dependent selves) and *in* the dependent self we're like the vessel which contains the water...we're like the body which the head operates... we're like the branch with the vine operates – we're one! And so we're conscious that the real Person...operating...living...acting is not we, it's He – Father, Son, Spirit! But you live...you live by consciousness, which is spontaneity. Your knowing is being mixed with a thing. Which means it's part of you, so you don't have to 'find' it. You just operate on that level. Just as I said before...going back on the human level...you are at home in your profession because it's got *inside* you. "Oh, I know how to build that house. I'm a builder." "I know how to teach that subject. I'm a teacher"...on that level. "I know how to handle medicine on certain levels," These are always developments, of course. "I know." "I know." "I know." It's perfectly spontaneous. You don't have to find it and work at it. So life's fun and ease. Interesting – because you *know* how to do it. You're always happy in doing what you know how to do, and this is what knowing means.

Now this is *real* knowing – when He and I form to be His manifested expressions – His own Son and then through His Son His sons and His manifested expression. Now when He and I are one like that, well we just *know* each other. We don't bother about it. We don't have to go and pray every day because that's what all life is about. It's just *being*. Praying is just being – recognizing. You don't do anything. You're just free persons. Stop being bothered by it. It's not you; it's He! Just the same as life. You have a profession. "Oh, I know that." So we live like this. This is 'the know' in knowing! And John, from that basis, which is not discussed in the letter of John – it comes in Romans...it comes in Galatians...and in other areas in the Bible – on this basis he's now saying now, what is the *product* of that Life. How does that Life work out as a person who has inner union – the living God and I as one – living in outer conditions, distorted conditions, conditions of this world? How does it work out? And so we went into that a little in the early chapters of John.

We found that first of all He's light. And when we first find Him – light is inner inspiration. Inner what? How do you put it into words? It isn't this outer light. God **is** light. We're *not* light – that's it! Light is inner inspiration. Realization. Knowledge. "Oh, yes, yes!" It registers in you. "This is it! That's light! This is it! I'm forgiven! God's become my Father! This is it! God loves me! He and I've got a purpose in life! This is it!" That's light. That's the *inner* light. Giving us this inner consciousness of this harmonious wonderful relationship in which He and I are familiars – in fellowship with Him.

Fellowship is familiars. I always say, one of the most illuminating things said of it concerning the heart of God. – in the Bible is when he called two humans his friends. He said, "Moses is My friend." "Abraham is My friend." In other words, God hungers for friendship. It's the Fall which has given us these fears of God. He's an awful Person. Come trembling and bow down before Him and all that stuff. Jesus Christ wiped all that out! That's a consequence of being 'out' with a person. When you're out with a person, you're polite to them. When you're 'in' with them you have fun with them. So you always know how you are with a person. So we have fun with God because we're in with Him. When you're out with God you're afraid. That's the old life. There's *no* fear in God. When you're afraid it's because you know you're wrong, not He's wrong. So your approach is like that. "Ooh, ooh, ooh." It isn't in Him, it's in you. But that's what Jesus Christ wiped out.

He became like that for our sakes – as if He was a person at outs with the Father. "My God, My God, why hast Thou forsaken Me?" In His death, which is the ultimate result of this 'out' life, He took the outer results of His out life when He died because dying is going to hell. The body dies, the spirit goes to hell. He went to hell it says for them – us now. Now, He went all the way because He was the Son representing the human race. He was the incarnate Son of God. He was the Creator representing the human race. He was representing the human race when He went there. So when He came up the whole human race came up! And when Satan couldn't hold Him – hell couldn't hold because He didn't belong there. So He'd been there, as if He was there for our sakes as us, made sin, bearing our sins. When it couldn't hold Him, and because He belonged to the Father...the Spirit of the Father, it says, raised Him. He was put to death in the flesh, quickened by the Spirit. The Spirit of the Father raised Him from the dead. His body came up with a new Spirit in it. This was the new union for us. Therefore there's no shadow of self between us and God! Fellowship, fun, friendship!

So I was saying God is a loving Person. Love likes freedom. Love likes fellowship. Love likes society. Love likes fun. Love likes fellow interests. That's God! So the light of God is when "He's my friend." Friendship has a certain connotation, a freedom in it. This is the relationship without a shadow between us – that's light. *We* are that Light – we're one. We are expressions of God. So He was Light – that's why Jesus says, *you're* the Light. Twice over Jesus said, "You're the Light." How are you the Light? You're darkness...you're human, but you're no longer human. That's an illusion. You're no longer a lonely human who's in darkness. *You're* in a unity. And in that unity you're just a branch of the Vine, and the Vine in that sense is equivalent to Light in that sense. So you're the Light – that's the proof of unity – because you love the Light.

Looked at as a human, you're not the light. How can you be the Light? It must be because you're a new Person. And that kind of Person isn't you, it's

He joined to you. Therefore you're the Light. So you see we've become God. You get the point? If He's the light and you're not the light, and now you are the Light something's happened! If He's the Light and you're darkness, not the Light, and now you are the Light, something's happened! And it can't be you. Something's happened *about* you, it's sure. Which is that your human spirit has become joined to His divine Spirit and you're One – and so you are God expressed. *You* are the Light. God is Light. You're the Light. We're God expressed. This is union!

And as I say, when we've moved in to this...because the whole way of all the ways we humans are made – the capacity of gaining experience by what we attach ourselves to – that's what we call *faith*. Some of these words need a re-interpretation. Faith isn't just mental belief; it includes that. You didn't come here by mental belief that there's a home here to which we were invited. You came here by saying, "I'll come." Now, that's faith. Faith is my free person attaching myself to something in which I mentally believe. So faith is the *inner movement of my inner self* in outer form, or it may be in some outer thing. And then I get to experience, the outer thing, by going there.

On the human level I take a car and come here, because that's on the human level. But it comes out of, not the car, it comes out of my *inner* self saying, "Yes, I'll go there." Now that's faith – I attach myself. In the *law* of faith – that's how you get experience. You experience the thing to which you attach yourself. In human form – you may take it like food, experience it. Or you may go there...experience it. Faith becomes fact because you experience by whatever means in the Spirit, of course. You experience it because the Spirit comes and does the automobile work...takes you there...on earth you drive it. That's all. It comes to the same thing. You come to something which is you, which is part of you. So being here...it isn't very hard for you to be here. It isn't very hard for you to recognize you're here. You don't have to spend all your time, "Am I here? Am I here? Am I here?" That's it. Life is spontaneity. Life is freedom. You *are* here.

Now when you are here you operate as being here...what you came for, which is sitting here looking bored, which you're very good at doing! That's what you came for. So when you are here you forget the thing you experienced and get working, or speaking, or whatever the situation is. Now that's the union consciousness. Forget God and live. Not remember God. Forget Him...because you *are* God. If you've got to always remember God you've got to remember yourself, too. You don't always remember yourself, do you? Am I here? Am I here? Am I here? You forget yourself and *be*. Life is expressing yourself...out from yourself...which you forget you are, which you are. Thinking, walking, talking, and so on is a consequence of being. But you forget the being and do the talking.

Now your *being* isn't you at all. Your being is God *and* you as one Person. Christ in you...the Holy Spirit in you...as one person. Forget Him! Don't think about Him – because you are as He! Now you operate on this level, and now He's saying what this letter is. How do you operate on that level? First of all it is that you have an inner consciousness – which is just the Light in you. Now when that got 'shadowed' then you know something's slipping in. He starts saying...He says we're human and self slips in. The self...as it were *detached*. It's an illusion! It says when sin gets you – Romans 7 – it deceives you. *Deceives* you – makes you *think* you are what you're not. And so when I'm tempted into sin, sin says, "Oh, you're not in Christ. You're just a self." It's a lie!

He deceives you into thinking...oh, you're yourself, you can go and do that. That's how he tempts you. "You'd like to do that wouldn't you?" Well, *deep down* we don't. The new I *doesn't* want to do that, but I'm tempted outwardly. Outwardly, "Oh, yes, I'd like to do that." So there's a division there between the new I, the real I in me who wants to express God in His love, and patience, and all the rest, and be a Godly person. This other thing tempts me and it pulls me as if I'm a *separate* person, "Just come on, come on." Now we can slip into that. That's where we learn there's no good answering by saying "I shouldn't." Because it's lying to you you're a separate person – as if "I shouldn't" *is* a *separate* person. "I shouldn't...." In that sense you're speaking as a separate person. "I shouldn't do that." *You* can't conquer it, because that separate "I" is the "I" geared to flesh. That's the flesh that's geared to *self*-interest...and *you can't conquer* self-interest. If you're tempted to hate, or tempted to lust, or tempted to fear, tempted to something, you can't conquer it – because if you look at yourself as a separate "I" you can't conquer it. So don't say "I shouldn't". You can't do it! "I oughtn't to...." You can't do it! That's no good. That's *how* you've got to learn this union. You're not a separate "I". So when you're tempted, deceived by sin into saying, "Come on, do this, do that," and deep down you don't want to, but on this surface area you do...and you forget that deep down what you really are is Jesus Christ. Christ is perfection. Christ is purity. Christ is love. You've forgotten that for a moment. Now, as if you're an independent person, you struggle.

That's no good because you *can't* conquer it, and so you get that guilty life. That's where the law comes in, as if I oughtn't to, then I go and do it! Then you're guilty. You're condemned because you've mistaken who you are. You've been deceived. You're not that at all! You're *not an independent* person who slipped into something. You've been deceived into that and therefore sin has stained you for a moment. Now that's not sin! Sin the *principal* of self-centeredness. That's out! The *principal* of self-centeredness is you live for yourself *period*. That's out. That's the devil. When you're born again, that's out! The basis of life isn't, "I'm just living for myself, to hell with everybody else." *That's out*.

This is a new life! So you don't *sin* again...but, you can be *tempted* to be called into the product of sin which is a little bit of self-gratification. And you do a little bit of self-gratification and you retaliate with hatred, or lust, or anger or something a little bit. And that's why the *way we learn* to live the new life is – it's this Person living it...not we! And when temptations come...this happens when I'm not quick enough...we say, "OK, God. You take over." As I say, "I'm bothered with that. That bothers me." Well it may..."God it's Your affair." Then you take it back to God. Then you're back in peace because it's God's affair...God's running it. Whatever it is you've done – "God, you're running that."

But the 'shadow' in life comes when this has *slipped in* and you are following through. You're following a worry through, or following a hate through, or following a lust through a bit. Maybe you haven't actually gotten into sin...maybe you're following through. Now something shadows you because you're acting under deceit – as if you are an independent person, when you're not. So you're not in the light, because the light is union. Light is – God and you are one! So when you're out from that there's a 'shadow'. And we read that in chapter 1 where "If we say that we walk in the light and walk in darkness, we lie and do not the truth." In other words what Light does for us is honesty...and honesty means the Light shows things as they are. Therefore, if I'm disturbed, or as the Africans put it, "My cup's not running over, and I'm not in the flow of the Spirit." I come to what I am in light. The light says, "You're not there. You've missed the way." And the light will show you how you've missed the way, because light exposes things. You can't hide from light. "Oh, yes, I have given in a bit there. I have given in." All right.

Now, God doesn't do that to bully us. He doesn't do that to condemn us, because the same light that shines on the sin shines on the blood. *He* doesn't see the sin ...because it's *disappeared* in the blood. We see the sin...but He sees the blood. So He doesn't come to condemn us. He comes to say, "OK, you've slipped a bit. You're human. I've been a human, too. I know what it is to be a human like you. I know what temptation is. OK. It'll *teach* you maybe to be a little quicker next time." That's all. He isn't bothered. It's *you* bothered. All this says is you'll be bothered until you get your freedom back. The bother's not with Him.

You'll be bothered because you've been caught out...and been deceived...and been fooled...and done the things you shouldn't do...or maybe continued in it a bit or something...and you'll be bothered because you're not in the light. You *are* in the light, but it doesn't *look* as if you are. You've been deceived...you've come out. So *you're* the one who's bothered. So He says, "To get your bother out you'd better confess it and get it right. I'm not bothered," He says, "but if you'll confess it, it will bring you back." The admission of it brings you back. God Himself says it's not there. "You've slipped. That's all. What *is* there is My forgiveness." What is there is the blood which is shed for you. Then when you come back, it says if you confess your sins...confess is not a big noise...confess is only admission.

I told you that last night. Confession is the Latin word, "say with." "Con" is "with." "Fess" is "fietor." In Latin, "Say with." So confess is "say with." Say with who? God, of course! We say, "What You say, God, is right. I tried to hide away, but what You say is right. I did lose my temper. I did do something." OK. So confession is all God asks of you. Come on. Respond to light. Be honest. Yes, you did get caught up by the deceit of sin. OK. He says, "If you'll confess your sins, He is faithful and just to forgive us our sins" because Jesus Christ took them. He's done that! He's just to forgive them. There's *no more penalty* for anybody to pay, because Jesus Christ paid the penalty. So He's just in forgiving.

He's faithful because He continues to be what He is. He doesn't change. Faithful is being what you are. He *never* changes. "I've always forgiven you. There's nothing there. Come on, now then." And so he gives us that reminder. Then he says, "You are faithful and just to forgive our sins and to cleanse us from all unrighteousness." Cleanses is my guilt – not in God, *in me*! I *feel* unrighteous. I *feel* I've done wrong. You see, I got 'caught up' a bit so I have this disturbed feeling...and I'm guilty and condemned. Not in God! In me! So this isn't getting God into the relationship. It's getting *me* back into the relationship. And so when we're cleansed, "Oh, it's not there!" And you're free! The thing's forgotten. It never was there in God's sight. Now

I'm back where I am. I'm not going to **try** to do better next time. I'll tell the Lord, "I'll do it again in 10 minutes unless You stop me. Stopping me is Your business. You're the real me. All right, be the real me in me! Get on with it." That's this life! That's this walking in the light!

So you see *we are* the Light in the light. So you see, John keeps saying, "We're in the union." As a consequence this has *practical* effects. It shows you up when you step out of the light and gives you *practice* in knowing...in knowing what the way back into the light is. You were always there...you never went away really...but you were forgiven because it was already done really. Forgiveness was already there. You just *recognize* that you're back. Use the word back if you like. There's no "away" with God. There was apparently on your side, because you'd slipped into this deceit. And you've come out of this deceit. OK. It's not there.

So he starts that, because in practical life these pulls are always coming to us. We don't live pulled. They come up anytime. These pulls are temptations of the flesh. Flesh is my humanity. I'm geared to this world...so my human response is to what's *in* this world. This world's here to attract me – the flesh. Attract me to self-ratification, and pride, and greed, and all these things. So the whole world pulls at my flesh all the time. So I know that beyond that I've got to learn how to live, because that's how I can be a light. When I can be a light and walk in God or walk in those situations, I've got what the whole world needs. Because everybody knows they *oughtn't* to be like that.

You see the whole human family is *in the being* of God. That's in Acts 17. Everybody is in the being of God...not the redeemed. Acts 17. It says, "He made of one blood all nations that dwell on the earth," verse 26. And then it says "They should seek after" Him. All nations of one blood. Not just us! This *isn't just* the saved. This is the whole world. And then he says, "Seek after God for in Him they live and move and have their being." Every single human being is *in God* and lives and moves and has their being in Him.

You don't know you're in His being because you're a *free* person. Forever a *free* person! You're a real person. So there's a paradox here. A dichotomy. It's always in life. As a free person in my self-*centeredness* – I don't know, because God is Self-giving love. Therefore, although I'm in the being of God while I'm a self-centered person...light and dark don't know each other (like that shadow)...don't know each other. So many people, while they're in the being of God, *don't know* they're in the being of God, because light and darkness don't know each other...and darkness is "I'm a self, geared to self-centeredness." So I'm a God-being operating for the devil.

The devil's a God-being operating for himself. God just *uses* the devil to get us self-blessed. He used the devil to crucify Jesus so we might get saved, so thank God for the devil! If he hadn't crucified Jesus we wouldn't have a Savior would we? So if you are wrong he uses you...if possible, *He* uses it to bless you! If He can't bless you He blesses others through you, despite you. That's all. In the being of God *without* knowing it until you're saved, because you're a real self...because as a real self you *are* what you *know*.

What you know is you're a self-centered person geared to Satan. You can't therefore know this other Person although you actually are a form of Him. That's the paradox! But you have to come back, as we say, to this way – to Who we are. I think I was saying this – I was saying we are in this world where the impact is, that *we* may be the Light shining to feed hungry people so everybody can want to be. Everybody knows they oughtn't to be bound up with these sins and things, which destroy them and which destroy other people...make a wreck of us (sins) and we're here to be lights. So there may be something about us which they see is different.

They maybe first of all kick and despise – something is different, because we've come into freedom of peace, and joy, and truth of Christ. But we've got to be **in** the world. We've got to be *tempted* by the world all the time. We never get free from that...so this is how we handle that. Then he went on from there into...we're to walk as He walked. As we said yesterday, we see that the top standard in this letter is that *we* are as He is in this walk – in light as He is in the light. In this next chapter we are to "walk as He walked." And then the end of this second chapter, "Righteous as He is righteous." And in the beginning of the third chapter, "Purify yourself as He is pure." Always, *as He is!*

And when he speaks of love in Chapter 4...his highest of all about love, "*You are* love." Not you *have* love. When you're in union you are love – because as He is *so are we!* Chapter 4:17: "As He is so are we in this world." Now, we immediately see, he goes on to say, "You have the faith...you conquer. You have the same faith Jesus had. That's how you conquer," (5:5). So that *now* you're faced with impossibility unless there's a union, because it's *impossible* for me *as an individual* to be like Jesus. I just don't do it. I'm not like that...I never will be! Because the human self is, as I say, the *falsehood* that God is separate – is a self-loving self. It's a lie! You're *no longer* separate...you *were*. You are no longer separate if you're redeemed. But looked at 'by yourself', of course you can't. You're for yourself...you can't be as Jesus. You're wasting your time trying!

So a gospel which teaches you to *imitate* Jesus is wasting your time. 'Be like' Jesus may be a nice little chorus, but it needs a little alteration in its doctrines. You can't do it! So this forces you to say, there's something else behind – either this man's phony and talking nonsense when he says we're to walk as He walked or there's a *hidden* trick there. Of course, the hidden secret, the mystery, as Paul says, "the hidden treasure made manifest to endless generations is *Christ in you...Christ as you.*" Because he goes *farther* than *in* you. In you is still you, too. *Christ* in *you*. But in Galatians 2:20 he says, "I'm not I, but Christ lives in me." He's taken my place. He's *as* me. I'm *as* Christ. "I, not" – it isn't Christ *in* me, it's Christ *as* me. I living...I live? No it isn't I living, it's *Christ* living. That's the final word! That's in Galatians 2:20.

Now, when that is so, as I say, we've dropped into this spontaneous recognizance – *be yourself* and you're walking as He walked, because it's He doing the walking. And you have the light as He has the light...because you're He!

So as we were saying on that level – the walking as He walks...righteous as He is righteous...and loving as He is love is sure, because it isn't you. It's He being Himself! It's you *are* that...but it *really* is expressing He – it's this paradox, this secret union. *You* are that! You're loving, you're walking, you're doing it. But it isn't you. The world has to catch that from the difference they see in you. You *inside* know what it's all about and why it's like that. So you see, you walk *as* He walks. Therefore you keep the commands. Remember the commands aren't that old law. Law had a threat in it, like the law of the country has. If you don't do this, you'll go to jail, because we're separate from the law.

When you're separate from the law you're *apart* from it, and likely to oppose it. So, like we say, if you don't do that you're in for trouble. *That's* not God at all. That's the only way in which God could speak – in a kind of outer form to those who didn't know Him. They didn't know He was the perfect God of love who does the whole thing Himself and moves you into His perfection and His ways. They didn't know anything about that. So the only way He could come to them was in a kind of guise of a warning, which is law, "Now, don't do that"...because while you break that law, you're going to have the consequence. The wrath wasn't in God...judgment wasn't in God. Judgment is in yourself! Acts 13 says you judge yourselves. When you judge yourself you *get* what you judge. It's what you are. Judging is what you *are*. We've judged ourselves as lost by remaining like that, *until* we're saved, of course. And the wrath, the judgment, the guilt, is what we get as a consequence of being out from the law. And so the law comes to us when we aren't it and don't like it. It threatens us so we *pretend* to do it, and can't wait until finally we admit our guilt. It's the first thing – it becomes the schoolmaster that leads us to Christ! Now the *law* really is *the way a thing works*. That's what the word law means – that law, a scientific law. That's the way it works.

A certain thing works and you go to the moon by the way it works, and you do everything by the way it works. That's those *outer* laws. The inner *law* of the being is God is love. The whole universe is the expression of love. It's nothing else. It may look distorted. It's nothing but love. The whole universe is the kingdom of heaven. It is God Who is love expressed in love.

We tend to see the distortion, the separation, because *you see what you are*, you know, and it reflects back to you what you're seeing. When you look at it separated then you see the world as separated. When you have a negative attitude, seeing bad it reflects back *as* bad. When you see God, it *reflects back* as God and you begin to see beauty, and love, and power, in fallen people. God's still working on them like He works on us. He's *there*. They're forms of God *gone wrong*, that's all, and you see that. Now you see, you're reflecting back what you are seeing! And this is the law.

Now then, when we come back to Christ we *are* that law. The law of the universe is God. Everything is an expression of His self-giving love, beauty, power, fulfillment, perfection, blessing...*nothing else* in Him! No wrath, no judgment...nothing in Him. That's only what's in us...where we're wrong. Now we've wiped out that wrong – that 'in us wrong' has gone out in Jesus Christ. Now we come back. We're in law, so we are the law now. So the law just is operating in us as *we* love, because we're loving just as God loves. *We* walk in light, because it's the same principal as I've said all along. Now the *commandment* is to help us humans to say, "This is the absolute." This is the absolute. It *must* be! The command is "You must love another." *This* is life. This is the only way life is life! So it's to help us to see what this is...and be that. Not by effort. Not by burden. We *want* to be. Not any wonder if we are because it's really He expressed in us.

So a commandment is where he says, "OK, God, that's it, I'm with that. I'll go along with you because that's You doing it. And when I tend to slip I'll confess. And so he says, if you walk, you'll keep the commandments. In this chapter, "You ought also to walk." If you don't keep the commandments you're a liar, vs. 4. Then he drops the hint of *how* we walk in verse 6 because he says, "You walk *because* you abide in Him and He in you." You walk because it's really He walking in you, of course. And then he says the commands you keep are the old commands. Many of the "Thou shalt nots," and so on. He says, "That's old stuff!" The *new* command which we now know is love, and love means God is for others. So he says this is the new commandment. It's *true in Him and in you*. So you see it's not something come to you. It's you *now*. It's in you, *in Him in you,* as one that is! If you walk in the light and hate your brother you're in darkness, it's a lie. If you love your brother you're in the light.

And so *that* love is the outer evidence, outer projections of this Person – loving men, not loving God, because we're not to see God in men. We're to see God in this human family, bringing His human family back to Himself. We're to see *God* in humans, and we're to love humans. We should love *in God*, so he says you love your brother. And then he puts that little bit in, now you'll find *this* as the basis of life! Loving your brother means you want to do what's best for him, whether you like it or not. You may not *feel* like that, but you learn that this soul feeling isn't the point! You may feel annoyed and hurt and dislike the way he treats you, but you say, "I'm not that person. That's self soul stuff. It isn't the real me at all. It's just the outer form; it's just the emotions and so on. In my inner form *I'm* God's love. I love with God's love, so I want what's best for my brother." If I do that there's *no stumbling* in me, because if you're living by what you see being best for your brother, that's right!

Stumbling comes when you're doing things...when you really want to do them *your* way. Then you'll find yourself stumbling, not in the way of self-loving self/other-loving self. We went through that. And we went through the phase where he spoke about the grades of understanding we have – little children, young men, and fathers. And these top standards will be accepted by you up to the grade at which you *catch on* to them. And the primary evidence that you are...whether young man, little child, or father...the evidence is, you have a new love. Because God is love and *you've* got the new other-love and the other-love is you love God! And so he says, the evidence that you're a new person is – the love of the Father is in *you*. Whereas there was the love of the world.

You *know* you're a born-again person because you *were* geared to self-gratification – love of the flesh, lust of the flesh, self-accumulation – what you can get for yourself. Lust of the eyes – self-aggrandizement. Pride of life – become what I want to be and build up *my own* status and be somebody. Those are the old self-loves. The evidence you're a born-again person is that those old loves have been replaced by the love of the Father, who's become *your* Father, and the Savior who died for you. And then for the family – that you want the whole world to become the family. The *other*-love! That's doing the will of God.

He then went into the next phase of the practical effects of this union relationship – is a knowing of the truth. This, the inner effects, still of the truth that there are many things *claimed* to be truth...many anti-Christs...many varieties of doctrines. You *know* the truth in *you*. You know the truth is Jesus Christ! The truth is that you've come into this light through Jesus Christ, Who both was the Author and the Redeemer and to Whom we're joined. And our peace and light and relationship with the Father comes through eternity in our relationship to Him. So this is the heart of truth – the Son. The Father and the Son. And therefore he says anything which denies the Son denies the Father – because the Father is only manifested and we're only restored to Him through the Son.

So if there are doctrines which *claim the Father* **without the Son**, they are lies. The inner truth, you know, is the knowledge which was retained, which is the inner true knowledge – which is that this new life is related to the eternal Father in fellowship with Him, joined to Him. He operating by us only through the Son as it comes into being – the creation's *through*...the Son coming into redemption...the Son joined to the son *now* as brothers with the Son, *co-heirs* with the Son. It *all centers* in the Son and the Son forever will be the means of manifestation the Father uses, but Son and sons *now* as co-heirs. So His purpose always has been through His Son with a vast family of redeemed sons lifted up into brotherhood. Through Him He will express His love-Self to the world. He'll develop whatever there is in the future time coming. We don't understand what's going to happen.

So the steadying point when we're walking in the world which attacks us with false doctrines and weird points of view, of course they think we're weird. But of course the flesh must think the Spirit is weird. The Spirit knows the flesh is weird. Therefore we are in a life when we can be diverted by view point. So have steady in you...inner knowledge. The Spirit's given you an unction by which *you* know all things and the inner knowledge you have is this – this truth is the whole world, *creation* of the Son, *redeemed* by the Son, *joined* back to the Father through the Son! And we're now *the Father operating* through us all as sons through an eternity of ecstasy and joy and fulfillment and perfection and total efficacy...each of us fulfilling. We've got instincts *to be* worth something. We're sure we're worth something! We're gods. We can have total instincts affirming where all we should be able to do, we'll do! Retain that. Not on some other theory – **only** on that in which the Father you're related to...through the Son. Keep the Son! Keep the Son! If a person denies the Son he denies the Father. So that's the next practical area where our viewpoints can get us distorted. That's the second area of the second chapter from verses 18 to verse 28.

The third area was you're living right. Again he puts things into focus for us. You live a right life now because you've exchanged wrong for right. Wrong is what's called sin, which is a person living the opposite way from God...really a non-person. Only God is truth. Only God is life. The other is negative, not really there...sort of appears to be there. And so living this old life for self, which is sin, is the wrong life...is really a non-life. But that's what we've been geared to – a life of sin. And he gives a time to show how we're freed in Jesus Christ from this sin relationship.

Sin, being understood to be – sin is misused self. Sin is not a thing. It isn't something we call evil. The only evil is selves *misusing* themselves. Misusing myself – means I'm using myself *for* myself – is Satan. I'm geared to living a life for self, as we read. That's transgression of the way the universe is run, which is the law. So it's a non-life. It's a death. It's an empty thing. That's why the Bible says, "What fruit had you in those things of which you're now ashamed." They're fruitless...nothing in them. Now he says, this will *clarify you* in the boldness of Who you are – that you're freed from this sin relationship because Jesus Christ came to destroy the works of the devil, the author of sin, it says here. The devil's sin was sin from the beginning. In Chapter 3:8, "He who commits sin is of the devil because his sin was from the beginning" and we *were* caught up with him. Now in Jesus Christ we're *cut off* from him. In His death and resurrection we're freed from any control, any indwelling of us by the devil and so on. That's sin. And so we never again, when we've come through the Cross of Christ, *are* sin again. He was made sin because we're sin. Sin is this character. He says, "You're never that again!" That's the character of Satan who was the indwelling god, and he's been replaced by God in His character, which is the opposite type. So salvation is really just a change of *inner* gods.

The vessel has the other God in it and so we're able to say we cannot sin. We cannot sin. That doesn't mean you can't be a little deluded for a moment – slipped out and be deceived for a moment – and come back. We've slipped into temporary expression of sin. That's not we; we've slipped and been deceived in a *temporary* expression. Sin is self-centeredness...some temporary expression of *self*-gratification. We've slipped into that. But we're not sin, so we cannot sin again, if we're born of God! And the evidence that we cannot sin is that we live the right life according to what we know to be the old commands of God – honesty and truth and right relationships and so on. And then above all, the new commandment, the new compulsion, which is loving your brother. Again he comes back – this is the whole truth because there is no truth but this!

Love fulfills the law. Paul said that! All law is fulfilled if the basis of my motivation is what's best for God and best for you. If that's the motivation, that *fulfills* all law. And I *don't* do the things which damage you, lie against you, steal your goods or damage you. I *don't* do those things. So love fulfills the law. So he comes back and says the only real expression of God through us is other-love...loving people. Not loving God, now, because this is where God is manifested, in people. But he says, here's one form in which I told you is how it affects you. If you're not in love you'll stumble. Love *being* love is for others. If your attitude toward others isn't love you'll stumble because you're being run by yourself, your self-motivations. If you're geared by what's *best for them* you never stumble. So it frees you to be a safe lover of others in your daily walk. That's the first form of love given us in Chapter 2.

In Chapter 3, the form of love is – you therefore give your life for your brother. Your life now is a laid down life. You're privileged to *be love* that gives itself for others. That's why the final title given in the bible to Jesus Christ is the Lamb on the throne, because, humanly, the lamb is a helpless creature. You can do what you like with it. A lamb doesn't fight you, doesn't retaliate. It does nothing. If you want to kill it, kill it. If you want to play with it, play with it. Do what you like with it. Now He's called the Lamb of God because whereas a human lamb is just helplessly available, the Divine Lamb is purposely available – I'm just that for you. I'll go any lengths. I'll do anything that is necessary to get you right – here I am! So you lay your life for others. So here you say this is one of the practical outcomes of love is that your attitude is – you'll do anything you can for your brother. That might take a major form where you lay down your life for your brother. Or it may...he says it's much more likely...take a minor form and you can help them in some practical way. He says, "If you have this world's goods and see your brother in need and don't help him, how's that love?"

I say in passing then don't get the idea we lose ourselves. We find ourselves and we still remain, but there's always this paradox – we still remain real selves. We enjoy ourselves! It isn't wrong to be a self that enjoys the self because your real self isn't you now. Your real self is Christ, but *you* are a self. It's this paradox, He and you are one. You keep your separate *personalities*, though you're one. There's a paradox! "I live; not I don't live, Christ lives in me." Now, he says, the life I now live I live by the recognition of that fact – *I* live a life. So we have to. So life isn't not enjoying yourself. You're just at ease and doing the things that please you, because you've got a new motivation for pleasure. Your basic motivation of course is God. But enjoy yourself meanwhile, and you'll find the Holy Spirit will make you give yourself where He wants you to. Don't fuss about running about giving yourself for other people. Don't do a thing. Try and stop it! Try and not give yourself to anybody. He'll make you! And then it comes out of Him.

So you see the difference between the redeemed self and the unredeemed self – the primary object in the unredeemed life was to please myself. That was my major objective. I might vary occasionally because I had to please somebody else. I didn't want to; I just had to a little bit. But my life was pleasing *myself*. Now that was the primary measure of life. A minor detail is I might be a little help to other people sometimes. Now in my *new* life my major objective is others. The minor objective is I please myself. So in pleasing others, I have a good time too! And I'm *meant* to have a good time. Be free, enjoy yourself! But you know there's a greater objective.

There's a great deal of *compulsion* to really enjoy yourself. You want to be able to get Christ to that person! You want to be able to serve them. So behind all your *rightful* compulsion – freedom, fellowship, involvement – the right things you're given. Whatever you're involved in...jump into the things that interest you...whatever you do in life! Behind all this, in the old life, that was all there was to it, just to please yourself, just to satisfy yourself, just to gratify yourself. In the new life you do those things! Some of you fellows are involved with sports and so on. Throw yourself into it! Throw yourself into everything you do. If it's a profession, throw yourself into it. If it's something scientific, throw yourself into it. We're meant to be

343

people who have variety of interests and variety of involvements, and we're free to be that.

The difference is underneath that *always is the new life*! Really, I'm this – that somewhere Christ in me can meet other people through this. The meaning of life is people becoming sons of God...until the new dimension when we all operate as sons of God *together*. That's the difference! And that chapter also touched on the – a touch there put in there on watching *against self-condemnation*. We mentioned that before. If your heart condemn you, God is greater than your heart. Watch therefore *against*...just the same as you watch against false doctrine...just the same as you watch against temptation trying to pull you out as if you wanted to be an independent self, following yourself. So you watch against self-condemnation...that old grave clothes sort of 'under the fall' feeling that "I'm no good, I'm a failure, I'm useless." Cut that out! Looking at yourself you may *feel* like that, or compare yourself to somebody else. You may feel like that. It's a lie! Cut that out, and begin to replace self-condemnation which ties you up, makes you feel, "I'm not much good," and so on...by saying "God is greater than my heart. *God* has approved me. I'm a delight to God. I'm His precious person. I'm His agent." So it's just as God approves me, now I approve myself! I've got to say I've got *all* these in God. Now, *I* haven't got them...I've got all in *God!* I've got all I need now. Let's go do it.

So we watch against forms of self-condemnation coming in. He reminds us again we have the witness of these facts within us, "hereby we know that He abides in us by the Spirit which He has given us." And it's by this inner knowing. As I say, light is inspiration. Light is knowing...inner knowing. The Spirit He's given us has born witness to us. So we know He abides in us because we have this witness.

Then he does add a bit again about the possibility of contrary spirits that declare (somewhat along the line as before) a false doctrine. They may declare they speak the words of God or works of God or something. And so he says, don't believe every spirit. Some people will proclaim that they're speaking the words of God and doing the works of God. Don't believe every spirit. And then he goes back again and says you test that by whether they confess Jesus Christ *has come* in the flesh. The basis of our faith is always the incarnation – that this Person has got us because He became us and then took us up. There's no way except He came down, became us, and took us up through His death and resurrection.

Therefore anyone who doesn't accept that the Son became man that man may come up and be sons of God is false!

So any kind of expression of a person who speaks by prophesy, or speaks by authority or some occult power or something, *unless it has as its center recognizing Jesus Christ come in the flesh* – in other words, Jesus Christ is my Savior and in *Jesus only* am I lifted up into union with God – is a lie. So it's exactly what this is – a test. If anybody's claiming something, test them on that. He puts that little interlude in, in Chapter 4: 1-6, and in doing so also he (John is always the person who exposes things to the roots) is the one who plainly shows how all humans are indwelt by God. He is the one here who says that you overcome the world because "Greater is He who is in you than he who is in the world" because as you're walking and affirming Him He's greater than in them. And he's therefore saying there's another spirit in the world, and he goes on to say, "Hereby we know that God hears us and doesn't hear them because hereby we know the Spirit of Truth and the spirit of error." That's verse 6.

So the *whole human race* has a spirit in them. The whole human race was captured by the false spirit, the false god...so the unredeemed have a god in them. "Greater is He that is in you than he that is in the world," verse 4. There's a He in you and there's a he in the world. It was a revelation when I saw that! There isn't only a Spirit in the redeemed, there's also a spirit in the unredeemed. That's the spirit of error. That's why the gospel is a *change of spirits*, not a change of person. The vessel remains the same, but the vessel was utilized...or the capacity of the vessel was utilized to express self-centeredness, the spirit of this world...self-love, self-gratification. In the new birth it's Jesus Christ, but the same personality. It's the new spirit, a change of gods, which expresses Christ through us.

He then goes on to the *final revelation* of the heart of what we may say – operating truth – and that is that God *is* love. *Never been said before.* God *is* love! That's *all* He is! And so in the new relationship we're geared to this One Whose *whole being* is love. He then says, because He is love and you're born of Him – *you* are love. He starts by saying, in verse 7, "Now let us love one another." Now mind you, love is an expression of two way love – give and take love. It's talking as well as giving. Sometimes I've got to learn to take as well as give. Loving one another. Each loving the other. *This* is the meaning of eternity – each loving the other. Now, he says, "Let us love one another for love is of God, everyone that loveth is born of God and knoweth God."

Love is of God. He hasn't said the whole truth there. He has to kind of correct that, because when you say "love is *of* God," you may see love as something separate from God, which He just gives you. If you're born of God, you're born of love because love is of God...so love. But there's a subtle snare there, because we humans separated *everything* off. We're separate people. We see things as separate forms and we see the character of God in separated form. We see peace as a separate form and power as a separate form – as if they're things, as if they're detached things because we've become thing-minded. That's separated. We've become fragmented now. Everything's bits and pieces. We're bits and pieces-minded. We're not unified-minded. We don't see unity.

So he starts by saying you love because love is of God, and therefore you love because you're born of God. Therefore you love. But then he goes on to say, "He that loveth not knoweth not God, for God is love." Now he's made a big jump. He's jumped from some characteristic expression of being a thing...like life is a thing, peace is a thing, an expression of a character...to being a Person. *God is love.* Now he's found the key to the universe! The whole universe is a Person. So it isn't, we get things from Him and utilize them. It's He Himself *expressing Himself* by us. It's the secret! The whole universe is God Himself's expression. The fallen world has misused that and made God's self-expression a form of self...self-expression. They've taken what is a form of God (but everybody is a form of God, everybody is God in human form) but in our freedom we've taken this expression of God which is ourselves and made it a *self*-expression. Then we come back and say...the truth isn't me apart from Him...it's He, it's the love. And so he says, therefore if you don't love you don't know God *because* God is love. Love is manifested not as forms by which you get for yourself. Love is giving yourself for others.

So he says we know God's love, in the next verse, because *He* manifested it...because Love is seen in practical form because He gave Himself that we might have Life. He gave Himself to come into the world that we might live. He gave up His life that we might live. That's love! And he says there are further manifestations. He says first of all that's love...that you give yourself for others, and your life is identified with being *for* them. That can make them be what they should be. You give *your* life that they might live. That's what he says here, in verse 9, "because God sent His only son into the world that we might live through Him." But he says love has a quality beyond that. It doesn't depend on whether they love you. "Herein is love, not that we loved God, but that He loved us." In love it doesn't matter what *you* think about me, it's what I think about you! I think about you as a precious person. So love overflows the reaction of "Why I can't stand that person and he can't stand me. Look at the way he acts toward me. How on earth...."

So we were saying that love is unadulterated. It has nothing to do with what the *condition* of the object of love is. It simply lives to perfect that object – that person! What he *is* isn't the point...so is his reaction to me. Not that we loved God...*He* loved us. "And sent His Son to be the propitiation for our sins." He took upon Him what should come to us – that's love! *Any* way in which I can take the place of another person...relieve him...*that's* practical manifested love. Now, he says, obviously, if God so loves us we ought to love one another. *Ought to* because, again, it isn't because *you've* got to do something. It is what you are! It comes out. That's the same as a command. Of course you do it! *That's* what it is. *Obviously* you ought to love one another.

And then he makes this very strong point...*very* strong point. Nobody has seen God at any time...he says in vs. 11-12. How do you 'see' God? If we love another that is God living and dwelling in us, and now *perfect in us* if we love one another. So you see, God is manifested in us by us as love. Love *is* God. So he says when you love one another that is God! This is how *you* know God. It isn't some mysterious person up here. That loving is God in you loving – God, other love, expressed through you! So when you're loving another, that's seeing God. Now that's *God* dwelling in you...is now perfect in you. And he says we know that because He's given us His spirit.

And he says that love also includes a world, basically the whole world – the disappearance of any barriers in this world. So he says. The other proof that this indwelling God Who is love in you *is you* – have a world mind. He says, vs. 14, "We have seen and do testify that the Father sent the Son to be the Savior of the world. Whosoever shall confess that Jesus is the Son of God, God dwells in him, and we have seen Him and do testify." Whoever shall confess that Jesus is the Son of God, God dwells in him and he in God. So in a sense this includes every human being, and that He came to save the world. Let's be big minded. Let's expect to see many come in! He came not to save a few; He came to save the world. And so we lose our sense of nationhood. You see nationhood disappeared!

347

There was one earthly nation which was preserved as God's nation because they were under God's law and had God's truth revealed to them that they might be a preparation for Him coming and forming the true nation. The true nation was not an earthly nation. It's a heavenly one. So with His coming...the Israelite nation...it broke up. The day that God especially blesses America or especially blesses Great Britain...that's not the point. God's busy fixing the world! And we have to get rid of this whole idea we're concerned about this nation and that. We gradually see the whole world is one people and the *one nation* is the body of Christ!

The *true* nation now is *those who have become the redeemed* of every nation...and God's blotted out those national distinctions. We're gradually coming up to that now in which I'm American, I'm British, I'm German and so on – it's disappeared. Who cares? That's just a variety of expressions of humans, and the human is one company. They're all, as Paul says, they're God's offspring...and that's all there is! So we can't see nations. We just see the whole world is God's offspring...and then God's redeemed children as the holy nation, which is to *embrace all who will come in* within this outer human situation. So gradually there has to die out this sense of nationhood that we have. And that God has a special blessing for Britain, a special blessing for America, and so on. No! Law fulfills itself – what you sow, you reap.

And thank God, whatever sows more righteousness will get more righteousness. Now this is a nation that does that. This is a giving nation. It's a *very great* thing – because a giving nation is a blessed nation because it *fulfills itself* in law. If you become a giving person you get back. "He that soweth bountifully shall reap bountifully." And so this nation has much bounty *because* it has some very fine characteristics in it. Where you sow selfishness you reap selfishness.

Now England has certain good things about it, but it has a selfish colonial system. It grabbed the world mainly for its own gain, so it grabbed India and grabbed parts of Africa and grabbed things making it the British Empire, mainly for what we can get out of it. There were certain benefits en route...but the main point, of course, was *our gain* from them. Therefore there's a *basis* of selfishness. Now then we are the losing nation, because we took for gain from them. Therefore Britain today is in a weak condition. It needs to be. It needs to learn. And God can pick us up again. We had to learn. You sowed to the flesh and in the flesh you'll reap corruption. And all your empire's disappeared and you're just a poor little quarreling nation now. God'll pick us up...but it *had* to be!

Now you're not that *yet*. Thank God for that! You're not that. You are a nation that has a world concern. God will bless you on that level, because what you sow you'll reap. God isn't basically interested in America, He's interested just as much in Communist China and Russia and Libya and all these places that make us pay for oil and so on. Nations don't matter to Him. People matter to Him...the whole people of this world. So He's broken this thing up...and among the people, the people of God...and the hope that all of them will become the people of God...as many as possible will become the people of God. Not a few!

But there is this – this *time* that they are moving in to become the people of God...this great wave of salvation going on in the world. So he's saying you love because you're indwelt by Him Who *is* love. If you love that's the evidence that *God* dwells in you. In verse 16, "God is love and He that dwells in love, dwells in God, and God in him." If you're governed by other-love, *that is God*. When you love your brother...that *is* God. So *this* is the evidence that we're in this God union. The motivation is – now in what way can we love each other, express our love for each other? And he puts little helpful hint in it. He says, "Now fear is not love." When you fear, you're off. Watch that fear. It means you're believing in evil, not believing in God who is love. So he says there's no fear in love. That's perfection! But fear destroys that perfection. So whenever in my relationship a certain fear comes in, watch out! I'm believing some evil happening. So you say, "God will handle this thing."

Even the difficulties, the difficult experience you're having. *God's* in this thing. I'm with God as His love...and God loves the people in this situation, and we shall *see* God operating in love. And so, "There's no fear in love." And once again he says, "Don't kid yourself, if you say you love God and hate your brother, you're a liar" (vs. 20). Because "if you don't love your brother whom you have seen, how can you love God whom you have not seen?" That's rather strange *until* you get the thing right. You can say, "Well, my brother isn't so nice to love. Why do you say..."If I don't love my brother who's nasty to love, I'm therefore not loving God who's nice to love?" Because God and your brother are one! You're to see your brother as a *form* of God, so whatever he *appears* to be, he's a form of God. Therefore, when you're loving your brother, you're loving God.

So it isn't that here's a sort of theoretically nice God out here whom we love and there's this nasty person you don't love. And how is it true to say if I don't love him I don't love God? Because what? And so Jesus says, "You don't feed the hungry, you don't feed Me. You don't visit the sick, you don't visit Me. You don't clothe the naked, you don't clothe Me." So He identified Himself with the whole human race. The whole human race *is God* in *human form* – is Jesus Christ in human form. And we minister to the human race...we minister to Christ. They haven't found Him, mind you, and they can be lost eternally if in their freedom they refuse to, but He's there, knocking at their heart's door, working on them so we can always be confident that God is in those folk, and they know what they ought to be. Everybody's meant to love. We want to love and be loved, and they're going to have that sense of alienation until they can come back to Him.

In the last chapter he repeats again what he's been repeating. How can we operate this pattern of life? We've done it *by faith*, he says, and so the last chapter's concerned with believing. And it says we're to love God and keep His commandments. They he says they are not grievous, vs. 3. His commandments are not grievous! They're grievous while you're in the *deceit of independent self*. "Oh, I can't help that!" No, you can't because you're not a 'little i'. You're not an independent self! You're Christ's...so while you try to run this thing yourself it's grievous. It's not grievous if you have the faith – if you're held by your faith. What faith? The same faith that Jesus had! It says in vs. 4 you overcome the world. "The victory that overcomes the world is your faith." What faith? He that overcomes the world is he that believes Jesus is the Son of God. How did Jesus overcome the world? *He saw Himself in the Father*. He didn't see Himself in Satan. He said the world overcame him, didn't it? They crucified Him. Now He says, "Overcome it!" Because *love overcomes* and God's truth in the end will overcome the whole world, of course. He overcame it in His own Self. He overcame the world by not seeing the world. "I see My loving Father. He puts Me through this. He means this to be My cup, which I'm to drink. OK. I'll drink it." After this He'll bring His new revelation of love and power and great salvation to the world – the resurrection! So you overcome.

Faith overcomes by what it's attached to. Faith is the inner ability by which things control you. You are controlled by the way you see a thing. And, as I say, if you are seeing a thing as evil, it comes back as what you see as evil. "Oh, what'll I do with that?" And most of our life is headshaking. "What shall I do with that? What shall I do with that?" Because we're seeing things with this negative faith which is from inside seeing evil. The *point* isn't evil. The *point is* I'm seeing it. My trouble is not evil, as I see it. You are controlled by what you see. That's all you are. All you have is your inner self. You're controlled by what you see because you're your inner self. When I see an evil, then I'm seeing the one who controls me. Now in one way it is evil. If you looked at it humanly it's an evil thing – now an evil because you look at it humanly. But then what do you do? You transfer your seeing.

Wait a minute! Seeing God is universal – the living God and love, they're all forms of it – everything that is a form of God. And He's standing in perfection behind all this. And they may be misusing a thing, and so on. It's all a form of God and He's working on this thing. He *purposed* that to *be* like that and evil to bring it out to His own ends. Now I see Him. Now you're an overcomer because I'm with Him and what He is I'm able to do because it's in Him. I'm able to do what He tells me to do, even if it's the Cross to overcome.

And then he goes on to give some reminders for emphasis. Believing on the Son is the *heart of all*. He goes back to that. He who believes on Him is God's Son and has eternal life. And he says you can know this because if you believe in the witness in yourself. Now you see, *faith* brings this experience! That's the way it is all along. It has the witness in itself. Now *outer* faith I told you – you commit yourself to something. You have the witness, here's the thing. I took this, here it is. In there, here I am. And the witness is an outer faith, outer witness.

And in this case, your real self's your inner consciousness. And in this case your inner faith has witness in itself because as you *believe*, there comes to your consciousness that it's so! So the Spirit bears witness. And, in you, you have the witness that this is the Son of God – and faith is the committal faith. Faith is a decisive moment. You don't act by *thinking.* You don't act by *mentally* believing. You act by faith which means "that's so." That's why the emphasis is put on the *word of faith.* Because the word confirms you, settles you in. And where you doubt, "Shall I do this, shall I do that? Well, you're doubtful. That's what I'll do. Inwardly you've got inner confirmation. That's it. That's settled. You're going to do it. So faith is only *inner* settlement. But it's the *word* of faith. It's not hanging around a thing. You don't see this unified life; you *say* it's a fact, given you in the word of God. "Faith comes by hearing and hearing by the word of God." The word of God first gives it to you, but it's got to become a *heard* word of God.

Heard means you're within hearing distance. Little children, young men, and fathers are different hearing distances. And "Oh, yes!" Now you're in a condition of faith. The word of God has said things through history. Millions of things. We said it this morning. Now, "Here He is." "Oh, yes." You catch it. Your ears have opened. Jesus said some people don't have their ears opened. Your ears are open. Now, when your ears are open, *that* isn't it. Say, "OK, God. That's so." That's the critical moment of life, always. Life always lived by the *words* of faith – a person's inner decisions of faith. You live that life. You operate on these inner decisions. The word matters. You didn't get Jesus by saying, "I'd like to have Him." You've got to say, "Jesus, I have You." You have to say, "I've accepted You." That's the word confirmed to you as well as making a fact a fact to you...made it the real thing to you. So the word of faith is that which bears a *witness*.

So he just goes on with a few more statements confirming us in this faith in the Son. "And we know the Son of God has come and gives us understanding and we know it's Him that is true." In His Son, Jesus Christ the true! This is the true God and eternal life, that's the end. Now he says, "Keep yourself from idols." Keep yourselves from the things that can divert you from Him in the center...and from detaching your affection to something else. That's this letter.

These last few verses of this chapter center on the word "know." Know. Know. We "know" we have eternal life. We "know" the Son of God has come. We "know" we have our requests filled in him. We "know" if He hears us we get what we ask and so on.

So his final word is, what we've already said, faith becomes fact. We've talked about this all along the way through. Now therefore in the inner faith – when it's by faith in Him, He comes back and confirms that to me and then faith becomes knowledge. So faith disappears and becomes knowledge. That's what the last word is. We just *know*...and that's how we know Him. The ultimate way by which we know Him – we just *know* Him. There's that in us which says, "That's it!" That's what God is. That's what this *holy suit* that fits me is – a God who is love – the Savior. That's it! This is the truth. I know. Yes, I know. That's what's become a reality to me. That's what we ultimately stand by. We can't do anything...but you've got yourself and you are what you are! And when your faith has become *knowing Him* like that, then we just live on this basis. That's the end of 1 John.

AFTERWORD

I still say that faith is the victory. We cannot help having heavy hearts, but when we give way to grief, we are really giving way to unbelief.

If we dare to believe the God of the impossible, then we honor Him by rejoicing when things are darkest.

Norman Grubb

In case you missed the BACK COVER

There are no better words than Hearts Set Free to describe the true and living reality Norman Grubb brought to the body of Christ in his rich 75 years of ministry. This truth of **our lives bound in unfettered freedom** in Christ is a treasure found in every book of the bible. As the Holy Spirit gives us eyes to see and ears to hear, this reality soars within us!

In these Epistle talks Norman thoroughly explores God's untold wealth for man by bringing him into his full inheritance of a life of **true** freedom in our union with Christ. This freedom begins in knowing we died when we received Christ as our Savior and that from that moment on we live in a union of spirits – our spirit in oneness with His Spirit! Norman saw this truth in 1920 when the Holy Spirit revealed Galatians 2:20, "I am crucified with Christ: nevertheless I live; **yet not I, but Christ liveth in me**..." and he wrote and spoke about this miracle the remainder of his life.

Hebrews tells us, "There remains a rest to the people of God. For he that is entered into his rest, he has also ceased from his **own** works, as God did from His." This *union rest* is *grounded* in Romans 6:6, "knowing this that our old man is crucified with Him, that the body of sin might be destroyed..." and also in John 17:22-23, "That they may be one, just as We are one; *I in them and You in Me*".

It is in *resting* in the finished work of Christ that we discover our freedom. Let each of us examine ourselves in the faith. "Is *my* heart set free? Do I *believe* 'yet not I, but Christ'? Am I **free** from trying harder to 'be like' *and* from self-condemnation?

"If the Son shall make you free, you shall be free indeed."

"The New Testament is a covenant of the Spirit, not a covenant of words, of letter...the only reality in the church of Christ is people – people who are born of the Spirit, and filled with the Spirit, and bearing fruit of the Spirit. That is the same as saying that we are expressing Christ. This is the only gospel there is, the only truth there is!"

Norman Grubb

ABOUT THE AUTHOR

Norman Percy Grubb was the son of an English clergyman. He married Pauline Studd Grubb, daughter of C.T. Studd, the founder the Heart of Africa Mission which became Worldwide Evangelization Crusade. After C.T.'s death Norman became General Secretary and traveled extensively developing the Mission and its outreach to bring Christ to unevangelized peoples. He retired as International Secretary in 1965.

In 1920 when Norman was a new missionary to the Congo, God gave him fresh insight to the Scriptures and His Being that set the course for the rest of his life. Norman had given his all to bring Jesus to the Africans, but soon found himself deeply disturbed because he feared he was bringing them just another set of rules and doctrines. He also faced the *aching* reality, that no matter how he tried, he could not love the African.

After much anguish, one day the Holy Spirit impressed upon him, "God *is* love." God then said to him that He would not give Norman love, but that He would *be* love in him. At the same time God revealed to him Galatians 2:20 ..."I am crucified with Christ: nevertheless, I live; **yet not I, but Christ** liveth in me and the life I live in the flesh, I live by the faith *of* the Son of God who gave Himself for me."[1] Norman then knew it was not his love, not his faith and not his life!

Norman called himself "a fiddle with one string" writing and speaking about our oneness and union with Christ. In his autobiography *"Once Caught, No Escape"* Norman says, "...there has been for me a vital difference between the second experience of discovering Christ living in me, and this third revelation of Christ all in all. The second experience left gaps where I did not yet see Him in everything everywhere, and all a form of Him, whether negatively of Him in wrath, or positively of Him in grace as light; and so there were separations, and callings on Him to be this or do that, in place of affirming that He is in fullness of His action everywhere...to be settled into this union which is unity, I had to go through a 'dark night of the soul' which affected no outward things, but the very inward vitals of my 'I and Thou' consciousness." [i] His oft written word of encouragement in signing his books was *"Not God and......but God only."*

Norman Grubb spent his life sharing these truths with anyone who would invite him into their home or church and also in writing countless books,

pamphlets and letters about Galatians 2:20...**our** lives being lived by the One who gave Himself for us.

With many great men of the Bible in their latter[ii] years, when their life's work seemed over, God had a new work...and it was so for Norman. He called it "God's redirection" in order that he might bring Paul's "mystery of the gospel, Christ in you, the hope of glory" to many he could not reach through W.E.C. Norman heard his 'Homecall' at 98 years of age on December 15, 1993. He is buried in Philadelphia next to his beloved wife, Pauline.

And from Norman's final letter shortly before his "Homecall"...

"By *faith* may you find the answers

that the Lord has for you.

May you always walk in faith

until we meet in the glory of God."

Printed in Great Britain
by Amazon

49956766R00214